Facebook Cookbook™

Other resources from O'Reilly

Related titles   FBML Essentials   JavaScript: The Good Parts
                      PHP Cookbook™   PHP Pocket Reference

oreilly.com   *oreilly.com* is more than a complete catalog of O'Reilly books.
                     You'll also find links to news, events, articles, weblogs, sample
                     chapters, and code examples.

   *oreillynet.com* is the essential portal for developers interested in
                     open and emerging technologies, including new platforms, pro-
                     gramming languages, and operating systems.

Conferences   O'Reilly Media brings diverse innovators together to nurture
                     the ideas that spark revolutionary industries. We specialize in
                     documenting the latest tools and systems, translating the inno-
                     vator's knowledge into useful skills for those in the trenches.
                     Visit *conferences.oreilly.com* for our upcoming events.

   Safari Bookshelf (*safari.oreilly.com*) is the premier online refer-
                     ence library for programmers and IT professionals. Conduct
                     searches across more than 1,000 books. Subscribers can zero in
                     on answers to time-critical questions in a matter of seconds.
                     Read the books on your Bookshelf from cover to cover or sim-
                     ply flip to the page you need. Try it today for free.

Facebook Cookbook™

Jay Goldman

O'REILLY®

Beijing · Cambridge · Farnham · Köln · Sebastopol · Taipei · Tokyo

Facebook Cookbook™
by Jay Goldman

Published by O'Reilly Media, Inc., 1005 Gravenstein Highway North, Sebastopol, CA 95472.

O'Reilly books may be purchased for educational, business, or sales promotional use. Online editions are also available for most titles (*http://safari.oreilly.com*). For more information, contact our corporate/institutional sales department: 800-998-9938 or *corporate@oreilly.com*.

Editor: Mary E. Treseler	**Indexer:** Fred Brown
Production Editor: Sarah Schneider	**Cover Designer:** Karen Montgomery
Copyeditor: Genevieve d'Entremont	**Interior Designer:** David Futato
Proofreader: Sarah Schneider	**Illustrator:** Jessamyn Read

Printing History:

October 2008: First Edition.

ISBN: 978-0-596-51817-2

[M]

1224014169

*To Bianca, whose face is tops in my book. I could
do nothing without you.*

Table of Contents

Contributors

The following people contributed recipes to this book:

Jayant Agarwalla: Recipe 2.4, *The Winning Formula for Facebook*

There aren't many people in the world who can claim to have a winning formula for building Facebook applications. Jayant is one of those very, very few. I had the pleasure of interviewing him on stage at the ICE08 conference, and I can honestly say that I've never met anyone with a deeper understanding of what it means to build a successful Facebook app. And he should know! At 21 years old, Jayant, who comes from Kolkata, India, is the cofounder of *http://scrabulous.com* and the Scrabulous application on Facebook (now called Wordscraper). He's currently the VP of business development and marketing for Scrabulous.

Will Pate: Recipe 2.21, *Community Gardening*

When I set out to find someone who could write eloquently about some good community gardening strategies, my list had exactly one person on it: Will Pate. From starting the Infinity BBS when he was still in high school, through cofounding Raincity Studios in Vancouver, to being the community manager for Flock, co-hosting commandN, and in his current role as community manager for VenCorps, Will has demonstrated an unparalleled understanding of how to grow a vibrant community. You can find him at *http://www.willpate.org*.

Alistair Morton: Recipe 2.22, *Finding Inspiration*

Al is one of the most talented designers I've ever met, and certainly the tallest. We've collaborated on a few projects, which has given me the opportunity to notice that even his on-the-phone doodles are individually perfect works of art. I asked him to contribute a recipe that's a little outside the regular scope you might have come to expect, and to shine some light on where he finds inspiration for his creative endeavors. You can find him at *http://www.peapod.ca*.

Rajat Agarwalla: Recipe 4.4, *Scalability*

I've never met Rajat, but I have had the pleasure of sharing a stage with his brother, Jayant. You might not recognize their personal names, but you've almost certainly lost hours and hours of your life to their creation: Scrabulous. Few Facebook developers have dealt with the scaling issues that they have! The brothers hail from Kolkata, India, and are cofounders of *http://scrabulous.com* and the Scrabulous application on Facebook (now Wordscraper). Rajat is the CEO and chief software architect.

Mark Slee: Recipe 4.6, *Cross-Language Development with Thrift*

I've only had the honor of meeting a handful of Facebook's development team members, which fortunately included Mark. I saw Mark present at the FSOSS07 conference on Thrift and immediately cornered him to contribute a recipe. He's one of the original authors of Thrift and is a product manager at Facebook. Prior to that, Mark was a member of the engineering team, focused on systems infrastructure, mobile applications, and general site development. He holds degrees in computer science and mathematics from Stanford University, and spends the better part of his spare time listening to and producing electronic music.

Ilya Grigorik: Recipe 4.8, *Advanced Caching with Nginx and memcached*

Every now and then, you run into a person who is so much smarter than you that you're really just dumbfounded. Ilya is one of those people. He's the founder and CTO of AideRSS (*http://www.aiderss.com*), an RSS filtering service designed to help you find and read what matters. In his downtime, he maintains a popular blog (*http://www.igvita.com*) where he talks about Ruby, Ruby on Rails, and best practices of scalable web architectures. The scope of his recipe is probably beyond all but the most advanced readers, though I encourage you to consider it in your architecture if you're planning an app that really needs to scale.

James Walker: Recipe 4.10, *Integrating Drupal and Facebook*

Since some of you will be experienced PHP developers, there's a good chance that you've played around with Drupal or even built some sites on it. What you may not know is that you can save yourself a lot of time and energy by building your Facebook app on it! James, known to his loyal followers as Walkah, is a High Priest in the religion of Drupal. He's also a father, a geek, a drummer, a (former) hockey goalie, a music nerd, a free software advocate, a beer drinker, a thinker, a Cancer, a flirt, a closet singer, a dork, a hugger, a clown, and alive. James and I have shared many conversations in which the answer ended up being "Drupal," so I was thrilled when the conversation about him contributing to this book started with "Drupal" and ended with "Yes." You can find him at *http://walkah.net/* and at *http://lullabot .com*, where he's the director of education.

Daniel Burka: Recipe 4.13, *Facebook's Global User Interface*

Daniel is one of the friendliest people I've ever met. Maybe it's because he's a fellow Canadian, but it's always such a pleasure to run into each other and catch up. You may not recognize his name, but you know his work: Daniel is a partner at Silverorange and the design director at Digg, as well as a cofounder of Pownce. You can find him at *http://deltatangobravo.com*.

Jason DeFillippo: Recipe 5.4, *Starting Out in PHP*

Many of you will be new to the world of programming or won't be overly familiar with PHP. I asked my good friend Jason DeFillippo to contribute a recipe on a simple but effective beginner PHP tip, which he happily did. Jason has been building websites professionally since 1994, working for companies such as Epson, Paramount, Technorati, and 8020 Publishing. He specializes in social media and blogging and is the cofounder and CTO of the Metblogs global network. Jason's blog can be found at *http://jpdefillippo.com*, and his awesome photos can be ogled at *http://aphotoaday.com*.

Martin Kuplens-Ewart: Recipe 6.5, *Web Standards*

Martin was a member of our team at Radiant Core and now consults on frontend development for Zerofootprint. He's a brilliant web designer and writes better HTML than almost anyone I've ever met, which makes him perfectly qualified to contribute a recipe about why web standards are important, even on Facebook. Martin has helped major groups and brands, including Microsoft, Mozilla, Toronto's Hospital for Sick Children, UNESCO, YMCA, and Zerofootprint, understand how to embrace web technologies and online community as part of their core business, and he has developed online solutions for these and other major organizations. He is an expert in the development of web applications using standards-compliant methodologies and is a 10-time judge of the Web Marketing Association WebAwards. Martin's consulting services can be found at *http://www .apolitic.com*.

Pete Forde with **Rowan Hick**: Recipe 8.5, *Advanced Relational Database Table Optimization*

Pete Forde is a cofounder of Unspace Interactive, one of the world's best Ruby on Rails consulting firms. He's also an amazing photographer, a charismatic leader of the tech community in Toronto, founder of our Rails Pub Night, and a co-organizer of the Ruby Fringe Conference. I asked Pete to contribute a recipe about optimizing database performance and got more than I could have hoped for when he dragged Rowan along for the ride. You can find Pete at *http://www.unspace .ca* or on Flickr at *http://flickr.com/photos/leftist*. Rowan is at *http://www.rowanhick .com*.

Alain Chesnais: Recipe 10.1, *Attracting Users Through Facebook Ads*

Alain is the vice president of product development for View 22, makers of the SceneCaster application. Their Facebook application, a portal into the world of SceneCaster, has quickly attracted over a million users. Alain has previously worked at Alias|Wavefront, ATI, Tucows, and TrueSpectra, and has forgotten more about the world of 3D than you or I will ever know.

Jeffrey Tseng: Recipe 10.6, *Measuring Your Success*

I was completely blown away when Albert Lai, Kontagent's CEO and an old friend of mine, showed me their demo. Albert's a very successful serial entrepreneur and has another great startup on his hands, cofounded with his CTO, Jeffrey Tseng. Kontagent is focused on providing next-generation social analytics tools for developers, and Jeffrey is well-suited to his roll, having previously been the founder of a startup that provided consulting services for wireless sensor networks. You can find them at *http://www.kontagent.com*.

Preface

One day, in the not too distant future, I fully expect my grandmother to ask me about Facebook. She's particularly hip, as grandmothers go, and is already all over email. She even occasionally "surfs" the Web to read up on the latest events in her native South Africa! You might not think she falls into Facebook's target demographic, but I would hate to be the person standing between her and her Mac if anyone told her that she could learn even more about her beloved Toronto Maple Leafs by registering for a Facebook account. She is, after all, their number-one fan.

There's an important takeaway in there for everyone who has picked up this book in a bookstore and is weighing the idea of building a Facebook empire: my grandmother, and millions of people like her, are waiting for you to build the application that lures them into the world's fastest growing social network. Please don't disappoint her, because I'm *her* number one fan, and I have no objection to getting a little rough in the corners, if you know what I mean.

Who Should Read This Book

The contents of this cookbook are primarily aimed at developers with a general background in web development who are interested in building Facebook web applications. Although Facebook Desktop and Mobile apps are covered where applicable, the content in here is really aimed more at the web side of things. There's a wide swath of material covered, from how to plan an app, to really gritty API details and FQL calls, to how to market and attract users, so there should be something for everyone.

Most cookbooks assume that the would-be chefs reading them have a basic knowledge of how to cook, and this book is no different. I assume you know your way around the following (even at a very fuzzy, somewhat-in-the-dark level): web development in the areas of HTML, CSS, programming (particularly PHP), and SQL/database design. You don't need to be a master of any of them, and I've asked a few friends to contribute some recipes to help you out if you're just getting started (particularly Recipes 5.4 and 8.5, respectively). I've also pointed out some excellent books if you need to brush up on some of the related topics.

What's in This Book?

Like all good cookbooks, this one is intended to be pulled off the shelf and rifled through when you need to know how to embed an MP3 on a Canvas page (`fb:mp3`: see Recipe 6.26), how to look up friend lists using FQL (`SELECT flid, name FROM friendlist WHERE owner = $uid;` see Recipe 8.33), or where to find inspiration when you're faced with App Developer block (all around you; see Recipe 2.22). You're welcome to read through it from cover to cover—and I hope you'll find it entertaining and worth a few laughs if you do—or to use it as a trusted reference while you take over the Platform world.

This book is organized into 10 chapters:

Chapter 1, *Introducing Facebook Platform*

> A general overview of Facebook, Facebook Platform, and an introduction to the incredible opportunity it represents.

Chapter 2, *Ideation and Strategy*

> If you don't have an idea in mind already for an app, this is the chapter for you. Learn about the Platform ecosystem, dig into the integration points and different strategies for using them, and pick up a few techniques for doing app design quickly and with the best possible results.

Chapter 3, *Hello World*

> Time to get started building your first app! This quick chapter will walk you through the classic Hello World first programming example.

Chapter 4, *Architecture and Design*

> This chapter covers the best architectures for Facebook apps, some solid recommendations for database performance, and an overview of the design and user experience of winning applications.

Chapter 5, *Setting Up Your Environment*

> Learn about all the things you need to download, how to add apps to Facebook, the secret trick to setting up a test account, and how to get the lowdown on the latest and greatest from Facebook.

Chapter 6, *Facebook Markup Language (FBML)*

> FBML is the magic that makes the Facebook Platform world go 'round. We'll cover all of the tags, dig into some surprising behaviors you might encounter, and explore some great tricks for building better frontends.

Chapter 7, *Facebook JavaScript (FBJS)*

> If JavaScript is the duct tape that binds the Web together, FBJS is the glue that makes Facebook apps stick (or something like that). This chapter explains why you can't just use regular JavaScript in your app, how to build great Ajax-like interactions using Facebook's Mock Ajax techniques, and goes into detail about all of the handy functions available to you.

Chapter 8, *Facebook Query Language (FQL)*
> As FBML is to HTML, FQL is to SQL. We'll take a look at the schema of the various database tables you have access to, and catalog some really useful (and fast) FQL queries you can use in your apps.

Chapter 9, *Facebook API*
> Ah, sweet, sweet API. We would be nothing without you! This chapter will show you the real power behind Platform, digging deep into the code that connects everything together. We'll go through each of the objects and methods you have at your disposal, and I'll give you some tips and tricks for desktop apps along the way.

Chapter 10, *Marketing Your App*
> Remember: if you build it, they won't come—without persuasion. Marketing is the art of persuasion, and this chapter goes over some general marketing options for Facebook apps and some great techniques for measuring your success.

Code Samples

Many of the PHP code samples in this book require the Facebook API to be included and instantiated before the sample can be run. Those precious few lines of code have been omitted throughout to save space, so stick these in when you need them:

```php
<?php
    include_once 'resources/includes/config.php';
    include_once 'resources/includes/facebook.php';
?>

<?php
global $api_key, $secret;

// Code Goes Here

?>
```

You'll need to adjust the paths in the `include_once` lines to match where you've put the files after downloading them. See Chapter 5 for more information on setting up your environment.

Although there's a lot of code in here that you could lift straight off these pages and drop into your app, remember that none of this has been extensively tested as production code and there's very little error checking. Since Facebook throws exceptions when things blow up, I'd suggest at least wrapping your code in some try/catch statements and doing something useful with your contained explosions.

Keeping Up with the Facebookers

As I was getting to the end of writing this book (mid-2008), Facebook announced that they were planning a major redesign of their Profiles and the way that applications integrate with them. That decision sure made for exciting times in these parts!

Luckily, the timing worked out nearly perfectly, and this book now contains information about the "Profile redesign" rather than the old way of doing things. The new design was still in the initial phases of being rolled out as we were wrapping up the manuscript, so some of the screenshots still show the old design we knew and loved, rather than the new design we're fumbling around with but are pretty sure is going to become our number-one squeeze. Fear not: the screenshots were updated anywhere that it was absolutely required. It's also possible that some of the information changed after we went to press, so check the Developers Wiki if you think that might be the case (*http://wiki.developers.facebook.com/*).

It's also worth noting that some of the applications profiled in this book are no longer, and that some have completely changed their look, feel, and very purpose in life. Scrabulous, for example, is consistently used throughout as a paragon of what to do right, but it has actually fallen prey to its legal battles and has been reborn, phoenix-like, as Wordscraper (*http://apps.facebook.com/wordscraper*).

Using Code Examples

This book is here to help you get your job done. In general, you may use the code in this book in your programs and documentation. You don't need to contact us for permission unless you're reproducing a significant portion of the code. For example, writing a program that uses several chunks of code from this book doesn't require permission. Selling or distributing a CD-ROM of examples from O'Reilly books does require permission. Answering a question by citing this book and quoting example code doesn't require permission. Incorporating a significant amount of example code from this book into your product's documentation does require permission.

We appreciate, but don't require, attribution. An attribution usually includes the title, author, publisher, and ISBN. For example: "*Facebook Cookbook* by Jay Goldman. Copyright © 2009 Jay Goldman, 978-0-596-51817-2."

If you feel your use of code examples falls outside fair use or the permission given above, feel free to contact us at *permissions@oreilly.com*.

Safari® Books Online

 When you see a Safari® Books Online icon on the cover of your favorite technology book, that means the book is available online through the O'Reilly Network Safari Bookshelf.

Safari offers a solution that's better than e-books. It's a virtual library that lets you easily search thousands of top tech books, cut and paste code samples, download chapters, and find quick answers when you need the most accurate, current information. Try it for free at *http://safari.oreilly.com*.

Comments and Questions

Please address comments and questions concerning this book to the publisher:

O'Reilly Media, Inc.
1005 Gravenstein Highway North
Sebastopol, CA 95472
800-998-9938 (in the United States or Canada)
707-829-0515 (international or local)
707-829-0104 (fax)

We have a web page for this book, where we list errata, examples, or any additional information. You can access this page at:

http://www.oreilly.com/catalog/9780596518172

To comment or ask technical questions about this book, send email to:

bookquestions@oreilly.com

For more information about our books, conferences, Resource Centers, and the O'Reilly Network, see our web site at:

http://www.oreilly.com

Thanks!

Writing this book was hard work, so I'm lucky to have been surrounded by so many great contributors who made gathering recipes so easy. To my gang of guest chefs: they say that too many cooks spoil the batter, but obviously they were never backed by a team like you. Your expertise and insight have made this book what it is. In the order they appear in the book:

- Jayant Agarwalla
- Will Pate
- Alistair Morton
- Rajat Agarwalla
- Mark Slee
- Ilya Grigorik
- James Walker
- Daniel Burka

- Jason DeFillippo
- Martin Kuplens-Ewart
- Pete Forde
- Rowan Hick
- Alain Chesnais
- Jeff Tseng

A special thanks to Will, who shot my Profile pic one cold day on a photo walk through Toronto's Junction neighborhood.

My gratitude to my reviewers, who helped turn my (sometimes incoherent) ramblings into the book you hold today. In no particular order:

- Jesse Stay (*http://staynalive.com*)
- Pete Bratach (*http://facebook.com*)
- Peter Meth (*http://softersoftware.com*)
- Michael Porterfield (*http://wealthengine.com*)
- Tim Consolazio (*http://tcoz.com*, *http://nabbr.com*)

Thanks also to the amazing crew at O'Reilly, who made life for this first-time author a whole lot easier. Particular thanks go out to Jacque McIlvaine for handling the administrivia; Sarah Kim, Maureen Jennings, Marsee Henon, and Laurel Ackerman for marketeering; Adam Witwer and Marlowe Shaeffer for handling my sometimes clueless questions; Genevieve d'Entremont for making my ramblings into readable copy; Sarah Schneider for turning this into a real book; Brady Forrest (and Jen Pahlka, even though she's not really an O'Reillyian) for the speaking gigs; and my editor, Mary Treseler, for putting up with me and for shared stories about dogs.

Apologies to Eli

In searching for an example ID I could use for applications, users, groups, networks and the like, I settled on 12345. It turns out, much to both my delight and surprise, that Facebook has actually assigned that ID to a user: Eli Richlin. So, my apologies to Eli for using him as an example throughout the book. Apart from being user 12345, Eli is apparently a Harvard graduate and an NYU grad student. Good luck with everything, Eli, and thanks for being such a model user!

CHAPTER 1
Introducing Facebook Platform

Many profound questions have haunted scholars and thinkers since the dawn of humanity: Why are we here? Does God exist? What is art? Where *does* the other sock go? The question of whether or not to build an application on Facebook[*] Platform is not one of them.

That said, since you're holding this book in your hands, you've likely already spent some time pondering this question. Perhaps you have recently been bitten by a zombie or been given some fish for an aquarium you didn't know you owned. Maybe you were challenged to a round of movie trivia or told that you were someone's Top Friend. If you're a Facebook user (and it's increasingly likely that you are), you've probably installed an application or been invited to install one by a member of your ever-growing social network.

Although it may seem impossible to live without those applications, Platform hasn't always been part of Facebook. Mark Zuckerberg unleashed Facebook Platform on May 24, 2007, at an event held at the San Francisco Design Center attended by 800 developers. For all the epic speechwriting and grandiose claims (Mark opened his presentation with, "Today, together, we're going to start a movement"), that day really did mark an important moment in the history of the industry. The enthusiastic and decidedly nervous founder of Facebook might just as well have been standing on that blue stage and waving a vial of gold over his head, yelling, "Gold! Gold! Gold from the American River!" Just as surely as Samuel Brannan's march through the streets of San Francisco heralded the start of the California Gold Rush, news of the Platform exploded onto the Web. Technorati shows nearly 500 blog posts with the term "Facebook Platform" from that day, up from practically none the day before (see Figure 1-1).

At the time of the announcement, Facebook counted just over 24 million active users (defined as people who have returned to the site in the last 30 days). At the time this book was written, its user base has exploded to more than 90 million[†] and continues

---

[*] Facebook is a registered trademark of Facebook, Inc.

[†] f8 Keynote Address (*http://www.new.facebook.com/f8*)

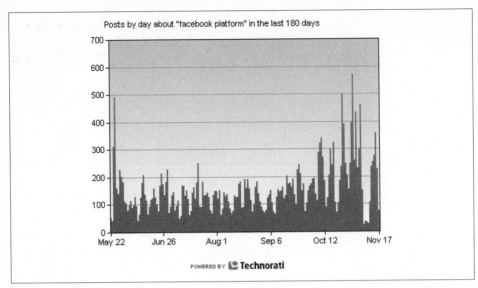

Figure 1-1. Blog posts about "Facebook Platform" since May 2007

to grow at the astounding rate of 200,000 new users per week. Numbers like that tend to be somewhat difficult to understand—if all those people impossibly stood on each other's shoulders, they'd reach 93,000 miles into the sky! But consider that San Francisco has a population just shy of 800,000 people, and now imagine each and every one of them sitting down in front of their computers and diligently joining Facebook in the same month. The current growth rate runs at about 3% a week, and if you consider that the world's population is only growing at a rate of about 1.14% a year, it becomes mathematically possible to calculate the Facebook Singularity: the point at which every human on the planet has been signed up and is filling your inbox with free gifts, pokes, and friend requests. Although it's difficult to figure out how much Platform has to do with that growth, it's notable that there have been over a billion installs of almost 24,000 apps, and that some of those apps (such as Slide's Top Friends and FunWall and Rock-You's Super Wall) are seeing well over a million daily users.

1.1 What Exactly Is Facebook Platform?

Chances are, if you're reading this book, you're comfortable with the concept of an operating system (OS), be it Windows, Mac OS, or Linux. In a lot of ways, you can think of Facebook Platform as an OS for social networking. Platform provides many of the important and underlying technologies that enable the *social graph*, a term Facebook uses to describe a social network.

The social graph is a representation of all the connections that make up a social network. Every member of the network has his own social graph, which represents that user's unique set of connections to other members of the same network. The example

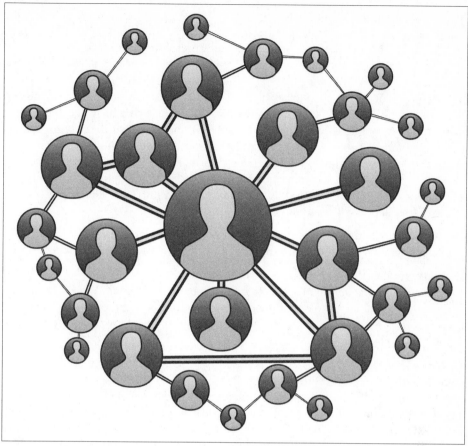

Figure 1-2. The social graph

shown in Figure 1-2 depicts the social graph of the person in the center, whom we'll call Mark. The people in the network who are directly connected to Mark are shown slightly smaller than him, the people he's indirectly connected to are shown even smaller, the next level even smaller, etc, etc. The social graph isn't unique to Facebook (although it's certainly one of the biggest on the Web); it is actually a common property of any network in which things are joined to other things. It's a useful visualization tool to show the structure of the interlinked nodes (the *topology* of the network), and it can also be used to calculate the value of any one node (usually based on the number of links it has to other nodes). Although it may not seem so at first, network value is a fascinating topic, especially when it's worth an estimated $15 billion.[‡] You can figure out the value of any network by applying *Metcalfe's Law*: the value of a telecommunications network is proportional to the square of the number of users of the system

[‡] *http://www.facebook.com/press/releases.php?p=8084*

(n^2). Robert Metcalfe, who coinvented Ethernet along with David Boggs and cofounded 3Com, first formulated his law to explain the network effects of things like joining computers or fax machines together, but it's just as useful for explaining social networks and the Web. The math behind the law is actually pretty simple and is easily illustrated by looking at the social graph just shown. If Mark is the first person to join Facebook, the value of the network is one ($1^2 = 1$). When Mark's friend Sarah joins, the network has become a lot more valuable because now Mark can stop poking himself and can now poke someone else. It's so much more valuable, in fact, that the value doesn't just increase by one but actually becomes four ($2^2 = 4$), meaning that the network is now four times more valuable to Mark and Sarah than it was to either one alone. Eventually, after every member of Mark's very extended circle of family and friends has joined, the network has 54 million users, the value of the network is too high to calculate on most calculators ($54,000,000^2 = 2,916,000,000,000,000$), and suddenly Microsoft is offering Mark $240 million for 1.6% of his company.

Before we get too far off topic, there's a reason why the value of the social graph is important, and it's one of the three pillars upon which Platform was launched:

Deep integration

> Two of the most popular Facebook applications are Photos and Videos, both written by internal Facebook developers. Your applications get the same level of integration as these do (known as *application parity*), and you have basically the same access to Platform.

Mass distribution

> Here's where the network value comes into play. Those of you old enough to remember television commercials from the 1970s may recall an ad campaign for a shampoo called Faberge Organics (with wheat germ oil!), which holds the distinction of being an almost entirely forgotten line of hair products whose marketing strategy has long, long outlasted the product it once promoted. One of their television commercials showed a blonde woman who had presumably just washed her hair with Organics. The voiceover said, "If you tell two friends about Faberge Organics shampoo with wheat germ oil and honey, they'll tell two friends, and so on... and so on... and so on...", which was accompanied by a Brady Bunch-esque splitting of the screen into more and more squares of smiling models. Now think of the social graph from Figure 1-2: if Mark does something interesting and Facebook automatically tells two of his friends, they might do the same interesting thing, and two of their friends will find out. Since most people on Facebook have a lot more than just two friends, the network effect does a lot more than just double at every point (if everyone on the site had an average of 10 friends, for example, the message would reach a million people in six generations). It's safe to say that Facebook offers an opportunity to distribute to a much larger audience much more quickly than virtually any other technology in history.

New opportunity

> This brings us to the bottom line: Deep Integration + Mass Distribution = New Opportunity. Building applications on Facebook Platform gives you a chance to get your software in front of 90 million people without having to spend millions on marketing, in an environment that is built to spread it to people who want to use it. The barrier to entry is very low and requires only that you retrain some of your existing web development skills (or learn some basic new ones), all of which you can master with this very book.

You're probably thinking that this all sounds a little too good to be true, and that if this book were a late-night infomercial, I would be telling you all of this from a sleek speedboat hurtling across my own private lake toward my towering mansion, accompanied by scantily clad models and drinking magnums of champagne. The truth is that champagne gives me nasty headaches, and that, although building apps on the Platform can be very profitable and lead to a satisfying career, it's not a breezy walk in the park. Like almost everything else in life, you'll still need an original idea, and you'll still need to roll up your sleeves and dig into some hard work. The rest of this book will help to make that as easy as possible by telling you how to get set up quickly, providing practical advice on what to build and how to evaluate your idea, working through the technical side of Platform, and showing you some proven marketing techniques for your new application.

1.2 Skills to Pay the Bills

Now that you know a little about Facebook Platform and the opportunity it represents, you may well be asking yourself what skills you'll need in order to take advantage of it. Facebook maintains an excellent high-level view of Platform on its Developers site (*http://developers.facebook.com*), as well as a wiki with the nitty-gritty details of Platform (API calls, FBML tags, FBJS, FQL tables, Platform Policy, etc.) along with user-contributed content (*http://wiki.developers.facebook.com*), but neither of these really covers the basics. Whether you're assembling a team to develop apps or you're going to bravely tackle it single-handedly, you're going to want:

Frontend skills

> The requirements here, as with the other realms we'll look at in a moment, are basically the same as if you were building a traditional website. A solid knowledge of HTML or XHTML is key, as is a good understanding of CSS. Although some of your HTML will be replaced with FBML, you still need to be able to build the structure around those tags and understand how they work. You'll want to have wrapped your head around JavaScript and Ajax if you're going to do any dynamic interface elements, as well as Adobe Flash or Microsoft Silverlight if you want to do any animations, audio, video, etc. Keep in mind that the only officially supported client library for Facebook is PHP (4 and 5), so you'll need at least some level of familiarity with that language if you're going to integrate directly with the

Facebook API (as opposed to relying entirely on FBML) or with your own backend. We'll cover these topics largely in Chapters 6 and 7.

Backend skills

As you'll see in the coming chapters, your application actually lives on your server, rather than being hosted by Facebook. This gives you a huge amount of flexibility in terms of how you architect and develop your backend, but it can give you equally huge hosting bills if you're not careful. If you're aiming to build a very successful application, you'll want to make sure you have some knowledge of industry best practices related to scaling and database design, as well as code optimization and server setup. We'll cover backend issues in Chapters 5 and 9.

Ideation, strategy, and marketing

The very early days of Facebook Platform were marked by an incandescent sense of optimism, as we watched applications such as Slide's Top Friends chart a meteoric rise toward millions of users in a matter of weeks. There was a pervasive sense of "if you build it, they will come" echoing among the cornfields of early developers as they leapt at the chance to mow them down and build baseball diamonds. However, it turns out that really does only work in the movies. Now that Platform has somewhat settled and Facebook has established more realistic rules around inviting friends to apps (which are much more focused—and rightly so—on protecting users from tidal waves of invitations at every login), it has become a widely acknowledged truth that successful application developers will need to spend some serious time on:

Ideation

Defined as "the capacity for or the act of forming or entertaining ideas." A lot of people lump "ideation" in with "synergy" as equally useless marketing terms, but both have very long histories that considerably predate our modern tech industry (the terms were first cited in 1818 and 1660, respectively, according to Merriam-Webster). Ideation, in the context of Facebook applications, means coming up with an original idea or twist on an idea. We'll cover this, plus strategy, in Chapter 2.

Strategy

Defined as "a careful plan or method." In the context of your illustrious future career as a Facebook application tycoon, strategy refers to how you plan to approach integration with Facebook Platform's myriad integration points, and the strategy you will use to spread your application.

Marketing

People often confuse marketing and selling, which are usually two sides of the same coin. For our purposes (and often in the world outside of Facebook), marketing is building demand for your service or product, whereas selling is satisfying that demand by exchanging your service or product for cold, hard currency. A whole world of application marketing is blooming alongside the world of application development, and we'll explore a bunch of those opportunities in Chapter 10.

1.3 Facebook Platform Off-Facebook

For the first half of a year that Facebook Platform was available, you could only build applications that ran inside the Facebook site itself. On December 12, 2007, Bebo launched its new application platform, which was carefully designed to use the same architecture and virtually identical tags as Facebook Platform (Bebo collaborated with Facebook on the development). Shortly thereafter, Facebook announced that it would be opening up the architecture and making it available to other social networks as a model for building out application platforms, and would even go so far as to license its technology to interested parties (see *http://developers.facebook.com/specification.php* for the high-level specification). In a world of things that are too new and young to predict, this is a particularly fresh area and it's difficult to anticipate the effects and consequences. The potential promise is that your Facebook application might run unaltered (or basically unaltered) on a variety of other websites in the near (or somewhat near) future, which really just sweetens the Platform pot, but don't count the proverbial chickens until they hatch.

Facebook Connect, launched in May 2008, takes the idea of Facebook Platform off-Facebook one step further by enabling you to include Facebook-like features in your own site. The topic is a little outside the reach of this book, but you can find more information on the Developers Wiki at *http://wiki.developers.facebook.com/index.php/Facebook_Connect*.

1.4 Facebook Platform Versus Google OpenSocial

Nobody likes a one-sided race: our competitive spirits take a beating at the unfairness of it all. Just when it looked like Facebook was going to single-handedly make a break for the cookie jar and steal all the cookies, competition popped up in the form of Google's OpenSocial Application Programming Interface (API). It's important to take a moment to understand what that means to you, the would-be Facebook developer, so that you can feel secure in your decision to write apps for this Platform.

What Exactly Is OpenSocial?

With much fanfare, Google launched OpenSocial on November 1, 2007. Now that you have the gist of Facebook Platform, think about how much more powerful it would be if your Facebook apps could run inside lots of other websites too. The promise of OpenSocial is that you can build an app that runs on *http://engage.com*, Friendster, hi5, Hyves, imeem, LinkedIn, MySpace, Ning, Oracle, orkut, Plaxo, salesforce.com, Six Apart, Tianji, Viadeo, and XING with little to no modification, giving you a potential audience of 200 million users (or double the size of Facebook, though it should be noted that installation on one of those doesn't guarantee or even cross-promote installation on others, and so the network effect of the social graph is lost). Unlike Facebook Platform, you don't need to learn a proprietary markup language, and you can take full advantage of Google Gears to have your application run on- and offline. The OpenSocial API includes three major areas of functionality, both accessible through JavaScript and via data APIs:

People
Information about individual people and their relationships to each other

Activities
Ability to post and view updates on what people are doing

Persistence
A simple key-value data store to allow server-free state-full applications

That definition obviously leaves a great deal out, and it's never wise to discount a company with more Ph.D.s per square foot than a NASCAR track has beer-drinking race fans. OpenSocial will evolve pretty quickly and a description is already beyond the scope of this subsection, so you should take a few minutes to familiarize yourself with the information Google has posted to its website (*http://code.google.com/apis/openso cial*). Like many arguments in the tech industry, some of this is going to come down to a religious war (see Mac OS versus Windows, etc.). A fair chunk of the rest is going to come down to the seemingly eternal struggle between Open and Closed, with Google and friends crusading under the Open banner and characterizing Facebook as the dark lord of Closed. There is some truth to that position: OpenSocial apps will run on any website that implements an OpenSocial container, and their environment is built on open technologies such as HTML and JavaScript, whereas Facebook requires developers to learn closed technologies such as Facebook Markup Language (FBML) and Facebook JavaScript (FBJS). The Facebook Legions would argue that Platform is really just extending the same open tech, that learning those extensions is almost trivial (as you'll soon see), and that their carefully developed and controlled environment means developers and users get more control, greater security, and easier interoperability. This is a theme that runs much deeper than the social network space, and anyone who has been in the industry for more than a few years has seen the same battle play out in any number of fields, from operating systems (Windows versus Linux) to browsers (Internet Explorer versus Firefox), and from content delivery formats (Flash versus HTML) to user interface markup languages (XAML versus XUL). The world of digital music is going through this as well in a classic, Hamlet-like struggle (to DRM or not to DRM: that is the question), and the mobile application space is about to have a similar shakeup with the release of Google Android and its push to open the previously walled gardens.

Who's Going to Win?

It's still the very early days in this battle, and therefore it's hard to predict the outcome. As of this writing, Orkut, hi5, Ning, and Plaxo have OpenSocial sandboxes or application containers enabled in some form, enabling some of their users to try Open-Social apps in the context of their sites. Anecdotal evidence from leading app developers—such as Slide, RockYou, and iLike—says that porting apps from Facebook Platform to OpenSocial is relatively trivial, which suggests that you can easily start with one and move to the other. Historical precedent indicates that some open platforms have a lot of success (Firefox has stolen a big share of the market away from Internet Explorer), whereas a number of closed systems have done even better (Apple's domination of the MP3 market is based largely on iTunes and iPods being completely closed).

Ultimately, the announcement of OpenSocial is a win for developers just like you, because it signifies a maturing marketplace backed by serious investment from major industry players. Mark Andreessen, founder of Netscape and now of OpenSocial partner Ning, agrees: "As an app developer, there's no real reason to choose between Facebook and OpenSocial. It's easy to do both. You've already put in most of the effort—creating a new set of frontend HTML and JavaScript pages is almost trivial, and that's all you need to do to have your app 'port' to Open Social...."§ Mark's proposed strategy (which is a very solid one) is to maintain a single backend with four sets of frontend pages, each optimized for different platforms:

- A set in normal HTML/JavaScript for consumption in regular browsers
- A set in FBML and FBJS for use in Facebook
- A set in normal HTML and using JavaScript to connect to the OpenSocial API for use in OpenSocial
- A possible fourth set adapted for use on mobile devices, such as Apple's iPhone

What Should I Do?

Calling Facebook Platform "mature" seems odd given how young it is, but it will always be nine months older than OpenSocial. Since the number of people who can access OpenSocial containers is currently smaller than the number of Facebook users, and since Facebook's social graph will make it easier for your application to pick up a larger user base in less time, you should start by building a Facebook version—but make sure to architect your backend services so that they are loosely joined to the frontend and can be used easily by an OpenSocial version later (we'll cover this in detail in Chapter 4).

1.5 Saddle Up!

You're about to embark on a big adventure! Just keep thinking of the gold in them thar hills while you ride across the wilderness of FBML. Don't forget to circle the wagons when you hear the hosting fees howling in the distance, and remember that the cavalry is just around the corner. It's not going to be an easy ride, but if you're dedicated and determined, you can definitely reap the rewards.

§ *http://blog.pmarca.com/2007/10/open-social-a-n.html*

CHAPTER 2

Ideation and Strategy

So! Now that you're ready to write your million-dollar Facebook app and retire to a life of luxury, there's only one small problem: what to build? You might already have an idea, or you might have come across an existing Facebook app that you think you can one-up. Maybe you have no ideas at all but are overflowing with web development fu and want to flex your coding muscles. Fear not, intrepid developer! This chapter will help you figure out the four Ws of Facebook application development:

Who should I build for?

Some of the most successful software products are born out of a need their developers felt wasn't satisfied elsewhere. If that's the case for you, build for yourself and your friends. However, many of you will be reading this book because you hope to make money from your work, in which case you need to consider your audience more carefully. Sometimes you and your friends aren't the ones who are going to pay for your villa in Maui, so make sure you spend the time to understand who is.

What can I build?

The sky is really the limit: if you can imagine it, you can probably build it. That said, before you start dreaming up the most complex application ever, keep in mind that you'll start earning users (and money) sooner if your app is released sooner, so consider how to tackle your problem in more manageable chunks. Also, keep in mind that throwaway apps that people install and play with once are much less successful (and profitable!) than apps that get used over and over. If you're new to this game, take the time (and $19) and read 37signals's *Getting Real* book, which you'll find at *http://gettingreal.37signals.com/*.

Where can I integrate with the Platform?

The Platform includes a number of "integration points," which you can use to tie your app into the everyday life of Facebookers. Simple math: the more points you hit, the more people will see your app. The more people who see it, the more who will add it. The more people who add it, the closer you get to mai tais, leis, and Maui.

Why should I build it?

That's a pretty metaphysical question! Why do anything, really? In this case, there are a few good reasons to build apps and a few less good ones. I can't promise I'll be able to satisfy all of your metaphysical needs, but keep on reading and I'll do my best to answer at least the Facebook-related ones.

More astute readers may be wondering what happened to the fifth W: when? The answer is so easy that we're not even going to cover it here: now! This really isn't rocket science, so get out there and build your first app today.

2.1 Which Types of Apps Are the Most Popular?

Problem

It's a big world out there and the sky's virtually the limit in terms of what I can build. Where do I start?

Solution

If you have no firm idea of which direction to go in, getting a feel for the pulse of Platform can definitely help. Just like doing a quick Google search and checking the number of results can help you get a feel for the amount of activity around a topic, the fastest way to get a sense of the relative popularity of app types is to look in the Facebook Application Directory (*http://www.facebook.com/apps/index.php*).

Discussion

Facebook's Application Directory lists all approved apps, organized by category. In early 2008 (and probably out-of-date before I even finished typing this), the Directory breakdown was as follows:

- Alerts (817)
- Business (746)
- Chat (1,051)
- Classified (265)
- Dating (1,194)
- Education (1,237)
- Events (796)
- Fashion (461)
- File Sharing (166)
- Food and Drink (429)
- Gaming (1,820)

- Just for Fun (7,142)
- Messaging (1,067)
- Mobile (237)
- Money (302)
- Music (870)
- Photo (704)
- Politics (543)
- Sports (1,667)
- Travel (442)
- Utility (1,481)
- Video (716)

Although there are nearly 10,000 more apps now (mid-2008) than there were then, the overall breakdown percentage-wise hasn't changed. Categories are determined by the apps' developers (you can pick yours by editing the About Page for your application), so keep in mind that this is a somewhat arbitrary and self-imposed categorization. If you've been using Facebook for some time, you probably won't be surprised to discover that the Just for Fun category has almost seven times more apps than the second biggest, Gaming. In fact, more Rain Man-like readers may have casually noticed that the list just shown adds up to 24,153 apps, even though at the time the official count sat at 16,409 (over 24,000 now). What gives? Since it's a little ambiguous whether your meticulously crafted "Go Fish" challenge should go in Gaming or Just for Fun, and since Facebook allows developers to pick up to two categories per app, you might as well stick it in both and be part of the 7,744 phantom duplicated app listings.

2.2 Which Apps Are Most Popular?

Problem

Riding onto the Platform battlefield means taking on over 26,000 opponents. Sun Tzu once said:

> Know thy self, know thy enemy. A thousand battles, a thousand victories.

Anyone can take on a thousand battles, but 26,000? That takes real courage. How can I possibly know thine enemy when there are so damn many of them?

Solution

You're probably wishing that someone had gone out and built some kind of thing that would tell you which apps have the most installs or active users. If that's true, it must be your lucky day! A few different people have done exactly that. There are two solutions with two very different approaches:

SocialMedia's Appsaholic

You can either install the Appsaholic Facebook application (*http://apps.facebook.com/appsaholic*) or register for an account on *http://www.socialmedia.com* and then use the web application. (If you're doing any work on Bebo or OpenSocial, go for the web version because it can track apps on all platforms.)

Deft Labs' AppHound

AppHound is available as a Facebook app (*http://apps.facebook.com/apphound*).

Discussion

Either one of those apps will help peel back the curtain and give you a glimpse into the sometimes bizarre world of Facebook app popularity. They won't, of course, tell you what made each of the apps as popular as it is, but they will help you develop an understanding of the kinds of apps people install, what motivates them to keep the app after installation, and general trends rippling their way across the Platform landscape.

Appsaholic (see Figure 2-1) has been around a lot longer than AppHound and is the basis for the so-called SocialMedia app network, which SocialMedia created to help developers track, monetize, and advertise their software. All of this is done through the sale and purchase of advertising spots on the Canvas pages of other apps, with the general idea being the creation of a marketplace in which developers effectively trade users back and forth. Using the calculator on its site (*http://www.socialmedia.com/market*), as of this writing, if your average user referred 1.25 additional users and you went through 10 levels of referrals, you could buy 8,513,225 new users for $50,000 (or $0.006/user). If you were able to sustain a 10% daily active rate (i.e., 10% of your users use your app every day), you would rank fifth on today's Top Apps scale. More realistically, if you saved yourself a doughnut and spent $5,000, you could buy (surprise!) 851,322 users, which might give you 8,513 dailies for a ranking in the top 1,000 apps.

AppHound might be more your cup of tea if you're not looking to monetize your app and just want a better understanding of the market. The user interface is simpler to navigate and it allows you to define "trackers," which are basically notifications when specified events occur (e.g., when your application's daily usage grows by more than 5%). An example screenshot of the AppHound Facebook app is shown in Figure 2-2.

Once you've decided what to build, you should jump into AppHound and add trackers for all the apps you consider competitive. Let's say you are going to write a quiz game and want to get a sense of how the genre is making out. Using AppHound's Browse feature, you can get an index of the top apps in each category of the Facebook Application Directory, ranked by total number of installs. A quick trip to the Gaming category will show you which quiz apps are doing the best, and you can throw a couple of trackers on them to receive alerts about changes in their popularity. Also, bonus points to Deft Labs for realizing that those of us who want to track Platform aren't doing our research as a social activity; AppHound doesn't publish a Profile Box or add stories to your feed.

Figure 2-1. Scrabulous in SocialMedia's Appsaholic web app and Facebook app

Figure 2-2. Scrabulous in Deft Labs' AppHound Facebook app

2.3 Test-Driving Ideas with Facebook Polls

Problem

I think I have an amazing idea for a Facebook app or a feature, but I want to test it out before I go and build the whole thing.

Solution

Facebook Polls offers a cost-effective way to get some real-time feedback on an idea before you invest a lot of time and effort. You can find out more about Polls at *http://www.facebook.com/business/?polls*, and you can jump straight into creating a new Poll at *https://secure.facebook.com/add_poll.php* (Figure 2-3).

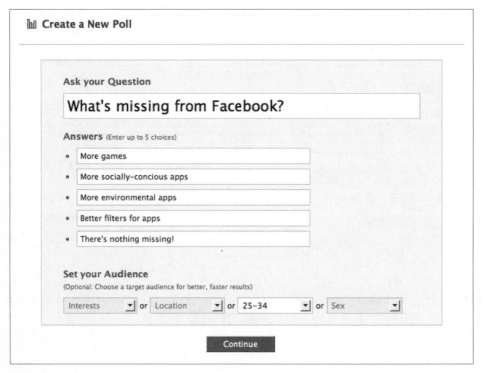

Figure 2-3. Create a New Poll, step 1

Polls consist of a short question and up to five multiple-choice options. You can filter your audience by one of Interests, Location, Age, or Sex in order to shrink your audience and get an answer faster, or you can just leave it open to anyone.

The second step (Figure 2-4) is all about the Benjamins: paying for your Poll.

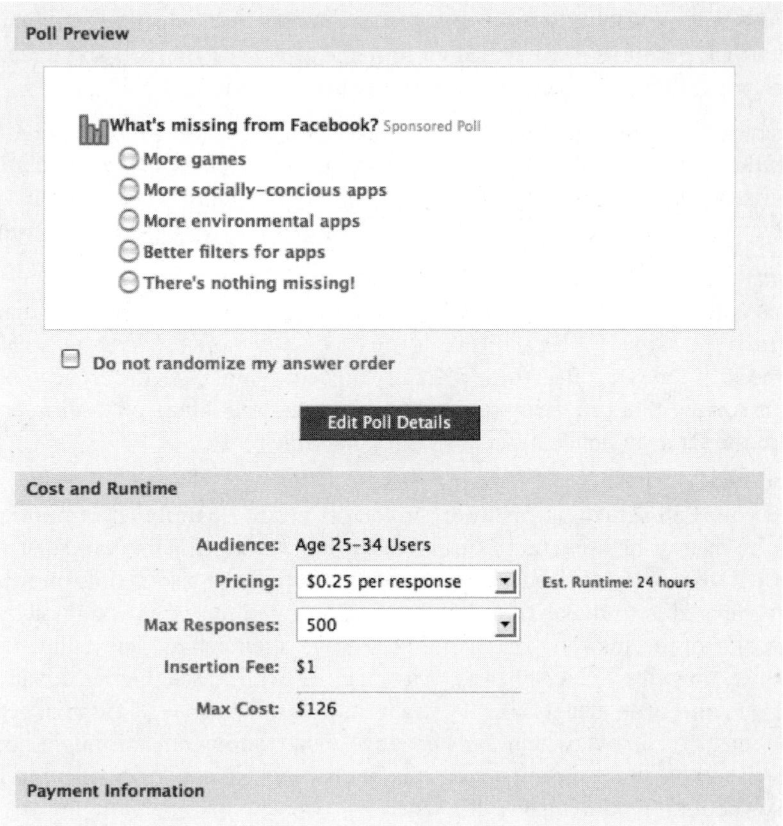

Poll Preview

What's missing from Facebook? Sponsored Poll
- ○ More games
- ○ More socially-concious apps
- ○ More environmental apps
- ○ Better filters for apps
- ○ There's nothing missing!

☐ Do not randomize my answer order

Edit Poll Details

Cost and Runtime

Audience:	Age 25-34 Users
Pricing:	$0.25 per response ▾ Est. Runtime: 24 hours
Max Responses:	500 ▾
Insertion Fee:	$1
Max Cost:	$126

Payment Information

Figure 2-4. Create a New Poll, step 2

The top of this screen gives a preview, the middle lets you configure how much you want to spend, and the bottom (omitted in the screenshot) gathers your credit card information. You'll note in the middle section that you pay a $1 insertion fee and can then select either $0.25 or $0.50 per response (with estimated runtimes of 24 or 48 hours, respectively), as well as a maximum number of responses. You may never get to that number if people don't feel like participating, so the maximum cost indicated here really is just an estimate until you see how the Poll plays out. You'll see the $1 fee hit your card immediately and the rest of the fee at the conclusion of the Poll.

You'll be given a URL for the dashboard of your Poll, where you can watch the results roll in as they happen. Facebook provides a demo poll (*http://tinyurl.com/4r3m84*), which shows you a "What's your favorite soft drink?" example that was answered by 148 users.

Discussion

In researching this book, I spoke to many accomplished developers who told me that using Polls was almost like a secret weapon in their success (which I humbly reveal to you with their permission): they had all started down a certain road and ended up on a completely different but very popular route thanks to the results of a Poll.

If you haven't done many statistics courses before (or if they were more slanted toward the math side of stats and less to their application in the social sciences), you might not be familiar with the ideas of reliability and validity. Both are critical to building any kind of survey if you're going to rely on the answers to make important decisions:

Reliability

> This is the constancy of your measurement. A survey is considered reliable if it returns the same result each time it runs (i.e., a person's score is reasonably the same each time she takes the test). This can be thought of as the "repeatability" of your survey. You can verify reliability by running the same Poll at different times with the same audience to see if you get the same result.

Validity

> Did your Poll actually measure what you set out to quantify? It's important that you're measuring an actual causal relationship, rather than a coincidence in the data. It's harder to construct an invalid Poll when you're asking only one question, but the goal is to make sure that the question you're asking is actually a direct outcome of the answers you've offered. People often behave very differently from the way they think they will, and so it can be difficult to ask them in advance what the outcome of an idea will be. If you asked, "Would you pay $5 for a widget app?", you might get an overwhelmingly negative answer; however, this might not be the case if you had built the app and it caught on, in which case respondents who now knew about it would answer differently.

Since Polls are really cheap to run, you should consider building out some part of your idea and then creating a series of reliable and valid questions that test your plans. Don't necessarily abandon them if the results don't jibe with your expectations, but keep an open mind about the possibilities that come out of the surveys.

2.4 The Winning Formula for Facebook

—Jayant Agarwalla (see his bio in Contributors)

Problem

What's the winning formula for creating a successful Facebook application?

Solution

Never build an application that you think will be successful. Always build an application that you *know* will be successful. Think carefully. Is your app going to have a seasonal appeal? Is it something that will not lose its charm after being used 100 times by a user? Are there any existing apps that are similar? If so, have you looked at their discussion boards and written down all the flaws? Getting a user to try a new app is difficult, but getting a user to switch from one app to another is nearly impossible. Try to build an application only when you see the need for it.

Discussion

Ever since Facebook launched its platform in May 2007, there has been a frenzy of activity amongst developers across the world. While there were only a handful of applications in the first couple of months, Facebook now has nearly 30,000 of them. Facebook applications have sublimely demonstrated the immense potential of a social network, in terms of entertainment as well as a solid revenue source.

Flipping the coin, however, shows us the darker side. In October 2007, a report prepared by a research team headed by Tim O'Reilly had revealed shocking results: 87% of application usage went to just 84 applications (out of around 5,000 applications at that time). And only 45 applications had more than 100,000 daily active users. Seven months hence, Facebook is healthier by more than 20 million users and 21,000 applications. But amazingly, only 50 applications now have more than 100,000 users! I think it's safe to say that more than 80% of application usage goes to not more than 120 applications today.

Why? It's simply because the developers are not planning for the long term. There are hundreds of applications out there that took perhaps thousands of dollars to build but have barely a few thousand active users. Many developers lose hope if their first application is not successful. We have learned a lot in the time since we created Scrabulous. Check out the following tips.

Try to build an application that is social in nature

Your application must be able to exploit the highly social nature of Facebook. If you build a top-notch Spades (card game) application that does not show top scores or best ratings of peers, it will disappear without a trace. There are tons of casual gaming sites, and it's nearly impossible to get someone to use a single-player application on Facebook. Keep in mind that the News Feed and Notifications are awesome tools to reach hundreds of thousands of users quickly. Use them to their full potential. This will also lower your costs on marketing and advertising.

Clean or vibrant look

Decide carefully whether your application will have more appeal as a highly colorful and bubbly app or as a more sober application. The "Who Has the Biggest Brain?" social game by Playfish is an excellent example of a flourishing application that uses a lot of graphics. No wonder it has made it to the top 20 so fast. With Scrabulous, we have done away with sounds and animations, but users are very happy with the way things are. The games load very quickly and there is no disturbance in game play.

Seasonal or long-term prospects

Working on seasonal apps such as Christmas greeting cards is not a bad idea. But try to have apps for most of the popular seasons or festivals so that users always think of your company when it comes to sending gifts or greetings. If you are planning for the long term, make sure that users will not get bored of the app. You should have enough resources to expand smoothly and meet user demands as quickly as possible. The moment you slow down, you will have stiff competition.

When to monetize

In case you are not just out to make a quick buck, it is highly recommended that you refrain from showing a crazy amount of ads, even if you think they will not be intrusive. Go simple. It's essential to retain users and provide them with excellent support. Spend more time reading discussion boards and walls than testing out the various ad networks.

Scalability

You have to be extremely cautious when it comes to making a scalable system. If your app is super cool but has high levels of downtime, users will soon lose interest in it. And once a user removes your app, getting him to add the app back is next to impossible.

Branding and appeal

Last, but definitely not least, make sure you have a powerful brand equity. Spend your spare time on weekends trying to think of the perfect name for your app. If you have a brand that users will love, they will talk about it and refer it to their friends as well. And make sure you book a domain of the same name. Having a strong identity might also help you secure financing more easily.

2.5 Where's the Money?

Problem

I'm totally excited about building my app, but something keeps bugging me. Where's the money in this game? How can I make mad cash through my apps?

Solution

If you're in this app-building game to make a quick buck, you're in the wrong game. There was a time when your app could attract a million users overnight, but those days are long gone (and probably for the better, since users hated being bombarded with constant app propaganda). Platform has evolved to become much more focused on keeping users happy, sometimes at the expense of app developers who had gotten used to attracting users through certain channels and are adverse to change.

That said, if you're determined and ready to put in the work, you can definitely still make a really good living from Facebook apps. There are lots of examples of developers (some of whom have contributed recipes to this book) doing very well off the apps they've built. Try to stay away from the tempting world of quick, throwaway apps, in which you build hundreds of them, keep the ones that make a little cash, and hopefully end up on top of the world. Sadly, this often just leads to lots of apps that don't make any money, and it upsets the small user base they attract when you stop supporting them, thereby guaranteeing that those users won't install any more of your apps and would firebomb your house if they only knew where you lived.

Discussion

Generally speaking, people who make money from Facebook apps do it by running ads inside of their apps. You're certainly not limited to doing this, and I encourage you to think up a completely new business model for making money on social networks (and then whisper it in my ear before you launch!). Most of the ad networks listed in Chapter 10, *Marketing Your App*, also provide developers with the ability to insert ads into their apps, so take a look at that list and check out their offerings. It's tough to get any real answers out of these networks about what you can expect to earn in terms of effective cost per thousand impressions (eCPM), so your best bet is to split up the available impressions you have between a few networks and monitor the amount they pay. Run that experiment for a week or two, and then start dropping the lowest paying networks until you've optimized your ad inventory sales to the highest margin buyers.

Here's a sample of the ways people have been monetizing to date, which might inspire some ideas for your apps:

Banner/skyscraper/text ads
> Any ad that you can run on an off-Facebook website also can be run on Facebook. Click-through rates tend to be lower on Facebook than off, but you can still earn

some money from running them. It's not a bad idea to design your pages so they have space for these ads, but don't count on them paying the mortgage.

Other apps

There's a whole underworld market of app developers selling each other installs, which can be a great way to line the pockets of developers who have popular apps while attracting lots of potentially interested users to your app. As you grow in popularity, you can earn a nice income by selling installs to other developers. Those installs work best when they're between related apps, so try to think of places in your app where it would logically make sense to suggest another app. Then, scope out some apps that would benefit from advertising in those spaces.

Product placement

There are lots and lots of brands that are still trying to crack the Facebook nut. If you do a really good job of monitoring your Facebook Insights statistics for your app and know your demographic, you can carefully engineer places to insert products and get paid for it. Consider, as examples, Facebook's own Gifts app and iLike, which are both excellent examples of product placement at work. Gifts recently included 250,000 free Indiana Jones fedoras to support the release of *The Kingdom of the Crystal Skull* (Figure 2-5).

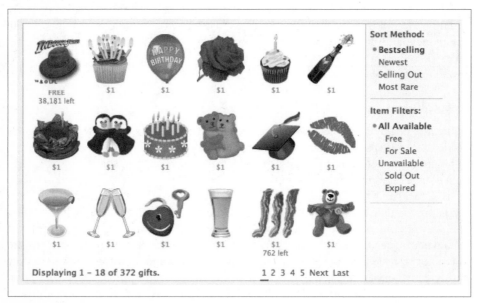

Figure 2-5. Facebook Gifts product placement

E-commerce

There hasn't been a lot of success in this area, mostly because Facebook currently doesn't offer developers a mechanism to accept payments through the site. You can create an integration to a third-party gateway such as PayPal or Google

Checkout fairly easily, but users have shown some resistance both to leaving Facebook and to paying for things that have traditionally been free (as they are in most of the apps in the Facebook ecosystem). Facebook has announced that it will be offering a payment gateway service to developers, so it's worth starting to plan out how you would take advantage of that.

Loss leader

Lots of apps on Facebook are extensions of off-Facebook brands or websites. Many of them are built on the premise that they can grab a chunk of the Facebook audience and gradually pull them into the off-Facebook site, where they can sell them upgraded accounts or show them more ads. This is a pretty solid idea, except that users on Facebook show a very strong resistance to leaving it. If you can figure out how to leverage their loyalty into upgrades to pay accounts without leaving the site, you might be on to something.

Guns for hire

If you're a crack team of Facebook developers but aren't big on ideas, don't discard the avenue of getting paid to build apps for other people. There's a lot of money out there in helping the world's agencies and brands establish their foothold on Facebook, and many of them are desperately looking for reliable resources who they can call on as needed. You can start by listing yourself in the Facebook Marketplace, but if you don't have a portfolio to call your own, you should get started on one. For those of you who are really pressed for ideas, consider finding a not-for-profit or charity whose work you dig and offer to build an app for them for free, provided they throw their marketing effort and budget behind building up users.

2.6 Google AdSense and Facebook

Problem

I'm using Google AdSense on my websites to run ads, and I really like the system. Can I use it inside Facebook?

Solution

You can, but it's a little more complicated than just dropping your AdSense code into place. Facebook's FBJS parser won't allow straight JavaScript through without adding all kinds of funky namespace and sandbox security to your code, which prevents Google's insertion script from working at all.

The generally accepted technique is to embed an `fb:iframe` tag in your Canvas page, which will load the AdSense ads inside your Canvas. Since AdSense works by selecting ads that are relevant to the content on the page, it's important that you create that context by passing some parameters to the page for use in the meta keywords, description, and page title:

```
<fb:iframe
 src="http://www.someserver.com/adsense.php?title=My%20Encoded%20Title&keywords=My%2
 0endcoded%20keywords&desc=My%20encoded%20desc"/>
```

Discussion

AdSense still pays out some of the best cost-per-click (CPC) rates around and has bigger reach than anyone else. However, it should be noted that the system isn't tailored to social networks, so you might get more relevance running ads from something like SocialMedia or Cubics.

2.7 Funding Facebook Development

Problem

I've heard that you can raise money if you're a developer with a good idea. Is that true?

Solution

A number of funds have been set up to back companies building Facebook applications, including:

Facebook's own fbFund
> fbFund gives grants between $25,000 and $250,000 (grants are awesome because you don't have to pay them back). There have been about nine grants so far, and the fund has plenty of money left in it. For more information, see *http://www.face book.com/developers/fbfund.php*.

Bay Partners' App Factory
> Bay Partners, a well-respected Valley-based venture capitalist (VC), has set up a fund called App Factory, which is "a fast-track program supporting entrepreneurs dedicated to developing applications for Facebook Platform." You can find more information at *http://www.baypartners.com/appfactory/*.

Altura Ventures' Altura 1 Facebook Investment Fund
> This fund exclusively backs developers of Facebook apps. You can get more info at *http://www.altura.com/* or in their Facebook group at *http://www.facebook.com/ group.php?gid=2392191727*.

Discussion

Investing in Facebook apps is really just like investing in non-Facebook apps, so there's no reason to limit yourself to the VCs and funds just listed. If you have a solid idea and the right team to pull it off, and especially if you have a monetization strategy in place and have built out some realistic projections, you should get in front of as many potential investors as possible. If you're unfamiliar with the world of VCs and angels, spend a little time reading their blogs and doing some Google research before you embarrass yourself in a pitch session. Start with *http://www.ventureblogs.com/*, which lists most of the good VC blogs.

2.8 Facebook Platform Integration Points

Problem

What are Facebook Platform's integration points?

Solution

It's tough to wrap your head around a limitless space that stretches on forever in every direction. How would you even start painting it? Limitations can be really helpful to get the creative mojo flowing in the right direction, even when those limitations don't actually impose many constraints. As a would-be Facebook developer, you need to know exactly where and how you can integrate with Platform so that you can wield your weapons most effectively.

Facebook Platform offers 10 official integration points that your app can hook into:

1. Application Directory
2. Application Menu
3. Facebook Canvas Pages
4. Profile Box
5. Info Sections
6. News Feed
7. Notifications
8. Attachments and the Publisher
9. Requests
10. Tabs

Discussion

Not all integration points are created equal, as we shall soon see. Facebook has made it easy for you to take advantage of all of them, and the most successful apps definitely do, so whenever you're designing a new product, keep the handy AAFPINNART acronym in mind (see the previous list). The bulk of this chapter goes through each of these points and gives you the quick rundown, and you can also check out Chapters 6 and 7 for more information about how to implement them.

2.9 Application Directory

Problem

What can I put in my Application Directory listing?

Solution

Every approved app gets a listing in the Application Directory; this is your place to shine when bored users are looking to spice up their Profiles. It's pretty rare for people to browse the Directory directly, since almost all application installs come as a result of the other integration points (unless they have a very specific Facebook itch that needs scratching). Don't overlook the Directory, though, since your app's About Page is part of it (which users will often view as a precursor to installing the app; see an example in Figure 2-6), and the description will appear in the right sidebar when users are adding your app. If you've never seen it before, you can browse the directory at *http://www .facebook.com/apps*.

Discussion

Five things make up your Application Directory listing (some of which make appearances elsewhere as well), and we'll examine them through the lens of the Causes application.

Application icon

You have a very, very tiny 16 × 16 pixel canvas to showcase your masterpiece. This icon will appear in the Applications menu, Message Attachment, and News Feed integration points, as well as in places like the Application Privacy Settings, so you want something distinctive that is going to stand out from the crowd but still represent your app. The Causes app uses a globe with two people in front of it, as shown in Figure 2-7.

It's really hard to draw something meaningful at this size, so do yourself a favor and find a designer to give your app some professional polish. If you don't know any, post a message to the Facebook Marketplace offering to trade some development resources for some creative ones, or take a look at sites like ProgrammerMeetDesigner (*http:// www.programmermeetdesigner.com*).

Figure 2-6. PackRat About Page

Figure 2-7. Causes icon

Application logo

You get to upload an image, up to 75 × 75 pixels, that will represent your application in the Directory listing pages. This is going to be the first impression users have of your baby when they see it listed among the other 1,067 Messaging apps, so get the same designer who made your icon to make the logo (you did get a designer to make the icon, right?). Causes uses a larger version of their app icon, as shown in Figure 2-8, which is a great way to build a brand through consistency.

Figure 2-8. Causes logo

Application description

You've just spent days toiling over your new app, and now you have to synthesize all that amazing functionality and mind-blowing cool into 250 measly characters. What to do? Take a look at the leading apps in your category (i.e., your competition) and see what they wrote. Stay away from describing your technological wizardry in favor of the awesome benefits that potential users will receive by installing it. In other words, break free from the tyranny of the Three-Letter Acronyms (TLAs), and avoid mentioning anything that isn't a real word. Try to use a more active tone ("Play Go Fish! Amaze your friends!") instead of a passive one ("You can play Go Fish"), since it adds more vibrancy to your message (and often takes up fewer characters). The description for Causes fits that model really well:

> Make a difference, on Facebook! Causes on Facebook lets you start and join the causes you care about. Donations to causes can benefit over a million registered 501(c)(3) nonprofits.

This text is also key because Facebook indexes this content for the search function in the Application Directory. You should try to get a bunch of relevant keywords in here so that you app turns up when people are searching for things like it.

Application picture

The picture is displayed on the app's About Page within the Application Directory. Although size restrictions are not actually listed on the upload page, your image will be scaled down to a maximum of 396 × 396 pixels, so you're better off working at that size from the beginning. These pictures are typically screenshots of the application, but feel free to get creative here and do something that really draws people in. And, of course, you don't need me to tell you to get your trusty designer to make it really shine, right?

Causes deviates slightly from the norm in that their Picture is a screenshot of the Profile Box rather than of the app itself, as shown in Figure 2-9.

Figure 2-9. Causes picture

Application categories

You'll have the option to choose two categories for your app from the full list of 22. Keep in mind that some of them are a lot more crowded than others, so if you can justify having your app categorized as File Sharing or Mobile, you'll be a much bigger fish in a much smaller pond (see Recipe 2.1, earlier in this chapter, for a full breakdown of categories). Causes is listed in the Education and Politics categories.

Measuring About Page success

The concept of A-B testing will be familiar to anyone who has tested speakers in a stereo store or built a sophisticated online marketing or e-commerce site. The name actually comes from the stereo test, in which two sets of speakers are connected to the same amplifier and are tested by flipping the A-B switch back and forth while the same music plays. The online version takes a little more work but a lot less crawling around in the dark trying to remember which side of the speaker wire is the positive connector. The same general principle applies: try two versions of something and see which gives the better result. This concept will come up again in Chapter 10 as a more general tool to stick in your tool belt, since it works equally well for things like invitations.

Think of this as an experiment in which you're going to gradually refine your About Page content until you've tweaked your visit-to-install ratio into install-base nirvana. We'll keep this example short by focusing on the Application Description. This will give you the general idea, which you can then apply throughout your app design. You'll need to track your success, so create a spreadsheet with different Descriptions in each row of column A, and then columns for each day you'll be running the experiment in columns B and up. I'd suggest keeping each iteration short but long enough to take into account different Facebook usage patterns on different days of the week. If you can spare a full seven-day period for each iteration, you'll have all your bases covered; if not, you can probably assume that most weekdays are the same and leave weekends out. Running a round is simple: at the start of the test period, swap the next version of the Description into your application, and then diligently record the number of installs over the interval (don't fret if you miss a day, since you can always look up your numbers through Facebook's Insights tool or on a third-party tool such as SocialMedia).

 You may be wondering why you need to go to the trouble of tracking this yourself, since there are other options out there that will track it for you. Good question! If you're content with the analysis they provide, save yourself the extra work and go with their numbers. If you'd like to be able to easily extract your stats into other reports or if you will be generating your own complex analysis or graphs, you'll want your own data set in an easy, spreadsheet-like format.

As with experiments in the real world, you have to follow scientific principles here and make sure you change only one variable at a time. If you change your app's Description and Photo at the same time, you'll have no way of measuring which one was responsible for an increase in uptake. Since we're focusing on the Description, try to keep everything else static while you refine just that piece. If you see a precipitous drop in installs right away, feel free to abandon all scientific reason and logic (no doubt setting countless scientific forebears spinning in their graves) and skip to the next variant. This kind of data unfortunately tends to be a closely guarded trade secret, so there's no established metric I can tell you to aim for. This makes it especially important to define your success criteria before you start or you'll be doing this forevermore. Establish a ratio that will make you happy, and stop when you hit it (but keep an eye on the ratio over time, since it will likely start to drop off and you'll need to begin again).

2.10 Navigating the Applications Menu

Problem

The Applications menu seems really sophisticated and slick. How does it work?

Solution

There used to be a Left Nav, which was the area that ran vertically down the left edge of Facebook's main content area and included the Facebook logo, search box, users' installed Applications, and a "skyscraper" format ad. That was removed in the Profile redesign of mid-2008, in favor of a site-wide Applications menu in the blue bar at the top of each page, as shown in Figure 2-10.

Figure 2-10. Page header with Applications menu

Clicking on Applications opens the menu shown in Figure 2-11.

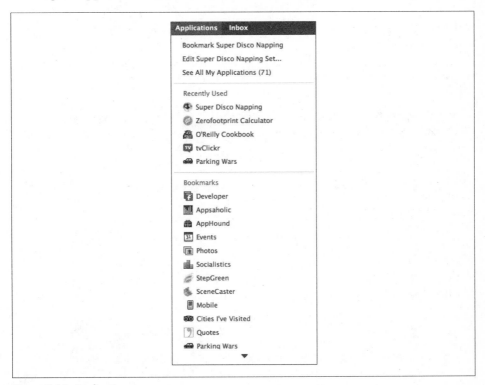

Figure 2-11. Applications menu open

The menu is divided into three sections: the top contains commands related to the current app or to all apps; the second lists the five most recent apps in which you've viewed at least one Canvas page; and the third lists all of the apps you've "bookmarked," which includes all of the apps you've added to your Profile.

Selecting "Bookmark [App Name]" opens a pop-up dialog (shown in Figure 2-12) with a checkbox indicating the current state of the bookmark.

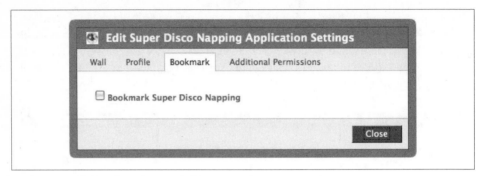

Figure 2-12. Bookmark application dialog

This is slightly confusing because the menu item should really be something like "Add Bookmark for [App Name]..." and should change to "Remove Bookmark for [App Name]..." if it's bookmarked. Selecting "Edit [App Name] Settings..." opens the same dialog but on the Wall tab instead of the Bookmark tab, as shown in Figure 2-13.

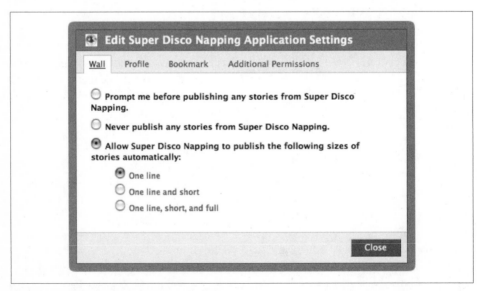

Figure 2-13. Edit Application Settings dialog

Finally, selecting "See All My Applications" goes to the full application listing page shown in Figure 2-14, where you can reorder your bookmarked apps.

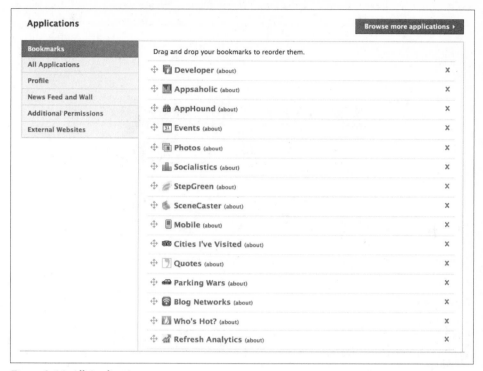

Figure 2-14. All Applications page

As a developer, this menu is of little interest to you, because you have no control over whether your application appears in it (you used to have an integration point on the Left Nav bar if users allowed it). That said, consider that your app's name and icon are still primary real estate because they will at least turn up on the "Recently Used" list, and you want to make sure that your entry is memorable.

2.11 Facebook Canvas Pages

Problem

Where do users go when they're actually using my application?

Solution

Every artist needs a canvas, and you're no exception. The Facebook Canvas is the area you work in when you're crafting your masterpiece of interface design and elegant code creation. App developers have the choice of building their apps as Canvas pages, which reside within the Facebook navigation frame, or as iFrames, which pull content from a different server and display it in place. Unless you have a make-or-break reason to use an iFrame, always go with the Canvas page option because then you'll be able to take full advantage of things like FBML and FBJS. The Canvas page, shown in Figure 2-15, is the blue square in Facebook's Deep Integration diagram (although it shows the old Profile design with the Left Nav rather than the newer design, which has a wider Canvas).

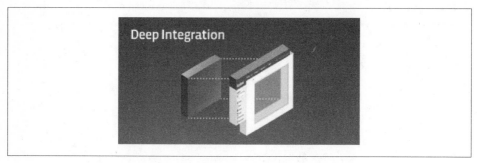

Figure 2-15. Facebook's Deep Integration diagram showing the Canvas page

Discussion

The most important thing to remember here, especially if you're building a Facebook version of something that already exists elsewhere on the Web (and especially if you're adapting a Flash movie), is that the Canvas area is only 760 pixels wide (up from 646 pixels in the old Profile design), so you may have to play with your layout to get it to fit. Calling this an integration point is a bit of a stretch, since Canvas pages are really only seen by users who are using your app (rather than their friends who are being exposed to it through the social graph), but you'll also spend the vast majority of your time building them, so pay close attention.

2.12 Think Outside the Profile Box

Problem

How do I get all this awesome data I have about my users out of the Canvas page and into their social graph?

Solution

One of the best ways to leverage the social graph is to show information about your users to their friends in way that inspires them to install your app as well. The best place to find information about a person is on their Profile, so it makes sense that the Profile Box is one of the best ways for you to share.

Discussion

Users have the option of allowing your app to display a Profile Box on their Boxes page when they install it (this is enabled by default), and they can then reorder and resize the box by dragging it up or down and from the wide to narrow column. As an app developer, you get to decide where your box goes by default and can build different layouts for both. Compare, for example, the difference between the Zerofootprint Calculator's two Profile Boxes, shown in Figures 2-16 and 2-17.

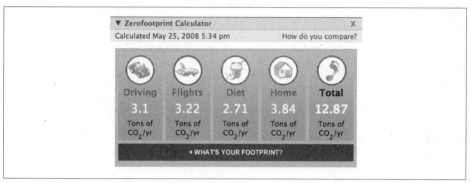

Figure 2-16. Profile Box (wide)

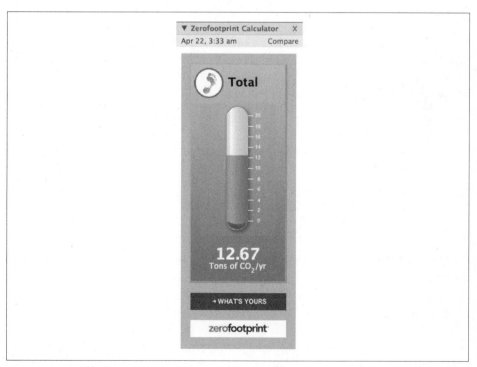

Figure 2-17. Profile Box (narrow)

The mid-2008 Profile redesign introduced a third size of box, which can reside in the left sidebar of the main Wall tab and is height-limited to 250 pixels. If your app includes a box of that size, your users can choose to add it to their main Wall tab instead of only on their Boxes tab.

2.13 Info Sections

Problem

I have some great structured data about my users, and I'd love for them to be able to publish it on their Profiles.

Solution

The Info tab, which debuted in the mid-2008 Profile redesign, gives apps the ability to publish structured data about users. Info sections are 540 pixels wide (including padding) and are dynamically sized vertically to fit your content. Your section will have a 25-character bolded title across the top, and Facebook will render a See All link if there's more content than will fit.

Your Info section is made up of field/value pairs, with each field's label being about 30 characters long (try to keep them to one line if possible). Facebook will automatically adjust the case of your title and add a colon (:) to the end if you forget. Values can be made up of text blocks (which you'll tokenize and add hyperlinks to) or objects (which can include pictures).

Discussion

The Facebook Groups app shows a good text-based section, as shown in Figure 2-18.

Groups — See All (5)

Member of: Franklin Pierce College Alumni UNDER 40, O'Reilly Tools of Change for Publishing, Business of Software, OSCON 2008, O'Reilly Media

Figure 2-18. Mary Treseler's groups (my editor!)

The Facebook Pages app renders a good example of an object-based section, shown in Figure 2-19.

See Recipe 9.25 for more information on setting Info sections.

Figure 2-19. Facebook Pages Info section

2.14 News Feed and Mini-Feed

Problem

How can I get my users to spread the good word about my app to their friends?

Solution

If success on Facebook is all about getting your message spread around the social graph, then the News Feed is your primary target. Think of it as the play-by-play announcer in a giant game of tag: almost every action you take on Facebook generates an item that appears in the Mini-Feed on your Profile. If it just stopped there it would still be a useful message-spreading tool, but luckily for us, the fun has just begun! Those same items can also appear in your friends' News Feeds on their home pages, announcing everything you've done to everyone who cares.

Facebook processes over a billion News stories per day, running them through a super-sophisticated algorithm that determines which tidbits about your friends will turn up in your Feed. The end result is that your app can publish one story about each user every 12 hours, all of which will appear in that user's Mini-Feed and some of which will get broadcast out to their friends via the News Feed.

Discussion

My News Feed (Figure 2-20) contains some subset of the stories that have been published about my friends, as determined by Facebook's top-secret algorithm, likely created by a crack team of ninjas and Tibetan monks.

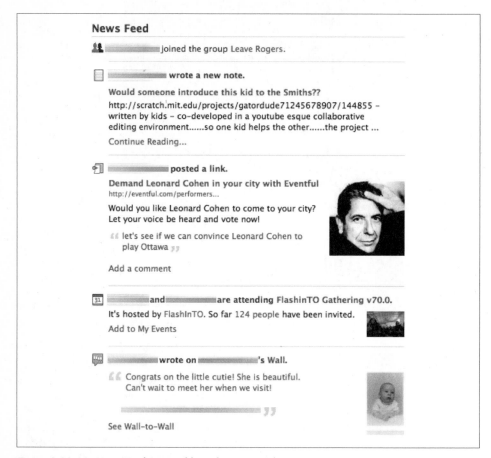

Figure 2-20. My News Feed (names blurred to protect the not-so-innocent)

As seen here, the Feed includes the icon of the application that published the story (in this case, Groups, Notes, Posted Items, Events, and Wall). Posts can include a *title* and a *body* (the Groups story only has a title, and the rest have both), and up to four images, which will be resized to fit within a 75 × 75 pixel area and cached by Facebook.

Each Facebook user also has a Mini-Feed, which appears as part of the Profile (see Figure 2-21).

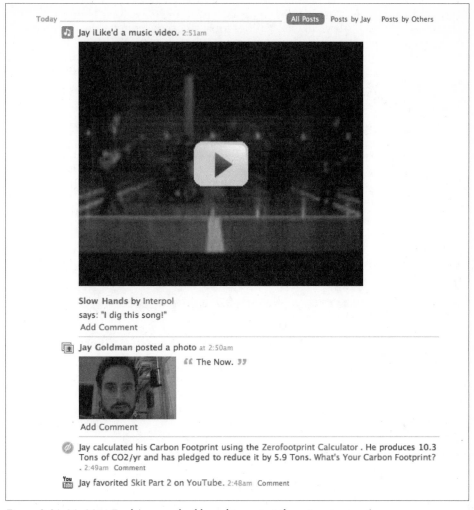

Figure 2-21. My Mini-Feed (names also blurred to protect the not-so-innocent)

Your Mini-Feed will contain every News story that gets published about you, regardless of whether your friends saw it in their News Feed. It also has the ability to import Mini-Feed items from external sites using the "Import" link in the box's subtitle, which is responsible for the YouTube story you see in my Mini-Feed. The Profile redesign launched in mid-2008 merged the previously separate Wall and Mini-Feed into a single tab of the Profile, with the ability to filter entries using the small filter control at the top of the screenshot in Figure 2-21 (setting the filter to "Posts by Jay" essentially makes it the Mini-Feed, and "Posts by Others" makes it the Wall).

Users now have a lot more control over how stories appear in their Feeds. Each entry can appear in one-line, short, and full sizes (assuming the developer of the app has provided templates for each size), and users can set an app-wide default, which they can override for each story. Overall settings for apps can be edited from the All Applications page, which brings up a settings dialog (Figure 2-22).

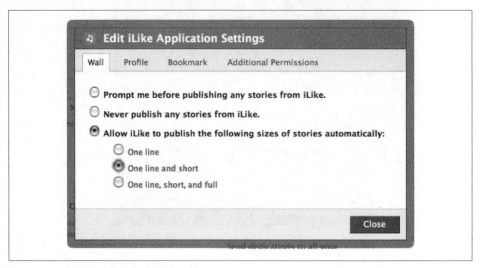

Figure 2-22. iLike application settings

Clicking on the blue pencil to the right of each story title on their Wall shows a pop-up menu with story-specific size options (Figure 2-23).

Figure 2-23. Feed story options

The iLike application has templates for each size: one-line, short, and full (Figures 2-24, 2-25, and 2-26, respectively).

Figure 2-24. iLike one-line story

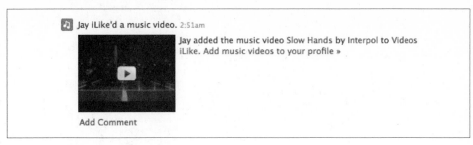

Figure 2-25. iLike short story

Figure 2-26. iLike full story

Facebook users can adjust their privacy settings (*http://www.facebook.com/privacy/?view=feeds*) to control the items that appear in their Mini-Feeds (and therefore in other users' News Feeds), as shown in Figure 2-27.

The best use of News Feed stories is to broadcast a significant action taken by a user of your application that includes some relevant information that the user's friends will find interesting. Remember that your primary goal is to get their friends to install the application, so think about adding a call to action that provokes their curiosity. Consider Facebook's own Photos app, which makes masterful use of the News Feed (Figure 2-28).

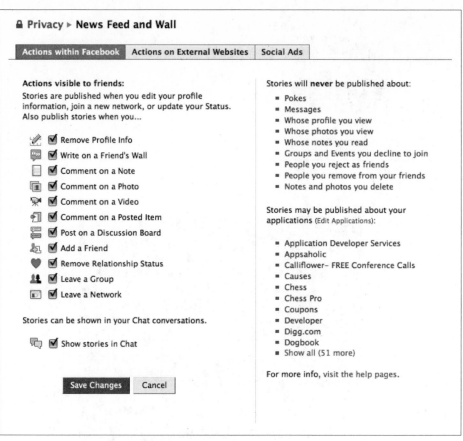

Figure 2-27. News Feed and Wall privacy settings

Figure 2-28. Photo app News Feed

Everything you need is in one place: information about your friends, what they did, a sample, and a very obvious call-to-action link to lure them into clicking.

2.15 Noteworthy Notifications

Problem

How can I keep my users coming back to my app after they've installed it?

Solution

Getting users to install your app is like G.I. Joe's message about knowledge: it's only half the battle. Your app's real success will be measured on your total install base and your percentage of active daily users, which is particularly relevant if you're planning to monetize by selling ads. You need to think about how you're going to get users engaged with your app on an ongoing basis. What's going to keep them coming back for more, and how are you going to let them know when there's more to come back to? Notifications are the key. Your app has the ability to send on-Facebook Notifications (and off-Facebook emails if users have opted into receiving them), letting your install base know about something relevant to them. It's important to keep them relevant or else users will start blocking your app, so try to think about things about which you can notify them that will really draw their interest. Scrabulous (and any game in which you challenge your friends) is a great example, since Notifications (like the one in Figure 2-29) are used to let you know that it's your turn to play.

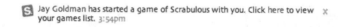

Figure 2-29. Scrabulous new game Notification

Discussion

As part of its ongoing effort to combat app spam, Facebook clamped down on Notifications in February 2008, implementing a scheme that grants applications a sliding cap on Notifications per user per day, based on how well your Notifications are being received by other users (i.e., if your Notifications get marked as spam, your available number per day will go down). You can check to see how many Notifications are available to you on the Allocations tab of the Stats area of your app in the Facebook Developer app (see Recipe 2.16 for more information). Remember that invitations from your app to another user count as a Notification, as do actual Notifications you send.

2.16 Understanding Allocations

Problem

I'm running into an allocated limitation on the number of emails I can send to users per day. I don't even understand what that means!

Solution

Back in the wild west days of the early Platform launch, you could basically send out as many Notifications and invitations per day as you'd like. This was great from a viral growth perspective, and apps like FunWall and Super Wall shot up into the millions of users range really quickly. The downside was the constant barrage of invites and Notifications that suddenly dropped Facebook's signal-to-noise ratio down the tubes (Internet tubes, naturally). Facebook responded by imposing a hard cap on the number of invites an app could send out at one time, but crafty developers found ways around it by using a succession of invite screens. Facebook responded again by imposing a hard limit on the number of invites per day, but that was limiting the majority of well-behaved apps to punish the minority of naughty ones.

So, in February 2008, Facebook responded by imposing a sliding scale system, based on how well the things you send out are received. This system, essentially a closed feedback loop, makes a good amount of sense: behave and your users will respond, thereby grading your behavior well and rewarding you with more Notifications that you can send to users who will grade your behavior, etc.

You can find out your app's allocations by visiting the Allocations tab of the Facebook Insights app at *http://www.facebook.com/business/insights/app.php?id=123456&tab= allocations* (replacing 12345 with your app's ID). Figure 2-30 shows an example.

Feedback–Based Allocations

Based on the affinity users show for your application's use of Facebook Platform through their interactions, your application is allocated certain abilities and limits. This is the functionality currently allocated to your application. These values will change over time depending on how users interact with your application. All integration points have a set of limit values and the threshold bucket column tells you which of these limits buckets your application is in for that integration point. Bucket 1 is the smallest allocation bucket.

Integration Point	Limit Threshold	Threshold Bucket
Notifications sends per user per day	15	6 out of 15
Requests per user per day	8	6 out of 13
Emails per user per day	3	4 out of 8
Email disable message location	Top	1 out of 2

Figure 2-30. Feedback-Based Allocations

Discussion

Allocations work by putting your app into a Threshold Bucket, which thereby imposes an actual threshold. If you take a look at Figure 2-30, you'll see that the app in the screenshot is allowed to send 15 Notifications per day, which is Threshold Bucket 6 of 15. That means I can move up nine more buckets, with each one giving me some higher number of allocated Notifications. They don't tell you how many extra Notifications are in each bucket, and it's not necessarily a linear scale, so it could turn out that buckets 14 and 15 each give you an extra 1,000.

The only allocation that really needs any extra explanation is the last one: "Email disable message location." Facebook will automatically append a link to disable emails from your app in every email that you send to users. It's obviously in your best interest that the link be at the bottom of the message, since users are less likely to see it way down there than they are if it comes before your content. In this case, there are only two Buckets, with the first being "Top" and the second being "Bottom."

 Jesse Stay, author of the excellent *FBML Essentials* (O'Reilly) and co-author of *I'm on Facebook—Now What???* (Happy About), gave me some great advice about Notifications. He suggested that you should build a queuing strategy into your app so that you send out less than the maximum number you're allowed, rather than running into the limit. Monitor the number of people who add/remove your app in the same period and increase the size of the queue (up to the maximum) in response to the add/remove ratio.

2.17 Attachments and the Publisher

Problem

According to Dave Morin, senior Platform manager, Facebook's servers process over a billion messages every day. Wouldn't it be fantastic if some percentage of them (even a small percentage!) included an attachment promoting my application?

Solution

Attachments are an easy way to make that happen. Prior to the Profile redesign of mid-2008, attachments were essentially limited to being attached to Facebook messages. The new Publisher—the strip of controls across the top of every Profile that enables users to publish content—now includes the ability to attach app content directly to Profiles. Every user who has your application installed will see your app's icon and Attachment Action listed in the Publisher, as shown in Figure 2-31.

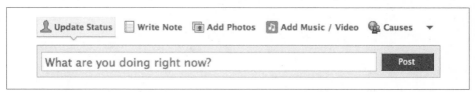

Figure 2-31. The Publisher

The "Add Music/Video" and "Causes" items in the screenshot appear because I have the iLike and Causes applications installed in my Profile. Clicking on the down arrow to the right of Causes shows a list of additional apps that offer attachments (from all of the apps I've installed), as in Figure 2-32.

Figure 2-32. Publisher attachments

Clicking on your app's link will bring up a dialog box with FBML inside, which gives your users the opportunity to customize their attachments (simpler apps might just use this box as a preview). iLike implements a fairly sophisticated mechanism, granting users a few different options for what they'd like to attach (Figure 2-33).

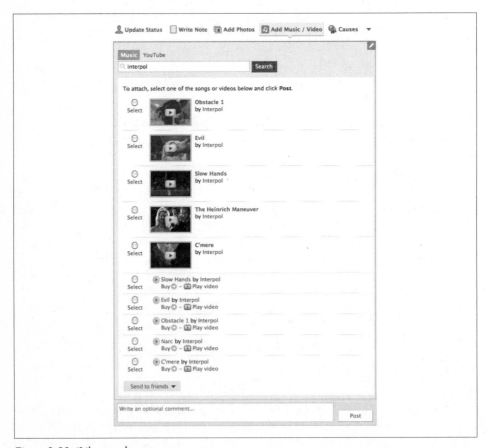

Figure 2-33. iLike attachment

Discussion

As with all of the other integration points, remember to make the attachment relevant to both the sender and receiver. The best attachments focus on something the sender is sharing with the receiver (e.g., check out my score on this quiz!) or something they want to give them (e.g., here's a gift to cheer you up!), and include a clear call to action that will bring the receiver into your app.

2.18 Requests

Problem

How can I ask users to come and do something in my app?

Solution and Discussion

It's easiest to think of requests as Notifications with an action. They carry a little more weight than general invitations into an application because they have a specific call to action associated with them, as shown in Figure 2-34.

Figure 2-34. Disco Nap request

The general idea is that you're requesting users to take an action in your app based on an action that another user has already taken. Requests tend to have a higher click-through rate than Notifications because they contain an obvious call to action, so carefully consider how you can leverage them.

2.19 Tabs

Problem

If my users really like my app, I'd like for them to be able to feature it more prominently on their Profile. Is there anything I can offer them?

Solution

You can give your app the ability to have its own Profile tab, which users can create by clicking on the + symbol tab when they're viewing their own Profile (Figure 2-35).

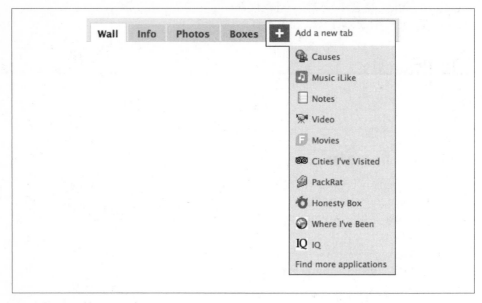

Figure 2-35. Add a new tab

Discussion

Your app will get a tab that defaults to roughly the first 15 characters of its name (although users can edit this and override it). Your tab is very similar to a Canvas page in that it has a width of 760 pixels, but different in that it loads in "passive" mode and can't autoplay any content or JavaScript until it's activated by a user.

2.20 Guiding Principles of App Strategy

Problem

Are there any general principles of Facebook app strategy that I should keep in mind while designing my app?

Solution

The Facebook team has published a set of Guiding Principles that they encourage all Platform developers to follow, grouped into three categories:

- Applications should be Meaningful.
- Applications should be Trustworthy.
- Applications should be Well-Designed.

You should try to follow all of the Principles in your app's design, particularly if you plan to apply to fbFund for funding. You can find the full list at *http://developers.face book.com/get_started.php?tab=principles*.

Discussion

The Facebook Guiding Principles are great, and you should read and practice them, but the full list is a little long. Here's a short list of things that will almost certainly make your app more successful, each of which includes some questions that you can ask yourself while you're designing your application, to help you stay focused:

Create value

People use things that add value to their lives and throw away things that don't. Your own use of Facebook apps will show the same trend: the ones that actually add value to your use of Facebook remain in your Profile and the rest get installed, stick around for a bit like a bad cold, and then get flushed down the toilet with the used tissues. Ask yourself, "What's the value this feature provides to my users?" as you work through your app's design.

Help users communicate and share information more efficiently

This is the key value proposition that the Facebook Social Graph offers: make it easy for people to find information about their friends and they'll add their own information to the network. If you can tap into an area of people's lives that they want to share with other people, you'll see much better adoption. Ask yourself, "What's the value of the information I'm helping people share?" and, "How can I make the process of sharing this as efficient as possible?"

Generate more meaningful activity

Facebook Platform is drowning in apps that deliver little value to their users because the activities undertaken in the apps are valueless. If your application doesn't include activities that users can do with each other (e.g., tagging their friends in photos), there's very little meaningful activity generated into the social graph, and consequently your app won't spread. Ask yourself, "What's the value of the activity my app adds to the social graph?" and, "How can I add value to the activities my users do with their friends both inside and outside my app?"

Provide valuable information to users

In a world in which you're competing with tens of thousands of apps for attention, the higher the value of the information you provide to your users, the more likely they are to return. This is a classic application of the signal-to-noise ratio principle. According to Wikipedia (*http://en.wikipedia.org/wiki/Signal_to_noise_ratio*):

> *Signal-to-noise ratio* (often abbreviated SNR or S/N) is an electrical engineering concept, also used in other fields (such as scientific measurements, biological cell

signaling), defined as the ratio of a signal power to the noise power corrupting the signal.

In less technical terms, signal-to-noise ratio compares the level of a desired signal (such as music) to the level of background noise. The higher the ratio, the less obtrusive the background noise is.

For our purposes, think of the valuable information your app provides as signal, and the valueless information you and the other 20,000 apps provide as noise. Ask yourself, "Can my users find the signal in all the noise?" and, "What can I do to amplify the signal and suppress the noise?"

Increase user trust

Every relationship is based on trust, including the one your users form with your app. The more that users trust your app, the more likely they are to invite their friends and to make it part of their Facebook experience. Remember that you can artificially earn trust, but you'll lose it all if users figure out that you've lied or misled them. Ask yourself, "Would I trust this app if I hadn't built it?", "Which aspects will make users lose trust?", and, "What can I do to build trust?"

2.21 Community Gardening

—Will Pate (see his bio in Contributors)

Problem

I'm an experienced developer, but now I want to build a community around my application.

Solution

Interact with your users every way you can. Listen, respond quickly, and always be friendly.

Think of a community like it's a party, and you're the host. You have to set the table, welcome the guests as they arrive, help them with anything they need, and do it all with a smile.

Discussion

Before you launch your application, create a short list of questions you would like to ask your users. "What do you like the most?", "What do you like the least?", and "What's missing?" are good questions to start with. Too many questions can be overwhelming, so embrace constraints.

Next, create a list of places to check regularly for feedback. Your application page can have discussion forums, reviews, and a Wall. Also keep an eye on community activity outside of Facebook with a Google Alert for your application name, so you can respond to blog and forum posts.

As you launch your application, be proactive and reach out to your early users. Ask them the questions you prepared, follow up on their answers, and answer any questions they may have. If a member engages with you in any way, be sure to thank them.

Ask your users to rate, review, and invite their friends to try out your application. If people seem unsatisfied, work on addressing their concerns before you ask them to tell their friends.

Pay particular attention to language. Most people are not developers, and they may not understand how you explain something. If that happens, they may feel like you are talking down to them or being dodgy. If you have to talk about technology, use clear language that is accessible to anyone.

Tone is also important. Be warm, positive, and excited. If you are pushy, negative, or lackluster, people will be turned off.

If something breaks, resist the temptation to get defensive or not respond until it's fixed. Apologize, accept responsibility, and clearly state how you are working to fix the problem. Give an ETA if you have one. When the problem is fixed, follow up to thank people for their patience and support. No reasonable person expects your application to be perfect, but they will be impressed if you act professionally when a crack shows.

2.22 Finding Inspiration

—Alistair Morton (see his bio in Contributors)

Problem

Sometimes it's hard to find a source of inspiration. I don't even know where to start looking!

Solution

Creativity isn't a system that can be learned easily. I've been told it's much like writing: the more you do it, the easier (and clearer) it gets. A great boss once told me that to be a good writer, you need to "flex" your writing muscles often. Creativity is much the same.

Discussion

Where you find elements of creativity will be quite different for different people. Let's begin with your immediate surroundings, as they will hold the keys for you to begin to visualize and associate differently. An average person, during an average day, is bombarded with television ads, art, architecture, print ads, billboards, and the like. Design and creativity simply surround us, but most of us have built up a resistance to the constant onslaught and become partially (if not fully) immune. While marketing companies fight to keep your attention, our built-in defense systems can really begin to neutralize the effect of these messages. To find a creative edge, we simply need to figure out how to turn it back on.

For some, this is something as simple as a sketchbook or a camera. Others can take in a great deal of their surroundings and process the things that speak to their creativity with ease. For the rest of us, keeping a keen eye on seeing past the messages to what might speak to people's interest is tougher, but it's possible when you store a mental note to remind yourself to try to see things slightly differently than you have before.

Similar to writing, this is an exercise you'll need to do regularly before you can really identify the patterns and inspirational elements you react to most strongly. Design tends to work in trends, and once you spend a little time making the conscious connection to it, the patterns and elements will become obvious. Just remember to keep switching off your mental filter, and you'll be surrounded by the beginnings of a creative glow in no time. Congratulations! You're part of the way there. Finding those patterns and elements is just the beginning of discovering your creative brain.

For me, in my work as a designer, the most important part of creating is always to work in an element of a style that I have honed as my own over the course of many years. I spend a great deal of time picking the brains of other creatives and programmers for elements of things that interest them. A creative genius might not always be available to the average person, but there are plenty of them blogging about their processes and designs, and most of them don't bite! You'll find that designers are pretty friendly as a rule and are more than willing to share their work with you. Here are a few of my favorite hangouts:

- *http://www.flickr.com/photos/splat/sets/981332/*
- *http://veerle.duoh.com/blog/*
- *http://www.31three.com/weblog/*
- *http://www.qbn.com/*
- *http://vectips.com/*

An important tip that I can't stress enough: don't be afraid to join in the discussions of the sites you find! A big part of creativity and inspiration is sharing.

Finally, it's very important to find the time to spend alone to let your creative process begin. If possible, find a place where you can avoid all the distractions of your normal everyday life. For me, this could be my home office or even a coffee shop in a neighborhood I don't really know. The latter is especially effective for me, but everyone will find a different place that suits them best. Many of my best designs have begun on a napkin or back of a receipt! Good ideas wait for no man, so it's really critical to get them down on paper as soon as they come. Try to learn to detail your creative ideas in ways that will help them make sense when you view them again later on.

Picasso said he could never have made any of his famous abstracts if he hadn't spent so much time initially learning the ins and outs of well-applied artistic theories and styles. His most simplistic work was his best, but developing his ability to do it with such a developed personal style was part of his life's work. The Web is much the same. Creative processing and learning to find inspiration is a road you must explore first, and then, in time, make your own. It's something that has to be done consciously, in order to unravel the direction you will take as you grow, but you have to begin by learning to flex your own creativity muscle.

CHAPTER 3

Hello World

"Hello World" is the *Citizen Kane* of computer programs: it's hailed as a classic by almost everyone, but seriously misunderstood the first time it's tried. If you've ever learned a new programming language, the odds are pretty good that your first program was some variation on Hello World: just enough complexity to get a flavor for the environment and to fill you with satisfaction at seeing those beautiful 10 letters paint across the screen, which is what this chapter is all about. Time to get Facebook Platforming!

3.1 Installing the Facebook Developer App

Problem

How do I actually add an app to Facebook? How do I configure and manage my apps? Where are the stats?

Solution

It's all about Facebook's Developer app, which acts as a control panel for managing all of your apps, a portal into the Developer Discussion Board, a listing of News published by Facebook, and a Marketplace listing that shows Platform-related jobs available and developers looking for gigs. It's also where you'll add a new app to Facebook, so install it here: *http://www.facebook.com/developers/*.

Discussion

You're going to spend a lot of time in this app, so it's worth taking a quick look around. Figure 3-1 shows the app's home page.

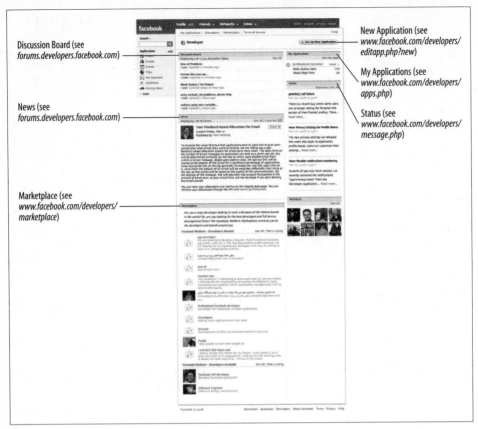

Discussion Board (see
forums.developers.facebook.com)

News (see
forums.developers.facebook.com)

Marketplace (see
*www.facebook.com/developers/
marketplace*)

New Application (see
*www.facebook.com/developers/
editapp.php?new*)

My Applications (see
*www.facebook.com/developers/
apps.php*)

Status (see
*www.facebook.com/developers/
message.php*)

Figure 3-1. Facebook Developer app

Let's take a quick tour of the major areas you'll be interacting with:

Setup New Application
> Starting in the top-right corner, you'll see the all-important "Set Up New Application" button. That's the key first step in adding a new app to Facebook, which we'll cover a little later in this chapter.

My Applications
> Immediately below that button, you'll find a listing of all the applications that you've added, including the number of daily active users and fans of the app's About Page.

Developer Status Feed
> If you're suddenly running into a problem that you didn't have before, or you want a quick hit of what's going on right now, check the Developer Status Feed list right under your applications. The Developers page pulls in the three most recent posts, but you can click through to the full list or subscribe to the RSS to stay absolutely up-to-date.

Discussion Board
> To the left of your application list is the Discussion Board, which pulls in the five most recent posts from the Facebook Developer Forums (see *http://forum.develop ers.facebook.com*). A lot of very knowledgeable developers are on the boards who are happy to answer questions, so try posting questions here if you get stuck.

News
> The rate at which Facebook makes changes to Platform is one of the biggest challenges in producing a book like this. Hitting a target that moves this quickly is like trying to bullseye womp rats from a T-16, if you know what I mean. Keep up-to-date with the latest schemes hatched by the Facebook team in the News section, located just below the Discussion Board. Since their announcements regularly have a significant impact on what your application can do, I recommend subscribing to the RSS feed and making it a daily read.

Marketplace
> If you're the kind of evil genius who has brilliant ideas but lacks the technical chops to build them, or the kind of brilliant developer who needs an evil genius, then cast your eyes toward the Marketplace, located below the News. Use it to post about your idea and recruit developers, or post about your mad skillz and find projects to work on.

> If you're anything like me and your RSS reader is subscribed to more feeds than a pig farm at lunchtime, you might want to use an RSS-to-email service to make sure you are alerted when Facebook posts updates that could affect your app. Check out *http://www.rssfwd.com/* or *http:// www.sendmerss.com/*, both of which will happily send the latest posts from any RSS feed right into your inbox.

3.2 Setting Up a New App

Problem

I'm rip-roarin' to go on my new app and have the Developer app installed and mastered. Now what?

> If you don't have the Developer app installed, check out Recipe 3.1. You'll also need to have hosting set up with a third-party hosting provider; if you don't, check out Recipe 5.12 for more information. For the purposes of this recipe, we're going to use *http://yourdomain.com* as the name of your third-party host.

Solution

Inside the Developer app (*http://www.facebook.com/developers*), you'll find a Set Up New Application button, shown in Figure 3-2.

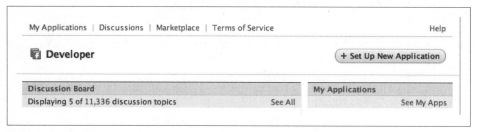

Figure 3-2. The fabled Set Up New Application button in its natural habitat

On the Developer app page, which lists all of your apps (*http://www.facebook.com/developers/apps.php*), you'll find a button that looks similar but is labeled Apply for an Application Key (Figure 3-3).

Figure 3-3. Set Up New App's evil twin, Apply for an Application Key

Click on either button to jump into the world's most deceptive form, shown in Figure 3-4. Sure, you could just provide an Application Name, check the ToS box, and ignore the innocent-looking Optional Fields area, but you'd be in for a nasty surprise when your app doesn't work.

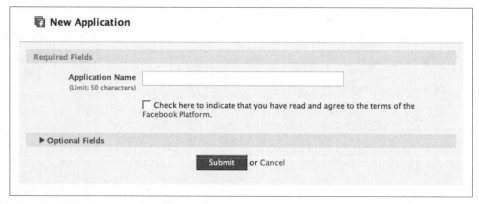

Figure 3-4. Simple version of the Set Up New Application form

Fill in the form to add your new Hello World app and get an API key, and then you're ready to start rocking. Take the extra few minutes to complete the full form here, even if you don't know all the details now. See the Discussion, next, for a description of each field.

Discussion

Some of the fields in the form are a little complex the first time through, so here's a quick guide.

Base Options

Developer Email Addresses (Contact and User Support)

Pretty self-explanatory, though worth noting that important things like ToS violation notices will get sent to the Developer Contact Email, so make sure you check it regularly. You should check the User Support address too, but it might be worth having them go to separate places so you can make sure you don't miss anything important from Facebook.

Suggested Hello World values: contact@yourdomain.com, support@your-domain.com.

If you don't have a bug tracking system in place, take a look at something like FogBugz from Fog Creek Software. Not only is Joel Spolsky one of the industry's leading brains on the development of quality software (see *http://www.joelonsoftware.com*), but FogBugz also has the ability to automatically check an email address and pull all the new messages in as support tickets. Their hosted Software-as-a-Service version is really inexpensive, and you can have it pull in all messages sent to the support address you specify here so you can easily track the issues your users are having. It also includes a wiki and discussion forum that you can open up to your users if you need to. More details are at *http://www.fogbugz .com*.

Callback URL

The address on your third-party server where Facebook will find the pages that actually make up your application. For more information, see *http://wiki.developers .facebook.com/index.php/Your_callback_page_and_you*.

Suggested Hello World value: http://www.yourdomain.com.

Canvas Page URL

Unless you have a really good reason for using an iFrame, you want to pick FBML here. You'll have a lot more control over your app's integration with Facebook and will have full access to things like FBML and FBJS when you're writing your code. Plus, it's what all the cool kids are doing. Think carefully about what you put in the URL here. It will be visible to everyone who uses the app, and it's best not to move it around or you'll break precious inbound links.

Suggested Hello World value: Unfortunately, you're not going to get "helloworld," so you might want to go with something like "jays-fantastic-demo." (You can't, of course, *all* use "jays-fantastic-demo"; only the first one of you to read this and nab it can.)

Profile Tab URL

Under the new Profile design launched in July 2008, applications can now give users the option to add a Profile tab that exclusively displays their content. If your app supports that functionality, you need to specify the URL here from which Facebook can get the FBML to display on the tab (note that it will always be a URL starting with *http://apps.facebook.com/*).

Suggested Hello World value: We're not actually going to add support for a tab here, but if we were, the URL might be something like *http://apps.facebook.com/ jays-fantastic-demo/profile-tab.php*.

Profile Tab Name

If you're providing a Profile tab URL, you need to also provide a name for your tab that will appear on the Profile tab itself. Facebook will use roughly the first 15 characters of the name on the tab.

Suggested Hello World value: Leave it blank, since we're not using it.

Application Type

This will be "website" for almost all of you, unless you're planning to build a desktop app that lives outside of Facebook and communicates with it via the API (e.g., photo uploaders, Outlook synchronization). Note that your selection here will change the other fields in the form.

Suggested Hello World value: website.

Mobile Integration

At the time this book was written, the mobile integration side of Facebook Platform hadn't taken off nearly as strongly as the website side. Some very powerful tools are available to you as an app developer, and it's always a good idea to consider ways to expand your user base, so think about adding in mobile support for your app. You can always check this option later if it's not part of your version-one plans. For more information about Facebook Platform for mobile, see *http://wiki .developers.facebook.com/index.php/Mobile*.

Suggested Hello World value: Leave this unchecked for Hello World.

IP Addresses

This is an optional security measure that can help prevent fraud in your app. If you're building something like a contest site and you want to make sure that the only servers that can communicate with Facebook belong to you, add in their IP addresses and Facebook's mighty firewall will block everyone else. This is probably overkill for most apps and can be a pain if you move servers and forget to update this, so I wouldn't recommend it unless you need it.

Suggested Hello World value: You can leave it empty for Hello World, but you should put the IP address of your *http://yourdomain.com* server in here for other apps.

IP Blocking Exceptions

If you're using the IP Addresses server to constrain your app to only accept requests from your server but you also have a client-side component making API requests, you'll need to set "Allow IP Blocking Exceptions" to "Yes" and make sure that those components use session secret keys for security.

Suggested Hello World value: "No" for Hello World, but "Yes" if the previous paragraph describes your need for other apps.

Can your application be added on Facebook?

This might be the most confusing field on the form. If your app can't be added on Facebook, why are you building it? The simple answer is that it might be a web-based tool outside of Facebook, or a desktop app that can't be added to a Profile. You'll almost definitely want to turn this on. Two whole new areas of the form will appear once you check this field. These areas allow you to adjust access privileges (make sure to lock your app down to just developers until you're ready to launch; see the Developers option, discussed later) and configure Platform integration points.

Suggested Hello World value: Yes.

TOS URL

You can use a Canvas page URL here so that users don't have to leave Facebook, or you can point them to an external URL if your legal department has carefully crafted a masterful ToS and wants everyone to read it on your website. If you don't have a ToS, you can leave this blank, but keep in mind that you're opening yourself up to potential legal troubles. It's not that hard to come up with a reasonable ToS for your app: go read a bunch of other ToSes and cobble together a new Franken-steinian version from the parts you like best. This will appear as a link when users are adding your application.

Suggested Hello World value: We're not going to add a ToS to the Hello World app, so you can leave it blank. Otherwise, a URL such as *http://apps.facebook.com/jays -fantastic-demo/tos.php* would work.

Developers

You'll have the option to have your app listed as having been built by everyone in this field or by a company when you edit the About Page information. Everyone you list in this field can access the application's settings (this page and the various additional pages), as well as the Insights stats on app usage. If you have the app locked down in Developer Mode, they're also the only people who will be able to add or use the app. Note that you need to be friends with anyone you want to add, so you'll need to do a friend request first. As with all the other fields on this form, you can change this later, so don't worry about listing everyone now.

Suggested Hello World value: You can just list your own name for the Hello World app.

Default iFrame Canvas Size

If you're not building an iFrame-based app, you can ignore this one. For those of you who have a really good reason to do so, this setting toggles your iFrame from being "smartsized" (Facebook automatically sizes it to fill the available space on the page) to being resizable (you have control via the JavaScript API). Remember: with control comes responsibility, which means you'll need to size it yourself and won't be able to rely on Facebook to handle it for you. This is one of the great trade-offs in life, second only to the eternal struggle over whether the toilet paper should roll off the front or back side (always bet on back).

Suggested Hello World value: We're not going to use an iFrame for Hello World, so you can leave it as smartsize.

 When you're editing the settings for an app you've already added, this section will also include a field for Connect Preview URL (the URL used to generate the account preview when a user is accepting a Facebook Connect request), as well as the app's icon, logo, and Facebook Connect logo.

Internationalization Options

Language Selection

As of late July 2008, developers can now take advantage of Facebook's Translations application to have their application translated into different languages. This option, which defaults to English, allows you to specify the default language.

Suggested Hello World value: Since you're reading this in English, that's probably a safe choice.

Installation Options

This section will be available to you only if your app is set in the Base Options as being able to be added to Facebook (see the earlier section for details).

Who can add your app?

Of all the dastardly user interface designs you're likely to encounter as a Facebook developer, this question has got to rank near the top. It's such a strange mix of controls that it deserves its own screenshot for posterity (Figure 3-5).

Where to even start? Perhaps with the lonely checkbox labeled Users. The difficult-to-understand distinction here is that you're enabling Users and/or Pages, which would be much more obvious if there were a checkbox for Pages with the three

Page-related options grouped underneath it. And speaking of those three blind mice: the All and None choices are pretty self-explanatory, but what to make of Some? Clicking on it will open a massive list of checkboxes that let you tailor the types of Pages (e.g., some combination of the 69 available Page types, which includes Actor and Model but lacks the all important Actor/Model combo).

Generally speaking, you want to turn on the Users checkbox so that individual users can add your app. You should think about what it means for your app to be available on Pages and should definitely go for it if you can, but make sure that you consider all the angles. If you're building the most awesome Go Fish game ever made, what would it mean for a Rental Cars or Religious Organization Page to have a Profile Box for it?

Suggested Hello World value: Pages are going to have to live without your Hello World app because we're making it available only to Users.

Figure 3-5. The bizarre mélange of controls that is the "Who can add your app" field

Post-Add URL

This one is simple: where do you want users to be sent once they've added your app to a Facebook Page? You're generally going to put a Canvas page URL in here, which will usually be the app's home page, but it might be a special welcome page or include a parameter in the URL to let your app know to display a welcome message. Consider having this point to an Invite Friends page that you show only to new users, which asks them to invite their friends into the app before they start using it (though this move is losing popularity as users feel more and more like they're being pressured to buy a used car from a guy in a bad suit, so you might want to skip it). For more information, see *http://wiki.developers.facebook.com/index.php/Post-Add_URL*.

Suggested Hello World value: We're not supporting Pages in this example, so you can leave this blank (or just use the value you put into Post-Authorize URL, described next).

Post-Authorize URL

This is similar to the Post-Add URL, but it's for users authorizing your app to access their Profile for the first time rather than for users adding it to a Facebook Page.

Suggested Hello World value: Since Hello World is really just for you and we're not worrying about inviting friends, we're going to keep this simple and use *http://apps.facebook.com/jays-fantastic-demo/*.

Application Description

If you're the kind of developer who has meticulously planned out every nook and cranny of your work of art well in advance, go ahead and fill in this box with your carefully crafted, 250-character marketing masterpiece. For everyone else, leave this field blank and come back to it after you've built the app and are ready to add it to the Application Directory.

Suggested Hello World value: Follow my advice and leave it blank for now.

Post-Remove URL

As George Santayana once said, "Those who cannot remember the past are condemned to repeat it." Wouldn't it be great if you could be notified whenever someone removes your app from a Facebook Page, so that you could track the circumstances and learn something from them? Well, you can! Enter a URL here and Facebook will ping it whenever your app gets un-added, and will provide some useful info, such as the person's UID and a timestamp. You'll find a whole lot more information, including some sample PHP, Rails, and pseudocode for handling the pings, at *http://wiki.developers.facebook.com/index.php/Post-Remove_URL*. An important note: this is different from the Post-Add URL because users won't be directed to it after they remove the app. Facebook will send a background ping to the URL, and users will continue on their merry ways.

Suggested Hello World value: Again, we're not supporting Pages and we don't really care who uninstalls Hello World, so leave this blank.

Post-Authorize URL

This is similar to the Post-Remove URL, but it's for users revoking authorization for your app to access their Profile rather than for users removing it from a Facebook Page.

Suggested Hello World value: Ditto here; we don't really care who uninstalls Hello World, so leave this blank.

Default FBML and Action FBML

The Profile Box and Profile Action links are two of the Platform integration points you'll be all over. Since the user has just added your app, you won't have anything to insert yet, so the two default boxes let you specify the FBML that should be used until you first make a call to `Profile.setFBML( )` (see Recipe 9.47). Leaving these blank will effectively make your app invisible on the user's Profile page until then, so think about sticking a "coming soon" message in there in the meantime. Your ultimate Bowling Score app might, for example, pop in a box containing "Scores coming soon!" and a link into your app for all of the user's bowling fanatic friends to follow.

Suggested Hello World value:

```
<fb:wide>Hello big, wide world!</fb:wide><fb:narrow>Hello narrower world!
</fb:narrow>
```

Default Profile Box Column

Users will have the option of dragging your Profile Box into either the wide or narrow column of the Boxes tab in their Profiles after it appears, and this gives you control over where it starts off. You can do completely different layouts depending on which width they choose, so pick the one you think is strongest as the default, but have a kick-ass backup in case they prefer the other size.

Suggested Hello World value: It doesn't make much difference, but since most apps go with wide, you might as well go narrow and appear higher up the page by default.

Developer Mode

The all-important Developer Mode switch lets you limit access to and the adding of your app to the people you've listed as Developers. Everyone else will get a 404 Page Not Found error when they try to hit any of the app's URLs, even if they had previously added the app.

Suggested Hello World value: On. This app isn't going to do much, so it's not really worth sharing with the wider world. If you'd like to show it to your friends, just add them as developers.

Integration Points

Like the Installation Options, this section will be available only if you set your app to be addable to Facebook Profiles.

Side Nav URL

This option used to provide the URL you wanted users taken to when they clicked on your app in their Side Nav (the sidebar on the left edge of the Profile, which doesn't exist anymore). Although this hasn't been renamed yet, it's now the URL you want users taken to when they select your app in the Applications menu in the blue header bar at the top of the Facebook window. Note that this has to be a Facebook Canvas page and can't be an external URL.

Suggested Hello World value: http://apps.facebook.com/jays-fantastic-demo/

Privacy and Help URLs

Both of these are links to static content within your app and can point to Canvas pages within Facebook or to external pages elsewhere (though the former is better than the latter).

Suggested Hello World value: We don't much care about private hellos or helping people, so leave 'em blank.

Private Installation

If you're building one of those rare apps that won't leverage the social graph to spread among users, you can turn on this option to disable News and Mini-Feed installation stories. This could be handy if your app is in a field such as health or finances, but you're generally going to want to leave this option off.

Suggested Hello World value: Leave it off.

Attachments

> Attachments are one of the most underused integration points, so you should think about how to take advantage of the scarcity of attachment options to give your app some good visibility in front of your users. You'll need two pieces of information in order to enable Attachments for your app: the wording to use as the action (which will appear next to your app's icon) and a callback URL (which will be loaded in the pop-up window to present the Attachment selection interface). For more information, see *http://wiki.developers.facebook.com/index.php/Attachment _Example*.

> *Suggested Hello World value*: Leave this blank, since we're not going to build attachments.

Publish Content to Friends/Self

> The Publisher, introduced in the Profile redesign of mid-2008, provides users with a very simple mechanism for publishing content on the Wall tab on their own Profile or their friends' Profiles. Specify URLs here for the Publishing Action and Callback Action the same way you do with Attachments, discussed earlier.

> *Suggested Hello World value*: Leave this blank, since we're not going to add Publisher support.

Info

> The Info tab, which was also introduced in the Profile redesign, contains information about the user whose Profile you're browsing. Apps can now populate their info into that tab, either in text-based or object-based formats, and will receive a ping at this URL when users edit the content so they can post-process it (i.e., tokenize and add URLs).

> *Suggested Hello World value*: Leave this blank, since we're not using the Info features.

3.3 Hello World

Problem

OK! I have my new Hello World application set up in the Developers app. Now what?

Solution

You have your app all ready to go, but when you go to your URL (one like *http://apps.facebook.com/jays-fantastic-demo*), you get a 404 error message (see Recipe 3.2 for more about setting up your app). The problem is that you don't have anything on your server for Facebook to display, so let's put something there. Make a new blank page in your favorite text editor (see Recipe 5.10 for a list) and stick this in it:

```
<p>Hello <fb:name uid="loggedinuser" firstnameonly="false" useyou="false"/>!</p>
```

Save the file to your *http://yourdomain.com* server as *index.php*, and then reload your new Facebook app.

Discussion

You should now have a fully functional Facebook application that only you can see. Congrats! This app can be used as a great test bed for all of your ideas as you work your way through the rest of this book.

3.4 Installing Your App: It's All About the About Page

Problem

Now that I have an app set up, how do people install it?

Solution

You probably know this already if you've ever installed an app, but the general case is that all installation roads lead to your About Page. It's worth noting that this used to be more true when you had to install an app before you could see any of its content, but it has become slightly less the case now that pages inside an app can be publicly visible. The URL to your application's About Page will take the form *http://www.face book.com/apps/application.php?id=8653633892* (obviously with your app's ID rather than the Zerofootprint Calculator's), which leads to a page profiling your masterwork.

The screenshot in Figure 3-6 shows the About Page for an application that I've added and for which I'm a developer. Contrast this with the page for tvClickr (Figure 3-7; see *http://www. facebook.com/apps/application.php?id=16534688290*), an app I haven't installed.[*]

In Figure 3-7, you'll note the big blue "Go to Application" button in the top-right, as well as the absence of the links that would enable me to edit the app's settings (which are present in Figure 3-6). Clicking on the button takes me to the "Log in to Application" page where I can grant the app access to my information, as shown in Figure 3-8.

Actually adding the application takes me to the post-add URL specified by the developer (see Recipe 3.2 for more information).

---

[*] I actually have installed it—and it's a great example of an app that thinks considerably outside the "box" of typical Facebook apps. Such is my dedication to you, the reader, that I uninstalled it for the purpose of this example.

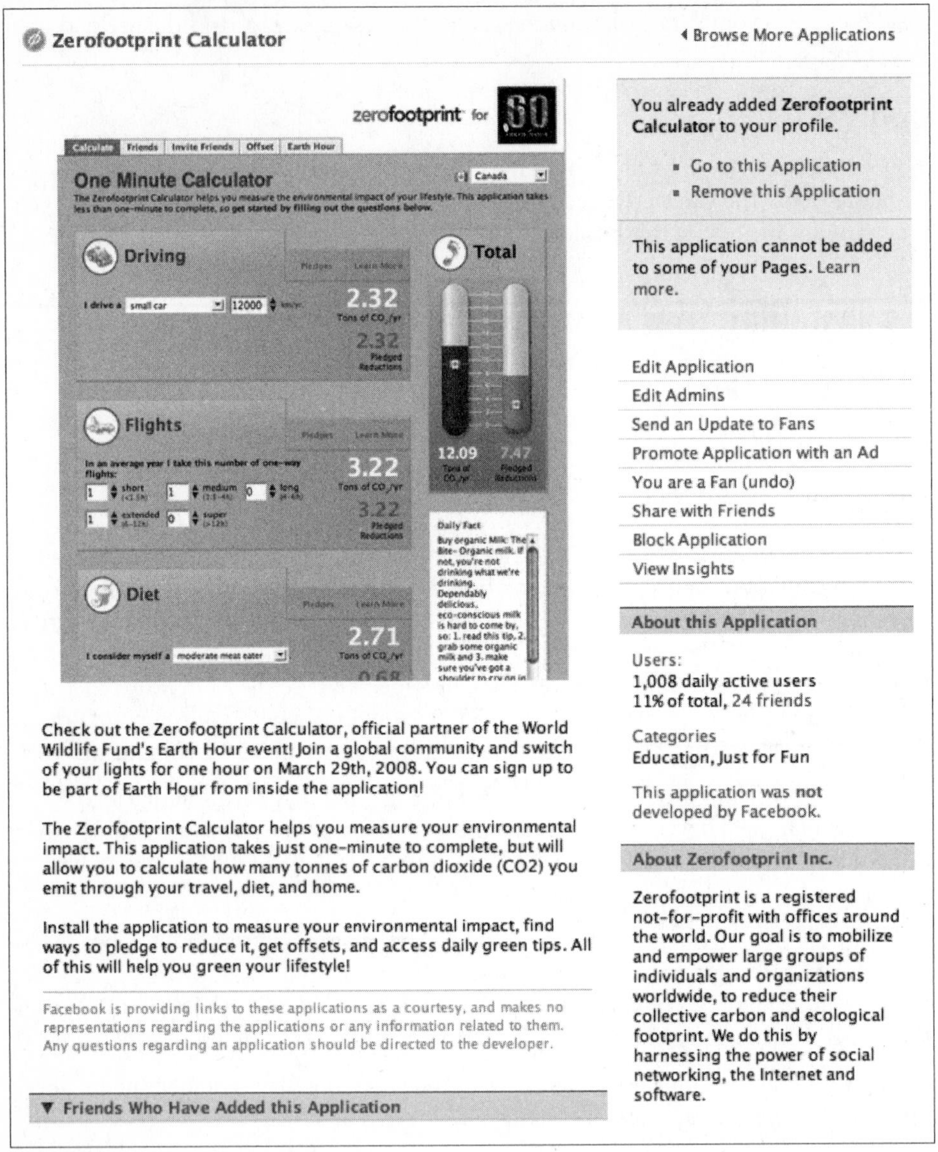
Zerofootprint Calculator
◂ Browse More Applications
zerofootprint for
Calculate Friends Invite Friends Offset Earth Hour
One Minute Calculator
Canada
Driving
I drive a small car 12000
2.32
2.32
Total
Flights
3.22
3.22
12.09
7.47
Diet
I consider myself a moderate meat eater
2.71
Daily Fact
You already added Zerofootprint Calculator to your profile.
Go to this Application
Remove this Application
This application cannot be added to some of your Pages. Learn more.
Edit Application
Edit Admins
Send an Update to Fans
Promote Application with an Ad
You are a Fan (undo)
Share with Friends
Block Application
View Insights
About this Application
Users:
1,008 daily active users
11% of total, 24 friends
Categories
Education, Just for Fun
This application was not developed by Facebook.
About Zerofootprint Inc.
Zerofootprint is a registered not-for-profit with offices around the world. Our goal is to mobilize and empower large groups of individuals and organizations worldwide, to reduce their collective carbon and ecological footprint. We do this by harnessing the power of social networking, the Internet and software.
Check out the Zerofootprint Calculator, official partner of the World Wildlife Fund's Earth Hour event! Join a global community and switch of your lights for one hour on March 29th, 2008. You can sign up to be part of Earth Hour from inside the application!
The Zerofootprint Calculator helps you measure your environmental impact. This application takes just one-minute to complete, but will allow you to calculate how many tonnes of carbon dioxide (CO2) you emit through your travel, diet, and home.
Install the application to measure your environmental impact, find ways to pledge to reduce it, get offsets, and access daily green tips. All of this will help you green your lifestyle!
Facebook is providing links to these applications as a courtesy, and makes no representations regarding the applications or any information related to them. Any questions regarding an application should be directed to the developer.
▼ Friends Who Have Added this Application

Figure 3-6. Zerofootprint Calculator's About Page

Figure 3-7. tvClickr About Page

Figure 3-8. tvClickr Log in to Application page

Discussion

There are a number of spots in this flow where the whole thing can go pear shaped and you'll lose potential installers. You need to put a lot of thought and effort into making sure your About Page is a gleaming model of marketing brilliance, carefully tweaked and toned to optimize the experience for would-be users. Keep in mind that your application's Photo and Description will be only two of the things people see, so you need to be a conscientious community gardener and keep close tabs on the Reviews, Discussion Board, and Wall Posts. Reply to people who have problems, encourage users to become fans and leave positive reviews, and provoke good conversations if your Boards are empty. The more activity that visitors see, the more likely they are to install and give it a try (remember that no one likes to be the first to the party, but everyone wants to get into the crowded bar).

CHAPTER 4

Architecture and Design

Building Facebook apps requires you to master the trifecta of dating: a pretty face, a winning personality, and a rock-solid architecture that can handle scaling tall buildings in a single bound.

Building an app is a lot like building a house: poor architecture and foundations will only lead to a rickety structure that falls over the first time the big bad wolf blows on it (and by "big bad wolf," I mean 100,000 users). Knowledge is power, so arm yourself with a thorough understanding of the way Facebook applications are structured, as well as some practical techniques for optimizing your app's underpinnings.

Once you have the basics down, bring out the best in your awesome framework by adding a beautiful and functional design. If you're more of a developer than a designer, don't make the classic mistake of applying lipstick to your pig: good user experience design is much deeper than a pretty skin.

 Most of this chapter is aimed at web developers who are building web-based Facebook apps, but a lot of the lessons in here can be abstracted to desktop apps as well.

4.1 Under the Hood: How Facebook Apps Work

Problem

I've heard that I have to host my own Facebook app, even though people access it through Facebook's site. I don't understand—how does this all work?

Solution

Facebook Platform architecture is brilliant from its perspective: you go and do all the hard work of building apps, and you have to pay for the hosting, too. The upside is, of course, that you get unparalleled access to a dedicated audience of 90 million users and the ease of building on a fairly mature and well-realized Platform.

The short solution is: yes, you host your app. You'll need to find a robust hosting provider who can scale up quickly if things go your way and who won't charge you an exorbitant fee if you exceed your allocated traffic (see Recipe 5.12 for more information about hosting choices).

Discussion

Let's take a look at what happens when someone requests a page from your app (Figure 4-1).

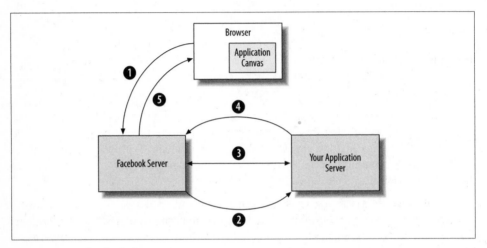

Figure 4-1. Facebook Platform

1. The user's browser requests *http://apps.facebook.com/myapp*.

   That address points to a cluster of servers in Facebook's data center. Their servers analyze the request, determine which app it's for, then look up the callback URL that the app developer provided and make a call to it behind the scenes.

2. Facebook server requests *http://www.myserver.com/index.php*.

   This call, which happens behind the scenes and is invisible to the user, goes into your application server. If you're hosted with Joyent or Amazon, you can take advantage of especially low latency rates, which speed this part of the process up considerably.

3. Your application server makes API calls to the Facebook Server as required by your page.

   This can, of course, include FQL calls made through the API's `fql.query( )` method. You may not need to do any calls, or you may need to do lots, but keep in mind that the user is waiting for his page while you do all this back and forth, so it's better to try and cache as much data on your server as possible.

4. Your application server returns FBML to the Facebook server.

   The end result of your app doing its thing should be an FBML document, which you'll send back to Facebook's server for processing.

5. Facebook's FBML parser turns your FBML into HTML and serves it to the user.

   This is the final step in the process and results in the browser rendering what appears to be a single Facebook page, made up of Facebook's HTML code around the edges with your parsed FBML in the middle.

This is a really clever piece of system design and makes for a lot of flexibility, but it also has some obvious spots where a slow network connection or poor page implementation can result in very slow page loads for your users. If you've ever run into a timeout error when you're trying to use a Facebook app, one of the five steps just outlined has probably taken too long. You can see it for yourself by inserting:

```
sleep(120);
```

into one of your PHP files and then requesting that page through Facebook.

4.2 Architecting for the Future: Open Web Apps

Problem

I'm following your advice and building for Facebook first, but I want to make sure that my app can be deployed elsewhere later. What steps should I take?

Solution

You should build one backend that is capable of serving your application's core data to several frontends, as shown in Figure 4-2.

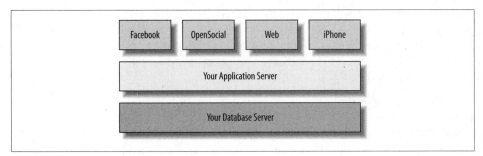

Figure 4-2. Facebook application architecture

Layered architecture diagrams always make me think of tasty cakes. This particular diagram makes me think of a tasty cake that comes in four excellent flavors but doesn't cost the baker much more in baking time. It also makes me think of Mark Andreessen, founder of Netscape and now of OpenSocial partner Ning. If you read the Preface, this probably comes as no surprise. If you didn't, you might find yourself grasping for a connection between a brilliant serial entrepreneur and baked goods. Look no further than this quote:

> As an app developer, there's no real reason to choose between Facebook and OpenSocial. It's easy to do both. You've already put in most of the effort—creating a new set of frontend HTML and JavaScript pages is almost trivial, and that's all you need to do to have your app "port" to OpenSocial.

As you start planning your application, think about ways in which you can consolidate your business logic, backend code, and data so that your application server is fairly independent of the particular API you need to use to render a page. Although the calls required to display a friend selector, for example, won't be the exact same on Facebook Platform as they are on OpenSocial, the data returned to your application will still be a selection of friends.

Discussion

There's a term that gets thrown around a lot in web development circles that always makes my sub-cockles[*] itchy: *future proof*. The idea that we can design something today that will be able to withstand whatever the future may throw at it is to give ourselves far too much credit. (Unless you're Danny Hillis, of course. Danny can give himself that much credit because he deserves it: anyone determined to build a clock that will last for 10,000 years on a hill in the Nevada desert gets pretty much all of my respect. See *http://www.longnow.org/projects/clock/*.)

At any rate, you don't need your application to last for 10,000 years, but you do want to try to see around the next curve in the road. There was a time, not too long ago, when everyone thought that Friendster was the best thing since Sir Tim Berners-Lee invented sliced bread, but now it's a relic of the past. If it had introduced a developer platform back when it was the flavor of the month, we might all still be Friendstering instead of Facebooking.

Following an architecture like the one described earlier frees you from being tied to something over which you have no control. Facebook has real momentum behind it now, so the risk is pretty low, but the Facebook team might also make a decision tomorrow about a new direction for Platform that could significantly affect the viability of your app. If you have no fallback strategy through other delivery channels, you have nothing.

---

[*] Thank you, Denis Leary.

4.3 Build Now, Scale Later: Getting Real

Problem

I've heard so many horror stories about developers who didn't think through their scaling issues at the beginning and ended up with 250,000 users and were madly running around trying to scale their app. I don't want to do that! I want to build in scaling right from the start. Isn't that a smarter approach?

Solution

Go watch this video: *http://youtube.com/watch?v=ntfEKmIg_VQ*.

(If that video isn't available, close your eyes and picture the iLike team madly driving around the Bay Area in a rental truck, begging, borrowing, and buying 150 rack-mounted servers and installing them in their data center, all in 48 hours.)

At the time when the iLike crew went on their mad dash, they already had six million users. The moral of this story is that you can always scale by throwing more money at servers later. It *is* important for you to take some time to think about scalability now, but if you plan to build out a carefully load-balanced, *n*-tier architecture for your zero users, you're going to spend the next six months figuring out how to do that while someone else just does it (to quote Nike) and has a six-month head start.

Discussion

Here's a fun exercise to get you into the right headspace. Start by drawing a line across this page, which would be defacing this book if I didn't do it for you (Figure 4-3).

Figure 4-3. A plain old line

Now take that plain old line and transmogrify it into a fancy, educated line by adding a sophisticated label full of $5 words (Figure 4-4).

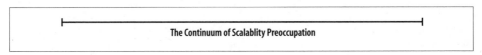

The Continuum of Scalablity Preoccupation

Figure 4-4. Fancy, educated-type line

Now let's add some points of reference to that line (Figure 4-5), and then I'll tell you a little cautionary tale.

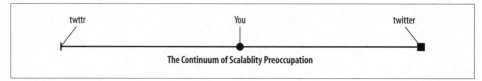

Figure 4-5. *You, bracketed by Twitters*

Once upon a time, Ev Williams and his cofounders built up Pyra Labs, created the Blogger platform, and sold it to Google. The web community looked upon this and said that it was good! Then Ev started a new company called Odeo and started to build it up, and the web community looked upon it and said that it seemed fairly interesting but that they were not, as of yet, entirely convinced. One day, whilst hard at work on Odeo, a member of their stalwart team named Jack Dorsey presented an idea that had been rattling around in his head for six years. The assembled other members looked upon this idea and decided it had real merit and so, on a lark, they cobbled together a working version and released it upon the world. And so it went that in October 2006, the world discovered the newly named twttr, 140 characters at a time.

Fast forward to May 2008. With over 1.7 million users sending more than three million tweets per day on the newly renamed Twitter, now owned by the newly minted Twitter, Inc., some serious scalability problems became apparent. In an interview with Robert Scoble,[†] taped on May 31, 2008, Ev notes (about 7 minutes and 35 seconds in) that their problem isn't money, Ruby on Rails, or servers, but is entirely architectural. When they built twttr, they had no idea that it would become popular or that it would even spread beyond the prototype built by Jack and Biz Stone. They had no scalability plan because they didn't think they would need one, and they followed the predominant Ruby on Rails mentality that dictates building software over spending time planning.

Ev mentions in the video that it's not usually worth considering scalability since most products never reach a point where it's needed, and he's mostly right. Looking back over the first year of Facebook Platform highlights a number of apps that skyrocketed into the Top 10 almost overnight, which is not an unrealistic proposition if you build a great application with broad appeal and leverage all of the viral integration points available. You should aim for the mid-point of the Continuum of Scalability Preoccupation: more than releasing an underengineered prototype, but less than worrying about handling three million messages per day.

† *http://scobleizer.com/2008/05/31/clearing-the-air-with-twitter/*

4.4 Scalability

—*Rajat Agarwalla (see his bio in Contributors)*

Problem

How do I scale my application so that it is not a victim of its own success?

Solution

Speed is critical. If your application does not load within milliseconds, it will tend to drive away users. Given the viral nature of Facebook, such a scenario can occur within weeks or even days of launching your application. Scalability needs to be ingrained within all aspects of the application: source code, database, hardware/operating system platform, user interface, and support systems. As there is no fixed formula for scalability, you need to monitor these aspects closely and tune the ones that you think will cause a bottleneck. Build your application to sustain at least three times more load than you initially expect.

Discussion

When we launched Scrabulous on Facebook in June 2007, we did not expect more than a few thousand users. Accordingly, Scrabulous was launched on a shared-hosting service and utilized a common database server with possibly 50 other websites. Two weeks into our launch and with less than 10,000 users on Scrabulous, we were introduced to the word "scalability." Our hosting service politely asked us to remove the application from their servers as it was causing a large amount of load! Even today, after having rewritten the entire source code *four* times and moving onto private dedicated servers, we still need to consider the scalability factors before launching a new feature on Scrabulous. For your application, you may want to consider looking into the following areas.

Monitoring software

This is the number one requirement. A number of free utilities can help you analyze your hardware resources (Cacti, MRTG, etc.). Use them as efficiently as possible. They are a tremendous help in letting you decide whether to add hardware or focus on the source code.

Application source code

The source code of your application may end up being a resource hog. In a hurry to launch applications, developers sometimes overlook the benefits of object-oriented programming (OOP). Even if you are not much into OOP, try to write your code in functions that can be loaded as required. For example, if you are writing your application in PHP, you can easily split functions into files and load the appropriate files based on the user's action. This will ensure minimal memory usage on page loads.

It is highly recommended that a versioning system, such as CVS or SVN, is utilized. Coding is more efficient and you can keep a history of changes, which helps when trying to tune the code for scalability.

Database

If your budget allows, start off with your database on a separate server within the same network as your primary server. This will allow you to tune the OS specifically for the database, removing all other applications and making more memory and CPU resources available to the database. Having a separate server will also let you cluster/replicate without affecting other aspects of the system.

Hardware/OS/software utilities

With the right hardware and OS platform, you can easily scale up. For example, if you are on Linux and using Apache as your HTTPD, it is very easy to convert your box into a load-balancing unit!

Simple utility software, such as memcached and various PHP accelerators, go a long way in easing out hardware resources. When we implemented memcached for Scrabulous, it reduced our database loads by 40%. You may also want to consider using Java or C++ servers for backend tasks (such as updating Facebook Profiles). Accordingly, you can schedule the backend tasks to run during off-peak hours.

User interface/support systems

Build your user interface so that it can grow with your application. Drastic interface changes drive users away. Try to imagine the largest possible feature set for your application and then see whether your interface can easily scale up to that level or not. This is an issue we faced with Scrabulous. There were too many useful features and too little space on the user interface to make them easily accessible.

Utilize a support system from day one so that all your user requests are handled in an efficient manner. This helps in bug solving and allows for easy handover to a support team when your application becomes successful.

4.5 Language Selection As Architecture

Problem

I hear Ruby on Rails is the best thing since Java, which was the best thing since Perl, which was once a great thing but is now a confusing thing, which is similar to but the reverse of PHP, which was a confusing thing but is becoming great. And then there's

JavaScript, which isn't Java at all and used to be the bane of everyone's existence but has come back as the golden child thanks to a household cleaner named Ajax. I'm confused. What should I use to build my app?

Solution

All languages are tools that ultimately can be used to achieve the same goal. Some languages are better at certain tasks, and others dominate different jobs. A paragraph like the question you just asked is sure to upset pretty much anyone with a language preference, which is the very nature of a "religious" war.

This question is, in a sense, like asking whether you should use only a hammer, screwdriver, or monkey wrench to build your house. Always use the right tool for the right job, and always remember to measure twice and cut once.

Discussion

At the risk of wandering innocently into the middle of said religious war, I recommend building Facebook applications using PHP 5. A number of different Client Libraries are available thanks to a very active developer community, but there is only one true ring, and it is known as PHP. You can choose to build your app on one of the other Libraries—and you probably should if you have, for example, an entire .NET stack or have spent the last 10 years becoming a Supreme Perl Monger—but keep in mind that those Libraries get updated after the official one and therefore run the risk of not having access to new features and of breaking when Facebook changes core pieces of Platform.

That said, if you're following the architecture recommended in Recipe 4.2, you can use a combination of different languages by adding a compatibility layer of web services, written in the best language for each frontend, which communicate to your shared backend through a standard data protocol like XML (see Figure 4-6).

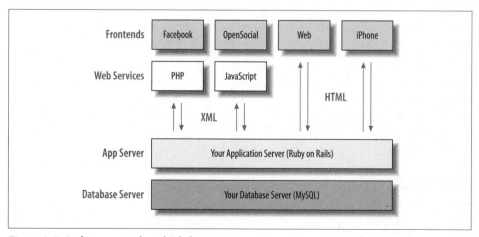

Figure 4-6. Architecture with multiple languages

Facebook actually uses a mixed language environment, and it is a big fan of the right-tool-for-the-right-job approach. The Facebook team built a framework called Thrift, which they use to do easy cross-language development, and which they have generously made available to the community at large as part of their Open Source Projects initiative (*http://developers.facebook.com/opensource.php/*). Mark Slee, one of the developers behind Thrift, has contributed a recipe explaining how you can make use of it in your own applications (see Recipe 4.6).

4.6 Cross-Language Development with Facebook Thrift

—Mark Slee (see his bio in Contributors)

Problem

I'm developing a large software system, and I'd rather not standardize on one programming language. I'd like to be able to make service calls and move data between languages, but it needs to be fast and easy to maintain.

Solution

Use Thrift, an open source framework developed by Facebook for cross-language data serialization and remote procedure calls in a high-performance environment.

Thrift facilitates performant interoperability between C++, Java, PHP, Python, Ruby, Erlang, Haskell, C#, Cocoa, Smalltalk, and even OCaml.

Discussion

Thrift uses code generation to enable rapid development of software spanning multiple programming languages. Data types and service interfaces are defined in *.thrift* files, which use a simple, language-neutral grammar. The Thrift compiler then generates all the necessary plumbing code in the languages of your choice to encode and transport data objects and make service calls, letting the developer focus on writing the actual application code.

For example, suppose you have created a web frontend in PHP. You want to build a service to efficiently search an object store, and you'd like to build this service in C++ to optimize memory usage and data structure layout. Here's how you might define such a service in Thrift:

```
search.thrift:
struct search_result_elem {
  1: i64 object_id,
  2: list<string> terms.
  3: i64 weight
}

struct search_result {
```

```
    1: i32 total,
    2: list<search_result_elem> matches
}

service search {
  search_result query(1:list<string> terms)
}
```

To generate all the framework code you need, you'd simply execute the following:

```
thrift -cpp -php search.thrift
```

Your C++ server stub is generated, and you just need to fill in the method implementation:

```
class searchHandler : virtual public searchIf {
 public:
  searchHandler() {
    // Your initialization goes here
  }

  void query(search_result& _return, const std::vector<std::string> & terms) {
    // Your implementation goes here
    printf("query\n");
  }
};
```

Similarly, all your PHP client code is generated. To make a call to the service, you simply write the following:

```
function call_search() {
  // Specify the server to connect to
  $transport = new TSocket('192.168.1.1', '9090');
  $transport->open();
  // Pick the protocol you want to use
  $protocol = new TBinaryProtocol($transport);
  // Make a client for your service
  $client = new searchClient($protocol);
  // Make the call!
  $results = $client->query(array('term1', 'term2'));
}
```

Thrift supports many advanced features, such as:

- Service inheritance
- Cross-language support for application-level exceptions
- Compatibility across application version changes
- Multiple encoding protocols (binary, JSON, etc.)
- Multiple transport mechanisms (TCP sockets, files, HTTP)
- Multiple server implementations (threaded, libevent, pooling)

For more information on Thrift, visit *http://developers.facebook.com/thift/*.

4.7 The Database Is Dead! Long Live memcached!

Problem

I'm designing a very database-intensive application that is going to need to do a lot of reads to render a page. I know this is going to get slow as the database fills up and I have a lot of users hammering on it, so what can I do to speed that up?

Solution

Use memcached, a caching application originally developed by Danga Interactive to speed up LiveJournal (*http://livejournal.com*) but now in use all over the Web (including YouTube, Slashdot, Wikipedia, SourceForge, Facebook, Digg, Twitter, and *http://ny times.com*). Memcached is a sophisticated caching engine designed to quickly return results from memory instead of making a trip to your database, which makes it fast. In answer to the question, "Is memcached fast?", Danga says:

> Very fast. It uses *libevent* to scale to any number of open connections (using *epoll* on Linux, if available at runtime), uses nonblocking network I/O, refcounts internal objects (so objects can be in multiple states to multiple clients), and uses its own slab allocator and hash table so virtual memory never gets externally fragmented and allocations are guaranteed O(1).

That's one of those blocks of text that you either understand on your own or, like me, have to read a few times before ultimately giving up and accepting that you can move on without knowing what a slab allocator is. You can find more information about memcached, as well as downloads, at *http://www.danga.com/memcached*.

Discussion

This is one of those places where it's worth building in scalability from the beginning. Thanks to the memcached libraries available for most languages, implementing is really easy and won't significantly slow down your initial code creation. Plus, if you build memcached in from the beginning and get a tidal wave of popularity, you won't have to scramble to track down all of the SQL queries in your code and rewrite them (unless you're smart and build them all into a Database Acess/Abstraction Layer). A number of memcached libraries are available in about 12 different languages from *http://www .danga.com/memcached/apis.bml*.

Instructions on how to implement memcached are outside the scope of this book, so if you're interested in more information I highly recommend Cal Henderson's excellent *Building Scalable Web Sites* (O'Reilly). Cal was the architect of *http://flickr.com*, so he knows a thing or four hundred about building really scalable sites (and he's a great guy to have a beer with!). He covers everything from providing content to an international audience all the way through buying hardware on a budget and coordinating a team of developers.

4.8 Advanced Caching with Nginx and memcached

—Ilya Grigorik (see his bio in Contributors)

Problem

I've built a popular destination (or an API server), and now I need to handle several thousand requests a second, but I don't have the time to rearchitect my code, or worse, rewrite in a faster language.

Solution

Memcached, the darling of every web developer, is capable of turning almost any application into a speed demon. No matter which language you're working in, your application server is usually the slowest part of the chain: no application server is faster than any web server, even if yours is written in C.

Nginx, a very popular HTTP and reverse-proxy server, by default comes prepackaged with a memcached module, which allows us to bypass the application server and serve cached responses from memcached directly. With minimal code changes, we've implemented this technique for AideRSS API servers, and immediately saw our request throughput improve by 400%—from 800 req/s to 3,700 req/s!

Discussion

Most popular open source web servers can be configured to serve cached data quickly and directly from one or more memcached server instances, rather than from your filesystem or an application server. Apache (see *http://code.google.com/p/modmemca checcache/*) and Lighttpd (*http://trac.lighttpd.net/trac/wiki/Docs*) require additional modules to enable this functionality, whereas Nginx (*http://wiki.codemongers.com/Main*) comes with native support and offers the most flexible implementation. A relative newcomer to the field, it is quickly gaining in popularity, and is currently the fourth most popular web server (*http://survey.netcraft.com/Reports/200806/*).

To get started, download the latest copy of the Nginx code base, and run configure, install—this takes less than a minute and has no additional dependencies. Also, make sure to browse the wiki and look at sample configuration files. If you're coming from Apache or Lighttpd, you'll be pleased to see that the configuration syntax is virtually identical.

Nginx comes with a built-in memcached module, which allows it to query the cache directly prior to forwarding the request to the application server. If the cache does not contain the item we are looking for, the memcached module will raise a 404 Not Found error, which we catch and redirect for processing on our application server:

```
upstream appserver  { server 127.0.0.1:9010; }
server {
```

```
location / {
    set  $memcached_key      $uri;
    memcached_pass    127.0.0.1:11211;
    error_page        404 = @dynamic_request;
}
location = @dynamic_request  {
    proxy_pass  appserver;
}
}
```

You can set the key with which Nginx will query memcached via the *memcached_key* variable directly in your configuration file. Any Nginx variable can be used to create the key: *uri*, *args*, *http_user_agent*, etc.

More complex keys can also be created with the help of the Perl module, which allows you to execute Perl directly within Nginx. To enable this module, specify `-with-http_perl_module` when running configure. Once installed, we can execute arbitrary code on the incoming request. For example, you can create an MD5 hash of the request URI, and set it as your memcached key:

```
perl_set $md5_uri '
    sub {
        use Digest::MD5 qw(md5 md5_hex md5_base64);
        my $r = shift;
        return md5_hex($r->uri);
    }
';

server {
    location / {
        set  $memcached_key      $md5_uri;
        ...
    }
}
```

If the cached item is not found in memcached, the request is passed on to your application server, which in turn should construct a response and send it to memcached so that Nginx can serve future requests directly.

It is a good practice to set a Time to Live (TTL) on the memcached record to avoid additional cache invalidations. Once the TTL timestamp expires, memcached will automatically return a 404 error, and the application server can repeat the pattern.

4.9 Standing on the Shoulders of Giants: Hosting with Amazon Web Services

Problem

I think my application could be a Top 10 app, so I want to make sure it has really solid hosting behind it that isn't going to ruin my profitability.

Solution

If I told you that you could hire the engineers who built and run one of the top 20 websites in the world to provide your hosting, all at pennies per GB, would you say I was crazy or would you say, "Oh! You must mean Amazon Web Services, you clever (and handsome) man"? If you said the latter, then you probably don't need me to tell you to build your stuff on their stuff and save yourself a lot of the green stuff (and from pulling out or graying a lot of the stuff on top of your head). Go there now: *http://www.amazonaws.com*.

Discussion

There are two whole recipes about getting set up on S3 and EC2 in Chapter 5: see Recipes 5.13 and 5.14.

4.10 Integrating Drupal and Facebook

—James Walker (see his bio in Contributors)

Problem

I have an existing site built with Drupal (*http://drupal.org/*) and I'd like to create an associated Facebook application quickly and easily. It's important to be able to reuse the existing content and user base for the new application.

Solution

Drupal for Facebook (*http://drupal.org/project/fb*) is an existing Drupal module with an associated FBML theme that can quickly and easily create one or more Facebook applications for an existing site.

Discussion

To begin, create your application on Facebook as you normally would, but leave the callback URL blank for now.

Next, download the Drupal for Facebook module from *http://drupal.org/project/fb* and install it per the included *README.txt*. The instructions here include downloading a copy of the Facebook PHP library and installing the associated FBML theme.

Once those steps are complete, it is time to enable some modules. The Facebook for Drupal package comes with several modules so that you can enable only the modules your application requires. A good starter set is "Facebook API," "Facebook Application," "Facebook Application Canvas Pages," and "Facebook User Management." Note, however, that there are modules for integrating things like the popular Views and Actions modules for Drupal.

Now we're ready to create applications. Go to Create content→Facebook Application, and fill out the form with information about the application you already created, such as the API Key, secret, and the app ID. You can also specify controls around user account handling and landing pages for users.

When that form is submitted, Drupal will generate a full callback URL that you can then use in the application settings on Facebook. Drupal will also generate Post-Add and Post-Remove URLs as well.

Congratulations! Your Drupal site is now a Facebook application.

For more information and hints on additional features and configuration, see *http://drupalforfacebook.org/* and the screencasts available at *http://www.dave-cohen.com/node/2246*.

4.11 App Design Process

Problem

I'm new to the whole idea of designing applications. What process should I follow?

Solution

Ever get that feeling like you're standing on the edge of a massive cliff and way down below you stretches an infinite plane upon which you can see large and very violent armies massing? Maybe it's just me. I tend to get that feeling whenever I'm overlooking what amounts to a religious war with no obvious winner, be it Java versus .NET versus Ruby on Rails, dogs versus cats (although dogs are clearly superior IMHO), or software design methodologies. Wikipedia lists 16 different approaches to application design (*http://en.wikipedia.org/wiki/Software_development_process*):

- Waterfall model
- Spiral model
- Model driven development
- User experience
- Top-down and bottom-up design
- Chaos model
- Evolutionary prototyping
- Prototyping
- ICONIX process (UML-based object modeling with use cases)
- Unified process
- V-model
- Extreme programming

- Software development rhythms
- Specification and description language
- Incremental funding methodology
- Verification and validation (software)

Most of these are overkill for your purposes, but you should take a few days out of your busy schedule and read up on them anyway. If you really are new to this and are coming at the question of methodology as pure as the driven snow, you should take the time to evaluate the strengths and weaknesses of the different armies before you dive into the battle.

In the end, you'll probably find that you need a really lightweight approach that adapts quickly to the changing demands of a platform such as Facebook. You might find that 37signals' *Getting Real* book has a lot of merit when it comes to Facebook app development—you can find out more about it, as well as pay your $19 to download the PDF, at *http://gettingreal.37signals.com/*.

The most important thing you can leave this recipe with is this: don't get stuck trying to pick a methodology at the expense of ever getting started. All of them are just tools in your toolbox, and although it's always easier to do a job with the right tool, you can still get it done with the wrong one. My own process is described next in the Discussion, but feel free to use anything you'd like, just as long as you get out there and use it.

Discussion

I agree with a lot of what 37signals says in their book, although I tend to prefer a more structured design process than they advocate. I've been on enough teams and built enough software to know that there is some real truth to the axiom that an hour of design saves 10 hours of programming. Here's the process I follow when designing a new application.

Know thy user

Start off by understanding who you're building for. Is your app targeted at males aged 17–24? Are you building for stay-at-home moms and dads in their 30s? Do you expect to attract predominantly French-speaking new immigrants who are trying to get established? The answer to this question is really the foundation of everything that comes after, so don't gloss over it and try to skip ahead. If you're serious about getting it right, consider using Alan Cooper's personas methodology to develop some personas for your key demographics. For more information, see his book *The Inmates Are Running the Asylum* (*http://www.cooper.com/insights/books/#inmates*) or Wikipedia (*http://en.wikipedia.org/wiki/Personas*).

Goooooooooooooaaaaaaaaaal!

Now that you know who your users are and have some personas built out to represent their opinions, what are they going to do in your app? Start with high-level goals and work your way down into lower-level use cases and bottom-level tasks. A quick break-down for the Facebook Photos app might look like this:

- Goal: See friends' latest photos
  - Use case: Browse through the latest photos from friends
    - Task: Go to the Photos app main page and see the list of newly uploaded photos, filtered to display only the current user's friends
- Goal: Share photos with friends
  - Use case: Create a new album and upload photos
    - Task: Click on the "Create new album" button, then enter a name and description
    - Task: Use the Java applet Photo Uploader to add photos to their new album
- Use case: Send photos to friends off-Facebook
  - Task: Copy the URL for a given photo or album from that photo or album's page and email to friends

Always remember the age-old adage KISS: Keep It Simple, Stupid. If your app is successful and attracts a lot of users, you're going to need to reconsider a lot of this anyway, so try to define the smallest set of goals and tasks that you can possibly get away with for the first version, and then start building them.

Frame the problem

It might be my human-factors background talking, but I never start writing code on a project until I have a full set of complete user experience sketches. A lot of the problems you'll run into writing code will become apparent as you design the user interface (UI), but the opposite doesn't tend to be true, and you end up with a so-called "implementation design": a user interface that exposes the underlying implementation, which is often irrelevant for your users.

I start this process by doing wireframes for every page and dialog so that I know what's going to be in them, what content I need to write for instructions, buttons, etc., and which graphics I'm going to need to produce (or get produced). There are about as many formats and techniques for doing wireframes as there are minutes in the day, so I suggest that you just experiment until you find something that works for you. Some people prefer to do wireframes in static HTML (and then use it as the basis for implementation), others prefer tools such as Visio or OmniGraffle, and others really dig old-school paper and pencil. The important thing at this point is to sketch out a UI and spend time thinking about how the different parts interact, rather than shading every button and getting the colors exactly right. Don't get hung up on how it looks just yet, but instead focus on where the big pieces are on the page and how they interact with each other. Think of this step as creating the architectural blueprints that will define your application rather than the interior design or construction technique you'll use to build it. The main page of the Photos app might look like Figure 4-7.

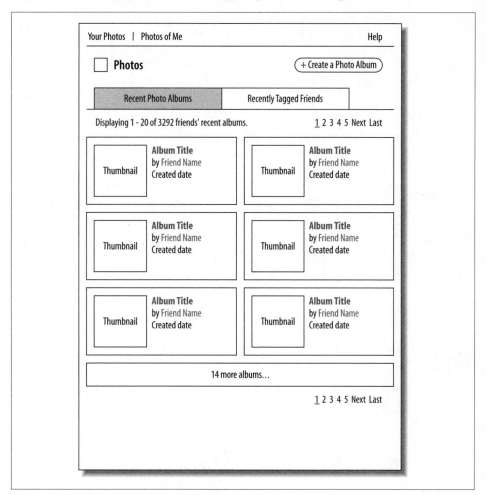

Figure 4-7. Photos app wireframe

Once you've laid out a page, go back through and make sure you know where each link and button goes. Plan out the interaction for any dynamic interactions (e.g., Ajax), and identify where you're going to use a standard Facebook control or roll your own.

If you went through the persona process in the earlier step, you can now use your personas to evaluate your wireframes as you go through this step. If you didn't use personas, or to supplement them, you can use wireframes as ultra-low-fidelity proto-types to run actual users or potential users through quick sanity checks. Sit them down and ask them to accomplish some of the goals from the previous step, using your wireframes as though they were real software, and see where they get stuck or confused.

Making a mockery

Now that you have your blueprint done, it's time to get creative! If you're not the designing type, find someone who is and pay them to do this step for you. User engagement increases dramatically when software looks good, and the tiniest details will make a huge difference to the overall impression of your app. Take a break from reading this recipe and have an honest moment with your ego over in the corner. Are you the right person to do this? Most developers aren't, so don't be afraid to admit that you might need some help here.

If your wireframes share a lot of similarities, there's no need to mock up all of them. Just concentrate on the differences between them, and you'll produce enough artwork to cover the development phase. If you have the time and resources to do so, it's well worth running your designs past some potential users to see what they think, but remember that everyone gets really emotional about design, so some of the feedback you get here will be very specific to the individual giving it and not particularly representative of your users at large. If you do this step properly, your mockup and your final build will end up being virtually identical. Based on the Photos app wireframe outlined in the previous step, the mockup might look like Figure 4-8.

Figure 4-8. Photos app mockup

Build it!

That's it! If you've made it to this point, you're ready to jump in and start building. If you like to have a plan of attack before you start slinging code, go through the wireframes and find all the tricky parts where you're unsure how you're going to do something, and build yourself some prototypes first. Don't forget about the Facebook Test Consoles on the Developer site (*http://developers.facebook.com/tools.php*); these can help you figure out FBML, API, and FQL without needing to write little test apps.

4.12 The Facebook User Interface Widgets

Problem

I really want my app to fit in on Facebook Platform, so I'd like to use as many of Facebook's native widgets in my interface as I can. Is there a style guide or widget library somewhere?

Solution

Unfortunately, Facebook hasn't published any official Human Interface Guidelines, so you're somewhat on your own. Luckily, they have provided a handful of FBML tags that will render standard controls, which means you don't have to worry about styling them now or changing them later when Facebook updates their look and feel. For more about why you should use their user interface (UI) widgets, see Recipe 4.13.

Discussion

First off: what's a widget? From Wikipedia (*http://en.wikipedia.org/wiki/GUI_widget*):

> In computer programming, a widget (or control) is an element of a graphical user interface (GUI) that displays an information arrangement changeable by the user, such as a window or a text box. The defining characteristic of a widget is to provide a single interaction point for the direct manipulation of a given kind of data. Widgets are basic visual building blocks which, combined in an application, hold all the data processed by the application and the available interactions on this data.

There are a whole bunch of UI widgets that you can easily implement with simple FBML tags, as well as a bunch of UI conventions that you should follow but that you'll have to code on your own. This is by no means an exhaustive list, so if you don't find what you're looking for here, take a browse through the FBML Wiki page (*http://wiki.devel opers.facebook.com/index.php/FBML*), or just go through the Facebook site and then take a look at its HTML/CSS.

Simple UI widgets

Thanks to the magic of FBML, implementing the following on your own is often as simple as inserting a few tags:

Page headers

Page headers (see Figure 4-9) can include links (or actions) across the top, a Help link, your app's name, and a Create button. These are all nested inside an `fb:dashboard` tag, which is explained in Recipe 6.36.

Figure 4-9. Facebook Photos header

Tabbed navigation

You can include as many tabs as you'd like, and full support is included for highlighting the current tab (see Figure 4-10). More information is in Recipe 6.37.

Facebook has adopted an informal UI convention related to the use of left- and right-aligned tabs in some of its apps. Generally speaking, left-aligned tabs are used to sort types of information, while right-aligned tabs are used for actions, as in Figure 4-11.

Figure 4-10. Facebook Photos tabs

Figure 4-11. Facebook Inbox with left- and right-aligned tabs

Errors and messages

It's particularly important to be consistent when delivering information to users, since they'll be used to seeing this kind of thing reported by Facebook. In order, from top to bottom, are `fb:error`, `fb:explanation`, and `fb:message` (see Figure 4-12), which are all documented in Recipe 6.39.

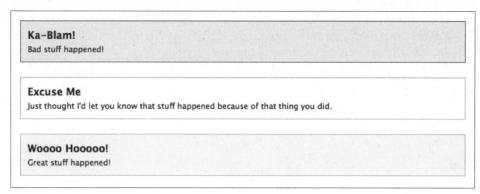

Figure 4-12. Facebook errors, explanations, and messages

UI conventions

Facebook has adopted some UI conventions that aren't available as simple FBML tags, but are worth following anyway:

Paging

> The convention here is to list on the left the number of objects on this page and the total number of objects, accompanied by a link back to an index (if applicable), with paging controls on the right and the current page indicated by an underline (see Figure 4-13). You can replicate this in your app by taking advantage of the fact that Facebook hasn't set a namespace on its own CSS classes, allowing you to use them, too:

```
<div class="bar clearfix summary_bar">
    <ul id="pag_nav_links" class="pagerpro">
        <li class="current">
            <a>1</a>
        </li>
        <li>
            <a href="/thingy.php?page=2" title="Page 2">2</a>
        </li>
        <li>
            <a href="/thingy.php?page=2" title="Page 2">next</a>
        </li>
    </ul>
    <div class="summary">
        <h4>
            Blobs 1 - 20 out of 24
            <span class="pipe">|</span>
            <a href="/stuffs.php?id=12345">Back to Jay's Stuff</a>
        </h4>
    </div>
</div>
```

I've made one small change from Facebook's code: it's generally a bad idea to have a page link to itself because it's not the expected behavior for links, so I've removed the href from inside the <a> around the current page.

Photos 1 – 20 out of 24 | Back to Bianca's Photos   1 2 next

Figure 4-13. Paging in Facebook Photos

Sidebars

Your home page on Facebook includes a sidebar with very subtle but effective divisions into sections (Figure 4-14). The sidebar is a 186-pixel-wide div floated right. The background on the sidebar is achieved by setting the entire Canvas's background to *http://facebook.com/images/newsfeed_line.gif*, which is a 646-pixel-wide and 1-pixel-tall image set to repeat vertically. Apply a sidebar_item_header class to your headers:

```
sidebar_item_header
    background:#E9E9E9 none repeat scroll 0% 0%;
    margin:0pt 5px;
    padding:3px 5px 4px;
    text-align:right;
}
```

Figure 4-14. Facebook Home sidebar

Canvas Footers

The Footer Bar runs across the bottom of Canvas pages and provides actions (usually contextualized to the current user: the earlier example is from the bottom of your Profile page; see Figure 4-15). You can replicate these easily with some simple HTML:

```
<div id="footerBar">
    <ul>
        <li><a href="/thingy.php">Thingy!</a></li>
        <li><span class="pipe">|</span></li>
        <li><a href="/stuffs.php">Stuffs!</a></li>
        <li><span class="pipe">|</span></li>
        <li><a href="/dudes.php">Dudes!</a></li>
    </ul>
</div>
```

and some equally simple CSS:

```
div#footerBar {
    background: #F7F7F7 none repeat scroll 0% 0%;
    border-top: 1px solid #DDDDDD;
    margin: 0px;
    overflow: hidden;
}
div#footerBar ul {
    list-style-image: none;
    list-style-position: outside;
    list-style-type: none;
    margin: 0px;
    padding: 10px 20px 25px;
}
div#footerBar li {
    float: left;
    line-height: 18px;
    padding: 0px 2px;
}
```

Profile Layout | Edit Extended Profile | Create a Profile Badge

Figure 4-15. Facebook Profile footer

4.13 Facebook's Global User Interface

—Daniel Burka (see his bio in Contributors)

Problem

I want to develop an application interface that will integrate smoothly and will adapt successfully with the global Facebook user interface.

Solution

By using user interface tools provided by Facebook and adhering to de facto standards, your users will find your Facebook application's user interface inherently intuitive, and your application will evolve smoothly as the main site changes.

Discussion

Facebook application developers are lucky to have a suite of user interface elements prebuilt for them by default. Designers often have a powerful desire to create original work that breaks with convention, but, particularly when developing Facebook applications, the benefit of adhering to standards (both explicit and implicit) far outweighs the potential benefit of originality.

In the case of developing a Facebook application, you will be developing an interface within an interface (see Figure 4-16). Your application will exist within the shell of the global Facebook interface and, possibly even more importantly, your application will live in a vibrant ecosystem of other applications made by Facebook developers just like you.

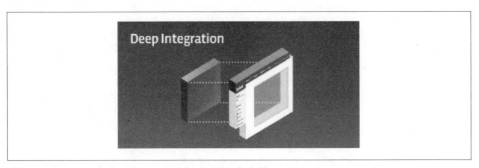

Figure 4-16. Your application within the Facebook shell

In many ways, the Facebook interface can be thought of like an operating system user interface. In developing their own default applications (such as the messaging system, your preferences, the News Feed, as well as the default applications) and the framework for the global user interface (such as the main navigational elements, error dialogs, and the footer), the Facebook design team has tackled many of the interface challenges you are likely to come up against. There are standards already developed for tabbed navigation, selectors, item lists, menus, icons, sliders, forms, dialogs, and many of the other interface elements you are likely to need for your own application (see Figure 4-17).

Figure 4-17. Tabbed navigation, menus, and buttons

The most robust and simplest way to take advantage of Facebook's existing user interface elements is to tap into them directly with FBML. Using this proprietary markup language, you can pull directly from Facebook's own toolkit to build tabbed navigation, dialog boxes, headings, forms, and other elements. The Facebook Developers Wiki has a full list of FBML tags and how to use them.

There are many advantages to using FBML. Most importantly, people who use your application are already familiar with these standard interface elements because they have been using them elsewhere on Facebook. FBML elements look familiar and behave in a consistent way across the site and across different applications, no matter what those applications are for. You can also avoid reinventing the wheel. Developing your application will be faster and will have fewer bugs by taking advantage of prefabricated FBML code that has been tested extensively. By relying on FBML, you will also be future-proofing your application. When Facebook upgrades its user interface, you will immediately reap the benefits because your own interface will be upgraded seamlessly. For instance, should Facebook improve its tabbed navigation design, your own tabs will reflect those improvements without any effort on your part.

Although FBML has many common elements, you will find occasions where custom interface elements are necessary. In these cases, try to fall back onto de facto standards—become familiar with Facebook's default user interface and how other Facebook application developers have tackled similar issues. If you can copy or mimic other common implementations of user interface elements, you will reap many of the same benefits as using FBML. Your users will find your application more intuitive if they are already familiar with elements you are using (for example, Figure 4-18). Facebook even documents on its Wiki how to copy some of the common elements that are available as FBML (*http://wiki.developers.facebook.com/index.php/Facebook_Styles*).

Figure 4-18. Two list table

All of this said, there is room for branding your application and inserting your own style into the work. Build a strong foundation of standard user interface elements to create a highly usable and efficient application, and then integrate your brand in a meaningful way.

CHAPTER 5

Setting Up Your Environment

The difference between churning out beautiful code and pounding your head against the wall can often come down to getting your environment configured properly. This chapter covers some of the things you need to do to become a Facebook developer, and also some of the things you should really check out to make your life a whole lot easier.

5.1 Creating a Test Account

Problem

I want to test my application as another user who isn't a developer, but the Facebook ToS prevent me from creating accounts that aren't linked to my real identity. What's a poor developer to do?

Solution

The Facebook team realized that they were caught in a vicious cycle in which developers were creating fake accounts for testing and the Facebook police were disabling them as fakes, thereby upsetting the developers who then created more accounts, thereby making more work for the police, etc., etc., ad infinitum. Facebook put an end to the problem by giving us the ability to mark an account as a "test account," which has most of the privileges of a real account but with the notable exception of not being able to see "real" Facebook users or owning Platform applications.

Making a test account is really easy: just create a new Facebook account and then go to *http://www.facebook.com/developers/become_test_account.php* while you're logged into it. You'll be shown a confirmation page (Figure 5-1) that reiterates that any applications owned by this account will be disabled, and you're one click away from testing nirvana.

Become a Platform Application Test Account

You are logged in as Bob Dylan.

Test accounts should not be used to interact with normal Facebook users. If you do so, your account may be disabled.

WARNING: Any applications owned by this account will be permanently disabled if you become a test account.

> Make Bob Dylan a Test Account

Figure 5-1. Becoming a test account

 This is very strong magic! Be very, very careful. Test accounts are like the Matrix: once you've swallowed the red pill (or gone to the URL just listed), there's no way to go back to living innocently in your pod. Don't do this step from your primary Facebook account or you'll have banished yourself into Test Account land.

Discussion

Here are a few useful tips on using test accounts:

- Test accounts can be really handy, but the fact that they can't own applications (which really means not being registered Developers of an app) means they can't see apps that are in Developer Mode and therefore can't be used to test an app that isn't yet public.

- You'll need a unique email address in order to sign up, but coming up with different addresses for each account can be a pain. If you have a Gmail account, take a look at so-called "dot addressing." Gmail doesn't recognize dots inside of your email address, so *bob.dylan@gmail.com* is the same thing as *b.obdylan@gmail.com* and *b.o.b.d.y.l.a.n@gmail.com*, in that they'll all get delivered to you. Facebook sees them all as different addresses and will let you sign up as different accounts. Gmail also has a much more useful "plus sign addressing" feature in which it ignores everything after a plus sign in your address (so *bobdylan+test1@gmail.com* is the same as *bobdylan+test2@gmail.com*), but unfortunately Facebook won't allow plus signs in emails.

- Facebook login sessions persist across all the tabs and windows in your browser through the use of session cookies, but they can't persist into different browsers. Since you're a kick-ass web developer and you already test in Firefox, Safari, and IE 6/7/8 on Windows and in Firefox and Safari on Mac, why not log into Facebook with a different test account on each platform? That way you cover different browsers and different users at the same time.

5.2 Facebook Clients

Problem

I have a good grasp on my idea and how to build it, but I need to find the right Facebook client for my development environment before I can get started.

Solution

Most of the resources you're going to need to get started can be found on the Facebook Developers site at *http://developers.facebook.com*.

Discussion

Facebook officially supports Client Libraries for PHP 4 and PHP 5, which you can find at *http://developers.facebook.com/resources.php*. Facebook has also recently launched a JavaScript Client Library (which was still in beta at the time this was written), which you can find at *http://wiki.developers.facebook.com/index.php/JavaScript_Client_Library*. There used to be an officially supported Java library, but it's been discontinued (presumably due to a lack of interest).

If you're intent on using a different language and don't mind that its Client Libraries might not be up-to-date, you'll find a full list on the main page of the Wiki at *http://wiki.developers.facebook.com/index.php/Main_Page* (including ASP.NET, Perl, Python, Ruby on Rails, etc.).

The PHP Client is currently missing four methods that are available through the API: `Photos.createAlbum( )`, `Photos.upload( )`, `photos.addTag( )`, and `Users.hasAppPermission( )` (see Recipe 9.57). You can use a third-party extension to get around the fifth method (see Recipe 9.45).

5.3 JavaScript Client Library

Problem

I'd like to use the JavaScript Client Library to access the API, but I want to make sure I understand any potential limitations and how to get set up before I jump in.

Solution

The JavaScript Client Library is a new addition to the Facebook family and was still in beta at the time this book went to press. The biggest advantage is that you can use it from an HTML page with no server-side code required, which can be served up by Facebook either inside an iFrame-based app or inside an `fb:iframe` in a Canvas-based app. This opens up the possibility of creating apps with really rich Ajax interactions, which can even run outside of Facebook (provided that the user is logged into Facebook in another window or tab).

Since there's no server-side code, there's nothing for you to download. The first step is to create what's known as a "channel page" on your server, which uses a library developed by Facebook to enable communications between your site and Facebook without running into cross-domain scripting limitations. Create a page on your site called *xd_receiver.html* and enter the following HTML into it (you can copy and paste from *http://wiki.developers.facebook.com/index.php/Cross_Domain_Communication _Channel*):

```
<!DOCTYPE html PUBLIC "-//W3C//DTD XHTML 1.0 Strict//EN"
    "http://www.w3.org/TR/xhtml1/DTD/xhtml1-strict.dtd">
<html xmlns="http://www.w3.org/1999/xhtml">
<head>
    <title>Cross-Domain Receiver Page</title>
</head>
<body>
    <script src="http://static.ak.facebook.com/js/api_lib/
v0.3/XdCommReceiver.debug.js" type="text/javascript"></script>
</body>
</html>
```

Now you can create the HTML pages for your app. Load the Client Library JavaScript into the <head> of each page:

```
<script type="text/javascript" src="http://static.ak.face
book.com/js/api_lib/v0.3/FeatureLoader.js"></script>
```

When you're ready to start making API calls, instantiate a Facebook API Client object, passing in your app's API key and a domain-relative URL to the *xd_receiver.html* page:

```
var api = new FB.ApiClient('1234567890123456789', 'xd_receiver.html', null);
```

That's about it for setup! Now you're ready to build your JavaScript-based app.

Discussion

If you're doing a lot of JavaScript development and aren't already using Firefox with the Firebug add-on installed, I highly recommend you make the switch (see Recipe 7.17 for more info about Firebug). Apple has recently added some fantastic developer tools to Safari, which is quickly becoming an excellent platform for building JavaScript apps. Microsoft's Internet Explorer 8 has some really compelling JavaScript features (particularly the debugger), but we won't see it in reliable production for some time yet.

There are eight methods in the JavaScript Client Library that give you control over the Canvas page that your app is running inside:

FB.CanvasClient.startTimerToSizeToContent( )
iFrames in Canvas pages are sized to fill the remaining space in the page by default. If you would like your iFrame to adapt to the content you put in it, call

`FB.CanvasClient.startTimerToSizeToContent( )` and Facebook will start a timer that regularly checks in on the content and resizes appropriately.

`FB.CanvasClient.stopTimerToSizeToContent( )`

When you are ready to have the iFrame stop resizing, call `FB.CanvasClient.stopTimerToSizeToContent( )`, and it will revert to the default behavior.

`FB.CanvasClient.setSizeToContent( )`

If you want to make a one-time adjustment to the size to match the content (rather than having it continuously adjust), call `FB.CanvasClient.setSizeToContent( )`.

`FB.CanvasClient.setCanvasHeight( )`

You can manually adjust the height of the Canvas by calling `FB.CanvasClient.setCanvasHeight( )`. Note that the width is always set to 646 pixels.

`FB.CanvasClient.add_windowSizeChanged( )`,
`FB.CanvasClient.remove_windowSizeChanged( )`

These two methods let you add a listener to the window's event so that you can be informed of changes to the window's size and adjust appropriately.

`FB.CanvasClient.get_timerInterval( )`, `FB.CanvasClient.set_timerInterval( )`

These final two methods let you get and set the timer interval used in `FB.CanvasClient.startTimerToSizeToContent( )`.

The Wiki's JavaScript Client Library page (*http://wiki.developers.facebook.com/index .php/JavaScript_Client_Library*) has some great sample code on it which demonstrates retrieving a user's friends and how to make a bunch of API calls in batched mode to save bandwidth and increase performance.

The library currently supports Internet Explorer 6 and 7, Safari 3, and Firefox 2 and 3 (the Wiki currently says that the beta of Firefox 3 is unsupported, but since the browser has shipped, support will certainly follow shortly if it isn't already provided). Facebook has promised to support Internet Explorer 8 when it ships.

5.4 Starting Out in PHP

—James DeFillippo (see his bio in Contributors)

Problem

I'm new to PHP and want some general tips on optimizing my application so that it can scale gracefully.

Solution

One of the easiest and most overlooked ways to optimize a PHP application is the proper use of double and single quotes when handling strings. Using double quotes only where they are entirely necessary can give your app the runway it needs to get off the ground.

For example, you wouldn't want to use:

```
echo "This is a simple piece of text with a single $variable";
```

when this is faster to execute with much lower memory requirements:

```
echo 'This is a simple piece of text with a single ' . $variable;
```

Discussion

When dealing with strings in PHP, there are two ways of using quotation marks to wrap your strings. One involves using single quotes (') and the other uses double quotes ("). There is a major difference—not only in functionality, but also in speed—when it comes to using the two different options.

PHP will take anything wrapped in a matching set of single quotes and treat that as a string literal. Literally anything in between single quotes is a string and should be treated as such, with no interference from the parser. If you wrap the string in double quotes, though, PHP will parse every element in that string looking for variables for reassignment. Even if none are present, it still has to look, which means if you are wrapping any piece of text in double quotes that does not have a variable in it, you're throwing compute cycles away and making your application slower for no reason.

On smaller and low-load applications, the difference in speed is not noticeable, which is why it's often overlooked during testing and ignored as a potential bottleneck. As your application grows in size, complexity, and traffic, the difference can be extremely troublesome and can hinder your ability to serve your clients or customers.

A recent application that I rearchitected to use proper quoting for strings saw an immediate speed increase of 35%! And all we had to do was make sure that the right quotes were used for the right job.

When assigning plain text strings, common practice is to use something like this:

```
$error_message = "Hey $username! Something's broken. Try again.";
```

Since there is a variable in the assignment, common thinking is to wrap the entire assignment in double quotes and call it a day. This works just fine from a functional standpoint, but from a speed standpoint you're wasting time and memory by having PHP look at every other word in that string to see if it also is a variable. The preferred method for assigning a string with a variable is the "." concatenation method. For example:

```
$error_message = 'Hey ' . $username . '! Something\'s broken. Try again.';
```

By breaking the line into two string literals and a simple variable replacement, we've taken the burden off of PHP when it comes to finding out exactly what each element of that assignment is. You will also note the \' in the previous example. When you're dealing with string literals and single quotes, you need to remember to escape your containing characters. The same thing goes for double quotes inside of a double-quoted string.

And quotes don't just matter when you're doing variable assignments or echos; they also matter when dealing with arrays, ifs, elseifs, and almost anything else you can use a string for. The following are a few of the more common things I've seen that can easily sneak into your code if you're used to using double quotes for all your string needs.

When manually initializing an array, you should always use single quotes for any strings:

```
// Don't
$foo = array("a", "b", "c");

// Do
$foo = array('a', 'b', 'c');
```

When accessing a named array slice, always (and I mean *always*) use single quotes:

```
// Don't
$foo = $array["slice"];

// Do
$foo = $array['slice'];
```

Often something like this can get by and turn into a massive loop:

```
for ($x=0;$x<100000;++$x)
{
    doSomethingWith($array[$x]["slice"]);
}
```

In this example, you're iterating over and over again on that array, and with every loop, PHP is taking the string "slice" and checking it to see whether it has any variables in it for reassignment. This wastes memory and cycles on a much larger scale than a single assignment or if statement.

When upgrading older code that uses a lot of double quotes to a single-quote model, the biggest gotcha can come from special escaped characters. These characters include \n, \t, and \r, which, when used in a double-quoted string, get replaced with a newline, tab, and carriage return, respectively. You can use the concatenation method for keeping these structures intact, though, and still save processor time and memory. For example:

```
echo 'This is a line with a newline at the end' . "\n";
```

Proper quoting of strings can sometimes be a pain, but the rewards over time in terms of speed, hardware costs, man hours, and your sanity can be extraordinary in any app that you want to scale to a global audience. And who doesn't want that?

5.5 Demo Applications

Problem

It would be so awesome if I had some demo applications I could download and play with!

Solution and Discussion

Lucky for you, there are a bunch of demo apps that you can grab and dig through. You'll find them on the Wiki at *http://wiki.developers.facebook.com/index.php/Demos*. The current crop of three demos includes:

Footprints
> An extremely basic application included with the PHP 4 and PHP 5 clients. You can play with a live demo at *http://apps.facebook.com/footprints/*.

Restaurants
> A more advanced demo showing some of the more complex features, including Mock Ajax, FBJS, and the Data Store API. It's backed by premade data on your MySQL server and/or the Facebook Data Store API.

Who's Showing Up
> Another "real" application, demonstrating building applications that are installable both for users and for Facebook Pages, such as those for businesses, bands, and brands.

In addition to the apps provided by Facebook, Jesse Stay (author of O'Reilly's excellent *FBML Essentials* and coauthor of *I'm on Facebook—Now What???*) has built an app that demonstrates almost all of the FBML tags; see *http://apps.facebook.com/fbmlessen tials*.

5.6 Developer Documentation

Problem

This book is the greatest thing since sliced bread, but I need more technical detail on a specific topic and/or long listings of sample code.

Solution

Facebook Platform launched with some official documentation (see *http://developers .facebook.com*, not to be confused with *http://www.facebook.com/developers*, which is the Developer app), but that quickly became out-of-date. Realizing that there was a veritable army of people who were happy to help keep the docs relevant, the Facebook team quickly launched a wiki and stopped updating the old docs, which languish as a reminder of days gone by. If you're looking for info or want to contribute to keeping it real, check out the Developers Wiki at *http://wiki.developers.facebook.com*.

Discussion

The Wiki is a real treasure trove of information but can be very difficult to navigate. Since it's essentially crowdsourced documentation, different authors have come up with very different ways to organize different sections, which leads to a palpable sense of disorientation (as an example, check out the excellent index page for the FBML section and the chaotic jumble of FBJS's single page). The joy of wikis is that we're all free to update and edit them, and so I encourage you to contribute back to the community by jumping in and helping to keep it orderly, up-to-date, and well-organized.

5.7 Test Consoles

Problem

It can be a real pain to set up a testing framework as a Facebook app if you just want to try out a few lines of API code. Surely there must be a better way!

Solution

Facebook makes three test consoles available to developers:

API Test Console

> Found at *http://developers.facebook.com/tools.php?api*, the API Test Console lets you pick an API call from a drop-down menu, specify any optional parameters, and see the returned XML for your logged-in user. It's very useful for figuring out what you'll get back from a given call so that you can write code to handle it. There isn't an FQL-specific Test Console, but you will find an `fql.query` option in the Method drop-down here.

FBML Test Console

> Found at *http://developers.facebook.com/tools.php?fbml*, the FBML Test Console lets you choose where your FBML will occur (*narrow profile box*, *wide profile box*, *canvas*, *email*, *notification*, *request*, *feed title*, *feed body*, and *mobile*) and lets you enter some FBML that will be rendered from the logged-in user's perspective (and shown in HTML source form).

Feed Preview Console

Found at *http://developers.facebook.com/tools.php?feed*, the Feed Preview Console is a really quick way to preview what a given story will look like in a user's News and Mini-Feeds. This is critical to making sure your feed items will make effective use of the social graph, so spend time in here tweaking to get them right.

Discussion

All three consoles use the Facebook session from your browser, so they'll work from the perspective of the logged-in user. If you want to see how different code will be seen by different users, use more than one browser and log into test accounts in the others (see Recipe 5.1). It's pretty easy to tweak the code in your main account and then copy and paste it into the console in other browsers to double-check.

5.8 Developer Forums: Help!

Problem

I've been through this book and I've read through the Wiki, but I'm really stuck and nothing is working. Help!

Solution

Gotham has the bat symbol, Metropolis has Superman, and we have the Developer Forums. Whether you're really stuck or are a super-talented dev master with knowledge pouring out your ears, the Forums are a great place to meet other developers, ask questions, and get help. You'll find them at *http://forum.developers.facebook.com*.

It's also worth checking to see when the next Facebook Developer Garage is happening near you, since these events are like being in the middle of a real-world forum with real people who can answer your questions (and who you can then buy drinks for!). Keep an eye on the Developer Garage Calendar at *http://wiki.developers.facebook.com/index.php/Garage_Calendar*.

Discussion

Don't forget to contribute back to the community! If you ask a question in the forums and get a helpful answer, make sure you come back when you've grown your developer chops and help out others who are just finding their footing. Also, if you're new to the world of online forums and discussion boards, spend a little time looking through the forums before you post to get a feel for the right tone and content, and to make sure that no one else has already asked your question and received an answer.

5.9 Facebook Bug Squashing

Problem

I've found an honest-to-goodness bug in Facebook Platform. Now what?

Solution

Platform bugs are actually very rare, so first off you should pat yourself on the back for a job well done. Then you should hit up the Facebook bug tracking system at *http:// bugs.developers.facebook.com/*.

Discussion

The Facebook bug tracking system is really Bugzilla with a prettier face. For those of you not familiar with Bugzilla, it's an open source bug tracker developed by the Mozilla Foundation and used by them to track defects in all of their products. It's not the most intuitive application but it is incredibly powerful, and Facebook has done a good job of cleaning up the user interface while still maintaining the irreverent humor Bugzilla is known for (try doing a search that returns no bugs).

One of the most powerful tools within the system is the ability to save searches, and you'll find that your shiny new Bug Tracker account comes with a predefined "My Bugs" search, which is accessible in the footer of every page. Once you've done a search, you'll find a "Remember search as" option at the bottom of the page, which will save your search under a new name.

5.10 Facebook Developer Software Toolbox

Problem

What software tools do I need to build Facebook apps? Is this going to be expensive?

Solution

The good news is that you can get away with entirely free software to build your app! The bad news is that there's only good news. So, I guess that's just good news, then! Phew.

Until Facebook released Facebook Open Platform, you couldn't build Facebook apps locally on your own computer because you needed the Facebook servers and parsers and other crazy software running. Now you can download Facebook Open Platform, which is licensed under a combination of the Common Public Attribution License (CPAL) and Mozilla Public License (MPL), get it running locally on your dev machine, and go to town. So, I guess there used to be a piece of bad news (you always needed to have a web connection available to test with), but it's now a mostly good piece (you can get it running locally if you're good at the server setup and software-compiling-type stuff). You can find out more about Facebook Open Platform at *http://developers.face book.com/fbopen/*.

Other than that, you'll need a text editor for writing code, an FTP client for uploading it to your server (see Recipe 5.12 for more info), and some sort of graphics editor for images. If you have a toolkit in place for doing web development now, you should be more than ready.

Discussion

I'm not going to cover getting Facebook Open Platform running, since that could be almost a book on its own given the number of possible operating system and server combinations out there. You're going to spend most of your time in your text editor, so that's the focus of this discussion.

Choosing the best text editor is a little bit like picking the best right hand. Editors disappear when you're comfortable in them, becoming a natural extension of your code-writing brain directly into your computer. Unless you're a heavy web designer (in which case you're probably quite at home in the Adobe Creative Suite), this is the piece of software you're going to use most often while building your app. The following are a few of the more popular options for different OSes.

Mac OS X

Mac-based developers tend to be in one of three camps:

Bare Bones Software's BBEdit
> The old-school choice of pros. I'm a BBEdit user myself, mostly because I've been using it for more than 10 years and I couldn't possibly face the idea of learning a new editor. Standing by its long-term slogan, Bare Bones maintains that "It doesn't suck.®", and I firmly agree. More info at *http://bbedit.com/products/bbe dit/*. The cost is $129 for an individual or $49 for an educational license.

MacroMates' TextMate
> A relative newcomer (compared to the venerable BBEdit), TextMate's slogan is, "The missing editor for Mac OS X." This is a full-featured editor with all the bells and whistles you would expect, and it is particularly popular in the Ruby on Rails world (though it has support for more than 50 languages). More info at *http:// macromates.com/*. The cost is €39 for an individual (which translated to about USD $64 in May 2008). Educational/academic licenses are available, though the price isn't listed.

Panic Software's Coda
> Coda is the newest contender for the Mac OS X editor throne. If you're a web developer who focuses on HTML/CSS/JavaScript and does PHP development, you should take a serious look at this app. It includes a full FTP/SFTP client based on Panic's popular Transmit client, file management, a great text editor based on the

Subetha Engine, a Preview window that uses WebKit (Safari's rendering engine), a WYSIWYG CSS editor, an integrated Terminal command-line window, and a built-in reference library of HTML, CSS, JavaScript, and PHP books. More info at *http://www.panic.com/coda/*. The cost is $79 for an individual, or $69 if you already own Transmit 3.

Windows

I'm less familiar with the world of Windows editors, being Mac-based myself. Short of advising you to switch to a Mac, I can offer the following list, solicited from my Windows-based developer-type friends:

E Text Editor
> If you're a fan of TextMate on Mac OS X, this is the editor for you (its slogan is, in fact, "The power of TextMate on Windows"). Full support for TextMate commands, snippets, and bundles makes this an excellent choice if you spend time between platforms, and it is a really solid editor in its own right. Get more info at *http://www.e-texteditor.com/*. The cost is $34.95 for an individual, with no obvious educational licensing.

Notepad++
> Notepad++ is an open source and entirely free replacement for Windows' built-in Notepad editor. This is a relatively mature editor with many of the high-end features you'll find elsewhere, including tabbed windows, syntax coloring, regexp, macros, and so on. More info at *http://notepad-plus.sourceforge.net/uk/site.htm*.

Helios Software Solutions TextPad
> This fairly popular editor was designed to follow the Windows XP user interface guidelines, so you should feel right at home if that's your operating system of choice. More info at *http://www.textpad.com/products/textpad/*. The cost is $33 for an individual, with educational discounts available on request.

Linux

If you're running Linux as your primary operating system, you certainly don't need my advice on text editors (and I'm certainly not about to step into the vi/Emacs war without at least a Pico or NEdit to shield myself with).

Eclipse

If you're into the idea of an open source, cross-platform editor, particularly one that is extendible through a veritable mountain of third-party plugins, check out Eclipse at *http://www.eclipse.org/*.

5.11 Weekly Facebook Pushes

Problem

How will I know when Facebook is going to push new code to its production servers? What if it breaks my app?!

Solution

Facebook generally does one weekly push of new code to their production servers, which is currently scheduled for Tuesdays. The details of the push (which is, essentially, the list of check-ins to Facebook's source control server) are available from the Wiki's Push Changes page at *http://wiki.developers.facebook.com/index.php/Category:Push_Changes*.

Discussion

If you're actively working on a new app or maintaining an existing one, you should make sure to test it on Wednesdays to see whether the push has broken anything for you. But don't fixate on that day of the week, as Facebook sometimes moves the actual push day to Monday. You can see when the push is scheduled by keeping up with the Platform Status Feed from the Developer app, which you can find at *http://www.facebook.com/developers/message.php?id=233*, or you can subscribe to it by RSS/Atom at *http://www.facebook.com/feeds/api_messages.php*.

As of mid-May 2008, Facebook has started pushing its release candidates to *http://www.beta.facebook.com* on the Monday prior to the Tuesday push to production, so that developers can test and report bugs. You should definitely take advantage of that testing window, so schedule some blocked-off time on Monday nights to make sure your babies haven't broken.

5.12 Hosting

Problem

I need to find reliable and scalable hosting for my Facebook applications.

Solution

Hosting a Facebook app doesn't have any real requirements, other than the ability to rapidly scale up if your app becomes popular.

Unclear on why you would need your own hosting since your app is on Facebook? Check out Chapter 4 for more information on the way Facebook apps work.

Facebook has negotiated with Joyent and Amazon Web Services to offer programs tailored to Platform developers. You can, of course, host your app anywhere you'd like, but make sure that your hosting provider doesn't have a really expensive ramp up if you exceed your plan. Your app could become the hottest thing on Facebook overnight, which would be awesome, but then you could get a bill from your provider for $100,000 in overages, which would suck (to say the least).

 If you're happy with your existing hosting and have already checked to make sure you're OK to become #1 with a bullet, you can safely skip the following discussion.

Discussion

Facebook's Developer Resource page lists two hosting partner programs: Joyent Facebook Developers Progam and Amazon Web Services (AWS).

Joyent Facebook developers program

A proud member and leader of the cloud computing world, Joyent provides scalable web application hosting using their Accelerator technology. From its site (*http://joyent.com/developers/facebook*):

> Facebook, Joyent, and Dell have partnered to provide free scalable, on-demand infrastructure from Joyent to Facebook developers. Joyent's Accelerator on-demand infrastructure (peered with Facebook's datacenter!) provides the very best load balancers, routing and switching fabric, x86 servers, and storage from Dell. Facebook developers can take advantage of Joyent Accelerators to quickly launch Facebook applications capable of scaling to millions of users. All for free.

Joyent's program offers one of its entry-level Accelerators for one year for free (up to certain levels, over and above which you have to pay), after which you have to start paying. A limited number of free Accelerators are available, so you might not get a spot if you want to take advantage of this program. We host our Zerofootprint application with Joyent (in a non-free account) and have been very happy with the service and support, so I can personally recommend it.

As of May 2008, the restrictions on the free Accelerator are as follows: you need to use your Accelerator within the first 30 days of signing up (or they release it back into the pool); you need to log into your Accelerator every 60 days by either *ssh* or *webadmin*; you have 512 MB of RAM and 10 GB of storage; you can use the Accelerator to host non-Facebook apps but need to have at least one active Facebook app (i.e., more than

50 total users); and you can have only one Accelerator account per person. If you want to bypass the potential hassle of waiting for a free account, pricing for regular Accelerators starts at $45/month for 5 GB of storage, 256 MB of RAM, and 1/16 of a CPU, and they range up to $4,000/month for 100 GB of storage, 32 GB of RAM, and 8 CPUs. The Joyent team has a post up on their blog about a presentation they did at the Graphing Social Patterns conference in 2007, which includes some price comparisons with Amazon Web Services, showing that you can save a considerable amount by going with Joyent's Accelerators: *http://joyeur.com/2007/10/10/graphing-social-patterns-joy ent-web-application-presentation*. Check the math for yourselves since prices may well have changed.

More info about Accelerators can be found at *http://www.joyent.com/accelerator*.

Amazon Web Services (AWS)

AWS may have started as an attempt by Amazon to leverage extra capacity in its data centers into a new revenue earner, but it's grown way beyond that. Its fourth quarter earnings report for 2007 revealed that traffic to AWS had exceeded traffic to Amazon's actual sites for the first time:

> Adoption of Amazon Elastic Compute Cloud (EC2) and Amazon Simple Storage Service (S3) continues to grow. As an indicator of adoption, bandwidth utilized by these services in fourth quarter 2007 was even greater than bandwidth utilized in the same period by all of *http://amazon.com*'s global websites combined.

Facebook and Amazon have partnered together to provide hosting in EC2 and S3 for Facebook apps, as well as some sample code, plug-ins, etc. See Recipes 5.13 and 5.14 for more information about setting up those services.

As of May 2008, the rough cost to host 1 GB worth of assets on S3 (1 GB of data inbound, 100 GB outbound, 1000 PUT/LIST requests, 1000 other requests) and to have a small instance of EC2 running for the full month (with 100 GB of data in and out) was $116. That won't handle a popular Facebook application, but it would serve up a smaller app without a huge number of graphic and rich-media resources.

More information about Amazon Web Services can be found at *http://www.amazonaws .com*.

5.13 Amazonian Backends: Simple Storage Solution

Problem

My app is going to require me to store a whole big heaping pile of rich-media files, which are huge and are going to gobble up my entire monthly bandwidth allocation in one bite.

Solution

Store your media files (or any files, for that matter) on Amazon Simple Storage Solution (S3), part of Amazon's growing family of web services. Don't just take it from me—Nat Brown, CTO of iLike, is a big fan of S3:

> S3 is a no-brainer if you need to scale out delivery of simple content or provide secure limitless storage. We chose S3 for expediency (we were up and running within a few hours) and usage-based pricing (instead of minimum commits and long-term contracts).
>
> Also, the active open source community, growing commercial ecosystem of products & services around AWS, and the high-quality tools for working with AWS are not only great resources for us but they also indicate that the community will be around for the long-term and so we feel comfortable basing more of our architecture on AWS.

You can read a full interview with Nat about how iLike uses AWS at *http://tinyurl.com/ 3j7hmw* (the actual Amazon URL is so long and embarrassingly full of weird parameters that it's actually unprintable).

Discussion

Back in the bad old days of the first bubble, it used to be that startups had to raise bucket loads of money, which they then handed straight to the network hardware and server makers in exchange for rooms full of gear, which they could then sell at fire sale prices when the bubble popped. The Web 2.0 revolution has turned that entire equation upside down, giving startups the ability to get going with almost no upfront cost by building entirely on services like S3. So many web apps are now built on Amazon S3 that a very irregular outage in early February 2008 nearly brought the Web to a crashing halt. Other than that single blip, S3 (and all of the AWSs) have been rock solid and completely reliable as they continue their inexorable march toward complete web backend dominance.

S3 is a godsend for developers on a tight budget because it brings the cost of storing and transferring data down to the point where they basically disappear. I store my personal library of photographs—about 30 GB—on S3, and I pay about $5/month for the storage and bandwidth to access them. For a server located in the U.S. (European servers are slightly more expensive), storage is currently $0.15/GB/month, $0.10/GB transferred into S3, and between $0.10 and $0.17 for data out, depending how much you pull. To get a better idea of pricing, you can play with the AWS Simple Monthly Calculator at *http://calculator.s3.amazonaws.com/calc5.html*.

Setting up your AWS account

The first step is to sign up for an AWS account at *http://www.amazonaws.com*. You will need to activate the S3 service on your account by visiting the S3 page (*http://s3.ama zonaws.com*) and clicking on the big "Sign Up For This Web Service" button on the right side, shown in Figure 5-2.

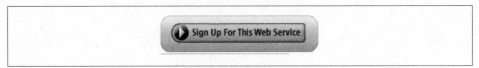

Figure 5-2. The eponymously named "Sign Up For This Web Service" button

S3 provides developers with API and secret keys (which will feel familiar to a Facebook expert like yourself), which you can collect by logging into your account and then selecting "AWS Access Identifiers" from the yellow "Your Web Services Account" drop-down menu in the upper-righthand corner of most pages (Amazon's URLs are unfortunately completely useless for sharing between users, so you'll just have to follow along; see Figure 5-3).

Figure 5-3. AWS menu

You can view your Secret Access Key by clicking on the Show link, as in Figure 5-4.

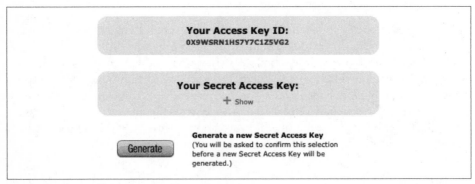

Figure 5-4. Amazon Web Services access identifiers

Getting foxy with S3Fox

Once you have those puppies, it's time to find an S3 client that you're comfortable with. You have quite a few options to choose from, including S3Fox if you're a Firefox user (*https://addons.mozilla.org/en-US/firefox/addon/3247*), or Panic's Transmit if you are on a Mac (the best FTP/SFTP client in the world; *http://www.panic.com/trans mit/*). If you'd like to use S3 for personal storage (as I do with photos), I highly recommend JungleDisk on both Macs and PCs (*http://www.jungledisk.com/*), though note that the automated file renaming it does makes it less useful if you're using S3 for web development. I'm going to use S3Fox as an example, mostly because it's cross-platform.

After you've installed the Add-on and restarted Firefox, you'll find a new "S3 Organizer" entry in the Tools menu, as shown in Figure 5-5.

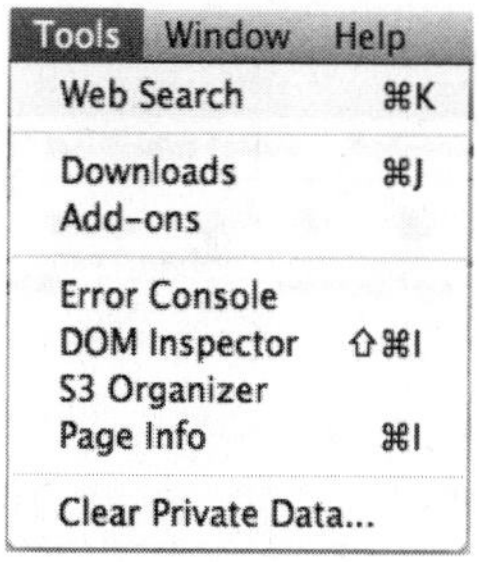

Figure 5-5. S3 Organizer in Firefox's Tools menu

Selecting that item will open the S3 Organizer, and when you open it for the first time, it will prompt you to enter your account info. Click on the "Manage Accounts" item in the top-left corner of the S3 Organizer window to open the Accounts window (Figure 5-6), into which you should carefully place your S3 credentials.

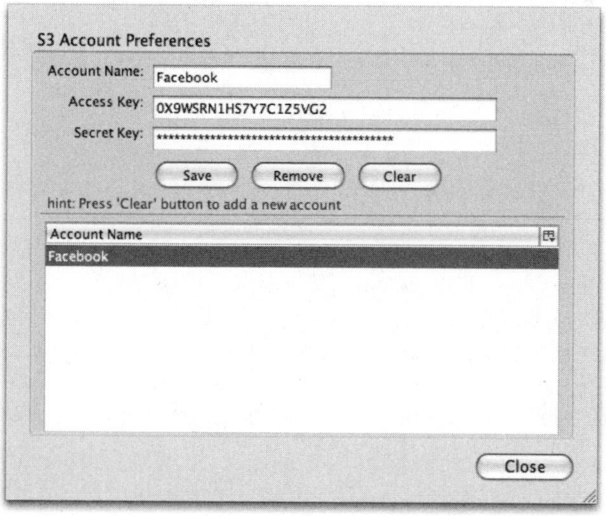

Figure 5-6. S3 Organizer account preferences

Clicking "Close" will close the Accounts window and should connect you to your S3 account on the right side of the S3 Organizer window (Figure 5-7).

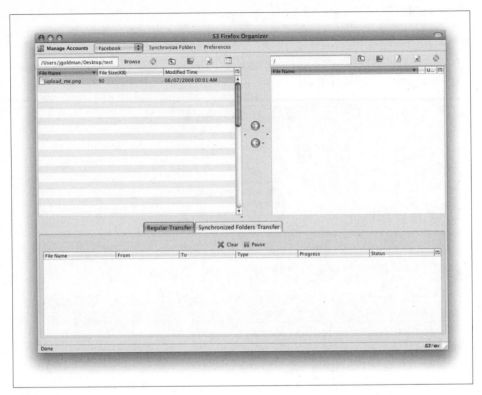

Figure 5-7. S3Fox Organizer window

Buckets of files

S3 is essentially a flat file system, in that it doesn't support nested hierarchies of folders. You can create "buckets" (which are basically folders), but you can't put them inside of each other. We're going to create a new bucket first, and you should do this for each of the apps for which you want to store files on S3. If your app's name is "Jay's Super Cool Facebook App," you might create a bucket called "jay.super.cool.app" (you're only allowed to use lowercase letters, and you never want to put spaces into filenames on servers). Click on the "Create Directory" button above the file list on the right (it's the little blue folder with the spark of life), and then name your new bucket (Figure 5-8).

Don't be confused by the fact that the button is called "Create Directory" and that the dialog box uses the terms "Folder" and "Bucket" interchangeably. You can now upload any files you'd like, either by selecting them on the left and clicking the blue arrow, or by dragging and dropping from right to left.

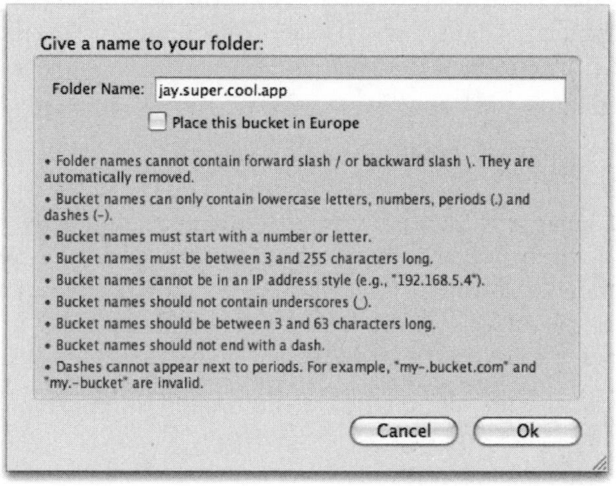

Figure 5-8. S3Fox new bucket

As a final step, you'll need to edit the permissions on your new bucket to allow "Everyone" to read the files, which you can do by selecting it in the list and clicking on the "Edit ACL" button (the Access Control List—the paper and pencil icon). Click on the red "X" in the Everyone/Read box to turn it into a green checkmark, turn on the "Apply to subfolders" checkbox, and then click Save (Figure 5-9).

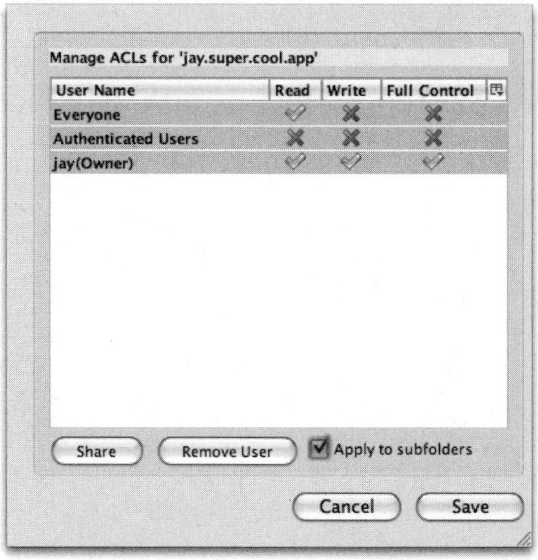

Figure 5-9. S3Fox ACL

That should set the permissions of everything in your new bucket to match. You can now embed those images right in your HTML (or serve up PDFs, embed videos, etc.) by using the URL of your bucket:

```
<img src="http://jay.super.cool.app.s3.amazonaws.com/my_image.jpg" />
```

Interacting with S3's API

Adding files to S3 manually is great if your app has a small number of images or media files, but what about handling user-generated content uploads? A very popular app might have a million users, and if 10% of them are active every day and a quarter of those upload a 100k image, you're looking at about 2 GB a day in new data. You certainly don't want to have to upload that by hand!

There are a number of different ways to interact with S3 via the AWS API, including some great Client Libraries for different languages:

Neurofuzzy's Amazon PHP class
http://neurofuzzy.net/2006/03/17/amazon-s3-php-class/

Edoceo, Inc.'s phps3tk
http://edoceo.com/creo/phps3tk

Undesigned's Amazon S3 PHP class
http://undesigned.org.za/2007/10/22/amazon-s3-php-class

"How to Serve Static Files From Amazon's S3" from the Ruby on Rails wiki
http://wiki.rubyonrails.org/rails/pages/howtoservestaticfilesfromamazonss3

JetS3t, an open source Java toolkit for Amazon S3
http://jets3t.s3.amazonaws.com/downloads.html

5.14 Amazonian Backends: Hosting on Elastic Cloud Computing

Problem

I want to make sure my app is able to scale up really quickly to meet demand. I've heard that Amazon's Elastic Cloud Computing (EC2) service lets me add on servers as I need them, really cheaply. How do I host my app there?

Solution

As Amazon S3 is to storage, EC2 is to hosting (see Recipe 5.13). You can realize some pretty dramatic cost savings by hosting on EC2, particularly if your app needs to scale suddenly to meet demand.

Discussion

Setting up and running an EC2-based hosting system isn't any easier than doing it the old-fashioned way, but it sure is cheaper. If you don't have experience administering Linux-based systems, you might want to skip this approach or find a friend (or new employee) who does. There's a pretty thorough tutorial on setting up and using AWS with Facebook available at *http://tinyurl.com/2fs9f6* (Amazon really needs to do something about the URLs on its website).

Getting started is pretty simple: if you don't already have an AWS account, you can sign up for one at *http://www.amazonaws.com*. You'll then need to add EC2 to your Amazon Web Services by visiting the EC2 page (*http://ec2.amazonaws.com*) and clicking on the big "Sign Up For This Web Service" button on the right side (Figure 5-10).

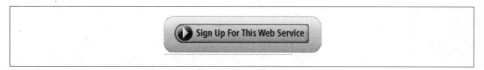

Figure 5-10. Can you guess what this button does?

You're going to need an S3 account to go along with your EC2 account, since EC2 stores and retrieves your Amazon Machine Images (AMIs) from S3. That will make more sense in a moment, but in the meantime you should go add S3 to your AWS account at *http://s3.amazonaws.com*.

Amazon will email you when your servers are available, so in the meantime you should make yourself an X.509 certificate. According to Wikipedia (*http://en.wikipedia.org/wiki/X.509*):

> In cryptography, X.509 is an ITU-T standard for a public key infrastructure (PKI) and Privilege Management Infrastructure (PMI). X.509 specifies, amongst other things, standard formats for public key certificates, certificate revocation lists, attribute certificates, and a certification path validation algorithm.

Amazon uses X.509 certificates to authenticate you when you connect to your server over SSH or SFTP. If you already have a certificate, you can upload it at *http://tinyurl.com/6jbnbu*. If you don't, it provides a service for creating a new certificate, which you can access at *http://tinyurl.com/5dm5cb*. That page will produce two files that you should download and store very securely: your Private Key file and your X.509 Certificate. Create a directory called *.ec2* in your home directory of your computer, and put those two files into it.

You'll need to figure out your EC2 username, which is your Amazon account number with the hyphens removed. If you don't have your account number, you can get it by selecting "AWS Account Activity" from the yellow "Your Web Services Account" menu, as shown in Figure 5-11.

Your account number will be listed at the top of the page, and it should take the form 1234-1234-1234. Drop the hyphens, and there you have your EC2 username (123412341234).

Figure 5-11. Amazon Web Services Account menu

Next up is grabbing the EC2 Command Line Tools, which are a set of shell scripts written in Java and available for Windows or Mac OS X/Linux/Unix. You can get them from the EC2 Resource Center at *http://tinyurl.com/2erefx*. Once you have them installed on your machine, you'll need to configure the `EC2_HOME` environment variable and will probably want to add the *bin* directory to your path. You can also make your life a whole lot easier by setting up the `EC2_PRIVATE_KEY` and `EC2_CERT` variables, which should point to the two files you stashed in your *.ec2* directory, so that you don't have to provide paths to them with every EC2 call you make. The instructions for doing so vary considerably depending on the operating system, so either consult your documentation or do a Google search.

You're all ready to fire up your first EC2 instance! Your path will deviate considerably from this point depending on what you're looking to accomplish, so I'm going to end this recipe here and point you to some resources that can take you further along in this process:

Amazon EC2 Getting Started Guide
> *http://docs.amazonwebservices.com/AWSEC2/2007-03-01/GettingStartedGuide/*

Hosting Facebook Applications on Amazon EC2
> *http://developer.amazonwebservices.com/connect/entry.jspa?entryID=1044*

Hello World Facebook Application AMI (a very useful AMI to load as a starting point, including a demo app showing how to list objects from an Amazon S3 bucket)
> *http://developer.amazonwebservices.com/connect/entry.jspa?categoryID=116&externalID=964*

If you're going to be running a large number of instances, you might want to consider using RightScale (*http://www.rightscale.com*) or Service Cloud (*http://www.servicecloud .com*) third-party systems that make managing 20 or more concurrent servers a piece of cake.

5.15 Staying Up-to-Date

Problem

How can I stay up-to-date with changes in the world of Facebook?

Solution

Facebook publishes four RSS feeds, and you should definitely subscribe to them. If you already subscribe to a lot of feeds, you might want to use an RSS-to-email service to make sure that these feeds don't get lost in the shuffle (or use a separate RSS reader just for them):

Facebook Developer Blog
> Updates from Facebook's team about upcoming changes to Platform.
>
> Website: *http://developers.facebook.com/news.php*
>
> RSS: *http://developers.facebook.com/news.php?blog=1&format=xml*

Facebook Platform Status Feed
> Updates on pushes, problems, etc.
>
> Website: *http://www.facebook.com/developers/message.php*
>
> RSS: *http://www.facebook.com/feeds/api_messages.php*

Facebook Blog
> The general blog maintained by Facebook.
>
> Website: *http://blog.facebook.com/*
>
> RSS: *http://feeds.feedburner.com/FacebookBlog*

Facebook Pages Blog
> The News Feed from the Facebook Pages Page, maintained by Facebook. This isn't directly related to Platform, but it is still a useful source of information if your app is installed on Pages.
>
> Website: *http://www.facebook.com/notes.php?id=10381469571*
>
> RSS: You'll have to visit the page to subscribe because it generates a unique RSS URL for each visitor.

There are at least two pages on the Facebook Developers Wiki that you'll want to watch closely. Unfortunately, there's no way to subscribe to them by RSS, but you can add them to your Watchlist within the Wiki:

Push Changes
> This page documents the changes included in each push of new code that Facebook makes, organized by date. See *http://wiki.developers.facebook.com/index.php/Push _Changes*.

Platform Changes
> This page documents the bigger-picture changes that Facebook has released. See *http://wiki.developers.facebook.com/index.php/Platform_Changes*.

Discussion

In addition to the news straight from the horse's mouth, there are also a number of excellent third-party websites maintained by the community at large:

FaceReviews
> Reviews of Facebook applications published by Gravitational Media, LLC. This is a great way to keep up-to-date on the competition and get some attention for your app when it's ready to go live.
>
> Website: *http://www.facereviews.com*
>
> RSS: *http://feeds.feedburner.com/facereviews*

Inside Facebook
> A wide and deep-reaching view into the world of Facebook, started by Justin Smith.
>
> Website: *http://www.insidefacebook.com*
>
> RSS: *http://www.insidefacebook.com/feed/*

AllFacebook
> A similar mandate to Inside Facebook, started by Nick O'Neill.
>
> Website: *http://www.allfacebook.com*
>
> RSS: *http://feeds.feedburner.com/allfacebook*

CHAPTER 6

Facebook Markup Language (FBML)

In the world of Facebook Platform, Facebook Markup Language (FBML) is to Hypertext Markup Language (HTML) as Facebook JavaScript (FBJS) is to JavaScript (JS) and Facebook Query Language (FQL) is to Structured Query Language (SQL). This may seem strange at first—almost like some sort of parallel universe in which you have been given two left feet and must dance the tango in double-time—but it's really not that bad. If you have any familiarity with HTML, you'll discover pretty quickly that FBML is really just like having a bunch of new dance moves available, having a bunch of your old ones updated and changed from 10-step-long sequences into a graceful one-stepper, and occasionally having to learn a different way to do the familiar foxtrot.

 You should be able to look up any of the tags covered in this chapter by adding them to the end of the Facebook Developers Wiki URL. As an example, if you want more info on `fb:name`, go to *http://wiki.developers.facebook.com/index.php/Fb:name*.

6.1 What Is FBML?

Problem

When I hang out around other Facebook developers (at a Facebook Developer Garage event, say), sometimes all I hear is FBML, FBML, FBML. I just got a handle on HTML! What's this new thing everyone is going on about?

Solution

FBML is Facebook Markup Language, an extension of HTML that works within Facebook Canvas pages (and some other spots, such as Profile Boxes) to render your content within the constraints of the Facebook Platform Sandbox. The FBML parser on Facebook's servers takes in your FBML, does its parsing magic, and spits out HTML, which your users' browsers render and display. FBML is very similar to HTML (and you can use a lot of regular HTML mixed in with your FBML), and is generally recognizable because all of the tags start with "fb:".

You can find documentation on every FBML tag on the Facebook Developers wiki at *http://wiki.developers.facebook.com/index.php/FBML*, and a high-level spec for FBML at *http://wiki.developers.facebook.com/index.php/FBMLspec*.

Discussion

Google touts that not needing to learn a new language is one of the big advantages of OpenSocial. It's not fair to call FBML a new language, since it's entirely based on HTML and is really just an extension that makes available a number of very handy tags.

Let's say that you want to insert a friend selector into your Facebook Canvas page so that your users could pick a friend to send a gift to. You're focused on user experience and you know that your users might have very long lists of friends, so you want to implement an in-place suggestion mechanism as they type.

If you were building your own web app, you'd have to create a text field, write a bunch of Ajax to take keydown and onchange events and pass them to your server, write a server-side function to receive them and return suggestions encoded in something like XML or JSON, and finally add some more client-side script to receive the suggestions, display them, and handle selections within the list. If that's something you've done before, you might have a library you've already written to handle some of it. If you're using a JavaScript library such as jQuery, you might use something like PengoWorks' Auto-complete plug-in (*http://www.pengoworks.com/workshop/jquery/autocomplete.htm*).

Since you aren't building a standalone web app, and since I've gone to the trouble of setting up such a carefully contrived example to prove that FBML can make your life easier, you're probably thinking that there must be a better way. Well, there is! Just drop the following code into your FBML page (or try it in the FBML Test Console at *http://developers.facebook.com/tools.php?fbml*):

```
<fb:friend-selector/>
```

That's it! If you include that inside a form, the Facebook ID of the user they entered will be added to your POST request (the variable will be called friend_selector_id by default, but you can override it by specifying an idname as a parameter inside the fb:friend-selector tag).

> If you're looking for more or different info than this chapter provides, I recommend the excellent *FBML Essentials* book (O'Reilly), written by Jesse Stay. Find it at better bookstores everywhere, including O'Reilly's own store at *http://oreilly.com/catalog/9780596519186/index.html*.

6.2 Categories of FBML Tags

Problem

There sure are a lot of FBML tags! Surely there must be some way to group them together to make some sense out of them.

Solution

Damn skippy! There sure is. FBML tags can be organized into types based on their intended use:

- Social (tags that leverage or expose the social graph, such as `fb:name`)
- Sanitization (tags that sanitize potentially insecure or dangerous content, such as `fb:swf`)
- Design (tags that provide Facebook-style elements much more easily than building the HTML, such as `fb:tabs`)
- Component (tags that provide actual user interface widgets, such as `fb:comments`)
- Control (tags that control what gets displayed on your page, such as `fb:visible-to-owner`)

The other way to slice and dice is based on the area of functionality they affect (see all of the tags grouped this way on *http://wiki.developers.facebook.com/index.php/FBML*):

- Dialog (display a Facebook-style dialog, either pop-up or contextual)
- Editor display (display a Facebook-style form with labels)
- Embedded media (embed media such as Flash, Silverlight, MP3s, etc.)
- Forms (enable images or text links to act as form submission controls)
- Message/Wall attachments (preview attachments to messages or Wall posts)
- Misc (things that don't fit somewhere else)
- Notifications and requests (content for the Notification and Request integration points)
- Page navigation (navigation widgets, including dashboards and tabs)
- Profile-specific (FBML that works only in Profile Boxes)
- Status messages (display Facebook-style errors and messages)
- Tools (assorted tools, including various friend selectors and Google Analytics)
- User/Groups (display information related to users)
- Visibility on Profile (control who can see what on Profiles)
- Wall (emulate a Wall-like environment in your app)

Discussion

One of the biggest differences between HTML and FBML is the context of the logged-in users. Tags in HTML always render the same content, regardless of who looks at them, so there's never a need to think about what someone will see depending on which state she's in. FBML is different, and the first grouping provides a handy way to remember which tags are affected by context and which ones aren't.

Social tags are very aware of who's logged in and what they can see. For example, the `fb:name` tag will render the specified user's full name to someone who is logged into Facebook, but only that user's first name to someone who isn't. The output of sanitization tags generally doesn't change from user to user, but the content they add to a page might (e.g., standard HTML `<form>`s will get some hidden fields automatically added, including the UID of the current user). Design and Component tags are almost all user-agnostic, as they tend to be shortcuts to blocks of HTML or advanced functionality rather than user-specific content that needs to be aware of privacy concerns. Control tags are highly user-aware, since their primary purpose is to control display of content based on who's looking at it.

6.3 FBML Versions

Problem

I know there are different versions of FBML and some tags require FBML 1.1, but how do I set or even know which version I'm using?

Solution

Wrap your FBML in `fb:fbml` tags and specify a version you want them executed with:

```
<fb:fbml version="1.1">
    <!-- FBML Here -->
</fb:fbml>
```

Discussion

You can include an `fb:fbmlversion` tag inside an `fb:fbml` tag to output which version is being used to parse that content, though you should note that this is really only intended for debugging purposes. As an example, the following:

```
<fb:fbml version="1.0">
    <p>This is <fb:fbmlversion /></p>
</fb:fbml>
<fb:fbml version="1.1">
    <p>This is <fb:fbmlversion /></p>
</fb:fbml>
<fb:fbml version="1.2">
    <p>This is <fb:fbmlversion /></p>
</fb:fbml>
```

will give you:

```
This is 1.0
This is 1.1
```

You might have expected to get a third paragraph for 1.2, but the FBML parser ignores it because that version didn't exist at the time this book was written. Using an `fb:fbmlversion` tag outside of an explicit `fb:fbml` tag should give you 1.0, since that's the assumed default if you haven't specified otherwise.

6.4 A Rose by Any Other Name: Forced Renaming

Problem

Facebook keeps renaming all of the `id`s in my HTML.

Solution

It's cool! Relax, man. You're in the Sandbox! The Sandbox is groovy.

No, seriously. The Sandbox is just doing its job, protecting the forces of good (namely, you) from the evil demon know as namespace clash. Sandboxes in the computer science sense are a security mechanism for safely running programs in a contained space, preventing them from having access to things outside the box. Think about it this way: picture a situation in which you've given a `div` in your page the `id` "supercalifragilicious," and by some unthinkably remote change, that happened to be the same `id` that Facebook had given to one of their `div`s. Aside from the invalid XHTML that would cause (`id`s have to be unique in a page), how would your CSS or JavaScript know which one to work with? To get around this situation, the Facebook Sandbox goes through your code and replaces things like:

```
<div id="supercalifragilicious">
```

with:

```
<div id="app12345_supercalifragilicious">
```

where 12345 is your app's ID. This is known as creating a "namespace," which Wikipedia defines as:

> In general, a namespace is an abstract container providing context for the items (names, or technical terms, or words) it holds and allowing disambiguation of items having the same name (residing in different namespaces).[*]

Discussion

The end result is that your application should be basically unaffected. The Sandbox is smart enough to also rename any occurrences of `#supercalifragilicious` in your CSS

---

[*] *http://en.wikipedia.org/wiki/Namespace*

files, so that they still match up to the renamed `ids` in your FBML. That said, be careful with classes! The Sandbox doesn't rename those, so:

```
<div id="supercalifragilicious" class="person">
```

will become:

```
<div id="app12345_supercalifragilicious" class="person">
```

This is OK within your app, but what happens when your classes conflict with Facebook's markup? Crazy, crazy things. For example, consider this line:

```
<div id="app12345_sample" class="so_sound_player">
```

That's not an entirely unlikely line of HTML for you to have written. Unfortunately, `so_sound_player` is a Facebook class already:

```
.so_sound_player{
    left: 0px;
    position: absolute;
    top: 0px;
    z-index: 1000px;
}
```

You'll notice pretty quickly that your `div` is misbehaving, and a quick trip into Firebug should tell you why, but you can avoid this problem by enforcing namespaces in your own CSS and then overriding Facebook's markup (or just renaming your class). Since Facebook automatically wraps your Canvas page in a `div` with the `id` `app_content_12345` (where 12345 is your app's ID), you can do this:

```
#app_content_12345 .so_sound_player{
    position: relative !important;
    z-index: auto !important;
    ...
}
```

This takes advantage of CSS's inheritance rules to contextualize the class named `.so_sound_player` within your app, and then to override Facebook's rules for them.

6.5 Web Standards

—*Martin Kuplens-Ewart (see his bio in Contributors)*

Problem

I want to create an innovative application that I can build on Facebook and also deploy to other platforms (such as OpenSocial, iPhone, etc.) in the future.

Solution

Build your application with standards-compliant techniques, including clean, semantic HTML (FBML) to mark up your content and page structure, hack-free CSS to style your application, and DOM scripting using JavaScript (FBJS) to interact with your application's backend code to make the whole thing work.

Discussion

Crucial for the success of a Facebook application is constant innovation and experimentation. The best applications keep refining interactions, implementing new features, and developing new ways for their users to engage with their friends.

As you plan out your application, it may be worth preparing to structure it in two parts: the Facebook interface elements that are viewed by the user, and your application logic, which is hosted and accessed independently of the Facebook environment. This kind of separation between the layers of your application will be crucial if you intend to deploy to other platforms down the road. See Figure 6-1.

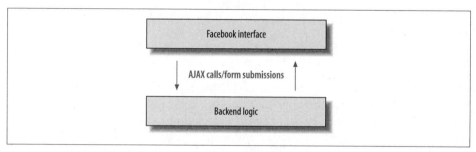

Figure 6-1. Separating interface and logic using Ajax calls

There are three elements to your standards-compliant development toolkit:

1. FBML (HTML), used for marking up content and establishing boundaries of elements and blocks of the page

2. CSS, used to add style and visual cues to guide your users, and to bring personality to the experience

3. FBJS (JavaScript), used to add complex functionality and behavior to your application

Stop! Is that a `<table>` I see in your page source? Unless you've been marking up tabular data, don't use that tag. There are two reasons for this: first, using tables to lay out your page forces you to rewrite your FBML (HTML) if you want to move an element or iterate the design and interactions. Second, remember your goals in building your Facebook application—growth, growth, and growth. Once your application's audience starts to grow, the extra markup associated with a table-based layout will start to ratchet up your hosting costs and potentially cause slowdowns if your server is unable to meet the demand.

Facebook provides an amazing environment for developing a following of passionate fans, but chances are you will want to expand your reach to other community platforms or even deploy your application to your own or other websites. If you've followed this advice and built your application with the trifecta of standards-compliant web development (and avoided the temptation of the `<table>` tag), porting your application could be as simple as adjusting CSS and updating link and form submission URLs. Soon your application architecture could go from a Facebook-only structure to something like Figure 6-2.

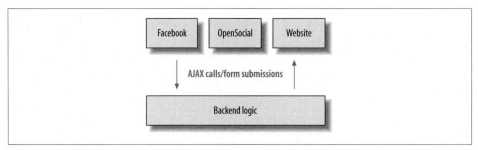

Figure 6-2. Addition of interfaces to the shared backend logic

A well-structured Facebook application built using standards-compliant techniques permits you to iterate presentation, content, and application behavior independently of each other. It allows you to determine the logic that will be followed as Facebook members use and share your application, and then adjust layout and copy to make that as simple (or complicated) as you like. Finally, it allows your markup to be lightweight and quick to transfer, keeping your bills down and user satisfaction up!

Resources

Two-Faced Django (http://www.lethain.com/entry/2007/dec/04/two-faced-django-part-1-building-project-exists-si/)
> A series of articles by developer Will Larson detailing how he created an application that works in both Facebook and as a simple web application outside the Facebook ecosystem.

W3C HTML Validator (http://validator.w3.org/)
> An indispensable tool. Make sure your HTML is fully standards-compliant before adapting it to fit the FBML format.

6.6 Displaying a User's Name

Problem

How do I display a user's name?

Solution

Use the `<fb:name>` tag. Among the many options you can include, specify the `uid` of the user whose name you want to display (you can also use `loggedinuser` or `profileowner`).

Discussion

This tag is interesting because of the various ways that different languages deal with possessive nouns and other grammatical structures, which I can never keep straight. (Is the participle dangling? What does that even mean?) This is a great example of FBML saving you from having to add giant `if`/`else` blocks to your code. The parameters are listed in Table 6-1.

Table 6-1. Parameters for fb:name

Name	Type	Default value	Description	They see	I see
uid	uid	N/A	The Facebook user ID (uid) of the user or Page whose name you want to show. You can also use `loggedinuser` or `profileowner`. This is the only required field.	"Jay Goldman"	"You"
capitalize	bool	false	Capitalize the text if useyou is true and loggedinuser is the uid.	"Jay Goldman"	"You"
firstnameonly	bool	false	Show only the user's first name.	"Jay"	"You"
ifcantsee	string	Empty	Alternate text to display if the logged-in user cannot access the user specified.	Specified text if they can't see me; "Jay Goldman" if they can	"You"
lastnameonly	bool	false	Show only the user's last name.	"Goldman"	"You"
linked	bool	true	Link to the user's Profile.	"Jay Goldman"	"You"
possessive	bool	false	Use the possessive form (his/her/your).	"Jay Goldman's"	"Your"
reflexive	bool	false	Use the reflexive form (himself/herself/yourself).	"Jay Goldman"	"Yourself"
shownetwork	bool	false	Displays the primary network for the uid.	"Jay Goldman (Toronto)"	"You"

Name	Type	Default value	Description	They see	I see
subjectid	uid	None	The Facebook ID of the subject of the sentence where this name is the object of the verb of the sentence. Will use the reflexive when appropriate. When subjectid is used, uid is considered to be the object and uid's name is produced.	See upcoming explanation in the text	
useyou	bool	true	Use "you" if uid matches the logged-in user.	"Jay Goldman"	"You" if true; "Jay Goldman" if false

The only one that really needs explanation is subjectid, which feels a little like you're being asked a question on *Jeopardy!* in the "Mind-Bending Grammar Rules" category for $500. It's easiest to understand in the context of an example from the Mini-Feed story that the Photos application pushes out:

```
<fb:name uid="561415460" capitalize="true" /> tagged
 a photo of <fb:name subjectid="561415460" uid="567770429" />.
```

In this example, 561415460 is my prison number and 567770429 is my wife, Bianca. I've just tagged her in a photo of our daring escape under the wall, and Facebook has helpfully pushed that story out to all of my friends, including Warden Norton. That sentence would get rendered for me as:

You tagged a photo of Bianca Gutnik Goldman.

When my wife sees the item in her News Feed, right before she yells at me for putting the cops on our tail, she'll see:

Jay Goldman tagged a photo of you.

When Warden Norton sees the item pop up in his News Feed, right before he jams the big red button on his desk and sends the boys in blue after us, he'll see:

Jay Goldman tagged a photo of Bianca Gutnik Goldman.

But wait! There's more. If I tagged a photo of myself, the FBML would look like this:

```
<fb:name uid="561415460" capitalize="true" /> tagged a photo
 of <fb:name subjectid="561415460" uid="561415460" />.
```

Now when I see the item, dejected and alone in a dingy roadside motel after Bianca left me for being stupid moments before being apprehended, the sentence would be rendered as:

You tagged a photo of yourself.

When Bianca sees it, celebrating in the Cayman Islands at her new beach-side bar, she'll see:

Jay Goldman tagged a photo of himself.

The moral of this story is that the Cayman Islands are a British overseas territory, which means they have an extradition policy and my wife is coming right back to join me in the slammer. Think carefully before you tag yourself in incriminating photos, folks (but not before you use `fb:name`, which can save you a whole world of trouble)!

6.7 He Said, She Said: Dealing with Pronouns

Problem

Gender issues are complicated. I could just use the third-person pronouns ("they" and "their") for everything, but that's really not grammatically correct. How do I figure out whether to use "he" or "she"? And what about people who didn't specify a gender on their Profiles?

Solution

The `fb:pronoun` tag will output the correct pronoun for the user specified by the `uid` parameter. The simplest form is:

```
<fb:pronoun uid="12345" />
```

Discussion

Just like the `fb:name` tag, the `fb:pronoun` tag gets itself into all kinds of trouble with possessives and reflexives and lots of other grammar ghouls that you don't want to have to deal with. Luckily, FBML will deal with them for you! See Table 6-2 for a list of the tag's parameters.

Table 6-2. Parameters for fb:pronoun

Name	Type	Default value	Description	They see	I see
uid	int	N/A	The Facebook user ID (`uid`) of the user or Page whose pronoun you want to show. You can also use `loggedinuser` or `profileowner`. This is the only required field.	"he"	"you"
capitalize	bool	false	Capitalize the pronoun.	"He"	"You"
objective	bool	false	Use the objective form (him/her/you/them).	"him"	"you"
possessive	bool	false	Use the possessive form (his/her/your/their).	"his"	"you"
reflexive	bool	false	Use the reflexive form (himself/herself/ yourself).	"himself"	"yourself"

Name	Type	Default value	Description	They see	I see
usethey	bool	true	Use "they" if gender is not specified.	"him" (but if I removed my gender, "they")	"you"
useyou	bool	true	Use "you" if uid matches the logged-in user.	"your"	"your"

6.8 Worth a Thousand Words: Profile Pictures

Problem

Profile pictures are awesome because they're so easy to recognize and they really draw people in! How can I display someone's pic?

Solution

The fb:profile-pic tag will display the Profile picture for the user specified by the uid parameter. The simplest form is:

```
<fb:profile-pic uid="12345"/>
```

Discussion

In addition to the uid, there are two optional parameters, listed in Table 6-3.

Table 6-3. Parameters for fb:profile-pic

Name	Type	Default value	Description
uid	int	N/A	The Facebook user ID (uid) of the user or Page whose pronoun you want to show. You can also use loggedinuser or profileowner. This is the only required field.
linked	bool	true	Link to the user's Profile.
size	string	thumb	Size of image to display (see the upcoming list).

Differently sized pics can be hugely useful in different scenarios. Using my current Profile picture (taken by my good friend Will Pate), the following list shows a breakdown of the options (note that you can use the short form listed in parentheses):

thumb (t): 50 pixels wide

small (s): 100 pixels wide

normal (n): 200 pixels wide

square (q): 50 × 50 pixels

6.9 Linking to Events

Problem

How do I link to an event from the Facebook Events application?

Solution

Use the `fb:eventlink` tag and specify the event ID:

```
<fb:eventlink eid="12345" />
```

where 12345 is your `eid`.

Discussion

This will insert the name of the event as a link to the event's page in the Events app.

6.10 Linking to Groups

Problem

How do I link to a group from the Facebook Groups application?

Solution

Use the `fb:grouplink` tag and specify the group ID:

```
<fb:grouplink gid="12345" />
```

Discussion

This will insert the name of the group as a link to the group's page in the Groups app.

6.11 Linking to Networks

Problem

How do I link to a Facebook network?

Solution

Use the `fb:networklink` tag and specify the network ID:

```
<fb:networklink nid="12345" />
```

Discussion

This will insert the name of the network as a link to the network's page.

6.12 Display Content to Group Members

Problem

How do I display content only to members of a specific group?

Solution

Use the `fb:if-is-group-member` tag and specify the group ID. The simplest form is:

```
<fb:if-is-group-member gid="12345">Private content goes here</fb:if-is-group-member>
```

Discussion

You can use this tag in combination with the `fb:else` tag to display alternate content to people who aren't in the group. The tag will default to checking for the `loggedinuser`, but you can also specify a different `uid` if you want to check a different member:

```
<fb:if-is-group-member gid="12345" uid="12345">
    Private content goes here
    <fb:else>
        Sorry! You're not in <fb:grouplink gid="12345"/>.
    </fb:else>
</fb:if-is-group-member>
```

Since groups support different roles (member, admin, officer), you can also use the `fb:if-is-group-member` to check for a user's access level:

```
<fb:if-is-group-member gid="12345" uid="12345" role="admin">
    Private content for admins goes here
    <fb:else>
        Sorry! You're not an admin of <fb:grouplink gid="12345"/>.
    </fb:else>
</fb:if-is-group-member>
```

6.13 Display Content to Network Members

Problem

How do I display content only to members of a specific network?

Solution

Use the `fb:is-in-network` tag and specify the network and `uid`s. The simplest form is:

```
<fb:is-in-network network="12345" uid="12345">Private
content goes here</fb:is-in-network>
```

Discussion

Although this tag doesn't start with the word "if", you can still use it in combination with the `fb:else` tag to display alternate content to people who aren't in the network:

```
<fb:is-in-network network="12345" uid="loggedinuser">
    Private content goes here
    <fb:else>
        Sorry! You're not in <fb:networklink nid="12345"/>.
    </fb:else>
</fb:is-in-network>
```

Note that the tag uses `network="12345"` and not `nid="12345"` as you might expect.

6.14 Displaying Content to App Users

Problem

How do I display content only to users who have added my app or accepted the Terms of Service for my application?

Solution

Facebook used to offer two tags that provided an easy way to limit the visibility of content, but only one is still supported. The `fb:if-user-has-added-app` tag, which is now deprecated, worked for all users who had added your app. The `fb:if-is-app-user` tag, which you should now always use, limits the display to users who have explicitly accepted your Terms of Service. The simplest use case is:

```
<fb:if-is-app-user>Thanks for installing my application! You rock!</fb:if-is-app-user>
```

Discussion

With no `uid` specified, the tag will automatically assume that it's for the current `loggedinuser`. You can specify a `uid` to check for a different user, as well as include the `fb:else` tag to provide alternate content:

```
<fb:if-is-app-user uid="12345">
    Here's <fb:name uid="12345" possessive="true" /> score: 55555!
    <fb:else>
        <fb:name uid="12345" /> hasn't signed up for this app!
    </fb:else>
</fb:if-is-app-user>
```

Note that these tags can be used only in a Canvas page.

6.15 Displaying Content to Friends

Problem

How do I display content only to friends of a specific user?

Solution

Use the `fb:if-is-friends-with-viewer` tag. The simplest form is:

```
<fb:if-is-friends-with-viewer>You're friends!</fb:if-is-friends-with-viewer>
```

Discussion

As with all `fb` tags that begin with `if`, you can use the `fb:else` tag inside the `fb:if-is-friends-with-viewer` to provide alternate content if they aren't friends. You can also specify a different `uid` if you don't want to check for friendship with the loggedinuser, and you can explicitly exclude the loggedinuser if you don't want to treat them as being friends with themselves (you will also be a friend of yourself unless you set includeself to false):

```
<fb:if-is-friends-with-viewer uid="12345" includeself="false">
    You're friends with <fb:name uid="12345" />. Yay!
    <fb:else>
        You aren't friends with <fb:name uid="12345" />. Boo!
    </fb:else>
</fb:if-is-friends-with-viewer>
```

6.16 Displaying/Hiding Content to/from Specific Users

Problem

How do I display content only to a specific user?

Solution

Use the fb:if-is-user tag. The simplest form is:

```
<fb:if-is-user uid="12345">You're it!</fb:if-is-user>
```

Discussion

As with all fb tags that begin with if, you can use the fb:else tag inside the fb:if-is-user to provide alternate content if the user isn't the droid you're looking for:

```
<fb:if-is-user uid="12345">
    You're it!
    <fb:else>
        You aren't it.
    </fb:else>
</fb:if-is-user>
```

You might sometimes want to check for a bunch of different users you want to exclude from seeing some content. The tag supports comma-separated uids, and you can use the fb:else tag to actually do the inverse of the example just shown:

```
<fb:if-is-user uid="12345,54321,11111,22222">
    <!-- No content here -->
    <fb:else>
        Everyone else sees this bit here.
    </fb:else>
</fb:if-is-user>
```

6.17 Displaying Random Content

Problem

I'd like to display some content on my Canvas page, randomly selected from a few different options.

Solution

The `fb:random` and nested `fb:random-option` tags are the answer. The simplest form is:

```
<fb:random>
    <fb:random-option>You're cool!</fb:random-option>
    <fb:random-option>You're awesome!</fb:random-option>
</fb:random>
```

Discussion

Profile Boxes are a really great use of the `fb:random` tag, which gives you the ability to have different content appear each time the page refreshes, even though Profile Box content isn't really dynamic.

You can assign weighting to the different options if there's something you'd like shown more often than the other options:

```
<fb:random>
    <fb:random-option weight="2">
        A: This will be shown twice as often as B
    </fb:random-option>
    <fb:random-option weight="1">
        B: This will be show half as often as A
    </fb:random-option>
</fb:random>
```

The weights can be any number greater than zero, and they are relative to each other rather than being relative to a fixed starting point (so a weight of 800 will still be shown twice as often as a weight of 400, not 800 times more often).

You can also have `fb:random` select more than one option by specifying a count of the number you'd like returned in the `pick` parameter. By default, `fb:random` will try to pick unique options (i.e., it won't return the same option more than once), but you can override that by specifying `false` in the `unique` parameter:

```
<fb:random pick="2" unique="false">
    <fb:random-option>You're cool!</fb:random-option>
    <fb:random-option>You're awesome!</fb:random-option>
    <fb:random-option>You're swell!</fb:random-option>
    <fb:random-option>You're rad!</fb:random-option>
</fb:random>
```

Note that specifying `false` won't guarantee duplication, but it means you will occasionally get back duplicates.

6.18 Displaying Content to Specific Browsers

Problem

I need to display content to specific browsers in order to get around some rendering issues.

Solution

Use the `fb:user-agent` tag. The simplest form is:

```
<fb:user-agent includes="ie 6">
    Your browser has lots of rendering issues!
</fb:user-agent>
```

Discussion

You might want to use this tag for reasons other than browser idiosyncrasies, but that's likely to be the main use. Every browser, crawler, indexer, etc. has a different "user-agent" string that represents the browser and company who make it. A few popular examples are given in Table 6-4.

Table 6-4. Some fun user-agent examples

User agent	Description
Googlebot/2.1 (*http://www.googlebot.com/bot.html*)	Google crawler
Mozilla/5.0 (Macintosh; U; Intel Mac OS X 10.4; en-US; rv:1.9b5) Gecko/ 2008032619 Firefox/3.0b5	Mozilla Firefox 3.0b5 on an Intel-based Mac running Mac OS X 10.4
Mozilla/4.0 (compatible; MSIE 7.0; Windows NT 5.1; bgft)	Microsoft Internet Explorer 7 on Windows XP
Opera/9.00 (Windows NT 5.1; U; de)	Opera 9 on Windows NT, running in German
Mozilla/5.0 (Macintosh; U; Intel Mac OS X 10_5_2; en-ca) AppleWebKit/ 525.13 (KHTML, like Gecko) version/3.1 Safari/525.13	Safari 3.1 on an Intel-based Mac running Mac OS X 10.5.2

For a full list of user agents, see the excellent *http://www.user-agents.org*, maintained by Andreas Staeding. You can also quickly find out the user agent for your browser by visiting *http://www.whatsmyuseragent.com*, which includes an excellent resource page about how to fake different user agents in your browser for testing purposes (*http://whatsmyuseragent.com/SwitchingUserAgents.asp*).

The tag supports include, exclude, and mixed modes, so you could also do:

```
<fb:user-agent excludes="Firefox">
    You should download Firefox!
</fb:user-agent>
```

and:

```
<fb:user-agent includes="Mozilla" excludes="Firefox/3.0">
    Time to upgrade to Firefox 3!
</fb:user-agent>
```

Note that the tag does appear to be case-sensitive, so "firefox/3.0" and "Firefox/3.0" aren't the same thing.

6.19 Displaying Your Application's Name

Problem

I'd like a way to output my application's name so that it will update automatically if I change it later. Also, I decided to put the word "message" in my application's name and have now discovered that I can't add it to things like my Mini-Feed and News stories, because Facebook won't let me put that word in those places.

Solution and Discussion

Use the very simple `fb:application-name` tag, which will output your app's current name as plain text. The simplest and only form is:

```
<fb:application-name />
```

6.20 Formatting Relative Time

Problem

I want to display time formatted and converted to my users' local time zones.

Solution

Use the `fb:time` tag. The simplest form is:

```
<fb:time t="212698800" />
```

If that doesn't look like a date and time to you, read on to the Discussion.

Discussion

The tricky part here is that you have to pass in `t` in what's known as "epoch seconds," or the number of seconds that have elapsed since the Unix Epoch, which was January 1, 1970. You think I'm making this up? You couldn't make this stuff up! No one would believe you. (See *http://en.wikipedia.org/wiki/Unix_epoch* for more information on why we use this seemingly bizarre method of encoding a date and time.) You might find yourself wondering how you're going to calculate that without doing a whole bunch of counting and skipping leap years and remembering that 30 days hath September,

April, June, and November. Easy! To display the current time, just take advantage of the PHP `time( )` function (or an equivalent in your language of choice):

```
<fb:time t="<?php echo time();?>" />
```

To display a different time, use the PHP `mktime( )` function, which generates the epoch seconds for any given date:

```
<fb:time t="<?php echo mktime(17, 35, 0, 4, 26, 2008);?>" />
```

The parameters, in order, are hours, minutes, seconds, month, day, and year. More info is at *http://www.php.net/manual/en/function.mktime.php*.

Note that `fb:time` makes the time display relative, so if `t` is on the same day as today, you'll just get the time (e.g., 5:35 p.m.); if it's in the same year, you'll get month, day, and time (e.g., April 26 5:35 p.m.); and if it's in a different year, you'll get the full thing (e.g., April 26, 2008 5:35 p.m.).

You can also include a time zone in your call to `fb:time` if you want to specify where and not just when:

```
<fb:time t="<?php echo mktime(17, 35, 0, 4, 26, 2008);?>" tz="America/Chihuahua" />
```

That would format April 26, 2008 at 5:35 p.m. in the Mexican state of Chihuahua, rather than inside a small, yappy dog. This won't include the time zone in the display, so you'd need to add it to the end (MST or MDT for Chihuahua, depending on whether daylight saving time is active). The `tz` parameter accepts any standard PHP time zone descriptor (you can find the full list at *http://ww.php.net/manual/en/timezones.php*).

Finally, you can pass in a `preposition` boolean to indicate whether you'd like "at" and "on" inserted into your date. For example:

```
<fb:time t="<?php echo mktime(17, 35, 0, 4, 26, 2008);?>" preposition="true" />
```

will give you:

at 5:35pm on April 26, 2008

6.21 Making Content Visible to Some Users in Profile Boxes

Problem

I'd really like to make some of the content in my Profile Boxes visible to only a select group of users.

Solution

The `fb:visible` family of tags will do exactly what you're looking for. Think of them as the big, burly bouncers who stand inside the velvet rope and won't let you into the club unless you're on the magic list. In this case, their clipboards actually contain eight different lists:

`fb:visible-to-owner`
> Content that is visible only to the owner of the Profile.

`fb:visible-to-user`
> Content that is visible only to the specified users. Include a `uid` parameter containing one or more comma-separated Facebook `uid`s to control who can see it.

`fb:visible-to-app-users`
> Content that is visible only to users who have also added the app and have agreed to the Terms of Service and been granted full permission.

`fb:visible-to-connection`
> Content that is visible only to friends of the user who owns the Profile, or fans of the Page if used on a Page. Note that this effectively replaces `fb:visible-to-friends`, which worked only on user Profiles.

`fb:18-plus`
> Content that is visible only to users who are 18 years old or older. Unlike the rest of the visible tags, this one and the `fb:21-plus` tag can both contain an `fb:else` tag (which displays alternate content) and can be used on Canvas pages.

`fb:21-plus`
> Content that is visible only to users who are 21 years old or older. As per the previous tag, this can contain an `fb:else` tag to display alternate content to people who are under 21.

Discussion

All of the previously listed tags will accept an optional `bgcolor` parameter, which lets you set the color of the block shown to users who don't meet the criteria. Let's say that you were going to include an encouragement to friends of your users to kick back and hang out with their friends, but you didn't want to encourage anyone under 21 to have a drink:

```
<p><fb:visible-to-connection bgcolor="#ccc">
    <fb:21-plus>
        Have a drink with your friend!
        <fb:else>
            Have a pop with your pal!
        </fb:else>
    </fb:21-plus>
</fb:visible-to-friends></p>
```

Users who are friends with the Profile owner and over 21 will see the message shown in Figure 6-3.

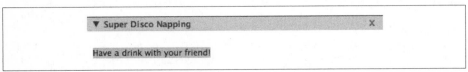

Figure 6-3. Visible to friends who are over 21

Underage users would see the same thing, but with the pop-related message. Users who aren't friends with the Profile owner would see the gray box in Figure 6-4.

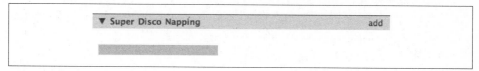

Figure 6-4. Visible to everyone else

It's very important to understand how the `fb:visible` tags actually work, since it affects the type of information that you should put in them. If you look at the HTML that the FBML parser renders for the "Have a drink" example (assuming you're over 21), you'll note that the part we don't want some people to see is right there in the source:

```
<p>
    <span style="background: #cccccc;"><span style="visibility: hidden;">
        Have a drink with your friend!
    </span></span>
</p>
```

That's not very well hidden, so *don't put really sensitive content in them*! You definitely don't want to use these tags for things like the following:

```
<p><fb:visible-to-owner>
    Your credit card number is 1234 5678 9012 3456!
</fb:visible-to-owner></p>
```

6.22 Hiding Private Profile Content

Problem

Privacy is such an important concern on Facebook, and I want to make sure my application follows all of the rules and regulations so I respect my users and don't get Terms of Service violations! How do I make sure I'm showing users only the Profile content from other users that they're supposed to see?

Solution

The `fb:if-can-see` tag gives you full control over whether to display one user's Profile content to another user. The simplest form is:

```
<fb:if-can-see uid="12345">You're allowed to see this</fb:if-can-see>
```

Discussion

The simplest case is probably not all that useful to you, since you're probably more interested in a specific part of the Profile rather than the whole thing. Add a `what` parameter and include any one of the following: `profile`, `friends`, `not_limited`, `online`, statusupdates, wall, groups, photosofme, notes, feed, contact, email, aim, cell, phone, mailbox, address, basic, education, professional, personal, seasonal:

```
<fb:if-can-see uid="12345" what="friends">
    You're allowed to see <fb:name uid="12345" possessive="true" /> friends
    <fb:else>
        You're not allowed to see them.
    </fb:else>
</fb:if-can-see>
```

Note that you can't chain the whats together, so you'll have to nest `fb:if-can-see` tags if you want to check for more than one permission at a time:

```
<fb:if-can-see uid="12345" what="profile">
    <fb:if-can-see uid="12345" what="friends">
        You can see <fb:name uid="12345" possessive="true" /> profile and friends.
    </fb:if-can-see>
</fb:if-can-see>
```

6.23 Hiding Private Photos

Problem

How do I know whether I can show a photo to a user?

Solution

Use the `fb:if-can-see-photo` and specify a photo ID (`pid`). The simplest form is:

```
<fb:if-can-see-photo pid="12345">
    <fb:photo pid="12345" />
</fb:if-can-see-photo>
```

For more information on `fb:photo`, see Recipe 6.25.

Discussion

The default behavior of `fb:if-can-see-photo` is to check for permission for `loggedinuser`, but you can specify a `uid` for a different user to check that person's permissions instead. As always, you can include `fb:else` to display an alternate image:

```
<fb:if-can-see-photo pid="12345">
    <fb:photo pid="12345" />
    <fb:else>
        <img src="images/default.jpg" alt="Can't see this!" />
    </fb:else>
</fb:if-can-see-photo>
```

6.24 Embedding an iFrame

Problem

I was smart and didn't build my app as an iFrame, but now I need to put an iFrame inside the page.

Solution

Use the `fb:iframe` tag to embed an iFrame inside of FBML. The simplest form is:

```
<fb:iframe src="http://www.someserver.com/" />
```

Discussion

The embedded iFrame actually gets all kinds of interesting goodies appended to the embedding URL (these are similar to the parameters added by the `fb:swf` tag; see Recipe 6.27), which you can use in that page to render more intelligent content. If you take a peek at the HTML rendered by the FBML parser, you'll see something like:

```
<iframe src="http://www.someserver.com/?fb_sig_in
_iframe=1&amp;fb_sig_time=1206929247.1825&amp;fb_sig_added=1&amp;
fb_sig_user=12345&amp;fb_sig_profile_update_time=1204849318&amp;fb_
sig_session_key=123456789&amp;fb_sig_expires=0&amp;fb_sig_api
_key=123456789&amp;fb_sig=123456789"></iframe>
```

Two important things to note: you can't use `fb:iframe` in a Profile Box, and you can't use FBML inside the iFrame, since it won't be parsed by the FBML parser. There are a bunch of additional options you can include as parameters in the `fb:iframe` tag, which are listed in Table 6-5.

Table 6-5. Parameters for fb:iframe

Name	Type	Default value	Description
src	string	N/A	The URL of the content you want to load into the frame. Facebook will automatically append a number of parameters to your URL, as noted earlier. This is the only required field.
frameborder	int	1	Sets whether the frame has a border (1) or not (0). Take careful note of this one because it isn't a boolean and it isn't yes/no.
height	int	None	Height of the iFrame, in pixels. Note that this may be overridden if you turn on `smartsize` or `resizable`.
name	string	None	This is required only if you're using `resizable` to resize the iFrame from the JavaScript API.
resizable	bool	false	Controls whether you can resize this iFrame dynamically using the JavaScript API. This can't be used when `smartsize` is enabled (so you have to pick one or the other), and you'll have to provide a name so that you can address it from your script.

Name	Type	Default value	Description
scrolling	string	yes	Controls whether the iFrame has scrollbars. Note that this one isn't a boolean or a 1/0, but rather one of "yes", "no", or "auto".
smartsize	bool	false	When set to true, smartsize will automatically size your frame to fill the remaining empty space in your Canvas page.
style	string	None	Anything specified in this field will be applied to the iFrame as an inline CSS style.
width	int	None	Width of the iFrame, in pixels. Note that this may be overridden if you turn on smartsize or resizable.

6.25 Embedding Facebook Photos

Problem

I know my users have some great photos in their Facebook Photos app and I'd really like to be able to embed them in my FBML.

Solution

Use the `fb:photo` tag to embed photos from the Facebook Photos app. The simplest form is:

```
<fb:photo pid="12345" />
```

Discussion

You'll likely have found the `pid` of the photo you're embedding through the Facebook API's `photos.get()` method (see Chapter 9 for more information). If you used FQL to find the photo, you'll need to include the `uid` that you used in the query to find the photo so that Facebook can make sure that user is allowed to view it:

```
<fb:photo pid="12345" uid="12345" />
```

You can also specify a `size` parameter, similar to the `fb:profile-pic` with the same allowable sizes: thumb (t), small (s), normal (n), and square (q). See Recipe 6.8 for a breakdown of the different sizes. The final optional parameter is `align`, which can be either `left` or `right`:

```
<fb:photo pid="12345" size="t" align="right" />
```

The `fb:photo` tag actually renders out a standard HTML `img` tag, so if I embedded a photo of my dog, Findley, from my Photos album of dog pictures, the FBML parser might ultimately insert this:

```
<img pid="2079254" uid="561415460" src="http://photos-g.ak.
facebook.com/photos-ak-sf2p/v168/16/97/561415460/n561415460_2079254_773.jpg" />
```

If you need to style the inserted image using CSS, just treat it like any other `img` tag.

6.26 Embedding MP3s

Problem

I want to embed a playable MP3 into my Canvas page.

Solution

Use the `fb:mp3` tag. The simplest form is:

```
<fb:mp3 src="http://host.com/file.mp3" />
```

Discussion

The Facebook MP3 player (Figures 6-5 through 6-7) is designed to match the rest of the Facebook interface and should look right at home on your Canvas pages.

Figure 6-5. Facebook MP3 player (closed)

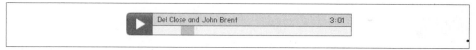

Figure 6-6. Facebook MP3 player (playing)

Figure 6-7. Facebook MP3 player (paused)

In these examples, the optional **song** and **artist** parameters were specified:

```
<fb:mp3
    src="http://someserver.com/my.mp3"
    title="How to Speak Hip, Side 2"
    artist="Del Close and John Brent" />
```

You can also specify a `width` and `height`, which will not actually scale the player but will cut it off (at the time this was written, the `height` parameter actually did nothing). Specifying a width of 20 will give you Figure 6-8.

Figure 6-8. Facebook MP3 player with 20 px width

As you may have guessed, the MP3 player is actually an Adobe Flash widget that gets inserted into your page by the FBML parser. If you want to position it using CSS, note that it gets added to a `div` with the class `mp3player_holder` and a unique generated ID (e.g., `mp3player_swf_fb_mp347f05b50e5add7c4380642047f05b50e5b392399159624`), so you can find it in the DOM and apply whatever styling you'd like.

This isn't the super-high-performance media-playing widget you might hope, so a few notes on compatibility and display:

- The player supports only MP3-formatted files, so formats such as WMV or Ogg Vorbis are out.

- The file's bit rate must be an increment of 11 KHz (11 KHz, 22 KHz, and 44.1 KHz all work).

- The `song` and `artist` fields have to be ASCII characters or they won't display properly, so non-ASCII foreign languages (e.g., Kanji) are out of luck.

- Adding `song=""` or `artist=""` will result in the title being displayed as "No Title" and the artist as "Unknown Artist," respectively (rather than not displaying them). Leave the parameters out if you don't want them in.

- Keep in mind that embedding multiple Facebook MP3 players on one page is entirely possible, but they don't have any intelligence built in to pause each other, so your users will end up with overlapping sound if they play more than one simultaneously.

6.27 Embedding Adobe Flash

Problem

I've made the most brilliant Adobe Flash piece ever created, and now I want to stick it in my FBML.

Solution

Use the `fb:swf` tag to embed Flash. The simplest form is:

```
<fb:swf swfsrc='http://www.youtube.com/v/12345"/>
```

Discussion

The FBML parser will automatically add a few Flash variables to your embed that you can then use in your Flash movie (these are similar to the parameters added by the `fb:iframe` tag—see Recipe 6.24), shown in Table 6-6.

Table 6-6. Flashvars added by the FBML parser

Name	Type	Description
allowScriptAccess	string	This parameter is always set to "never" by Facebook, so that your embedded Flash movies can't access any page-level scripts.
fb_sig_profile	int	If this Flash is being loaded in a Profile, this is the uid of the Profile owner. If it's being loaded in a Canvas page, this will be blank.
fb_sig_time	int	A timestamp of when this signature information was generated.
fb_sig_user	int	The uid of the current user (a.k.a. loggedinuser).
fb_sig_session_key	string	The current Facebook session key.
fb_sig_expires	int	The session expiration time.
fb_sig_api_key	string	Your application's API key, which the Flash movie will need if it's going to make any API requests.
fb_sig_added	bool	Indicates whether the current user has added your application.
fb_sig	string	An MD5 hash of all the parameters with names that start with fb_sig_ plus your application's secret key. See the section called "Enhancing security in your Flash" later in this recipe for how to use this to enhance security.

There are a number of additional parameters you can use to tweak your Flash, listed in Table 6-7.

Table 6-7. Parameters for fb:swf

Name	Type	Default value	Description
Swfsrc	string	N/A	The URL of the Flash you want to embed. This is the only required field.
Align	string	left	Pick either "left", "right", or "center".
Flashvars	string	None	Include any variables you want passed to your Flash movie here, making sure to URL encode them first. Facebook will automatically append a number of variables to your embed, as mentioned earlier.
Height	int	None	Height of your Flash, in pixels.
imgclass	string	None	CSS class to apply to the image specified in imgsrc.
imgsrc	string	*spacer.gif*	The image that will be shown in place of your Flash when it can't be displayed or in places where the user needs to click to activate it (e.g., in Profile Boxes). The default value is *http://static.ak.facebook.com/images/spacer.gif*, which will render your Flash unusable in Profile Boxes since it will be invisible, so make sure you specify this if you want to embed it there.
imgstyle	string	None	Inline CSS styling for the image specified in imgsrc.
loop	bool	false	Setting this to true will cause your Flash to loop endlessly.
quality	string	None	This can be any one of "low", "medium", or "high".
salign	string	None	This is the same as the salign variable you specify in a normal Flash embed, which can be "l" (left), "r" (right), "t" (top), "b" (bottom), or a combination ("tl", "tr", "bl", "br").

Name	Type	Default value	Description
scale	string	None	Choose one of "showall", "noborder", or "exactfit".
swfbgcolor	string	#ffffff	A hex-encoded background color that will be shown behind the movie.
waitforclick	bool	true	Setting this to false will autoplay your Flash whenever Facebook allows that behavior (i.e., anywhere other than Profile Boxes).
width	int	None	Width of your Flash, in pixels.
wmode	string	transparent	Standard Flash window modes: "transparent", "opaque", or "window".

Here are some important things to note:

- Facebook requires users to have the Flash 9.0 plug-in or greater, so take that into account when you're building your movies.
- Your Flash will be inserted into a `div` with a generated `id` (such as `15021277386_fbswf_47f06eeeae3c29499214985`) and no `class` set.

Enhancing security in your Flash

It's a good idea to make sure that your Flash is actually embedded in a Facebook page, because it tells you that the `uids` passed in are valid and have been authenticated by Facebook. If you don't verify this, someone could download your Flash that actually does some action on people's accounts, embed it in another page, pass in someone's ID, and do bad things. The `fb_sig` variable that Facebook passes into your Flash will help you do this, but you need to follow a few extra steps in order to be really secure.

The basic intent of `fb_sig` is to provide your app with an MD5 hash of all of the `fb_sig_` variables and your app's secret key, so that you can create a hash in your Flash movie and then check that it matches the hash passed in. Checking that will definitely prove that you were passed the correct key and that it's likely your Flash is inside of Facebook, but it's also possible that some malicious hacker type installed your app, grabbed the URL to your Flash from the page, downloaded *myBrilliantFlash.swf* onto their machine, and then reverse engineered it to extract your secret key. That would be bad, so the answer is not to put the key into your Flash. But if you don't do that, how will you check the hash?

It's actually not that hard. Instead of putting the key into your Flash, create a simple service on your backend that will accept the `fb_sig_` variables and the hash, and validate it, returning a boolean to indicate whether it passed the sniff test. The simplest way to do this is to add a page (written in PHP, or whatever you'd prefer) to your server, which accepts the `fb_sig_s` and hash as parameters:

> *http://www.someserver.com/myapp/checkMD5.php?fb_sig_profile=12345&fb_sig
> _time=12345&fb_sig_session_key=12345&fb_sig_expires=12345&fb_sig_api
> _key=12345&fb_sig_added=1&fb_sig=9e107d9d372bb6826bd81d3542a419d6*

The page will recreate the **fb_sig** string and then compare it to what gets passed in, returning **true** if they match and **false** if they don't. Here's the PHP version:

```php
<?php
    // Copy the $_GET params into a local array and sort it by the keys
    $nameValueArray = $_GET;
    ksort($nameValueArray);

    // Iterate through and create a string out of all the name/values pairs
    $nameValueString = '';
    foreach($nameValueArray as $key=>$value){
        if($key != 'fb_sig'){
            $nameValueString .= strtolower(substr($key, 7)) . '=' . $value;
        }
    }

    // Append the app's secret key
    $nameValueString .= $your_apps_secret_key_goes_here;

    // Encode as an MD5 hash
    $nameValueString = md5($nameValueString);

    // Check to see if they match and decide what to output
    if($nameValueArray['fb_sig'] == $nameValueString){
        echo 'true';
    }else{
        echo 'false';
    }
?>
```

Substitute your app's secret key on line 15, and you should be in business. Here's some ActionScript 3 code you can use in Flash to send the request and deal with the response (I put it in frame 1 of the movie, but you might have somewhere else you'd rather stick it):

```
var nameValue:String = "";

try {
    // Step through the parameters and keep any which are part of fb_sig
    var keyStr:String;
    var valueStr:String;
    var paramObj:Object = LoaderInfo(this.root.loaderInfo).parameters;
    for (keyStr in paramObj) {
        if (keyStr.substr(0,6) == "fb_sig") {
            valueStr = String(paramObj[keyStr]);
            if (nameValue!="") {
                nameValue += "&";
            }
            nameValue += keyStr + "=" + valueStr;
        }
    }
    nameValue = "http://someserver.com/checkMD5.php?" + nameValue;

    // Setup the URLLoader
    var loader:URLLoader = new URLLoader();
```

```
        loader.dataFormat = URLLoaderDataFormat.TEXT;
        loader.addEventListener(Event.COMPLETE, onMD5Check);
        // You should add more listeners for IO_ERROR, SECURITY_ERROR, and HTTP_STATUS
        loader.load(new URLRequest(nameValue));
    } catch (e:Error) {
        // Handle your errors here
    }

    function onMD5Check(ev:Event) {
        try {
            if (ev.target.data == "true") {
                // Your key matched! You can continue
            } else {
                // Your key didn't match. Something fishy going on so deal with it
            }
        } catch (e:TypeError) {
            // Handle your errors here
        }
    }
```

The check should still work even if you pass additional **flashvars** into the Flash that start with **fb_sig_**, but you should generally avoid that and use your own prefix if you want to have one.

 A really crafty hacker could still get around this by observing the URL to which you're sending the security check then using some network trickery to route requests to that address to a different page that just returns true without doing the check. The truth about software security is that there's always someone with more time and willingness to break your code than you can invest in preventing them, so it's probably safe to assume you're reasonably secure (unless your Flash app launches nuclear missiles, in which case you probably don't need my advice).

6.28 Embedding Flash Video

Problem

I've encoded some great video as FLV files and now I need to embed this in my FBML.

Solution

Use the `fb:flv` tag to embed Flash Video (FLV) files. The simplest form is:

```
<fb:flv src="http://someserver.com/greatEncodedVideo.flv" />
```

The player fits right into the Facebook look and feel, as shown in Figure 6-9.

Figure 6-9. Facebook Flash Video player

Discussion

The `fb:flv` tag really is just that: a tag that plays FLV files. This is not a generic video player, meaning it won't handle anything but FLV files, so don't throw it *.mov*, *.wmv*, or *.avi* files and hope they'll work. The three optional parameters let you set the `width` and `height` (which you should do if you can because some reports indicate that Internet Explorer will collapse your video down to a single gray dot if you don't), and a title, which will be passed into the video as the Flash variable `video_title`.

6.29 Embedding Microsoft Silverlight

Problem

I love using the latest and greatest technologies, so I've gone and built a kick-ass Silverlight movie that I want to embed into my app.

Solution

Use the `fb:silverlight` tag to embed your Silverlight objects. The simplest form is:

```
<fb:silverlight silverlightsrc="http://someserver.com/kickAss.xaml" />
```

Discussion

As with embedding Flash (see Recipe 6.27), your Silverlight objects will play automatically when embedded on a Canvas page and will load and display the image specified in `imgsrc` when embedded in a Profile Box, which will require a click to start playing. The `fb:silverlight` tag shares some of the same optional parameters as `fb:swf`, and these are listed in Table 6-8.

Table 6-8. Parameters for fb:silverlight

Name	Type	Default value	Description
silverlightsrc	string	N/A	The URL of the Silverlight you want to embed. This is the only required field.
height	int	None	Height of your Silverlight, in pixels.
imgclass	string	None	CSS class to apply to the image specified in `imgsrc`.
imgsrc	string	*spacer.gif*	The image that will be shown in place of your Silverlight when it can't be displayed or in places where the user needs to click to activate it (e.g., in Profile Boxes). The default value is *http://static.ak.facebook.com/images/spacer.gif*, which will render your Silverlight unusable in Profile Boxes since it will be invisible, so make sure you specify this if you want to embed it there.
imgstyle	string	None	Inline CSS styling for the image specified in `imgsrc`.
swfbgcolor	string	#ffffff	According to the Facebook Developers Wiki, that is the correct name for the parameter, even though it's not a SWF. The attribute doesn't appear to do anything either way.
width	int	None	Width of your Silverlight, in pixels.

The FBML parser will embed your image in a `div` with the `id silverlightImage` and your actual Silverlight in a `div` with the `id silverlightControlHost`. Since both of those are IDs rather than classes, it suggests that you can embed only one Silverlight movie per Facebook page. It's so early in the wild Silverlight frontier that it's hard to say whether anyone has used this tag in production, so keep that in mind when you're choosing a technology for your interactive media bits.

6.30 Wide Versus Narrow Profile Boxes

Problem

I know users can drag my Profile Box from the wide body of their Boxes tab into the narrow sidebar, and I'd really like to be able to display different content when they do. How can I send different info to Facebook?

Solution

Facebook provides two tags that differentiate where the content should be shown: `fb:wide` and `fb:narrow`. It will be left as a task for the reader (that would be you) to determine which is which. There are no parameters for either tag.

Note that these tags aren't used on a Canvas page in the same way as many of the other tags in this chapter. You'll need to pass your FBML as a parameter to the Facebook API's `Profile.setFBML( )` method, which will update the cached Profile Box for the specified user. For more information, see Recipe 9.47.

Discussion

If you call the Facebook API's `Profile.setFBML()` and don't pass in `fb:wide` or `fb:narrow` tags, everything you do pass in will be placed in both locations. Neither box has a height constraint, so you're free to make your content as tall as you'd like (though keep in mind that people are more likely to remove your box if it takes over their entire Profile). The wide box is 388 pixels wide with an 8-pixel left margin and no right margin, so if you want them to be balanced, go for a width of 380 pixels. The narrow box is 190 pixels wide, with a left margin of 10 pixels and no right margin, so go with 180 pixels if you want balanced margins.

Don't forget that there are settings for your application that will determine whether you end up in the sidebar or body by default ("Default Profile Box Column: Wide or Narrow"), as well as what default FBML to display in the Profile Box before the user has done anything in your application ("Default FBML"). For more information on setting these, see Recipe 3.2.

6.31 Tabling Users

Problem

I love the Mutual Friends table of users I see on people's Profile pages, and I'd really like to display a similar listing of users in my app.

Solution

The good news is that you can use the `fb:user-table` tag to display a table of users without worrying about the formatting and extra HTML. The bad news is that it will only work in a Profile Box and can't be used in a Canvas page. The simplest form is:

```
<fb:user-table>
    <fb:user-item uid="561415460" />
    <fb:user-item uid="561415460" />
    <fb:user-item uid="561415460" />
    <fb:user-item uid="561415460" />
    <fb:user-item uid="561415460" />
    <fb:user-item uid="561415460" />
</fb:user-table>
```

That'll give you an awesome table filled with links to my Profile; see Figure 6-10.

Figure 6-10. User table filled with my Profile

Discussion

You can add a `col` parameter to control the number of columns you want in your table. For example, the following:

```
<fb:user-table cols="2">
    <fb:user-item uid="561415460" />
    <fb:user-item uid="561415460" />
    <fb:user-item uid="561415460" />
    <fb:user-item uid="561415460" />
    <fb:user-item uid="561415460" />
    <fb:user-item uid="561415460" />
</fb:user-table>
```

will give you a two-column table, as shown in Figure 6-11.

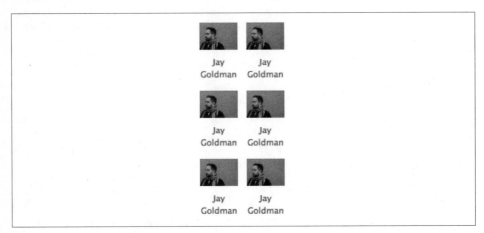

Figure 6-11. A two-column-wide user table

6.32 Page and Box Titles

Problem

Page titles are a really important element of Search Engine Optimization, and they also provide users with better bookmarks and history list entries. How can I set titles for the different pages in my app?

Solution

Use the `fb:title` tag to set the title of your page. When used on a Canvas page, this will append the included text to the title of the window. The simplest form is:

```
<fb:title>Title Here</fb:title>
```

If your app is called "Super Disco Napping," and you set the fb:title to "Invite Friends to Nap," and you're running Firefox 3 on Mac OS X (which you should be!), the window title bar will look something like Figure 6-12.

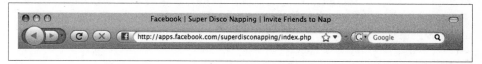

Figure 6-12. Window title

You can also use the fb:title tag to set the title of the various boxes you can place the tag in, including Profile Boxes and the like. When used inside of a wide Profile Box, you'll get something like Figure 6-13.

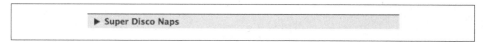

Figure 6-13. Profile Box text

Discussion

The fb:title tag is often used with the fb:subtitle tag to create a header like the one you'll see in Profile Boxes on users' Profiles. For example, the following:

```
<fb:title>Super Disco Naps</fb:title>
<fb:subtitle seeallurl="http://apps.facebook.com/superdisconaps/all">
    Displaying 10 of 2587 naps
    <fb:action
        href="http://apps.facebook.com/superdisconaps/nap.php">
        Take a Nap!
    </fb:action>
</fb:subtitle>
```

will give you something like Figure 6-14.

Figure 6-14. Title and subtitle

See Recipe 6.33 for more information on the fb:subtitle tag.

6.33 Profile Box Subtitles

Problem

I want to add one of those cool bars I see at the top of other Profile Boxes to mine so that I can give people more information about what's in the box and some useful links to draw them into the app.

Solution

Luckily for you, subtitles aren't just for foreign films anymore. Use the `fb:subtitle` tag to add a bar to the top of your Profile Boxes that contain more info. Note that this tag is usually used with the `fb:title` tag, which is included in the following examples. The simplest form is:

```
<fb:subtitle>
    Displaying 10 of 2587 naps
</fb:subtitle>
```

which will give you Figure 6-15.

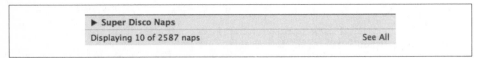

Figure 6-15. Super Disco Naps subtitle

Discussion

You can add a `seeallurl` parameter to the `fb:subtitle` tag, which will add a "See All" link to the right edge of your bar. For example, the following:

```
<fb:title>Super Disco Naps</fb:title>
<fb:subtitle seeallurl="http://apps.facebook.com/superdisconaps/all">
        Displaying 10 of 2587 naps
</fb:subtitle>
```

will give you Figure 6-16.

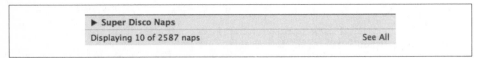

Figure 6-16. Super Disco Naps subtitle with "See All"

You can also add an `fb:action` tag within the `fb:subtitle`, which will add an action link next to the "See All" link (or in place of it if you don't include a `seeallurl` parameter):

```
<fb:title>Super Disco Naps</fb:title>
<fb:subtitle seeallurl="http://apps.facebook.com/superdisconaps/all">
        Displaying 10 of 2587 naps
        <fb:action
            href="http://apps.facebook.com/superdisconaps/nap.php">
            Take a Nap!
        </fb:action>
</fb:subtitle>
```

That code will give you Figure 6-17.

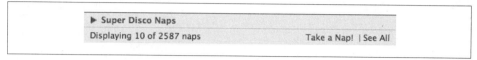

Figure 6-17. Super Disco Naps subtitle with an action and "See All"

6.34 Forms the Facebook Way

Problem

I need to display a form in my app and would really like to use the same layout and fields that Facebook uses for its forms so that my app matches the rest of Platform.

Solution

The `fb:editor` family of tags gives you the ability to quickly create a Facebook-style form. The layout gets wrapped in `fb:editor` tags, with the rest of the family inserted between your opener and closer to fill in the form itself:

```
<fb:editor action="http://someserver.com/somePage.php">
    <fb:editor-custom label="About You">It's all about you!</fb:editor-custom>
    <fb:editor-text label="Your Name" name="name"/>
    <fb:editor-textarea label="Comments" name="comments"/>
    <fb:editor-divider/>
    <fb:editor-time label="Current Time" name="time" value="<?php echo time();?>"/>
    <fb:editor-month label="Current Month" name="month" value="4"/>
    <fb:editor-date label="Current Date" name="date" value="<?php echo time();?>"/>
    <fb:editor-divider/>
    <fb:editor-custom label="Favorite Ice Cream">
        <select name="iceCream">
            <option value="chocolate" selected="selected">Chocolate</option>
            <option value="vanilla">Vanilla</option>
            <option value="strawberry">Strawberry</option>
            <option value="moosetracks">Moose Tracks</option>
        </select>
    </fb:editor-custom>
    <fb:editor-divider/>
    <fb:editor-buttonset>
        <fb:editor-button value="Give me Ice Cream!"/>
        <fb:editor-cancel />
```

```
    </fb:editor-buttonset>
</fb:editor>
```

The code here shows all of the various subtags, which are covered in great detail in the upcoming Discussion. This code will render out to a form that looks like Figure 6-18.

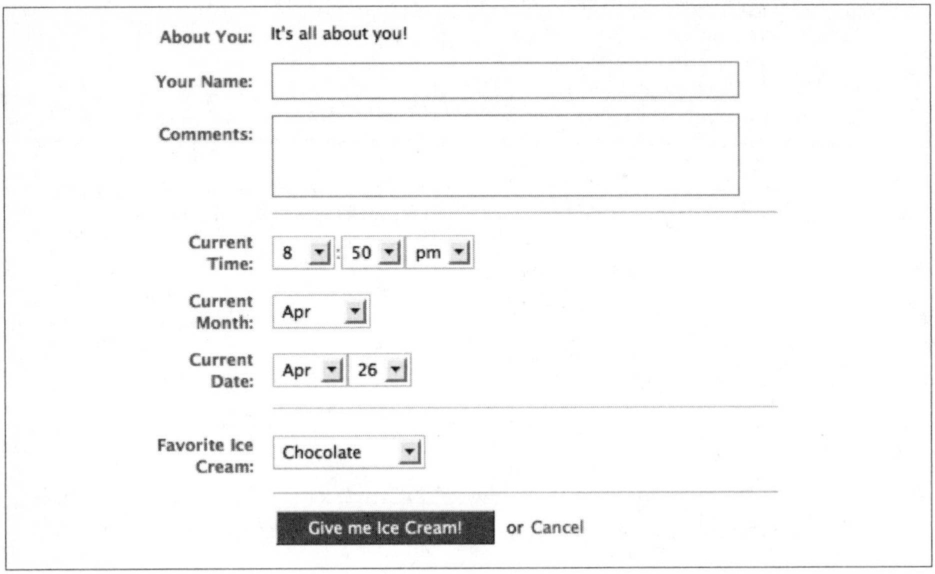

Figure 6-18. Facebook form

Discussion

The FBML parser renders the `fb:editor` form as a table with two columns, and so the example ends up looking like this:

```
<form action="http://someserver.com/somePage.php" method="post"><table
class="editorkit" border="0" cellspacing="0" style="width:425px"><tr
class="width_setter"><th style="width:75px"></th><td></td></tr>
    <tr><th class="detached_label"><label>About You:</label></th><td
class="editorkit_row">It's all about you!</td><td class="right_padding"></td></tr>
   <tr><th><label>Your Name:</label></th><td class="editorkit_row"><input type="text"
name="name"/></td><td
class="right_padding"></td></tr>
    <tr><th class="detached_label"><label>Comments:</label></th><td
class="editorkit_row"><textarea name="comments"></textarea></td><td
class="right_padding"></td></tr>
    <tr><th></th><td colspan="2"><divclass="divider"></div></td></tr>

    <tr><th><label>Current Time:</label></th><td
class="editorkit_row"><select name="time_hour" id="time_hour"><option
 value="1">1</option><option
value="2">2</option><option value="3">3</option><option value="4">4</option><option
value="5">5</option><option value="6">6</option><option value="7">7</option><option
value="8" selected>8</option><option value="9">9</option><option
```

```
value="10">10</option><option value="11">11</option><option
value="12">12</option></select><span>:</span><select
name="time_min" id="time_min">

<option value="00">00</option><option value="05" selected>05</option><option
value="10">10</option><option value="15">15</option><option
value="20">20</option><option value="25">25</option><option
value="30">30</option><option value="35">35</option><option
value="40">40</option><option value="45">45</option><option
value="50">50</option><option value="55">55</option></select><select
name="time_ampm" id="time_ampm"><option value="am">am</option><option value="pm"
selected>pm</option></select></td><td class="right_padding"></td></tr>

    <tr><th><label>Current Month:</label></th><td class="editorkit_row"><select
name="month" id="month"  ><option value="-1">Month:</option><option
value="1">Jan</option><option value="2">Feb</option><option
value="3">Mar</option><option value="4" selected>Apr</option><option
value="5">May</option><option value="6">Jun</option><option
value="7">Jul</option><option value="8">Aug</option><option
value="9">Sep</option><option value="10">Oct</option><option
value="11">Nov</option><option value="12">Dec</option></select></td><td
class="right_padding"></td></tr>

    <tr><th><label>Current Date:</label></th><td
class="editorkit_row"><select name="date_month"
id="date_month" onchange="editor_date_month_change(this,
'date_day','');" ><option
value="1">Jan</option><option
value="2">Feb</option><option
value="3">Mar</option><option value="4"
selected>Apr</option><option
value="5">May</option><option
value="6">Jun</option><option
value="7">Jul</option><option value="8">Aug</option><option
value="9">Sep</option><option
value="10">Oct</option><option
value="11">Nov</option><option
value="12">Dec</option></select><select
name="date_day" id="date_day"><option
value="1">1</option><option
value="2">2</option><option value="3">3</option><option
value="4">4</option><option
value="5">5</option><option
value="6">6</option><option value="7">7</option><option
value="8">8</option><option
value="9">9</option><option
value="10">10</option><option
value="11">11</option><option value="12">12</option><option
value="13">13</option><option
value="14">14</option><option
value="15">15</option><option
value="16">16</option><option
value="17">17</option><option
value="18">18</option><option
value="19">19</option><option
```

```
value="20">20</option><option
value="21">21</option><option
value="22">22</option><option
value="23">23</option><option value="24">24</option><option
value="25">25</option><option
value="26">26</option><option
value="27">27</option><option value="28"
selected>28</option><option value="29">29</option><option
value="30">30</option><option
value="31">31</option></select></td><td
class="right_padding"></td></tr>

    <tr><th></th><td colspan="2"><div
class="divider"></div></td></tr>
    <tr><th class="detached_label"><label>Favorite Ice
Cream:</label></th><td class="editorkit_row">
        <select name="iceCream">
            <option value="chocolate" selected="selected">Chocolate</option>
            <option value="vanilla">Vanilla</option>
            <option value="strawberry">Strawberry</option>
            <option value="moosetracks">Moose Tracks</option>

        </select>
    </td><td class="right_padding"></td></tr>
    <tr><th></th><td colspan="2"><div class="divider"></div></td></tr>
    <tr><th></th><td class="editorkit_buttonset">

        <input type="submit" class="editorkit_button action"
  value="Give me Ice Cream!" />
        <span class="cancel_link"><span>or</span><a href="#">Cancel</a></span>
    </td><td class="right_padding"></td></tr>
</table></form>
```

 It's worth noting that this XHTML is actually invalid. Challenge your powers of perception and go find the two validation errors! Back? Got 'em? No? OK, I'll tell you, but only this time. The various `select` `option`s that are marked as selected should be marked as `selected="selected"` in XHTML, and the `textarea` is missing the `rows` and `cols` attributes.

Each of the tags within the form has its own set of optional parameters (with the exception of `fb:editor-divider`, `fb:editor-buttonset`, and `fb:editor-cancel`, which are simplicity defined), discussed next.

fb:editor

The `fb:editor` tags wrap the whole kit and caboodle, defining the start and end of the form. These replace the HTML `form` tag, so you don't need to include one in addition to them. Its parameters are listed in Table 6-9.

Table 6-9. Parameters for fb:editor

Name	Type	Default value	Description
action	string	N/A	The URL to post the form to. This is the only required field.
width	int	425	Width of the fields column, in pixels.
labelwidth	int	75	Width of the labels column, in pixels.

Note that the total width of the table will be `width + labelwidth`, and so it defaults to 500 pixels.

fb:editor-custom

The `fb:editor-custom` tag is used to insert any valid block of FBML into your form. In the example shown earlier, it's used to both display some static text in the field column and include a `select` with ice cream flavors. Its parameter is listed in Table 6-10.

Table 6-10. Parameter for fb:editor-custom

Name	Type	Default value	Description
label	string	N/A	Label to display in the label column.

fb:editor-text

The `fb:editor-text` tag is equivalent to an HTML `<input type="text">`. Its parameters are listed in Table 6-11.

Table 6-11. Parameters for fb:editor-text

Name	Type	Default value	Description
label	string	N/A	Label to display in the label column.
name	string	N/A	Name of the control, which will become the variable containing the value in the POST.
value	string	N/A	Default string to put into the field.
maxlength	int	N/A	Maximum number of characters to allow in the field.

fb:editor-textarea

The `fb:editor-textarea` tag is equivalent to an HTML `textarea`. Its parameters are listed in Table 6-12. You can use this tag in either the self-closed or open modes, depending on whether you want to include content or not. For example:

```
<fb:editor-textarea label="Comments" name="comments"/>
```

or:

```
<fb:editor-textarea label="Comments" name="comments">
    Put your comments in here
</fb:editor-textarea>
```

Table 6-12. Parameters for fb:editor-textarea

Name	Type	Default value	Description
label	string	N/A	Label to display in the label column.
name	string	N/A	Name of the control, which will become the variable containing the value in the POST.
rows	int	N/A	Height of the text area in rows.

fb:editor-time

The fb:editor-time tag creates a series of selects with options for setting the hours, minutes, and a.m./p.m. values for a time field. Its parameters are listed in Table 6-13.

Table 6-13. Parameters for fb:editor-time

Name	Type	Default value	Description
label	string	N/A	Label to display in the label column.
name	string	N/A	Name of the control, which will be prepended to _hour, _min, and _ampm to create the variables containing the values in the POST (e.g., if you set this to "current", you'll get current_hour, current_min, and current_ampm in POST).
value	int	4:00 p.m.	The time in epoch seconds. See Recipe 6.20 for a description of epoch seconds and how to work with them.

fb:editor-month

The fb:editor-month tag creates a single select to pick a month of the year. Its parameters are listed in Table 6-14.

Table 6-14. Parameters for fb:editor-month

Name	Type	Default value	Description
label	string	N/A	Label to display in the label column.
name	string	N/A	Name of the control, which will become the variable containing the value in the POST.
value	int	"Month:"	Number of the month to select by default (January=1, and so on). If you don't specify a value, this will default to the text "Month:", which appears as the first option in the select and prompts users to make a choice.

fb:editor-date

The fb:editor-date tag creates two selects to pick the month and day of the year. Its parameters are listed in Table 6-15.

Table 6-15. Parameters for fb:editor-date

Name	Type	Default value	Description
label	string	N/A	Label to display in the label column.

Name	Type	Default value	Description
name	string	N/A	Name of the control, which will be prepended to _month and _day to create the two variables containing the values in the POST (e.g., if you set this to "current", you'll get `current_month` and `current_day` in the POST).
value	int	"Month:"	Number of the month to select by default (January = 1, and so on). If you don't specify a value, this will default to the text "Month:", which appears as the first option in the `select` and prompts users to make a choice.

fb:editor-button

The `fb:editor-button` tag, which should appear inside an `fb:editor-buttonset` tag, renders a Facebook-style submit button. Its parameters are listed in Table 6-16.

Table 6-16. Parameters for fb:editor-button

Name	Type	Default value	Description
value	string	N/A	Text to display on the button. This is the only required field.
name	string	N/A	Name of the control, which will become the variable containing the value in the POST.

6.35 Heads Up! Heading Your App Pages

Problem

I want to display my app's icon and a title at the top of my pages.

Solution

Use the `fb:header` tag:

```
<fb:header />
```

which will give you your app's icon and name, as shown in Figure 6-19.

Figure 6-19. Empty fb:header tag

You can also put text in the tag:

```
<fb:header>This is a Page in my App</fb:header>
```

which will keep the icon but substitute your text for your app's name, as shown in Figure 6-20.

🐢 **This is a Page in my App**

Figure 6-20. fb:header with text

Discussion

You can pass in a false value for `icon` to switch off the icon display:

```
<fb:header icon="false">This is a Page in my App</fb:header>
```

You can also pass in a `decoration` string set to either `add_border` or `no_padding` (but not both), which gives you control over whether you want a one-pixel gray border (#cccccc) along the bottom edge of your header or the default 20 pixels of padding. For example, the following:

```
<fb:header decoration="add_border">This is a Page in my App</fb:header>
```

will give you Figure 6-21.

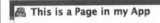

Figure 6-21. fb:header with border

Alternatively, this code:

```
<fb:header decoration="no_padding">This is a Page in my App</fb:header>
```

will give you Figure 6-22.

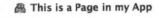

Figure 6-22. fb:header with no padding

 If you're looking for a full dashboard at the top of your page, including actions, help, and a Create button, try the `fb:dashboard` tag. See Recipe 6.36 for more information.

6.36 Dashing Dashboards: Heading Your App Pages

Problem

I've noticed that some Facebook apps have their app icon and name at the top, along with a really nice Create button relevant to what the app does. That looks swanky! How I do get that?

Solution

Use the `fb:dashboard` tag, along with its children, `fb:action`, `fb:create-button`, and `fb:help`. The simplest form is the `fb:dashboard` alone:

```
<fb:dashboard />
```

which will give you Figure 6-23.

Figure 6-23. Simple dashboard

Adding in the `fb:create-button` gives you Figure 6-24.

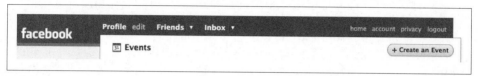

Figure 6-24. Dashboard with fb:create-button

Finally, adding some `fb:action`s and an `fb:help` gives you the full Events header, as shown in Figure 6-25.

Figure 6-25. Full dashboard

Discussion

Using `fb:dashboard` is a great way to give your app a Platform-native look and feel very quickly. The tag will automatically render your icon next to your app's name (if your app has an icon, which it should). The tag will ignore anything you put in it that isn't one of its children, so:

```
<fb:dashboard>
    No dice!
</fb:dashboard>
```

and:

```
<fb:dashboard />
```

both give exactly the same result (a dashboard with the app name and icon, but nothing else).

You might want to display a different dashboard depending on whether users have installed your app. You can't use any of the `fb:if` tags inside of an `fb:dashboard`, but you can wrap the dashboard in the `if` tags:

```
<fb:if-user-has-added-app>
    <fb:dashboard>
        <!--Dashboard Stuff-->
    </fb:dashboard>
<fb:else>
    <fb:dashboard>
        <!--Dashboard Stuff, Plus...-->
        <fb:action href="http://apps.facebook.com/add.php?api_key=12345">Add
this app</fb:action>
    </fb:dashboard>
</fb:if-user-has-added-app>
```

You can have as many `fb:action` links inside an `fb:dashboard` as you'd like, but keep in mind that they'll start to wrap onto a new line if you exceed the width of the Canvas, as shown in Figure 6-26.

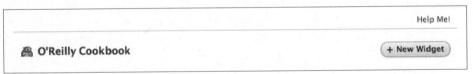

Figure 6-26. Lots of fb:actions

You can have only one `fb:create-button` and one `fb:help` per `fb:dashboard` (you can put more into your code, but only the first one will appear). Both tags require an `href` parameter that points to a Canvas page on Facebook. For example, the following:

```
<fb:dashboard>
    <fb:help href="other_canvas.php">Help Me!</fb:help>
    <fb:create-button href="canvas.php">New Widget</fb:create-button>
</fb:dashboard>
```

will give you something like Figure 6-27.

```
                                                                    Help Me!
   ─────────────────────────────────────────────────────────────────────────
     🎮 O'Reilly Cookbook                                      ( + New Widget )
```

Figure 6-27. Dashboard with fb:help and fb:create-button

You can have as many `fb:dashboard`s as you'd like per page, and you can put them inside of `div`s (and the like) if you want to position them:

```
<div style="width:30%; float:left;">
    <fb:dashboard>
        <fb:create-button href="canvas.php">Work It!</fb:create-button>
```

```
        </fb:dashboard>
    </div>
    <div style="width:30%; float:left;">
        <fb:dashboard>
            <fb:create-button href="canvas.php">Make It!</fb:create-button>
        </fb:dashboard>
    </div>
    <div style="width:30%; float:left;">
        <fb:dashboard>
            <fb:create-button href="canvas.php">Do It!</fb:create-button>
        </fb:dashboard>
    </div>
    <div style="clear: left;">
        <fb:dashboard>
            <fb:action href="canvas.php">Makes us...</fb:action>
            <fb:action href="canvas.php">Harder</fb:action>
            <fb:action href="canvas.php">Better</fb:action>
            <fb:action href="canvas.php">Faster</fb:action>
            <fb:help href="canvas.php">Stronger!</fb:help>
        </fb:dashboard>
    </div>
```

This would uselessly (but very Daft Punkingly) give you Figure 6-28.

Figure 6-28. Multiple fb:dashboards

 If you're just looking for your app's name and icon, try `fb:header` instead. See Recipe 6.35 for more information.

6.37 Tabs Ahoy!

Problem

I want tabs in my app just like I see all over Facebook. Tabs are the greatest! Tabs! Tabs! Tabs!

Solution

Woah! Easy there. Tabs *are* pretty great, especially when they're as simple as this:

```
<fb:tabs>
    <fb:tab-item href="http://apps.facebook.com/myapp/some.php"
  title="First Tab!" selected="true"/>
    <fb:tab-item href="http://apps.facebook.com/myapp/page.php" title="Second Tab!" />
</fb:tabs>
```

which will give you Figure 6-29.

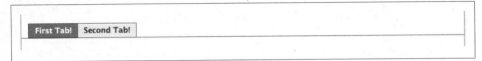

Figure 6-29. Easy tabs with fb:tabs

Discussion

You can have as many tabs as you'd like, but note that they'll either get cut off on the right edge of the Canvas or wrap around onto additional lines with somewhat unpredictable results. Each `fb:tab-item` must have an absolute `href` and `title`, and can optionally have `align` (either `left` or `right`; see Figure 6-30) and `selected` (`true` or `false`) parameters. Setting more than one tab to be `selected` will highlight only the first tab.

Figure 6-30. fb:tab-items with align left and right

6.38 Media Headers

Problem

I want to display a bunch of media that all belong to a user, so I'd like some way of showing that.

Solution

Use the `fb:mediaheader` tag along with its children, `fb:header-title` and `fb:owner-action`:

```
<fb:mediaheader uid="561415460">
    <fb:header-title>Jay's Photos</fb:header-title>
    <fb:owner-action href="http://facebook.com/photos">Facebook</fb:owner-action>
    <fb:owner-action href="http://flickr.com">Flickr</fb:owner-action>
</fb:mediaheader>
```

which will give you Figure 6-31.

Figure 6-31. fb:mediaheader as viewed by the owner

Note that I will see the Facebook and Flickr links in this image (because they're owner-actions), but other people will see a standard set of links relating to me (Send a Message, Poke, etc.), depending on privacy settings.

Discussion

Unlike tags such as `fb:help` (in `fb:dashboard`), the `href` in the `fb:owner-action` tag doesn't have to be a Canvas page URL.

6.39 Errors, Explanation, and Success: Displaying Messages (Oh My!)

Problem

I'd like the different types of messages displayed in my app to match Facebook's look and feel.

Solution

Facebook provides a family of tags that display text using their familiar user interface standards: `fb:error`, `fb:explanation`, and `fb:success`. They all follow the same pattern, in that they have two modes of use. For example, the following:

```
<fb:error message="Ka-Blam! Bad stuff happened!" />
```

will give you the message in Figure 6-32.

> **Ka-Blam! Bad stuff happened!**

Figure 6-32. Facebook error with inline message

The following is a slightly more complex mode:

```
<fb:error>
    <fb:message>Ka-Blam!</fb:message>
```

```
        <p>Bad stuff happened!</p>
    </fb:error>
```

which will give you Figure 6-33.

Figure 6-33. Facebook error with title and message

Discussion

Using the Facebook-native appearance is valuable because users are familiar with the look of errors and messages and will extend their understanding of them into your application. Figure 6-34 shows the three types of message displays.

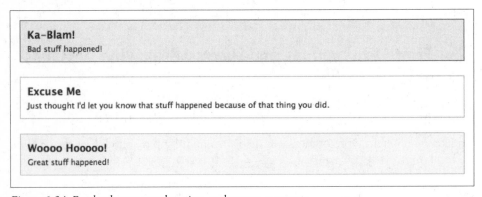

Figure 6-34. Facebook error, explanation, and success messages

The only optional parameter is `decoration`, which can be either `no_padding` (removes the 20 pixels of padding that normally surround the message) or `shorten` (removes the 20 pixels of padding from the bottom of the message). Facebook's CSS for these messages is pretty flexible, so they'll adapt if you put them inside a `div` with a specified width, as shown in Figure 6-35.

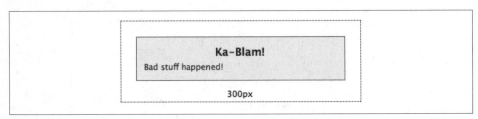

Figure 6-35. Facebook error inside a 300-px-wide div

6.40 Discussion Boards Made Simple

Problem

I'd love to have a discussion board in my app, but it's so much work to build one from scratch, and I'm not sure how easy it would be to convert an existing board to run inside of Facebook. What to do?

Solution

Facebook released the `fb:board` tag into a full public beta on December 7, 2007, so it can now be used in any application. This tag will render a full discussion board within your app and handle all of the subpages and additional functionality required to run the board. The simplest form is:

```
<fb:board xid="my_quick_and_easy_board" />
```

which will give you something like Figure 6-36.

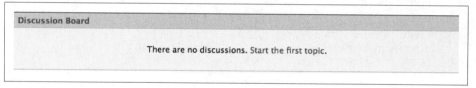

Figure 6-36. The simplest form of fb:board

 You might consider using a Wall post–type comments system instead of a discussion board, depending on whether you want a conversation or more of a one-way message board. See Recipe 6.41. Note that the implementation of both tags is almost identical, so you might have a striking sense of déja vu if you've already read that recipe.

Discussion

The `xid` parameter needs to be unique, so go nuts and make up something that no one else will have thought of. You're limited to alphanumeric characters (Aa–Zz, 0–9), hyphens (-), and underscores (_). You'll see why it needs to be unique once you have the board on your page and you can see the URLs it uses for internal pages, which all point back to the same set of PHP pages for every board, passing in your `xid` to identify which board it should load content for.

You can control the number of topics that appear in the initial view by passing in a `numtopics` parameter (which defaults to 3):

```
<fb:board xid="my_quick_and_easy_board" numtopics="6" />
```

Four optional parameters control permission for the current user: `canpost`, `candelete`, `canmark`, and `cancreatetopic`. Other than `candelete` (which defaults to `false` for obvious security reasons), they all default to `true`. The only one that isn't immediately obvious from its name is `canmark`. You might think this means they can mark things as favorites, but it actually enables or disables the ability to mark posts as relevant or irrelevant.

The last two options give you control over the URLs used by the board. Both default to the current page, but you can choose to load a configuration from a different URL by specifying a `callbackurl`, or to have people pop out of the discussion boards onto a different page by specifying a `returnurl`. The documentation for `fb:board` warns that every page load within the board will reload the configuration, so you should consider using the `callbackurl` to point Facebook to a page that is served from a potentially lower-cost or higher-bandwidth/reliability server, just in case hundreds of thousands of users storm down your door to talk about their favorite adolescent magicians.

Finally, you can specify your own title for your board by throwing an `fb:title` tag into the `fb:board`:

```
<fb:board xid="potter_chatter_board"
    numtopics="6"
    canpost="true"
    candelete="false"
    canmark="false"
    cancreatetopic="true"
    callbackurl="http://superrobustserver.com/board_config.php"
    returnurl="http://apps.facebook.com/potterchatter">
    <fb:title>Talk about Harry!</fb:title>
</fb:board>
```

Keep in mind that this feature is still marked as beta, so it might behave a little differently than you're expecting it to. If you run into any problems, jump into the Facebook Bug Tracker (*http://bugs.developers.facebook.com/*) and post about them so that the Facebook team can get right on fixing them.

6.41 Giving Users a Voice: Wall Posts in Your App

Problem

I'd really like to have something like the Profile Wall in my app so that users can leave comments.

Solution

Don't settle for something like the Wall; have the Wall! Use the `fb:comments` tag to add a real, live Wall to your Canvas pages. The simplest form is:

```
<fb:comments xid="my_quick_and_easy_wall" />
```

which will give you something like Figure 6-37.

Comments	
No one has said anything... yet. Write Something.	

Figure 6-37. The simplest form of fb:comments

 You might consider using a Discussion Board–type system instead of a Wall, depending on whether you want a one-way message board or more of a conversation. See Recipe 6.40. The implementation of both tags is virtually identical, so this might all seem very familiar if you've already read that recipe.

You could also use the `fb:wall` and `fb:wallpost` tags if you wanted to format content to look like Wall posts, but since they don't provide any mechanism to create new posts, they are much less useful. You can find more information about them on the Platform Wiki if you're curious.

Discussion

The `xid` parameter needs to be unique across all of Facebook, so put on your imagining cap and make up something that no one else will have come up with (note that you're limited to alphanumeric characters (Aa–Zz, 0–9), hyphens (-) and underscores (_)). You'll see why it needs to be unique once you have the Wall on your page and you can see the URLs it uses for internal pages, which all point back to the same set of PHP pages for every Wall, passing in your `xid` to identify which Wall it should load content for.

You can control the maximum number of Posts you want visible by passing in a `numposts` parameter:

```
<fb:comments xid="my_quick_and_easy_wall" numposts="6" />
```

Two optional parameters control permission for the current user: `canpost` and `candelete`. The former defaults to `true` and the latter to `false` (for obvious security reasons). Facebook will automatically adjust the text about the number of visible posts, as seen in Figure 6-38. The default behavior for posting is to include the "Write Something" link (see the earlier screenshot in Figure 6-37), but you can switch to an inline form by setting `showform` to `true` (the page will refresh after posts to show the new ones; see Figure 6-39).

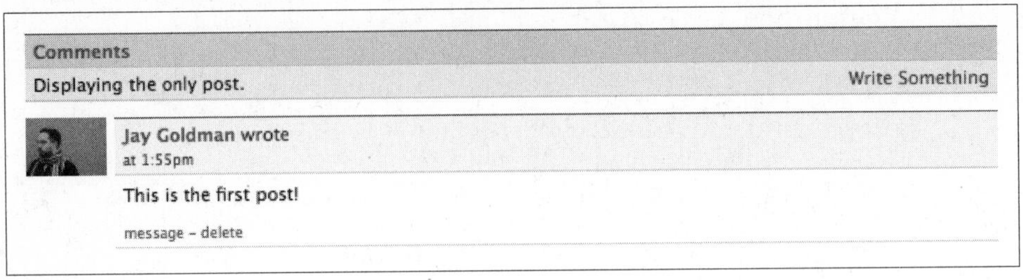

Figure 6-38. *The fb:comments Wall with one post*

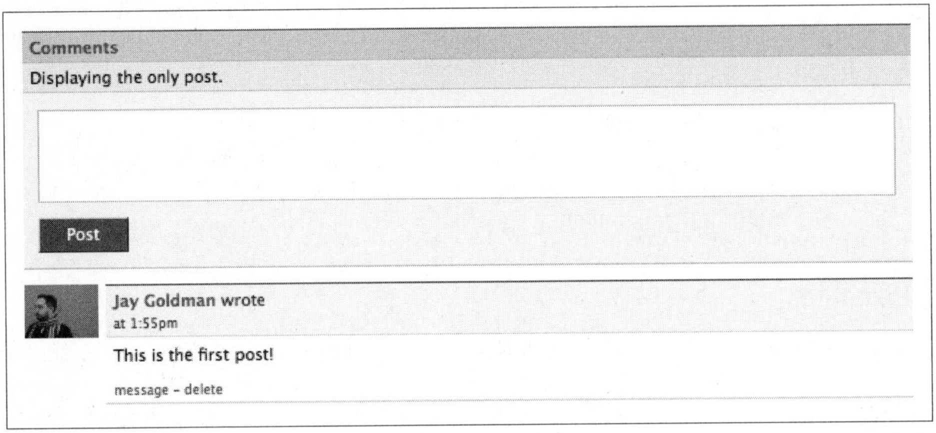

Figure 6-39. *The fb:comments Wall with showform set to true*

Note that you'll (obviously) need `canpost` set to `true` to use the form.

You might want to receive a Notification every time someone posts a comment so that you can jump in and check out what they've written. Pass in your `uid` as a `send_notification_uid` parameter. It unfortunately accepts only one `uid`, so set it to someone who will either keep up with the Wall herself or do a good job delegating.

The last two options give you control over the URLs used by the board. Both default to the current page, but you can choose to load a configuration from a different URL by specifying a `callbackurl`, or to have people pop out of the Wall onto a different page by specifying a `returnurl`. The documentation for `fb:comments` warns that every page load within the Wall will reload the configuration, so you should consider using the `callbackurl` to point Facebook to a page that is served from a potentially lower-cost or higher-bandwidth/reliability server, just in case hundreds of thousands of users storm down your door to talk about their cat's penchant for ignoring them, demanding food, and sleeping a lot.

Finally, you can specify your own title for your board by throwing an `fb:title` tag into the `fb:comments`:

```
<fb:comments xid="awesome_go_fish_game_wall"
    numposts="6"
```

```
        canpost="true"
        candelete="false"
        send_notification_uid="12345"
        showform="true"
        callbackurl="http://superrobustserver.com/comments_config.php"
        returnurl="http://apps.facebook.com/awesomegofish">
        <fb:title>Talk about AGF!</fb:title>
</fb:comments>
```

6.42 Adding Profile Boxes and Info Sections

Problem

How can I give my users the opportunity to add a Profile Box if they don't have one,
or to add my app's info to the Info tab of their Profile?

Solution

Use the `fb:add-section-button` to give users the ability to add either Profile Boxes or
Info sections:

```
<fb:add-section-button section="profile" />
<fb:add-section-button section="info" />
```

Discussion

This will render Facebook's Add to Profile and Add to Info buttons, shown in Figure 6-40.

Figure 6-40. Add to Profile and Add to Info buttons

The Add to Profile button will appear only if you have previously called
`Profile.setFBML( )` for this user and he doesn't already have your box on his Profile (on
either the Wall or Boxes tab). Likewise, the Add to Info button will appear only if you
have previously called `Profile.setInfo( )` and the user doesn't already have your Info
section on his Info tab. See Recipe 9.47 for more on Profile Boxes and Recipe 9.25 for
more on setting Info.

Clicking the Add to Profile button will show a confirmation dialog like the one in
Figure 6-41.

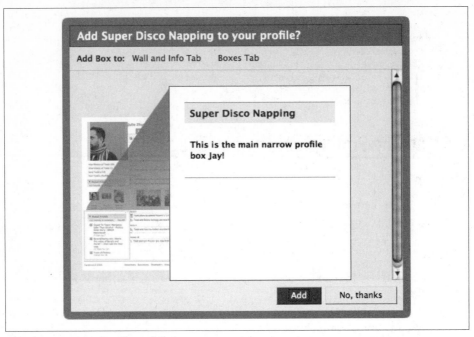

Figure 6-41. Add to Profile confirmation

Clicking on Add will take users to their Profile (on either the Wall or Boxes tab, depending on which tab they select in the subtitle of that dialog) and highlight the new box for them, as shown in Figure 6-42.

Figure 6-42. Keep Profile Box

Clicking on the Add to Info button will also show a confirmation (Figure 6-43).

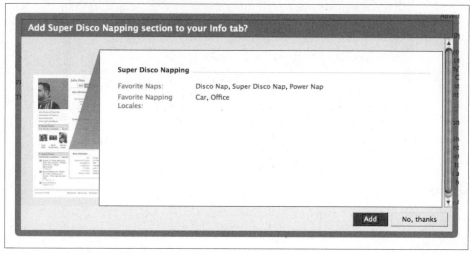

Figure 6-43. Add Info section confirmation

Clicking Add takes them to the Info tab but doesn't highlight the new section in the same way that the Profile button highlights the new box.

6.43 Prompting for Extended Permissions

Problem

I need to get permission from users to send them email, get an infinite session, update their status, upload and tag photos, and create or modify Marketplace listings. Is there an easy way to do that?

Solution

Sure is! Use the `fb:prompt-permission` button, which was added in the mid-2008 Profile redesign:

```
<fb:prompt-permission perms="set_status">Can we set your status?
  </fb:prompt-permission>
```

The tag will display the text (or any other FBML) you put into it as a link that opens a confirmation dialog like the one shown in Figure 6-44.

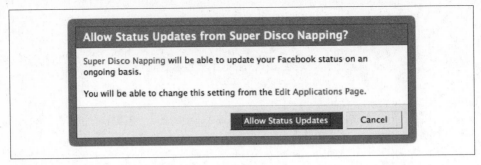

Figure 6-44. Prompt permissions confirmation dialog

Discussion

The following extended permission strings are available:

- `email`
- `offline_access`
- `status_update`
- `photo_upload`
- `create_listing`

Facebook will show links (or other FBML) only for permissions the user hasn't already granted you. You can optionally pass a `next_fbjs` parameter into the `fb:prompt-permission` tag to specify an FBJS function that you'd like called after permission has been granted, which gives you the option of hiding the link.

6.44 You Can Pick Your Friends

Problem

I need to give my users the ability to pick one of their friends. How can I give them a text field that will filter their friend list as they type?

Solution

Use the `fb:friend-selector` tag to render a predictive text field into your forms. The simplest form is:

```
<form name="some_form" action="http://apps.facebook.com
/myapp/handle.php" method="post">
    <fb:friend-selector />
    <input type="submit" value="Send it!"/>
</form>
```

which will give you a form field like the one in Figure 6-45.

Figure 6-45. *The fb:friend-selector field before typing any text*

When users start typing in the field, it will immediately show them potential matches, as in Figure 6-46, which can then be selected using the up/down arrow keys.

Figure 6-46. *The fb:friend-selector field after text has been entered*

Discussion

You can specify a `uid` for the selector if you'd like to give people the option of selecting from someone else's friends. Facebook will take care of the potential privacy violation by not listing any friends if the `loggedinuser` shouldn't see them (by default, the selector uses `loggedinuser` as the `uid` so that they're picking from their own friends).

The control works by using JavaScript to set the value of a hidden field when your user makes a selection in the predictive list. Pass in `name` and/or `idname` parameters to set the names of the actual selector field and the hidden field, respectively:

```
<form name="some_form" action="http://apps.facebook.com
/myapp/handle.php" method="post">
    <fb:friend-selector
        uid="4"
        name="marks_friends"
        idname="selected_friend"/>
    <input type="submit" value="Send it!"/>
</form>
```

Your *handle.php* file will receive the current contents of the `name` field and the last user selected in the `idname` field (using, in this case, `marks_friends` and `selected_friend` as keys in `$_POST`).

> Facebook CEO Mark Zuckerberg has the lowest Facebook `uid`: 4. The numbers stopped being consecutive at some point, so although my `uid` is 561415460, I obviously wasn't the 561,415,460th user.

There are three parameters that give you control over the contents of the list: `include_me`, which takes a boolean value that defaults to `false` and sets whether to include the `loggedinuser` in the selector; `exclude_ids`, a comma-separated list of `uids` to exclude from the selector; and `include_lists`, which takes a boolean value that defaults to `false` and sets whether to include friend lists in the selector.

If the user types a value into the field that doesn't match any of the friends in the selector, `name` will be the string they entered and `idname` will be blank. If they enter no text at all, the `idname` field will not appear in the POST variables. This actually introduces the potential for a misleading form submission in which the user picks a valid user in the selector and then erases their entry or enters some text that doesn't match. In the first case, you'll get an empty string for `name` and the `uid` of the user they had selected in `idname`, and in the second case you'll get whatever they type into `name` and the `uid` in `idname`. You shouldn't accept the `uid` in either of those cases because they didn't actually mean to submit it, so you should probably do a sanity check and make sure that `name` matches the name of `idname`, just to be safe:

```
if(isset($_POST['friend_name'])
    && isset($_POST['friend_uid'])
    && checkName($_POST['friend_name'], $_POST['friend_uid'])){
    // They match, so do your thing in here
}

function checkName($friend_name, $friend_uid){
    global $api_key, $secret;

    $facebook = new Facebook($api_key, $secret);
    $user = $facebook->require_login();

    // Retrieve the user
    $user_details = $facebook->api_client->users_getInfo($friend_uid, 'name');

    if($friend_name == $user_details[0]['name']){
        return true;
    }else{
        return false;
    }
}
```

6.45 You Can Pick Your Friends (in Batches)

Problem

I need to give my users the ability to pick a bunch of friends at the same time. How can I give them a text field that will filter their friend list as they type?

Solution

Use the `fb:multi-friend-input` tag. The simplest form is:

```
<form name="some_form" action="http://apps.facebook.com/myapp/
handle.php" method="post">
    <fb:multi-friend-input />
```

```
        <input type="submit" value="Send it!"/>
    </form>
```

It's hard to get much simpler than that! This is a great example of FBML saving you a huge amount of work. That piece of code will give you a simple text box shown in Figure 6-47.

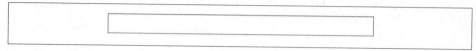

Figure 6-47. multi-friend-input box

When users put focus into the field, they'll get some instructions, as shown in Figure 6-48.

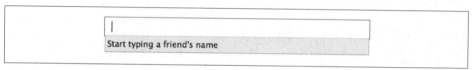

Figure 6-48. multi-friend-input with instructions

As they start typing a name, Facebook will display a list of matching friends below the field (Figure 6-49).

Figure 6-49. multi-friend-input with prediction

So far, this looks a lot like the `fb:friend-selector` tag covered in Recipe 6.44. The difference is in what happens after the user picks her first friend—in this case, she can keep adding more and more friends to the field, as you can see in Figure 6-50.

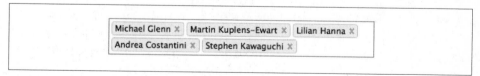

Figure 6-50. multi-friend-input with friends

Clicking on the "X" next to the name will, of course, remove it from the field, as will backspacing over a name.

Discussion

You can have only one of these per page. Well, you can add more, but they won't do anything.

In the example shown earlier, the *handle.php* page will receive a parameter called ids, which is an array containing the Facebook IDs of each friend listed in the field. You can step through the members of that array quite easily:

```
$friends = (isset($_REQUEST["ids"])) ? $_REQUEST["ids"] : 0;
if( $friends != 0 ){
    $counter = 0;
    foreach($friends as $friend){
        echo '<p>Friend ' . $counter . '\'s ID: ' . $friend . '</p>';
        $counter++;
    }
}else{
    echo "<p>You didn't pick anyone!</p>";
}
```

Given the field shown earlier in Figure 6-50, this would output:

Friend 0's ID: 512293981

Friend 1's ID: 759805472

Friend 2's ID: 505031822

Friend 3's ID: 548340659

Friend 4's ID: 725395385

There are a few optional parameters you can pass into the tag, which are listed in Table 6-17.

Table 6-17. Parameters for fb:multi-friend-input

Name	Type	Default value	Description
width	int	350px	The width of the field.
border_color	string	#8496ba	The color of the border.
include_me	bool	false	Setting this to true will allow people to add themselves to the field.
max	int	20	Limits the number of friends who can be added.
exclude_ids	array	N/A	Comma-separated list of IDs to exclude from the field.
prefill_ids	array	N/A	Comma-separated list of IDs to automatically pre-fill into the field.
prefill_locked	bool	false	Setting this to true will lock the list of pre-filled IDs (if you included one), preventing users from deleting them. This will have no effect without a prefill_ids list.

6.46 Invitations and Requests

Problem

I want to give my users the ability to invite their friends to install my app.

Solution

There are a bunch of different ways to handle the actual invitation controls, but they all stem from the use of the `fb:request-form` tag. The general principle is that you start with an `fb:request-form` tag and include parameters that define what you want to do, and then you include some combination of `fb:multi-friend-selector`, `fb:multi-friend-input`, `fb:friend-selector`, and `fb:request-form-submit`. Let's start with a look at the following example:

```php
<?php
$inviteContent = htmlentities('<fb:name uid="' . $user . '" firstnameonly="true"
 shownetwork="false"/> says this is the most awesomest Super Disco Napping
 application ever made. Come take naps with <fb:pronoun objective="true"
 uid=" ' . $user . '"/>!');
$inviteContent .= htmlentities('<fb:req-choice url="new_napper.php"
 label="Take Naps with Me!" />');
?>

<fb:request-form
    action="index.php"
    method="post"
    invite="true"
    type="Disco Nap"
    content="<?php echo $inviteContent?>">
    <fb:multi-friend-selector actiontext="Tell all your friends! Tell the
whole bunch!" />
</fb:request-form>
```

It's a good idea to put the name of the user sending the invites or requests right into the content so that it has some context for the recipient. The `fb:req-choice` tag creates a button in the actual invitation that gets sent. You can add more than one button here, with the caveat that they all have different URLs specified in the `url` parameter; otherwise, only the last of that group will appear. According to the Platform Wiki, it's important to encode the content that you want to have in the invitation so that things like < become < and © becomes ©, which the PHP `htmlentities` function will handle for you. See the Discussion in this recipe for a full breakdown of the parameters. If you're awarding any kind of points or want to track who has been sending invites, you could also append the ID of the sender to the URL in the `fb:req-choice` tag(s) and then include some code on that page to log them to your database:

```php
$inviteContent .= htmlentities('<fb:req-choice url="new_
napper.php?referrer=' . $user . '" label="Take Naps with Me!" />');
```

On to the contents of the `fb:request-form`. Facebook has given you a lot of flexibility here, though there are few occasions when you'll need to take advantage of it. In this case, we've put in an `fb:multi-friend-selector`, which will give us essentially the full-page version of the control with our `actiontext` listed across the top. If you're doing an invite type of page, this is what you want to use: it's big and commanding and gives lots of space for people to select their friends. As mentioned earlier, you can also use any combination of `fb:multi-friend-selector`, `fb:multi-friend-input`, `fb:friend-selector`, and `fb:request-form-submit`, although combining them can result in a pretty strange form. The other options are covered in the Discussion.

Discussion

The parameters for `fb:request-form` are listed in Table 6-18.

Table 6-18. Parameters for fb:request-form

Name	Type	Default value	Description
type	string	N/A	The type of invitation will appear on the recipient's Notifications page and in the title of the invitation itself (e.g., "You have received a Disco Nap invitation"). This is required.
content	string	N/A	The content to put in the invitation itself. This should be encoded for HTML entities so that they can appear properly, which you can do by using something like PHP's `htmlentities` function. It should contain at least one `fb:req-choice` button and will automatically have an Ignore button appended to the end. This is required.
invite	bool	false	Set to `true` to send an invitation, and `false` to send a request. This will affect the action button on the form and the format of the notification sent to the recipients.
method	string	get	Set to either get or post as you would with any HTML form. Depending on how many friends your user selects, there can be a lot of parameters in the URL and you can send them to URLs off Facebook, in which case post is probably a better choice for security reasons (it will hide all of the Facebook IDs of their selected friends). Then again, this isn't an HTTPS connection, so it's not all that secure either way.
action	string	N/A	The URL to send users to after they complete the form. This can be on- or off-Facebook, and it will receive two GET or POST variables (depending on what you specified for the method parameter): `typeahead` and `ids` (an array). See the rest of the Discussion for details.

The choice of which control to put in your `fb:request-form` depends on what you plan to use it for.

Inviting/requesting friends in bulk

Use the `fb:multi-friend-selector` in either full or condensed modes. The page identified in the `fb:request-form`'s action parameter will receive a GET or POST parameter called `ids`, containing an array of the Facebook IDs of the friends selected by the user. `fb:multi-friend-selector`'s parameters are listed in Table 6-19.

Table 6-19. Parameters for fb:multi-friend-selector

Name	Type	Default value	Full	Condensed	Description
actiontext	string	N/A	•		Title text displayed above the full version. This is required for the full version.
condensed	bool	false		•	Triggers condensed mode when set to true. This is required for the condensed version.
max	int	The number of remaining friend requests	•	•	The maximum number of friends the user can invite, ranging from 1 to 35. Facebook will automatically cap this at the number of remaining daily friend requests this user has in your app.
exclude_ids	array	N/A	•	•	Comma-separated list of IDs that should be excluded. See later in the Discussion for code to remove friends who already have your app.
bypass	string	skip	•		Choose the text you want listed on the skip button. Options are skip, step, and cancel, which will render "Skip", "Skip This Step", or "Cancel", respectively. Anything other than those three values will default to skip, and there's no way to set the top and bottom bypass buttons individually.
rows	int	5	•		The number of rows of friends to show in the selector without scrolling (i.e., the height of the box in rows). Any whole integer between 3 and 10 is allowed.
showborder	bool	false	•		Turns on a 10-pixel-wide light blue border with one pixel of darker blue on the inside edge, all the way around the selector.
unselected_rows	int	6		•	Number of rows of friends to display in the "unselected" part of the control. Whole integers between 4 and 15 are allowed.
selected_rows	int	5		•	Number of rows of friends to display in the "selected" part of the control. Whole integers between 5 and 15 are allowed, or set this to 0 to get a single box for "unselected" and "selected."

If you're using this tag to provide your users with a mechanism to invite their friends into the application, you might want to consider using exclude_ids to exclude friends who already have the app installed. Some relatively simple PHP code and FQL will give us back a list of who belongs in that group and will parse it into a comma-separated list for use in the tag (this is original code by the developers of PickPocket, from *http://wiki.developers.facebook.com/index.php/Fb:request-form*):

```php
<?php
global $api_key, $secret;

$facebook = new Facebook($api_key, $secret);
$user = $facebook->require_login();

// Use FQL to find the list of users who have installed this app already and are
// friends with this user
$friends = $facebook->api_client->fql_query("SELECT uid FROM user
 WHERE has_added_app=1 and uid IN (SELECT uid2 FROM friend WHERE uid1 = $user)");

// Parse into a comma-separated list
$excludeList = '';
if($friends){
    $excludeList .= $friends[0]['uid'];
    for( $counter = 1; $counter < count($friends); $counter++ ){
        if($excludeList != ''){
            $excludeList .= ',';
        }
        $excludeList .= $friends[$counter]['uid'];
    }
}

// Build your invite text
$inviteContent = htmlentities('<fb:name uid="' . $user . '" firstnameonly
="true" shownetwork="false"/> says this is the most awesomest Super Disco
 Napping application ever made. Come take naps with <fb:pronoun
 objective="true" uid=" ' . $user . '"/>!');
$inviteContent .= htmlentities('<fb:req-choice url="new_napper.php"
 label="Take Naps with Me!" />');
?>
```

Now you're ready to output the FBML for your selector:

```
<fb:request-form
    action="http://www.someserver.com/post_invite.php"
    invite="false"
    type="Disco Nap"
    content="<?php echo $inviteContent?>">
    <fb:multi-friend-selector
        actiontext="Here's a list of friends who don't take Super Disco Naps:"
        <?php if($excludeList != ''){?>exclude_ids="<?php
 echo $excludeList?>"<?php }?>/>
</fb:request-form>
```

Inviting/requesting a small number of specific friends

Use `fb:multi-friend-input` when your users will have very specific friends in mind (rather than when they want to browse through all of their friends). This is particularly true when your layout doesn't have space for an entire `fb:mutli-friend-selector`, even in condensed mode. See Recipe 6.45 for details. Note that you'll need to include an `fb:request-form-submit` tag if you use `fb:multi-friend-input`, since it won't render its own submit button.

Inviting/requesting a single user

Use `fb:friend-selector` when you need to prompt your users for one friend. This is particularly useful when they're doing something like challenging a friend to a game or sending someone a gift and you only support one-to-one interactions. See Recipe 6.44 for details. Note that you'll need to include an `fb:request-form-submit` tag if you use `fb:friend-selector`, since it won't render its own submit button.

 For information on actually sending Notifications and the like, see Chapter 9.

6.47 Predicting the Future with Type-Ahead Controls

Problem

I love the type-ahead control that Facebook provides in the `fb:friend-selector` (see Recipe 6.44), but I want to use it for things other than friends.

Solution

Use the `fb:typeahead-input` tag, which is currently in beta. The simplest form is:

```
<fb:fbml version="1.1">
<form name="some_form" action="http://apps.facebook.com/myapp/handle.php"
  method="post">
<fb:typeahead-input name="color">
    <fb:typeahead-option value="red">Red</fb:typeahead-option>
    <fb:typeahead-option value="yellow">Yellow</fb:typeahead-option>
    <fb:typeahead-option value="green">Green</fb:typeahead-option>
</fb:typeahead-input>
</form>
</fb:fbml>
```

This tag is supported only in FBML v1.1, so you'll need to make sure to wrap it in the `fb:fbml` tags or you'll get an error about it not being supported in this version.

Discussion

In the example just shown, the *handle.php* page will receive the value of the form as the color parameter. If you don't provide a name for your field, you won't be able to access the value later, so it's probably a good idea.

You can use FBML inside of the `fb:typeahead-options` tag if you'd like to include dynamic information, including names of users:

```
<fb:typeahead-option value="12345"><fb:name
    uid="12345" linked="false" useyou="false" /></fb:typeahead-option>
```

The type-ahead field is particularly useful when combined with an API call to provide users a choice from a long list of Facebook-related content. You could, for example, use the API to pull in a list of all of the groups this user is a member of:

```
<fb:fbml version="1.1">
<form name="some_form" action="http://apps.facebook.com/myapp/handle.php"
 method="post">
    <fb:typeahead-input name="groups">
        <?php
            global $api_key, $secret;

            $facebook = new Facebook($api_key, $secret);
            $user = $facebook->require_login();

            $groups = $facebook->api_client->groups_get(12345);
            foreach($groups as $group){
                echo '<fb:typeahead-option value="' . $group['gid']
. '">'. $group['name'] . '</fb:typeahead-option>';
            }
        ?>
    </fb:typeahead-input>
</form>
</fb:fbml>
```

 As with anything marked beta, remember that this might not work the way you expect it to. If you encounter any behavior that looks like a bug, feel free to report it using the Facebook Bug Tracker (*http://bugs .developers.facebook.com/*).

6.48 Using FBML Inside FBJS

Problem

I have a whole big function working perfectly in FBJS, but now I want to use some FBML as an output inside of it. Putting the FBML into the FBJS directly doesn't work, so how can I get it in there?

Solution

Use the `fb:js-string` tag. The simplest form is:

```
<fb:js-string var="myName">
    <fb:name uid="561415460" linked="false" useyou="false" />
</fb:js-string>
```

Any FBML you put inside the `fb:js-string` tag will become available in the FBJS on your page as the variable named in `var` (in this case, I'd now have a variable in my FBJS called `myName` with the value "Jay Goldman").

Discussion

This tag comes in handy when you want to do things like display a bunch of content or a number of options inside something like a dialog (see Recipe 6.49) using FBJS:

```
<fb:js-string var="iceCreams">
    <p>What's your favorite ice cream flavor?</p>
    <select id="iceCreamSelector">
        <option value="" selected="selected">(Pick a flavor!)</option>
        <option value="chocolate">Chocolate</option>
        <option value="vanilla">Vanilla</option>
        <option value="strawberry">Strawberry</option>
        <option value="moosetracks">Moose Tracks</option>
    </select>
</fb:js-string>

<script type="text/javascript">
<!--
    var myDialog = new Dialog(Dialog.DIALOG_POP);

    myDialog.showChoice('Ice Cream', iceCreams, button_confirm='Mmmm!',
        button_confirm='Ewww!');
-->
</script>
```

That will give you something like Figure 6-51.

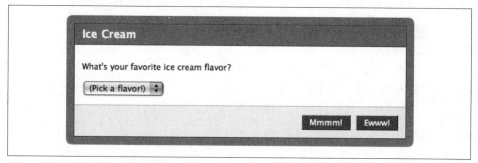

Figure 6-51. FBJS dialog using fb:js-string

 There's an easier way to create this particular example if you don't need to do it from inside FBJS—just use the `fb:dialog` tag. See Recipe 6.49 for more info.

6.49 Dialogs That Pop

Problem

I need to show my users some information in a way that really grabs their attention. I've seen some pop-up dialogs around Facebook that are like overlays (rather than JavaScript alerts) and I really dig 'em. Especially the semi-transparent smoky edges!

Solution

Another great example of FBML making something complicated really simple. Use the `fb:dialog` tag to show a simple pop up with some content:

```
<fb:dialog id="ice_cream">
    <fb:dialog-title>I Scream! You Scream! We All Scream!</fb:dialog-title>
    <fb:dialog-content>For Ice Cream!</fb:dialog-content>
    <fb:dialog-button type="button" value="Yay!" />
</fb:dialog>

<input type="button" value="Click me!" clicktoshowdialog="ice_cream" />
```

which will give you Figure 6-52.

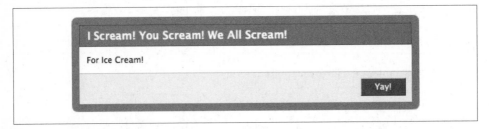

Figure 6-52. Simple fb:dialog

Notice the very important `clicktoshowdialog` attribute on the button, which tells Facebook to trigger the dialog when the button gets clicked.

Discussion

The `clicktoshowdialog` attribute can be applied to things that typically aren't clickable, such as `div`s:

```
<div id="my_dialog_trigger" clicktoshowdialog="my_dialog">Click Me!</div>
```

The `fb:dialog-content` tag can contain entire forms if you want to do something more than just display info to your users. For example, the following:

```
<fb:dialog id="ice_cream" cancel_button="true">
    <fb:dialog-title>I Scream! You Scream! We All Scream!</fb:dialog-title>
    <fb:dialog-content>
        <form id="ice_cream_flavors" action="http://www.someserver.com">
            <p>What's your favorite flavor?</p>
```

```
            <select name="flavors">
                <option>Chocolate</option>
                <option>Vanilla</option>
                <option>Rocky Road</option>
                <option>Moose Tracks</option>
            </select>
        </form>
    </fb:dialog-content>
    <fb:dialog-button type="submit" value="For Ice Cream!"
 form_id="ice_cream_flavors" />
    </fb:dialog>
```

will give you Figure 6-53.

Figure 6-53. fb:dialog-content with a form

 You can take advantage of Facebook's Mock Ajax to do form submission and return from inside of your `fb:dialog`. See Recipe 6.51 for more information.

The `fb:dialog-title` tag needs no further explanation, other than to note that you can format the content with HTML tags such as **strong** and em, and by applying CSS:

```
<fb:dialog-title>
    <strong>I Scream!</strong>
    <em>You Scream!</em>
    <span style="text-decoration:underline;">We All Scream!</span>
</fb:dialog-title>
```

The `fb:dialog-button` tag, on the other hand, does need some explanation because it has a few optional parameters, listed in Table 6-20.

Table 6-20. Parameters for fb:dialog-button

Name	Type	Default value	Description
type	string	N/A	The type of button to render. Can be either button for a generic button or submit for a form submitter (make sure to include a form_id for a submit button). This is required.

Name	Type	Default value	Description
value	string	N/A	The text to put on the button. This is required.
close_dialog	bool	false	Specifying true will close the dialog when this button is clicked.
href	string	N/A	The URL to take users to when they click on the button. Can be external to Facebook.
form_id	string	N/A	If this button submits a form, you need to specify the form's id here (e.g., <form id="some_id">).
clickrewriteurl	string	N/A	If you're using Mock Ajax with this dialog, you need to specify the URL from which Facebook will retrieve your response. See Recipe 6.51.
clickrewriteid	string	N/A	If you're using Mock Ajax with this dialog, you need to specify the id of the element that will be replaced with the response when it comes back (typically the id of the fb:dialog this button is in so that the whole dialog gets replaced, but it could be a div within it). See Recipe 6.51.
clickrewriteform	string	N/A	If you're using Mock Ajax with this dialog, you need to specify the id of the form whose values this button will submit to the URL specified in clickrewriteurl. See Recipe 6.51.

6.50 Dialogs in Context

Problem

Sometimes I want a dialog, but I don't really want it to pop up over everything else. Can I attach it to something on my Canvas page?

Solution and Discussion

The fb:dialog FBML tag won't give you the power you want, but you can definitely do this with FBJS. See Recipe 7.14.

6.51 Dialogs with Ajax

Problem

I have an fb:dialog with a form in it, which I'd like to submit to my server and have the result displayed back in my fb:dialog.

Solution

Facebook's Mock Ajax is perfect for this kind of application, taking a lot of the pain out of doing things such as dynamic form submission without having to reload the page. The setup is pretty simple, requiring an fb:dialog, a trigger control, and a response page. Let's start with the fb:dialog, which can be defined anywhere in your

FBML (or in an included file if you're going to use it in a few places throughout your app):

```
<fb:dialog id="ice_cream" cancel_button="true">
    <fb:dialog-title>I Scream! You Scream! We All Scream!</fb:dialog-title>
    <fb:dialog-content>
        <form id="ice_cream_flavors">
            <p>What's your favorite flavor?</p>
            <select name="flavors">
                <option>(Please choose a flavor!)</option>
                <option value="chocolate">Chocolate</option>
                <option value="vanilla">Vanilla</option>
                <option value="rockyroad">Rocky Road</option>
                <option value="moosetracks">Moose Tracks</option>
            </select>
        </form>
        <div id="ice_cream_image"></div>
    </fb:dialog-content>
    <fb:dialog-button
        type="submit"
        value="For Ice Cream!"
        clickrewriteurl="http://www.someserver.com/ice_cream_maker.php"
        clickrewriteid="ice_cream_image"
        clickrewriteform="ice_cream_flavors"/>
</fb:dialog>
```

 Some of you out there in reader land are inevitably going to read this example and say, "Moose Tracks!? He's just making this stuff up." I pity you. Go out to your nearest vendor of frozen treats and demand a big waffle cone of Denali Original Moose Tracks® and eat the whole thing before you read one more sentence. You can find a store here: *http://www.moosetracks.com/page/locator*. Go now! We'll wait for you. (But bring me one back, m'kay?)

Now we'll need a trigger for the dialog so that it knows when to open. As covered in Recipe 6.49, you can use pretty much anything as a trigger provided you specify a `clicktoshowdialog` property on it. In this case, I've used Flickr's awesome Creative Commons search to find a photo of some tasty ice cream ("Trio of Summer Fruit Ice Cream" by jessicafm) that we'll use as a button:

```
<img src="http://farm2.static.flickr.com/1339/855848513_515a9f66ba_m.jpg"
    alt="Trio of Summer Fruit Ice Creams by jessicafm"
    clicktoshowdialog="ice_cream"/>
<p>Photo credit: jessicafm, http://flickr.com/photos/jessicafm/855848513/</p>
```

So far, we have a button on our page, shown in Figure 6-54.

Photo credit: jessicafm, http://flickr.com/photos/jessicafm/855848513/

Figure 6-54. Dialog trigger

Clicking on our button gives us our dialog overlaid on our Canvas, as shown in Figure 6-55.

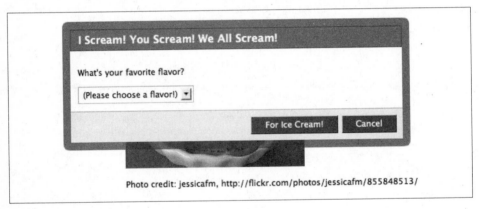

Photo credit: jessicafm, http://flickr.com/photos/jessicafm/855848513/

Figure 6-55. Dialog triggered

Now we need to put our response page in place so that clicking the "For Ice Cream!" button will go fetch the resulting FBML and display it. You need to use a URL for `clickrewriteurl` that isn't on Facebook (but can be on the server that hosts your app), so instead of something like *http://apps.facebook.com/myapp/ice_cream_maker.php*, go straight to the source at *http://www.myhostingserver.com/ice_cream_maker.php*. Normally, you would build some slick server-side processing here that would take the person's favorite flavor and perform some deep business analysis using data warehouse cubes to calculate an executive dashboard charting flavor versus education level versus bed linen thread count. We're just going to return a photo of the ice cream flavor they asked for. The most important thing to remember about what you return is that it needs to be wrapped in FBML tags:

```php
<?php
$flickr = 'http://farm2.static.flickr.com/1339/855848513_515a9f66ba_m.jpg';
$credit = 'jessicafm';

switch($_POST['flavors']){
    case 'chocolate':
        $flickr = 'http://farm2.static.flickr.com/1036/1072040703_6f657ebdbe_m.jpg';
        $credit = 'Zesmerelda';
        break;
    case 'vanilla':
        $flickr = 'http://farm2.static.flickr.com/1126/932883287_821c96d904_m.jpg';
        $credit = 'skye820';
        break;
    case 'rockyroad':
        $flickr = 'http://farm2.static.flickr.com/1132/734813872_63e3105b62_m.jpg';
        $credit = 'jessicafm';
        break;
    case 'moosetracks':
        $flickr = 'http://farm2.static.flickr.com/1401/1064233083_18445730bb_m.jpg';
        $credit = 'lucianvenutian';
        break;
}

echo '<fb:fbml version="1.0"><img src="' . $flickr
. '" /><p>Photo credit: ' . $credit . '</p></fb:fbml>';
?>
```

OK! That should just about do it. Now when you click the "For Ice Cream!" button, you see one of the Flickr photos below the drop-down, as shown in Figure 6-56.

Finding CC Photos on Flickr

The Flickr Advanced Search is a great resource to find Creative Commons–licensed photos for just about anything. You can find the search at *http://flickr.com/search/advanced/*, and you'll want to scroll down to the bottom and turn on at least the "Only search within Creative Commons (CC) licensed content" and "Find content to use commercially" options. If you plan to modify the content (like putting text over the image or manipulating it in any way), add in the "Find content to modify, adapt, or build upon" option as well. The CC license terms for each photo can be found in the righthand sidebar when you're on the photos page, and you'll see that some don't even require attribution (though I always give it if I can). If the search isn't finding what you need, try the actual CC search at *http://search.creativecommons.org/*. And remember, kids: you should license your photos under a CC license so that other people can benefit from them, too.

Figure 6-56. Dialog with Ajax result

Since this is an Ajax-based form, changing the drop-down and clicking the "For Ice Cream!" button again will just load a different image in place of the first one (though I have no idea why anyone would stray from the path of Extreme Moose Tracks).

Some of you may be using slower servers and may have seen a delay between clicking the button and getting your ice cream, thereby ruining the whole instant-gratification angle. It's generally considered good practice to implement a loading indicator to show that something is happening, but unfortunately Mock Ajax doesn't have any built-in methods for doing so. Thanks to the contributors to the Facebook Developers Wiki, we have a handy way to do this (see *http://wiki.developers.facebook.com/index.php/Mock_ajax*). The first thing you'll need is some type of spinner animation, which you can build for yourself at the excellent *http://www.ajaxload.info*. Once you have your image and have it saved to your server, update the FBML just shown to include the spinner in the `div` for `ice_cream_image` and set it to be hidden by default:

```
<div id="ice_cream_image">
    <img id="spinner" src="http://www.someserver.com/spinner.gif"
 alt="Loading" style="display: none";/>
</div>
```

Now update the FBML on the `fb:dialog-button` so that it shows the spinner when clicked:

```
<fb:dialog-button
    type="submit"
    value="For Ice Cream!"
```

```
clickrewriteurl="http://facebook.cheshoax.com/cookbook/ice_cream_maker.php"
clickrewriteid="ice_cream_image"
clickrewriteform="ice_cream_flavors"
clicktoshow="spinner"/>
```

As long as the `id` specified on the image matches the `id` specified in the `clicktoshow` parameter for the button, your image should appear as soon as you submit the form. This method is effective because Facebook automatically overwrites the inner HTML of the element you specify in `clickrewriteid`, thereby overwriting the spinner when the response comes back from your server. If you want to be really sure to display one, add it in to the final `echo` in the PHP code just shown so that a new spinner image gets returned with the response and is ready for the next time the button is clicked:

```
echo '<fb:fbml version="1.0"><img src="' . $flickr .
'" /><p>Photo credit: ' . $credit . '</p><img src=
"http://www.someserver.com/spinner.gif" id="spinner" style="display:non
e;"/>';
```

The one downside to this method is that it will leave your spinner control visible on the page if your Ajax call fails, since Mock Ajax doesn't provide any kind of callback capability on failure.

6.52 Facebook Share Buttons

Problem

I'd like to include a Facebook Share button in my app to encourage my users to share items on their Profile or to send them to friends.

Solution

Use the `fb:share-button` tag. The simplest form is:

```
<fb:share-button class="url" href="http://apps.facebook.com/myapp/somePage.php" />
```

That will give you the standard Share button, shown in Figure 6-57.

Figure 6-57. Facebook Share button

Clicking on the button shows the Share dialog, with a choice between sending a message or posting to your Profile, as shown in Figure 6-58.

Figure 6-58. Share dialog

If your URL includes content and images, your users will have the option of selecting what they would like to include in the message or post.

Discussion

There are two modes (or "classes") for the Share button: URL and meta. The URL class is easier and can be either an on- or off-Facebook URL, as seen earlier in this recipe. Meta class requires a little more effort on your behalf, but it also gives you more control over what appears in the Share dialog and in the message or Profile post. As an example, let's say that you wanted to include a Facebook Share button to this great video of my friend Leo Laporte interviewing my friend Kris Krug (of Raincity Studios) on the *Lab with Leo* show, talking about this shiny new social network called Facebook (which some of you may have heard of). The video can be found on YouTube at *http://www .youtube.com/watch?v=2IIHFEvpszU*, which we can use to define a meta-based `fb:share-button` tag:

```
<fb:share-button class="meta">
    <meta name="medium" content="video"/>
    <meta name="title" content="Facebook Applications Platform (f8) Overview"/>
    <meta name="video_type" content="application/x-shockwave-flash"/>
    <meta name="video_height" content="355"/>
```

```
<meta name="video_width" content="425"/>
<meta name="description" content="Kris Krug talks with Leo about
Facebook's new platform for Applications."/>
    <link rel="image_src" href="http://img.youtube.com/vi/2IIHFEvpszU/2.jpg" />
    <link rel="video_src" href="http://www.youtube.com/watch?v=2IIHFEvpszU"/>
    <link rel="target_url" href="http://www.youtube.com/watch?v=2IIHFEvpszU"/>
</fb:share-button>
```

Now that we've told Facebook where to find a bunch of the useful meta information about the video (hence the "meta" class), our Share dialog gets a lot smarter (Figure 6-59).

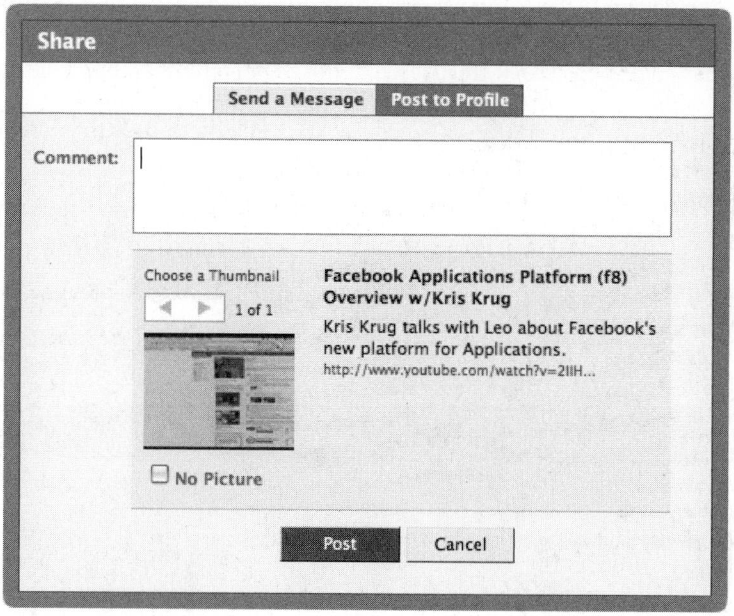

Figure 6-59. Share dialog using the meta class

The `fb:share-button` tag supports `audio`, `image`, `video`, `news`, `blog`, and `mult` mediums, and it has a whole bunch of different types of information you can send into it. The full documentation can be found at *http://www.facebook.com/share_partners.php*, though make sure you click on the unobvious "How do I make sure the Share Preview works?" link at the bottom to expand the content you're looking for.

6.53 Feed Forms: Publishing Feed Stories from FBML

Problem

I'd like to give my users the ability to publish Mini-Feed stories about themselves or about their friends by completing a form in my app.

Solution

To create a form through which users can publish stories to their own Mini-Feed, include an HTML form with the special fbtype attribute to signify that Facebook should use it as a Feed Form:

```
<form fbtype="feedStory" action="http://someserver.com/feed_handler.php">
    <input type="text" name="status" />
    <input type="hidden" name="template_id" value="12345678901" />
    <input type="submit" label="Publish" />
</form>
```

You can include any fields, content, and controls you'd like in the form. On submit, Facebook will send the form to the URL specified in the action, and will then take your JSON-formatted response back and use it to render a preview of a story. For the example just shown, your server-side *feed_handler.php* page could be as simple as:

```
{"method":"feedStory", "content":{
    "next":"http://apps.facebook.com/myapp/somepage",
    "feed":{
        "template_id":"<?php echo $_POST['template_id']?>",
        "template_data":{"status":"<?php echo $_POST['status']?>"}}}}
```

Depending on what template 12345678901 contained, the story preview for this example might look like Figure 6-60.

Figure 6-60. Feed Form preview

Discussion

We aren't, of course, setting the status in the previous example, though we could quite easily, as the next field in the JSON response tells Facebook where to send the user after he closes the preview box. By making that a page in your app that sets the status, you could make this example fully functional.

In addition to the feedStory outlined earlier, you can also create a multiFeedStory to give users the ability to publish into their friend's Mini-Feeds as well. The principle is exactly the same as feedStory, but you need to include one of fb:multi-friend-selector, fb:multi-friend-input, or fb:friend-selector:

```
<form fbtype="multiFeedStory" action="http://facebook.cheshoax
.com/superdisconapping/feed_handler.php">
    Take a nap with: <fb:multi-friend-input>  </fb:multi-friend-input>
    <input type="hidden" name="template_id" value="12345678901" />
    <input type="submit" label="Zzzzz!" />
</form>
```

You'll also need to modify your server-side handler so that it lists `mutliFeedStory` as the method:

```
{"method":"multiFeedStory", "content":{
    "next":"http://apps.facebook.com/superdisconapping/",
    "feed":{
        "template_id":"<?php echo $_POST['template_id']?>",
        "template_data":{}}}}
```

In this particular example, assuming a template like this:

```
{*actor*} took a nap with {*target*}.
```

we have no additional fields, so our `template_data` return is empty. Facebook will automatically provide the {*actor*} token based on the user who is publishing the story and the {*target*} token from the friends they selected.

6.54 Redirecting to a Different URL

Problem

I'd like to redirect users to a different URL from one of my Canvas pages.

Solution

Use the `fb:redirect` tag. The simplest (and only) form is:

```
<fb:redirect url="http://jaygoldman.com" />
```

Discussion

This tag will only work on a Canvas page, so you can't use it in a Profile. It's a bit of an awkward tag, since it will immediately redirect to a new URL when someone hits it, which means you'll need to wrap it in some page logic if you don't want the page it's on to just send them on their way. You might, for example, use it inside a tag such as `fb:if-is-group-member`:

```
<fb:if-is-group-member gid="12345" uid="12345">
    Private content goes here
    <fb:else>
        <fb:redirect url="http://apps.facebook.com/myapp/safe-page"/>.
    </fb:else>
</fb:if-is-group-member>
```

6.55 Painless Image Submitting

Problem

I've spent hours making beautiful image buttons that I want to use to submit forms, but I can't get them to work. Help!

Solution

Help is on the way. Use the `fb:submit` tag to wrap your images:

```
<form method="post" action="http://someserver.com/somePage.php">
    <fb:submit><img src="http://someserver.com/images/button.jpg"></fb:submit>
</form>
```

Discussion

Image buttons are all well and good, but make sure that they actually look clickable, or people are going to have a whole lot of nasty things to say about your app when they can't make it work.

6.56 Hunting for Robots: CAPTCHA in Your App

Problem

I'm worried that people will use scripts to hack their way into my app! How can I verify that my users are real people?

Solution

Use the `fb:captcha` tag to display a CAPTCHA (Completely Automated Public Turing test to tell Computers and Humans Apart) on your page. The simplest form is:

```
<form method="post" action="http://someserver.com/somePage.php">
    <fb:captcha />
</form>
```

which will give you something like Figure 6-61.

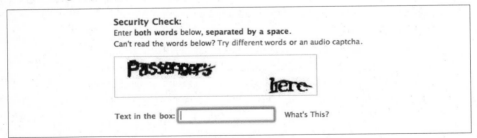

Figure 6-61. Facebook CAPTCHA

Discussion

CAPTCHAs were originally created in 2000 by Luis von Ahn, Manuel Blum, Nicholas J. Hopper (all of Carnegie Mellon University), and John Langford (then of IBM). The general idea is to present users with a distorted image of a word, which computers would find very difficult to decipher but which people should be able to read quite easily. Early CAPTCHAs were quickly defeated by sophisticated algorithms, but more modern ones have surpassed all but the most dedicated of hackers (or hackers smart enough to outsource the work of cracking them to people in places such as Russia, who are reputedly paid $3/hr to interpret image after image). The acronym is an extension of the concept of a Turing test, first proposed by Alan Turing and postulated as the ultimate test for artificial intelligence: the ability to convincingly pass as human (i.e., to demonstrate intelligence). This is almost a reverse Turing test in that it's really designed to separate the people from the machines rather than to unite us all under the Skynet banner.

When a form containing a correct CAPTCHA is submitted, you'll find an extra POST parameter called `fb_sig_captcha_grade`, which will be set to 1. The parameter doesn't show up when the CAPTCHA is false, so make sure you're checking for it to exist rather than for it to be `true` or `false`.

The Facebook CAPTCHA is smart enough not to display itself to verified users by default (i.e., users who have logged into their account and already proven to Facebook that they're human), but you can force them to by adding the `showalways` parameter:

```
<fb:captcha showalways="true" />
```

I wouldn't suggest adding these on every page of your app—they get annoying pretty quickly—but if you're doing anything that people might want to automate (entering contests, signing up for free stuff, etc.), you're entirely justified in sticking one in your form.

 Facebook's CAPTCHAS are actually provided by a really interesting service called reCAPTCHA, which is a Carnegie Mellon project. According to their website, people around the world solve over 60 million CAPTCHAs a day, which at about 10 seconds each adds up to over 150,000 hours of lost time. They realized that human processing time could be used for something valuable, and so their CAPTCHA images are actually text that various book digitizing projects have identified as being impossible for Optical Character Recognition (OCR) software to understand. Every time you solve a reCAPTCHA, you're helping a project to digitize two more words from our collected knowledge and history. For more information (including details about implementing reCAPTCHA on your own website), see *http://www.repcatcha.net*.

6.57 FBML Caching

Problem

I'd like to take advantage of Facebook's FBML caching to store a block of FBML that I use often.

Solution

Use the `fb:ref` tag. There are two ways to use it, depending on how you've architected your app:

By handle

If you're developing heavily in the Facebook API, this is probably the better method for you. Use the API call `setRefHandle` to initialize your handle:

```
$facebook->api_client->fbml_setRefHandle("MyUniqueAppHandle", "Some FBML Content");
```

Then insert the `fb:ref` tag in your FBML to pull the block out and display it:

```
<fb:ref handle="MyUniqueAppHandle" />
```

Now when you want to update the content, just call `setRefHandle` again with new FBML and it will change everywhere you've put `fb:ref` tags.

By URL

If your app is based more on different files or pages on a server, you can still put FBML into the cache by giving it a unique URL. Create a page that only renders out the block you'd like stored, and then use the alternate form of the `fb:ref` tag:

```
<fb:ref url="http://www.someserver.com/cacheThisPage.php" />
```

When you want to change the content, update your page on your server and then make a simple API call to tell Facebook that it needs to reindex that URL:

```
$facebook->api_client->fbml.refreshRefUrl("http://www.someserver
.com/cacheThisPage.php")
```

Discussion

There are lots of places you might use this—really wherever you have a block of relatively static content you want to display—but the best use is probably for Profile Boxes that aren't user-specific. In that case, you'll want to pick one of the methods discussed earlier and then embed the `fb:ref` tag inside your call to `profile.setFBML` so that the Profiles all contain the `ref`. Once you do that, you can go ahead and update either your handle or your URL, and all of the Profiles will update automatically.

 You can retrieve an `fb:ref` using the `FBML.setRefHandle( )` from the Facebook API. See Recipe 9.21 for more information.

6.58 Analyzing Traffic with Google Analytics

Problem

I want to know more about what users are doing within my application, and I really love using Google Analytics on my off-Facebook site, but dropping its code into my Canvas page didn't work. How can I use it?

Solution

Use the `fb:google-analytics` tag to insert your tracking code for you. The simplest form is:

```
<fb:google-analytics uacct="UA-9999999-99" />
```

where `uacct` is the `_uacct` variable from your Google-provided code block. The FBML parser will render that into:

```
<script src="https://ssl.google-analytics.com/urchin.js" type="text/javascript">
</script>
<script type="text/javascript">
    _uacct = "UA-9999999-99";
    urchinTracker();
</script>
```

Discussion

The first thing to note is that this tag still produces the old-style Analytics code that calls the `urchinTracker( )`, rather than the new-style code:

```
<script type="text/javascript">
var gaJsHost = (("https:" == document.location.protocol) ? "https://ssl."
 : "http://www.");
document.write(unescape("%3Cscript src='" + gaJsHost + "google-analytics.com/
ga.js' type='text/javascript'%3E%3C/script%3E"));
</script>
<script type="text/javascript">
var pageTracker = _gat._getTracker("UA-9999999-99");
pageTracker._initData();
pageTracker._trackPageview();
</script>
```

One of the features of the new code is the automatic detection of HTTP versus HTTPS, which would be wasted inside of Facebook because there are no secure connections to Facebook apps at this time. It also offers you the ability to track specific events that you won't be able to use, so try not to design your tracking and marketing strategies around any of the new features until the tag gets updated. You can read all about the new tracking code on the excellent Analytics Talk blog, maintained by Justin Cutroni: *http://www.epikone.com/blog/2007/10/16/gajs-new-google-analytics-tracking-code/*.

Facebook exposes the `urchinTracker` object to you via FBJS, so you can explicitly record some actions within your app:

```
<a href="http://www.someserver.com" onclick="Facebook.urchin
Tracker('/outgoing/example.com')">
```

Most Analytics users will be happy with this, but if you're the type who likes to really get under the hood and do things with the stuff, you can pass in a wide variety of Urchin Traffic Monitor settings to tweak the performance; see Table 6-21.

Table 6-21. Parameters for fb:google-analytics

Name	Type	Default value	Description
page	string	N/A	The argument given to the `urchinTracker( )` function, either a page or a virtual page.
ufsc	bool	1	Turns the client info flag on (1) or off (0).
udn	string	auto	Domain name for cookies. Can be auto, none, or domain.
uhash	string	on	Turns the unique domain hash for cookies on or off.
utimeout	int	1800	Inactive session timeout in seconds.
ugifpath	string	/__utm.gif	Path to the __utm.gif file.
utsp	string	|	Transaction field separator.
uflash	bool	1	Turns the Flash version detection option on (1) or off (0).
utitle	bool	1	Turns the document title detection option on (1) or off (0).
ulink	bool	0	Turns the linker functionality on (1) or off (0).
uanchor	bool	0	Controls whether the use of anchors for campaigns is on (1) or off (0).
utcp	string	/	Cookie path for tracking.
usample	int	100	Sampling percentage of visitors to track (a whole number from 1 to 100).
uctm	bool	1	Turns the campaign-tracking module on (1) or off (0).
ucto	int	15768000 (6 months)	Timeout in seconds.
uccn	string	utm_campaign	Name of the campaign.
ucmd	string	utm_medium	Campaign medium. Can be one of cpc, cpm, link, email, or organic.
ucsr	string	utm_source	Campaign source.
uctr	string	utm_term	Campaign term or keyword.
ucct	string	utm_content	Campaign content.
ucid	int	utm_id	Campaign ID number.
ucno	string	utm_nooverride	Whether to override the campaign.

6.59 Translations

Problem

I'd like to be able to offer my application in other languages, but I only speak and write English.

Solution

Facebook has made their amazing Translations app available to all developers. When added to your FBML, the following family of tags represents the Translations capability on your pages:

`fb:intl`
> Wrap content you want to make translatable in this tag.

`fb:intl-token`
> Replaces a token contained within an `fb:intl` tag with its content.

`fb:tag`
> Renders an HTML tag that has translatable attributes.

`fb:tag-attribute`
> Contains the translatable attributes of an HTML tag specified by the enclosing `fb:tag` tag.

`fb:tag-body`
> Contains the contents of an HTML tag specified by an enclosing `fb:tag`.

`fb:date`
> Renders a locale-specific date based on the settings of the viewing user.

`fb:fbml-attribute`
> Contains and makes translatable the value of an attribute of an FBML tag.

The Translations app isn't intended to provide translations for user-generated content within your application (which you hopefully have if you've built a good Facebook app), but rather for all of your static text (application description, About Page content, etc.), FBML content, Notifications, requests, and Feed stories.

Using the tags is quite simple and will become second nature as you write new FBML. Assuming you haven't built a gargantuan app with hundreds of pages, you should be able to go back and retrofit the Translations tags fairly quickly. As an example, consider this FBML:

```
Share a Pan Galactic Gargle Blaster with <fb:name uid="12345" useyou="false"/>?
```

You could make it translatable by adding a few tags:

```
<fb:intl desc="Asking whether user wants to share a drink">
    Share a {drink} with <fb:name uid="12345" useyou="false"/>?
        <fb:intl-token name="drink">Pan Galactic Gargle Blaster</fb:intl-token>
</fb:intl>
```

A few things to note about `fb-intl` and its children:

- The `fb:intl` tag that wraps the whole block makes this text translatable.
- The optional `desc` in the `fb:intl` tag provides context to the translators so they understand what they're translating.
- Wrapping part of the text in curly braces—{ and }—turns it into a token that can then be defined using the `fb:intl-token` tag. This is important because it helps translators know what they need to translate and what they don't. In this case, we're assuming that the Pan Galactic Gargle Blaster is truly pan-galactic and therefore doesn't need to be translated.
- Facebook will automatically turn the `fb:name` tag into a second token when presenting this phrase to translators: "Share a {drink} with {name}?"
- You'll need to load the FBML pages containing translation tags once before they appear in the Translations app (i.e., go through your site after adding tags so other people see the phrases).

The other main set of Translations tags have to do with translating HTML tags with attributes and content. Consider the following:

```
<div id="share_drink" class="share_something" title="You've shared 10 drinks.">
    <img src="http://someserver.com" alt="Drink photo" />
    Share a {drink} with <fb:name uid="561415460" useyou="false"/>?
</div>
```

Setting that same block up for translation considerably increases the amount of code but is still far less work than trying to translate it all on your own:

```
<fb:tag name="div">
    <fb:attr name="id">share_drink</fb:attr>
    <fb:attr name="class">share_something</fb:attr>
    <fb:attr name="title">
        <fb:intl desc="Status display">
            You've shared {numDrinks} drinks.
            <fb:intl-token name="numDrinks">10</fb:intl-token>
        </fb:intl>
    </fb:attr>
    <fb:tag-body>
        <fb:intl desc="Asking whether user wants to share a drink">
            Share a {drink} with <fb:name uid="561415460" useyou="false"/>?
            <fb:intl-token name="drink">Pan Galactic Gargle Blaster</fb:intl-token>
        </fb:intl>
    </fb:tag-body>
</fb:tag>
```

A brief explanation:

- The `fb:attr` tag contains an attribute of the enclosing `fb:tag`, in this case the `id`, `class`, and `title` for the `div`.
- `fb:attr` tags can contain `fb:intl` tags in order to make those attributes translatable, as per the `title` shown in the example.

Once you've wrapped your tags and been back through your app, you can keep tabs on translation progress inside the Translations app itself. All of your apps have their own Application Admin Panel, which you'll find at the URL *http://www.new.facebook .com/translations/admin/dashboard.php?app=12345* (where 12345 is your app's ID, not the API key).

Discussion

Translating, localizing, globalizing, and internationalizing might well be considered swear words if you've previously gone through any of those processes. Although the end result is fantastic, the journey to get to a multilingual website or web app is often a torturous, bumpy, and highly repetitive process.

Trust Facebook to save the day! When faced with the enormous task of translating their site into lots and lots of languages, the Facebook team built an extremely clever crowd-sourcing application that lets their members do all of the hard work (a task they took to in droves). For every page on Facebook, members have the ability to translate any string into a different language, which is then voted on by other Translations users. So far, in the French translation of the Facebook site itself, 9,437 translators have submitted 65,887 translations.

The Translations app presents users with a list of phrases that need to be translated, like the page shown in Figure 6-62.

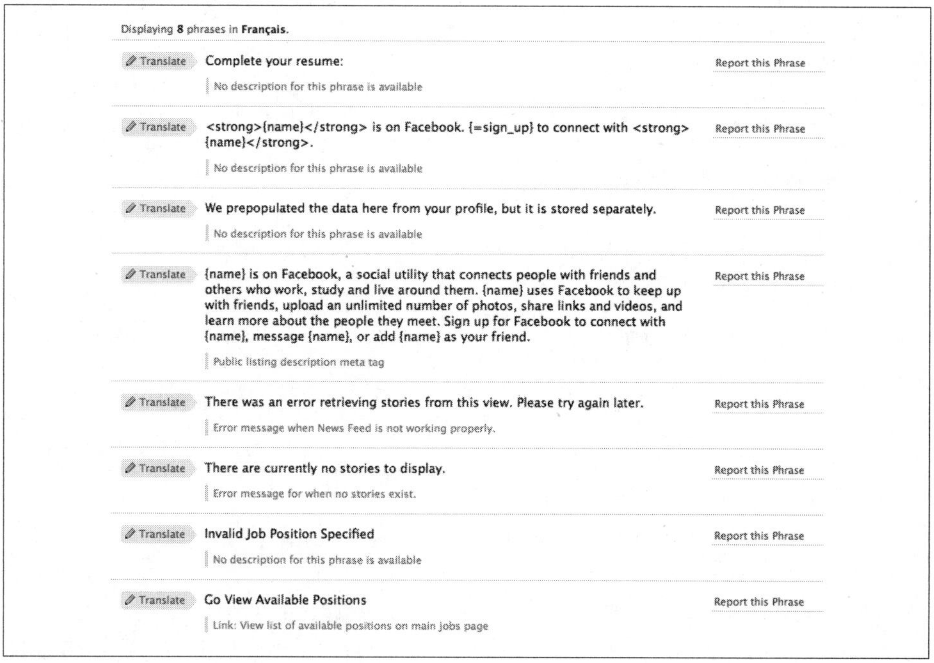

Figure 6-62. Translations list

Clicking on the Translate link next to a phrase opens a contextual dialog to enter your translation, as shown in Figure 6-63.

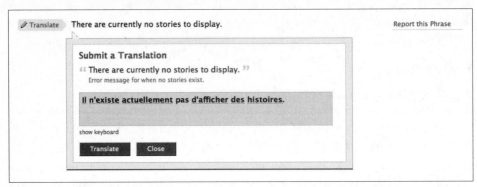

Figure 6-63. Submit a translation (mediocre French translation courtesy of Google Translate)

For incomplete languages, such as Georgian, you can get a sense of how much work is left on the Translations home page (after you've picked it as your language); see Figure 6-64.

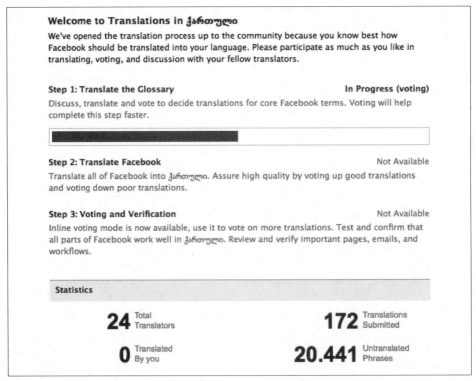

Figure 6-64. Translating Georgian

Voting on translations is actually a lot of fun, and primarily involves voting potential translations up or down, as in Figure 6-65.

Figure 6-65. Voting on translations

The "Discuss this Phrase" link takes you to a discussion board if you're unclear on a translation or want to debate the finer points of a phrase.

Each of your apps has an Application Admin Panel inside of the Translations app, which you can get to by selecting Translations from the app's menu in the Developer app (Figure 6-66).

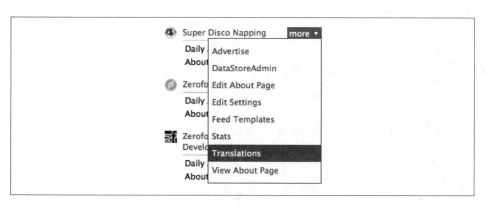

Figure 6-66. Translations in the Developer app's More menu

A newly translatable app will have no phrases complete and will look something like Figure 6-67.

Clicking on a checkbox next to a language enables that language for translation and changes the Publish column from a disabled Not Open to an enabled Publish. Clicking on a language in the Language column shows you the voting and translation interfaces for that language, and clicking on the Manage link in the Language Managers column lets you appoint users to be managers for that language.

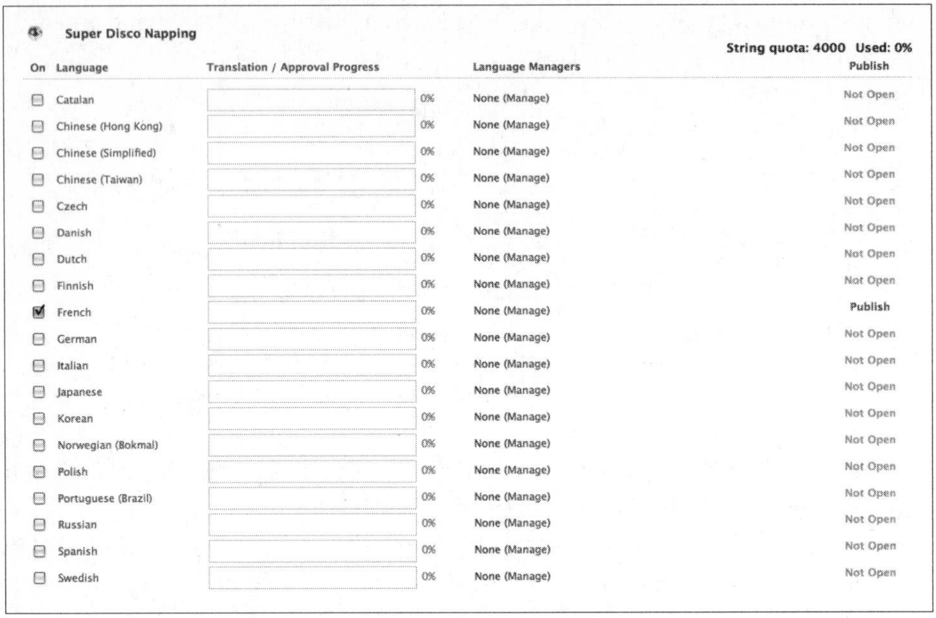

Figure 6-67. *Translations application Admin Panel with French enabled*

Finally, Facebook has published a series of Internationalization Best Practices, which I highly recommend you read as they represent the learnings of a team that has gone through a massive translation effort and lived to tell the tale. Find it at *http://wiki.de velopers.facebook.com/index.php/Platform_Internationalization_Best_Practices*.

6.60 Valid HTML Tags

Problem

FBML sounds great, but sometimes I just want to use good ole HTML. What can I get past the parser?

Solution

There's actually quite a lot of standard HTML you can use inside an FBML page. Keep an eye on the Wiki for an up-to-date list (*http://wiki.developers.facebook.com/index.php/FBML*), but this should give you a good idea:

a	code	h2	legend	script	textarea
abbr	dd	h3	li	select	tfoot
acronym	del	h4	link	small	th
address	dfn	h5	meta	span	thead

b	div	h6	old	strike	tr
bdo	dl	hr	optgroup	strong	tt
big	dt	i	option	style	u
blockquote	em	img	p	sub	ul
br	fieldset	input	pre	sup	var
caption	font	ins	q	table	
center	form	kbd	s	tbody	
cite	h1	label	samp	td	

Discussion

You'll note that head and body aren't included as valid tags, because you shouldn't include them in Canvas pages. This may go against everything you know when it comes to building valid HTML pages, but you'll actually get an error if you include them.

6.61 Facebook and CSS: FBSS?

Problem

I think I'm getting a handle on this FBML thing, but what about CSS? Is there an FBSS?

Solution

Actually, no. You're pretty much free to do whatever you'd like from a CSS perspective, and you can definitely follow best practices, such as linking to external CSS files rather than putting everything inline.

Discussion

You'll likely run into some things that don't work quite the way you expect them to, but for the most part, CSS on Facebook is the same as CSS off Facebook. A few things to look out for:

- CSS files, like images, are cached by Facebook's server, so you need to change the name every time you change the contents of the file; otherwise, the Facebook server will continue to serve up the old version. See Recipe 6.62 for two ways around this.

- Absolute positioning is one of the few things that is a little wonky. In the early days of Platform, it was possible to absolutely position elements from inside your app outside of the Canvas page frame, making them look like they were part of the Facebook interface. Since this posed obvious security issues, the div that contains your application's content (which will have an id like app_content_12345) has the canvas_rel_positioning class applied, which sets it to position: relative. Since absolutely positioned elements inside of a relatively positioned element are positioned within their parents, that resets your top, left, bottom, and right values to being context-sensitive to your Canvas area. The class also sets `overflow: hidden`, which will hide any content you try to position outside of the Canvas. You can test this easily by throwing the following code into a test page inside your app:

```
<style type="text/css">
    div#full{
        background-color: red;
        height: 200px;
        width: 200px;
    }

    div#half{
        background-color: red;
        height: 200px;
        right: -100px;
        position: absolute;
        top: 0px;
        width: 200px;
    }
</style>

<div id="full">This is a full div.</div>
<div id="half">This is half a div (but the other half still exists over here!).</div>
```

You should get most of a Canada flag, as seen in Figure 6-68.

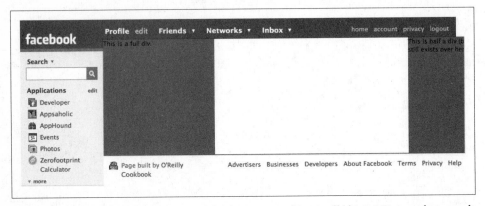

Figure 6-68. Positioning an element outside of the Canvas will cut it off (this is 100 px and one maple leaf short of a Canada flag!)

- You'll need to import CSS files using a `<link>` rather than a `<style>` tag with an `@import` in it. Your CSS files should be stored on your server, and you should use an absolute URL to pull them in:

```
<link href="http://someserver.com/resources/css/screen
.css" rel="stylesheet" type="text/css" media="screen" />
```

6.62 Beating the CSS, JavaScript, and Image Cache

Problem

I keep changing my static files on my server, but they're not reloading in Facebook! How do I get my CSS and JavaScript files and my beautiful images to load?

Solution

Facebook's servers cache your static files when they first serve them up so that your app loads faster for subsequent requests. To get your files to load after you've made a change to them, you'll need to change the file's name so that Facebook notices it's different and grabs the new one. If you're a server admin master and are running Apache (or are super server ninja and are running IIS), skip down to the Discussion. If you're less sure of your server admin powers, keep reading.

All you need to do is change the name of your static files and any references to them when you make a change. This is tedious and will quickly get annoying, but it will work every time and won't require you to mess around under the hood of your web server. If you had a file named *hawt_stylez.css*, you could start with *hawt_stylez_1.css*, then rename it to *hawt_stylez_2.css*, and so on. Make sure that you update the <link> that loads it into your pages as well:

```
<link href="http://someserver.com/resources/css/hawt
_stylez_1.css" rel="stylesheet" type="text/css" media="screen" />
```

If you use that file (and a number of others) on every page of your app, the easiest thing is to make an include file that contains all of your various <link>s, and then include that at the top of each page:

```
<?php require_once 'resources/includes/page_header.php'; ?>
```

Now you can just edit the include file and don't have to worry about tracking down all of the references in other pages.

Discussion

This Discussion is for you if you just read through the Solution and thought of the mind-numbing hours you were going to have to spend renaming files. Thanks to the brilliant minds at Particle Tree (*http://www.particletree.com*, makers of the awesome *http://www.wufoo.com*), this solution will completely remove any need to manually rename files in exchange for about five minutes of server reconfigurations. You'll find the original version on their blog at *http://particletree.com/notebook/automatically-ver sion-your-css-and-javascript-files/*. Note that this was written for developers who are building PHP apps running on Apache with *mod_rewrite* installed, but there's no reason you couldn't adapt this to work in other languages and server environments.

If you're not familiar with *mod_rewrite*, you might find this a little confusing. It's basically a way to run grep on the URLs your server is serving up (if you're not familiar with grep, this may be a little too far outside your comfort range). Brian Moore, quoted in the official documentation for *mod_rewrite*, says, "Despite the tons of examples and docs, *mod_rewrite* is voodoo. Damned cool voodoo, but still voodoo." So consider yourself warned. You'll find the documentation at *http://httpd .apache.org/docs/1.3/mod/mod_rewrite.html*, or you can pick up *Sams Teach Yourself Apache 2 in 24 Hours* by Daniel López Ridruejo and Ian Kallen, which includes some in-depth *mod_rewrite* mojo.

We're going to configure the server so that we can insert version numbers into filenames without it even noticing, and then we're going to use a function to insert filenames into our documents that automatically calculates the version number based on the last time the file changed. This example assumes a file path of *resources/css* and *resources/js* for your CSS and JavaScript files, respectively, as well as a path of *images/* for all images, but feel free to adjust this to suit your personal storage preferences:

1. Assuming your server has *mod_rewrite* already running properly, drop an *.htaccess* file into the root directory of your site (or edit your existing one). This is a plain text file.

2. We're going to add two rules to that file, one for images and one for everything else. These rules tell Apache to treat *hawt_stylez.1.css* as *hawt_stylez.css*, and to do the same for images (JPGs, GIFs, and PNGs) and JavaScript that have a version number after the first period and before the file type extension:

```
RewriteEngine    on
RewriteBase /
RewriteRule ^(.+)/images/(.+)\.(.+)\.(jpg|gif|png)$ $1/images/$2.$4 [L]
RewriteRule ^(.+)/resources/(.+)/(.+)\.(.+)\.(.+)$ $1/resources/$2/$3.$5 [L]
```

3. You could use this technique at this point by updating your filenames wherever they're referred to in your code, without needing to change the actual filenames to match, but that still requires manual labor on your end, and that sucks. The next step is to define a PHP function that will take in a filename and then figure out a timestamp of the last time it was modified and insert that as the version. Create a new PHP file called *autoVer.php*, stick it wherever you keep includes, and drop this function into it (note that you could rewrite this to skip passing in the server if you're always pulling your static content from the same server; just hardcode it into the function). Don't worry about what it does just yet; that's explained later:

```
function autoVer($server,$file){
    $path = pathinfo($file);
    $ver = '.'.filemtime($_SERVER['DOCUMENT_ROOT'].$file).'.';
    echo $server . $path['dirname'].'/'.str_replace('.', $ver, $path['basename']);
}
```

4. You'll need to include your new *autoVer.php* file into all of your other files. If you already have a header you're including, stick it in there. Otherwise, drop this into the top of your other pages:

```php
<?php require_once 'resources/includes/autoVer.php'; ?>
```

5. Last step! Wherever you previously referred to a static file, replace the reference with a call to our new function:

```
<link href="<?php autoVer('http://www.someserver.com',
'resources/css/screen.css'); ?>" rel="stylesheet" type="text/css"
media="screen" />
```

That's all the magic you need. The reference to *screen.css* in this example will automagically become something like *resources/css/screen.1206750843.css*, with the timestamp changing every time you make a change to the CSS file (the PHP `filemtime` function returns the last modification timestamp for a file). Facebook will note the new filename and request that from your server, which will disregard the version number and return your CSS. The last modified timestamp will remain the same until you touch the file again, so Facebook's cache will continue to speed things up until you don't want it to. It's hard to get more elegant than that.

I ran this solution past my good friend Jason DeFillippo (*http://www .jpdefillippo.com*), the mastermind behind some of the best PHP you've ever unknowingly used (including Technorati and *http://jpgmag.com*) and contributor of Recipe 5.4. He really dug it, but added that he would "write an update script that builds a conf file that you can trigger via cron or manual update that includes in the particulars and caches it via *apc* or memcache so it's not doing a `filemtime` every time the script is called. Can be hard on the disk for apps with larger traffic." If that sentence makes any sense to you, you know what to do. For the rest of you, move along. There's nothing to see here.

CHAPTER 7

Facebook JavaScript (FBJS)

JavaScript is not unlike the Force (and duct tape): it has a light side and a dark side, and it holds the universe together. Back in the dark days of JavaScript, before the light of Ajax shone upon the land, it mostly got used for doing things like validating form input on the fly (inevitably making it really hard to complete forms amidst the onslaught of `alert( )` boxes) and putting counters on pages. Now that we are firmly ensconced in the land of Web 2.0, JavaScript is the prodigal son, returned to make every web experience animated, dynamic, and completely incompatible with all assistive technologies. All kidding aside, the ability to build richer and more desktop-like user interfaces (UIs) within browsers, combined with some impressive libraries—such as the Yahoo! User Interface Library (YUI), jQuery, Scriptaculous, Prototype, and Dojo—has breathed new life into the web application space and made it a whole lot more fun to work in.

There's no reason that your Facebook application need be any different.As we saw with FBML in Chapter 6, Facebook has imposed a sandbox on JavaScripts running inside of applications by creating a variant of JavaScript (Facebook JavaScript, or FBJS). It's not a dramatic variation from the actual language, and primarily exists to protect its users from the potentially massive security and privacy holes you could otherwise open. Allowing third-party developers to run scripts within an existing website is a well-known quandary, and most platform providers solve it by forcing developers to run their JavaScripts within an iFrame which loads content from a different server. Since browsers prevent Cross-Site Scripting (XSS), this effectively prevents the script running inside the iFrame from accessing the Document Object Model (DOM) outside of it. Consider the gaping hole that would be opened, for example, with the following script:

```
<script type="text/javascript">
<!--
    function doBadStuff(menu){
        for(var i = 0; i < menu.length; i++){
            if(menu[i].childNodes && menu[i].childNodes.length > 0){
                doBadStuff(menu[i].childNodes);
            }

            var item = menu[i];
```

```
            if(item.tagName == 'A'){
                var pageHref = item.href.split('http://www.facebook.com/');
                item.href = 'https://www.securefacebooklogin.com/' + pageHref[1];
            }
        }
    }

    doBadStuff(document.getElementById('navigator').childNodes);
//-->
</script>
```

If you followed that recursive bit of naughtiness and knew in advance that Facebook's main menu bar has the `id` "navigator", you would understand that all of the links in the navigation had been deviously rewritten to point to the fictional *http://www.secure facebooklogin.com* site. Users going to that site could be presented with an entirely authentic-looking Facebook login page, which would capture their usernames and passwords and then redirect them to their destinations without them ever realizing that their accounts had been compromised. That's obviously a problem, and so if you try to run this code from a Facebook Canvas page, it will fail with an error very similar to "`a12345_document.getElementById("navigator")` has no properties" (which might give you a clue as to how the Sandbox works).

Here are two main areas that FBJS locks down:

The JavaScript namespace
> Any identifiers used in your JavaScript code (function names, variable names, etc.) could collide with names used by Facebook elsewhere on the page, and so your JavaScript will automatically be rewritten to prepend your application ID to all of them (hence the earlier error). For example, the following code block:

```
function foo(bar) {
    var obj = {property: bar};
    return obj.property;
}
```

> would automatically become:

```
function a12345_foo(a12345_bar) {
    var a12345_obj = {property: a12345_bar};
    return a12345_obj.property;
}
```

 I'll be using 12345 as the Facebook application ID throughout this chapter. If you look at your own app, you'll find a different ID in its place.

Accessing and modifying the DOM tree
> Many of the standard function calls and properties remain, but a number of them behave differently (e.g., setting the `innerHTML` property of an object only allows text

and will remove all `childNodes` of the element it's called on) or don't work at all (e.g., you can't access the `document.form` property directly). There are a number of very useful functions for setting and manipulating the style of objects, as well as handling events, working with Ajax, and displaying dialog boxes.

This chapter focuses on the most common FBJS-related objects you'll want to complete, but it's worth noting that the full scope of using JavaScript in Facebook applications could fill a few books on its own. We cover the basics in the rest of this chapter, including some handy recipes for stuff you'll want to do frequently.

 If your JavaScript skills are a little rusty and you want to brush up before jumping into FBJS, check out David Flanagan's *JavaScript: The Definitive Guide* or Shelley Powers's *Learning JavaScript*, both from O'Reilly.

7.1 Dealing with Sandbox Renaming

Problem

The Facebook Sandbox keeps renaming my objects and functions.

Solution

Don't sweat it! That's what the Sandbox is there for. The good news is that it should be renaming them consistently throughout your application (in your HTML and in your JavaScript), so that your DOM manipulation still works properly.

Discussion

As mentioned in the introduction to this chapter, the Sandbox is really there to protect Facebook's users from the nasty things you might (advertently or inadvertently) do to them. Let's say, for example, that you gave a `div` in your HTML the very common `id` of `content`. That would clash with the `id` of the Canvas area of the Facebook page, which is a problem because no two HTML elements on the same page can share the same `id`. Ever spent time around one or more people who share your name? It gets confusing pretty quickly, especially when someone is trying to manipulate your style object. This isn't as big of a deal when you're applying CSS based on `id` (e.g.,`#content{font-weight: bold;}` would just be applied to both), but it is when you try to grab one of them through JavaScript (e.g., what gets returned by `document.getElementById('content')`?).

The solution is the same for JavaScript as it is for HTML. As we saw in Chapter 6 for FBML, the FBJS Sandbox rewrites your code to prepend your application ID to things such as object, function, and variable names. Let's take a look at a quick example that should allay your fears.

If your carefully constructed Canvas page contained this HTML and JavaScript:

```
<script type="text/javascript">
<!--
    function checkIt(){
        var title = 'Are you sure?!';
        var content = 'You really want to change it? The world could end!';
        var confirm = 'Yup!';
        var cancel = 'Oh geez!';
        var doIt = new Dialog();
        doIt.onconfirm = changeIt;
        doIt.showChoice(title, content, confirm, cancel);
    }

    function changeIt(){
        var it = document.getElementById('it');
        it.setStyle('background', 'red');
    }
//-->
</script>

<div id="it" style="background: blue;">This is it!</div>

<input type="button" value="Click me!" onclick="checkIt();" />
```

Facebook would rewrite it to something like:

```
<div id="app12345_it" style="background: blue none repeat
  scroll 0% 0%;" fbcontext="f5b362fe8409">This is it!</div>

<input type="button" value="Click me!" onclick="a12345_checkIt();"/>

<script type="text/javascript">
    function a12345_checkIt(){
        var a12345_title = 'Are you sure?!';
        var a12345_content = 'You really want to change it? The world could end!';
        var a12345_confirm = 'Yup!';
        var a12345_cancel = 'Oh geez!';
        var a12345_doIt = new a12345_Dialog();
        a12345_doIt.onconfirm = a12345_changeIt;
        a12345_doIt.showChoice(a12345_title, a12345_content, a12345_confirm,
            a12345_cancel);
    }

    function a12345_changeIt(){
        var a12345_it = a12345_document.getElementById('it');
        a12345_it.setStyle('background', 'red');
    }
</script>
```

Here are a few important things to note:

- The id of the div changed from it to app12345_it, as we saw in Chapter 6.

- The name of the function changed from `checkIt` to `a12345_checkIt`. Sandbox renaming for JavaScript prepends `a###` instead of the `app###` used in FBML. All of the variables within the function were likewise renamed.

- The call to set the `onconfirm` handler for the `doIt Dialog` was automatically changed from `changeIt` to `a12345_changeIt` to match the new function name.

- Finally, even though the `div` itself has been renamed `app12345_it`, the call to `a12345_document.getElementById` still refers to it as plain old `it`. Since this is no longer a call to `document.getElementById` but has instead been contextualized to your app's sandbox, you're now making a call to a prototype function defined in `fbml.js` (look for `fbjs_main.prototype.getElementById` near line 72). The new version of the old standby basically translates between the Sandbox and the DOM, prepending your app's ID to a standard `getElementById` call and then passing the resulting object back to you. There are a number of standard JavaScript objects that get similarly remapped, so don't worry if you see things like `Math` getting renamed to `a12345_Math`. Here's the full list:

—`Ajax` (Facebook-specific)

—`console`

—`Date`

—`Dialog` (Facebook-specific)

—`document`

—`escape`

—`Facebook` (Facebook specific)

—`Math`

—`RegExp`

—`setInterval`

—`setTimeout`

—`String`

—`undefined`

—`unescape`

The end result should be that you don't even need to think about this, but sometimes bad things happen to good code. As we'll see in Recipe 7.15 later in this chapter, very complicated and fragile code constructions might break given the translation into FBJS, particularly if Facebook makes any changes to the way Platform interprets code. If you remember the primary rule of all programming—Keep It Simple, Stupid (KISS)—you should be fine.

7.2 Losing Your < >s

Problem

The angle brackets (< and >) keep disappearing from my rendered FBJS code.

Solution

Facebook suggests wrapping code within `<script>` tags in standard HTML comments to prevent the FBJS parser from removing < and > characters (or turning them into their equivalent < and > HTML entities):

```
<script type="text/javascript">
<!-
    function someFunction(){
        // Do stuff!
    }
//-->
</script>
```

This will likely change at some point as the FBJS parser matures, so you may not find it necessary, but YMMV (Your Mileage May Vary).

Discussion

This was standard practice for a long time to support older browsers that didn't handle `<script>` tags properly. Then again, we also used to build websites that degraded gracefully when people didn't have JavaScript enabled in their browsers (or were using browsers that—heaven forbid—didn't even support it). If you take a look at the source of one of your app's rendered pages, you'll find that a lot of the Facebook JavaScript that gets added to your app isn't escaped, so this recipe will likely be out-of-date pretty quickly (you'll also notice that the FBJS parser removes them when it renders your final JavaScript). That said, it certainly doesn't hurt to have the comment tags in there, so you might as well add them.

7.3 Retrieving DOM Elements

Problem

I need to retrieve a DOM element from my page.

Solution

Use the old standby `document.getElementById( )`:

```
var someElement = document.getElementById('aDiv');
```

Discussion

Document is one of the standard JavaScript objects that gets mapped from the renamed Sandbox format to the actual object in fbml.js (see Recipe 7.1 for more information), so there's no need to worry about it breaking in your code.

 Make sure you haven't named any of the elements in your page with the same ids. Not only is that part of the HTML and XHTML specs, but it's also just good practice. If you don't follow it, document.getElementById( ) will get confused and not know which one to return. This is just as true on Facebook as it is off.

7.4 Manipulating DOM Elements

Problem

I want to dynamically add DOM elements to my page.

Solution

You can use most of the JavaScript calls that work outside of Facebook to make programmatic changes to the DOM:

```
function addNewDiv(){
    var parentDiv = document.getElementById('parentDiv');

    // Appending a child
    var firstDiv = document.createElement('div');
    firstDiv.setId('appendedChild');
    firstDiv.setStyle('color', 'black');
    firstDiv.setTextValue('This div rocks!');
    parentDiv.appendChild(firstDiv);

    // Insert before
    var secondDiv = document.createElement('div');
    secondDiv.setStyle('color', 'red');
    secondDiv.setTextValue('This div rocks more!');
    parentDiv.insertBefore(secondDiv, firstDiv);

    // Remove the first div
    parentDiv.removeChild(firstDiv);

    // Clone the second node
    var thirdDiv = secondDiv.cloneNode();
    thirdDiv.setStyle('color', 'blue');
    thirdDiv.setTextValue('This is the third div to be created.');
    parentDiv.appendChild(thirdDiv);
}
```

Assuming you have a `div` in your HTML with the `id parentDiv` when you run the script, the end result will have it contain the text:

This div rocks more!
This is the third div to be created.

(with the text in the appropriate colors), along with anything else it might have contained already.

Although `appendChild( )`, `insertBefore( )`, `removeChild( )`, and `cloneNode( )` all work the same way they do off-Facebook, you'll run into problems with many of the other JavaScript object manipulation functions. Most of the ones you've come to know and love are available, but they've been changed to getters and setters instead of direct functions. Table 7-1 shows the mappings.

Table 7-1. JavaScript DOM manipulation function mappings

JS function	FBJS getter	FBJS setter	Description
accessKey	getAccessKey	setAccessKey	
checked	getChecked	setChecked	
childNodes	getChildNodes	N/A	Returns an array of childNodes.
className	getClassName	setClassName	See rest of recipe for more info.
clientHeight	getClientHeight	N/A	
clientWidth	getClientWidth	N/A	
cols	getCols	setCols	
dir	getDir	setDir	
disabled	getDisabled	setDisabled	
firstChild	getFirstChild	N/A	
form	n/a	N/A	No direct access to forms. Use document.getElement ById('formid') instead. (You gave your form an ID, right?)
N/A	getRootElement	N/A	Equivalent to docu ment.rootElement. Returns the top-level element of a Canvas page or Profile Box.
N/A	getAbsoluteTop	N/A	Returns the element's absolute position relative to the top of the page. Use this instead of offsetParent.
N/A	getAbsoluteLeft	N/A	Same as getAbsoluteTop, but horizontal-wise.
href	getHref	setHref	
id	getId	setId	

JS function	FBJS getter	FBJS setter	Description
innerHTML	N/A	setInnerFBML	Can throw an error if you try to put the FBML in as a string. Create an `<fb:js-string>` in your code first, and then pass the variable name instead.
innerText/ textContent	N/A	setTextValue	Only allows text: no HTML or FBML. Removes all `childNodes` of the element it is called on.
lastChild	getLastChild	N/A	
location	N/A	setLocation	
name	getName	setName	
nextSibling	getNextSibling	N/A	
OffsetHeight	getOffsetHeight	N/A	
offsetWidth	getOffsetWidth	N/A	
parentNode	getParentNode	N/A	
previousSibling	getPreviousSibling	N/A	
readOnly	getReadOnly	setReadOnly	
rows	getRows	setRows	
scrollHeight	getScrollHeight	N/A	
scrollLeft	getScrollLeft	setScrollLeft	
scrollTop	getScrollTop	setScrollTop	
scrollWidth	getScrollWidth	N/A	
selected	getSelected	setSelected	
selectedIndex	getSelectedIndex	setSelectedIndex	
src	getSrc	setSrc	
style	N/A	setStyle	
tabIndex	getTabIndex	setTabIndex	
tagName	getTagName	N/A	
title	getTitle	setTitle	
type	getType	setType	
value	getValue	setValue	

7.5 Manipulating CSS Styles

Problem

I want to make things pretty programmatically.

Solution

Facebook Platform provides a very handy `setStyle()` method that does exactly what it sounds like it should. The very simplest form lets you set one style attribute at a time:

```
obj.setStyle('color', 'green');
```

Basically, pass in an attribute name (e.g., `color`) and a value (e.g., `black`). You can also set multiple attributes at the same time:

```
obj.setStyle({color: 'green', background: 'white'});
```

Discussion

`setStyle()` is one of the most useful shortcuts provided by Facebook Platform. If you master it (and the bar is not exactly high on that task), you'll find dynamic styling a lot like a big slice of tasty chocolate cake. There are only a couple of things you need to look out for:

- Be aware that names usually including a hyphen (e.g., `text-decoration`) need to be spelled out using so-called camel case (i.e., drop the hyphen and capitalize the first letter of the next word):

  ```
  obj.setStyle('lineHeight', '120%');
  ```

- If you're working with an attribute that's measured in a given unit, note that you have to include the unit in the value:

  ```
  obj.setStyle('top', '20px');
  obj.setStyle('fontSize', '9em');
  ```

- Be careful with that last one when you're calculating the value in JavaScript, because it means you need to tack the unit onto the calculated number:

  ```
  var newWidth = (someValue + someOtherValue) / somethingElse;
  obj.setStyle('width', newWidth + 'px');
  ```

- Note that there is no getter method to complement `setStyle()`, so you can't get back an array of style information.

7.6 Manipulating CSS Class Names

Problem

I've done a great job of setting up my CSS so that I can make things pretty in a very modular and semantically correct fashion while keeping a flawless separation between presentation and content. But how can I apply that CSS programmatically?

Solution

In addition to the nearly standard `getClassName()` and `setClassName()` methods, Facebook has added a handful of fantastically useful methods:

`obj.addClassName(newClass)`

Adds the `newClass` class name to the object's `className` string, checking first to see that it isn't already there.

`obj.removeClassName(oldClass)`

Does the exact opposite of `addClassName( )`, but you already knew that.

`obj.toggleClassName(someClass)`

If `obj` already has `someClass` in its `className` string, the class is removed. Contrary-wise, if it doesn't already have it, the class is added.

`obj.hasClassName(someClass)`

If `obj` has `someClass` in its `className` string, returns `true`. Otherwise, returns `false`.

 See Recipe 7.4 for an explanation of why you can't just look at the `className` property of an object.

Discussion

If you're not using one of the Ajax-type libraries (which is impossible given the Sandbox renaming), manipulating CSS through JavaScript can be a bag full of pain, crammed with sharp-ended bits of code that do lots of `className` checking and poke you in the ribs repeatedly. Facebook's new functions take a whole bunch of those sharp bits and round the corners off, so it's more like a dull throbbing ache than a real hurty poke. Let's look an example:

```
<style type="text/css">
    div{
        margin: 20px;
    }

    div.redDiv{
        background-color: red;
    }
    div.blueDiv{
        background-color: blue;
    }
    div.greenDiv{
        background-color: green;
    }

    div.funDiv{
        float: left;
        height: 100px;
        width: 100px;
    }

    div.bordered{
        border: 1px black solid;
    }
```

```
    div#control{
        clear: left;
    }
</style>

<script type="text/javascript">
<!--
function dullAche(){
    var firstDiv = document.getElementById('firstDiv');
    var secondDiv = document.getElementById('secondDiv');
    var thirdDiv = document.getElementById('thirdDiv');

    firstDiv.addClassName('bordered');
    secondDiv.removeClassName('blueDiv');
    secondDiv.addClassName('redDiv');
    thirdDiv.toggleClassName('greenDiv');
    if(!thirdDiv.hasClassName('greenDiv')){
        var butNotGreen = new Dialog().showMessage('Not Green',"But
 it's not green!",'True');
    }
}
//-->
</script>

<div id="firstDiv" class="redDiv funDiv"></div>
<div id="secondDiv" class="blueDiv funDiv"></div>
<div id="thirdDiv" class="greenDiv funDiv"></div>

<div id="control"><input type="button" value="Ouch!" onclick="dullAche();" /></div>
```

Before you click on the "Ouch!" button, you should see three colored squares and a
button, as in Figure 7-1.

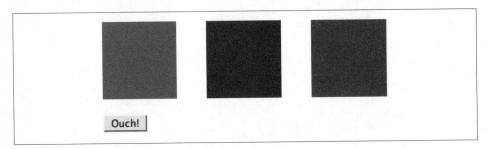

Figure 7-1. Before clicking "Ouch!"

When you click on the button (see Figure 7-2), the first div gets the bordered class
applied (so it now has a black border), the second div loses the blueDiv class and gains
the redDiv one (so it becomes red), and the third div toggles the greenDiv class to off
so that it disappears (and we get a pop-up Facebook dialog to let us know it's not green
anymore).

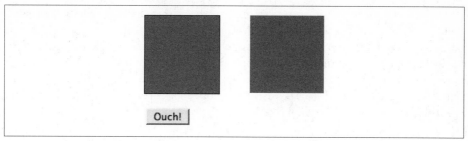

Figure 7-2. After clicking "Ouch!"

7.7 Dynamically Setting Content

Problem

Now I want to set the contents of an element on my page programmatically.

Solution

Facebook Platform makes two methods available to you:

`obj.setInnerFBML(newContent)`
> Similar to using `obj.innerHTML = newContent` in traditional JavaScript, but with a few differences. Note that actually passing a string instead of a variable will usually cause a JavaScript error (`fbjs_private.get(fbml_ref) has no properties`), so you should instead use the `<fb:js-string var="newContent">` FMBL tag on your page to define an FBJS string that you can pass instead (i.e., wrap the content in opening and closing `<fb:js-string>` tags). Also, note that `setInnerFBML()` will replace all of the existing children of `obj` in the same way that setting `innerHTML()` will.

`obj.setTextValue(newContent)`
> Sets the text displayed within an object but will *not* accept FBML or HTML. This is really useful for doing things such as status updates, where you don't really need anything beyond a text update, especially if you're setting the text value of a `div` with a class applied for formatting (e.g., `<div class="statusMessage"></div>`).

Discussion

Setting text values is pretty self-evident, but `setInnerFBML` needs a little bit more explanation, mostly because of the weirdness around passing a string versus setting up a JavaScript string.

If you've read the chapter on FBML (Chapter 6), you'll know that a lot of the power of building on Facebook Platform comes from the ease of throwing in tags that display user interface widgets and a lot of content. It's much easier to toss in a `<fb:name uid="<?php echo $user?>"/>` than it is to use the PHP API to extract the person's name and output it. It's also way simpler to drop in an `<fb:tabs>` block than it is to build your own from scratch, and these blocks have the added benefit of being Platform-native. You could build your FBML as a string literal in your function call to `setInnerFBML`, but odds are that you'll end up having to untangle a whole bunch of nested quote characters that will need to be properly escaped, and you'll end up with one long line of rendered HTML instead of your meticulously formatted and easily readable version. Do this instead:

```
<script type="text/javascript">
<!--
    function showInvite(){
        var fp = document.getElementById('friendPicker');
        fp.setInnerFBML(fpContent);
    }
//-->
</script>

<fb:js-string var="fpContent">
<fb:fbml>
    <fb:request-form
        action="index.php"
        method="POST"
        invite="true"
        type="Your App"
        content="Your text goes here.">
        <fb:multi-friend-selector
            showborder="false"
            actiontext="Invite your friends!">
    </fb:request-form>
</fb:fbml>
</fb:js-string>

<div id="friendPicker"></div>

<div id="controls">
    <input type="button" value="Show Invite" onclick="showInvite();" />
</div>
```

7.8 Textbox Selections

Problem

I need to get or set the selection (or contents) of a **textarea** or an **input** of type **text**.

Solution

Facebook Platform provides a pair of methods for getting and setting the selection in text fields:

`obj.getSelection( )`
Returns an object with start and end properties:

```
selIndexes = document.getElementById('myTextarea').getSelection();
selStart = selIndexes.start;
selEnd = selIndexes.end;
```

`obj.setSelection( )`

    Sets the selection within the text field, taking a required start and an optional end:

```
// Put the cursor into the field after the 5th character
document.getElementById('myTextarea).setSelection(5);

// Select the 5th to 10th characters
document.getElementById('myTextarea).setSelection(5,10);
```

Discussion

This isn't much different from the way you would access the same properties through normal JavaScript, except than an abstraction layer has been added to smooth over Internet Explorer's lack of support for `selectionStart` and `selectionEnd`. The Fabulous Selection Getter and Setter twins will help you do all kinds of amazing manipulation of the cursor and text selection regions, but they won't help you actually retrieve the value of the text in the field (or, by extension, of the selected text in the field). Here's a useful function that accepts the `id` of a text field and returns the full value if nothing is selected, or returns just the selected text if something is:

```
function getText(targetField){
    var indexes = document.getElementById(targetField).getSelection();
    var fullText =  document.getElementById(targetField).getValue();
    if(indexes.start == indexes.end){
        // There's nothing selected so return the whole thing
        return fullText;
    }else{
        // Substring out the part that's selected and return it
        return fullText.substr(indexes.start,(indexes.end - indexes.start));
    }
}
```

 You'll note a call in there to `getValue( )`, which you might not recognize. It's a handy function provided by Facebook Platform that will figure out what type of object you've called it on and will then use the appropriate methods to retrieve and return the value of it. See Recipe 7.4 for more information.

7.9 Limiting the Length of Text Fields

Problem

I have a text field in my app, and I want to limit the number of characters someone can type into it.

Solution

You're looking for a combination of getValue( ) and setValue( ), a pair of getter/setters implemented by Facebook as a shortcut to manipulating the value of various object types. If your Canvas page is set up something like this:

```
<div id="message">
    <textarea id="messageField" onkeyup="limitLength(this,200);"></textarea>
    <div id="messageCount">0/200 characters</div>
</div>
```

then give this a shot:

```
function limitLength(targetField,maxLength){
    var currentLength = targetField.getValue().length;

    if( currentLength > maxLength){
        targetField.setValue(targetField.getValue().substring(0, maxLength));
        currentLength = maxLength;
    }

    document.getElementById('messageCount').setTextValue(currentLength + '/200
        characters');
}
```

Discussion

There are lots of occasions in which you might need to do something like limit the length of a text field, so it's always better to try to write functions like that as general-purpose utilities rather than one-time-use tools. That function could have been written as checkMessageField( ) without passing in the field or length, but then you'd also need checkProfileField( ) and checkDescriptionField( ), etc. Since FBJS allows you to include external JavaScript files, do yourself a favor and put things like this into a utilities.js, which you can just include in pages where you need them (see Recipe 7.16).

7.10 Creating Elements Dynamically

Problem

I want to dynamically create DOM objects and pop them into my page.

Solution

Use document.createElement( ), the same way that you would in traditional JavaScript.

Discussion

This is one of the things that doesn't change in FBJS, so your knowledge of off-Facebook JavaScript can be applied directly.

One special exception to note: `document.createElement( )` can be used to create FBML elements, but it is currently limited to `<fb:swf>` (not even `<fb:flv>` or `<fb:silver light>` work). The call is basically the same:

```
var newFlash = document.createElement('fb:swf');
```

Once you've created your object and attached it to the DOM (using a call such as `appendChild( )`), you will not be able to move it around the DOM, and it will be rendered by the FBML parser into a standard `<embed>` tag.

7.11 Adding and Removing Event Listeners

Problem

I want to add an event listener to or remove an event listener from a DOM object. (In other words, I have a thing I want to be able to click on and have it do something.)

Solution

FBJS supports the standard `addEventListener( )` and `removeEventListener( )` methods that you know and love from traditional JavaScript. Calling them is as simple as finding your target in the DOM and passing in your event type and function name:

```
var myObj = document.getElementById('someId');
myObj.addEventListener('click', otherFunctionName);
myObj.removeEventListener('click', otherFunctionName);
```

Discussion

This is pretty simple, as long as you keep in mind that `otherFunctionName` needs to be a defined JavaScript function, and that your new listeners will join any that were added in the FBML code (e.g., `<div id="someId" onclick="aFunctionName( );">`).

7.12 Retrieving Data via Ajax

Problem

I want to do a call and/or response to my server without causing the current page to refresh. For example, I might want to dynamically populate some content, or update a section of my page, or maybe check to see whether some text entered into a field is valid.

Solution

Ajax can be used for such a wide variety of uses that it would require a whole other book to run down all the various permutations and combinations (conveniently, you can pick up any number of O'Reilly books on the topic, including *Understanding AJAX:*

Using JavaScript to Create Rich Internet Applications and *Ajax for Web Developers*). As a simple example, we're going to use a text field in which users would enter the username they'd like to use, and then we'll check on the fly to see whether it's available. You'll need a text input on your Canvas page:

```
<div id="registration">
    <div id="usernameFields">
        <label for="username">Username:</label>
        <input type="text" id="username" onchange="checkUsername(this);" />
        <span id="usernameAvailable"></span>
    </div>
</div>
```

The JavaScript for `checkUsername( )` is surprisingly simple because of the Ajax object provided by Facebook Platform, which really makes your life easy:

```
function checkUsername(usernameField){
    if(usernameField.getValue() == ''){
        document.getElementById('usernameAvailable').setTextValue('');
        return;
    }

    var encodedUsername = escape(usernameField.getValue());
    var checkUsername = new Ajax();
    checkUsername.responseType = Ajax.JSON;
    checkUsername.ondone = function(data){
        var message = '';
        console.log(data);
        if(data.available){
            message = 'Great! That username is available!';
        }else{
            message = 'Ooops! That username is taken. Sorry!';
        }
        document.getElementById('usernameAvailable').setTextValue(message);
    }
    checkUsername.post('http://www.yourserver.com/checkUsername.php?
        username=' + encodedUsername);
}
```

Finally, you're going to need to create a page on your server (or a servlet, depending on your server-side language of choice) that the Ajax script in your Canvas page can call to send data to and/or receive data from. Since this is just a simple example, the *checkUsername.php* file on our server contains:

```
<?php
if($_GET['username'] == 'jay'){
    echo '{"available": true}';
}else{
    echo '{"available": false}';
} ?>
```

 Your Ajax call will fail if you try to use a Facebook URL as the callback. It's very important that the script call a URL that is not on Facebook, but it could still sit on the same server that your app is served from.

That should really be it! If you're following along at home and have recreated the code just shown, you can now try entering a username in the field. As soon as the field loses focus, the onchange event will fire and cause the checkUsername( ) JavaScript function to execute, which will prepare and fire off an Ajax request to your server and then parse the JSON-formatted response and update the contents of the usernameAvailable <span>.

Discussion

Even though the solution presented here is one of the simplest cases, it provides a pretty flexible foundation for building more complicated Ajax calls. You would use an almost identical function if you just wanted to update data on your server (e.g., moving the pieces in a chess game might call a chessMove.php page and pass it player and move, and then parse a result value and update the displayed board on the Canvas page). You could also use a similar function and a call to setTimeout( ) to create a rotating banner ad system that doesn't need to refresh the page when changing ads.

The Ajax implementation in Facebook Platform provides a good deal more functionality than we've covered, including:

onerror

An error handler function that you would set the same way we've set the ondone handler in the earlier example.

requireLogin

A boolean attribute you can set on your Ajax object to indicate that the user has to log into Facebook before the Ajax call can be made. This is particularly useful if you're using a public Canvas page but need access to the user's Facebook account information in order to calculate the return value of your Ajax method.

abort

Some quick testing shows that the Facebook Platform Ajax object has a default timeout of about 10 seconds, which you can't adjust. If you think you might need to bail out sooner (or need to kill an in-progress request for any number of other reasons), call the myAjax.abort( ) method.

responseType

This is covered in the earlier example (we're using Ajax.JSON), but you have the choice of three values:

Ajax.JSON

Your server will return a response encoded using JavaScript Object Notation (JSON), which will automatically be decoded for you. Any attributes you encode on the server side will become attributes of the data object, which you can then access using dot-notation (e.g., if you send back an attribute called available, you can access it using data.available). Generally speaking, this is the preferred approach because it keeps a proper separation between your data and display layers, meaning that the return from the server contains no formatting codes, and therefore isn't tied to Facebook Platform (for example, you could call the same server-side function from a mobile version of your app and then parse and display the result using something like XHTML Mobile Profile). For more information on JSON, see *http://json.org*.

`Ajax.FBML`

Your server's going to do all the calculations and formatting of the result and return it in FBML, all ready to display. You can pass this directly into the `setInnerFBML()` function. This approach means less client-side processing (since you can just dump the result straight to screen), but it also means that you're tying your data and display layers very tightly together, and you might not be able to use the same server-side function in non-Facebook environments.

`Ajax.RAW`

Your server will return raw data that you'll deal with client-side on your own. You might use this if you have an existing server-side function that returns something like XML and have an XML parser implemented in FBJS separately.

post

There's no real magic in the `post` method, but it is worth noting that the earlier example uses the simpler form and passes the variables as a `GET` request. Since we were passing only one variable, we just used the JavaScript `escape()` function to handle the URL encoding, in case someone enters a username with funny characters in it. Sometimes you'll need to pass a whole whack of variables to the server, which is happily accommodated by passing an array of variables instead:

```
var queryParams = {'username': username, 'firstName': firstName};
myAjax.post('http://www.yourserver.com/process.php', queryParams);
```

The FBJS parser will automatically encode all of the values so that you don't have to worry about them. It's important to note that this will change your request from a `GET` to a `POST`, so if you're looking for these variables on the server side and you're writing PHP, make sure to look in `$_POST` instead of in `$_GET`.

In keeping with the Facebook design methodology evident in apps such as Photos, this framework isn't intended to provide the kind of overwhelmingly complete feature set you'd find in libraries such as jQuery, Prototype, or Dojo (to name a few). You're not likely to need a whole lot more than is listed here for the simple interactions that most Facebook apps exhibit, and you might even find this overkill, in which case take a look at Recipe 6.51.

7.13 Displaying Pop-Up Dialogs

Problem

I want to display a pop-up dialog in the style seen throughout Facebook (well, I really want to display an alert but I'm not allowed to in FBJS, so I'll settle for this).

Solution

Facebook Platform provides a very simple implementation of a Dialog object that can easily be used to display pop-up dialogs with a confirm button (Figure 7-3):

```
var myDialog = new Dialog(Dialog.DIALOG_POP);

// Show the dialog with only a confirm button
myDialog.showMessage('Title Here', 'Text Here', button_confirm='Okay!');
```

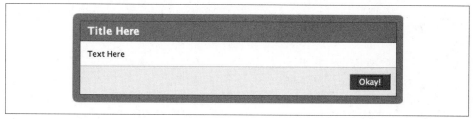

Figure 7-3. Simple dialog

If you'd like to have the confirm button do something other than just hiding the dialog, you can set an event handler for it before you call showMessage( ):

```
myDialog.onconfirm = eventHandlerName;
```

Your event-handler function can do whatever processing you'd like and should return **true** to hide the dialog (e.g., you have validated some input in the dialog) or **false** to leave it open (e.g., the input didn't validate and the user needs to re-enter it). If you are asking for input, you probably want to add a cancel button (Figure 7-4):

```
var myDialog = new Dialog(Dialog.DIALOG_POP);
myDialog.onconfirm = handleConfirm;
myDialog.oncancel = handleCancel;
myDialog.showChoice('Title','Body',button_confirm='Okay!', button_cancel='No!');
```

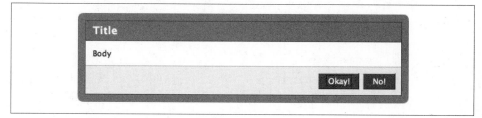

Figure 7-4. Dialog with confirm and cancel buttons

Discussion

As mentioned in the Solution, the showMessage( ) form of dialog is a useful replacement for the traditional JavaScript function alert( ). The showChoice( ) version is a little more useful in that you can ask users simple yes-or-no questions ("Are you sure you want to put the chocolate in the peanut butter?"), but what if you need to ask them something with more than two possible answers? Luckily for you (and for ice cream lovers everywhere), you can pass an <fb:js-string> as the text parameter in the call to showChoice( ) and use it to render a much more complex query:

```
<fb:js-string var="iceCreams">
    <p>What's your favorite ice cream flavor?</p>
    <select id="iceCreamSelector">
        <option value="" selected="selected">(Pick a flavor!)</option>
        <option value="chocolate">Chocolate</option>
        <option value="vanilla">Vanilla</option>
        <option value="strawberry">Strawberry</option>
        <option value="moosetracks">Moose Tracks</option>
    </select>
</fb:js-string>

<script type="text/javascript">
<!--
    function showDialog(){
        var myDialog = new Dialog(Dialog.DIALOG_POP);

        myDialog.onconfirm = handleConfirm;
        myDialog.oncancel = handleCancel;

        myDialog.showChoice('Ice Cream', iceCreams, button_confirm='Mmmm!',
            button_confirm='Ewww!');
    }

    function handleConfirm(evt){
        // Get the flavor value from the selector
        var flavor = document.getElementById('iceCreamSelector').getValue();

        // Make sure something was selected
        if(flavor != ''){
            // Do something with this new found knowledge

            // Close the dialog
            return true;
        }else{
            // Don't close the dialog
            return false;
        }
    }

    function handleCancel(evt){
        // Close the dialog
        return true;
    }
//-->
```

```
</script>

<input type="button" value="What's your favorite?" onclick="showDialog();" />
```

That should give you a dialog something like Figure 7-5.

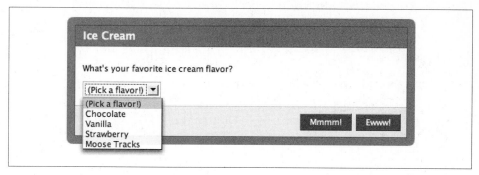

Figure 7-5. Dialog with an embedded <fb-js:string>

7.14 Displaying Contextual Dialogs

Problem

I want to display a nifty contextual dialog that points to one of my DOM objects.

Solution

Contextual dialogs are really a variation of the pop-up dialog covered in Recipe 7.13, so take a moment to read that recipe first. The main differences are in your call to the `Dialog( )` constructor and in the call to `setContext( )`, which establishes which DOM object the dialog should point to (see Figure 7-6):

```
var myDialog = new Dialog(Dialog.DIALOG_CONTEXTUAL);
myDialog.setContext(document.getElementById('attachToMe'));
myDialog.showMessage('Look at Me!', 'Check this out!', button_confirm='Cool!');
```

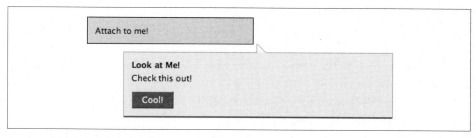

Figure 7-6. Contextual dialog

Discussion

All of the same tidbits that apply to pop ups apply to contextual dialogs as well, including the ability to set up an `<fb:js-string>` for use as the body:

```
<fb:js-string var="messageText">
    Hi <fb:name uid="<?php echo $user?>"
            firstnameonly="true"
            linked="false"
            useyou="false"/>!
</fb:js-string>

<script type="text/javascript">
<!--
var myDialog = new Dialog(Dialog.DIALOG_CONTEXTUAL);
myDialog.setContext(document.getElementById('attachToMe'));
myDialog.showMessage('Message for you!', messageText, button_confirm='Thanks!');
//-->
</script>
```

That should give you a dialog something like Figure 7-7.

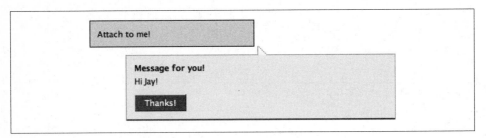

Figure 7-7. Contextual dialog with an embedded <fb:js-string>

7.15 Avoiding Heartache When the DOM Changes

Problem

I've built an amazing piece of JavaScript that has suddenly stopped working because Facebook has changed the structure of the page!

Solution

Be careful when you architect your code so that you don't build very specific DOM structures into it:

```
this.getElementByTagName('div')[1].getFirstChild()
.getLastChild().setStyle('color', 'white');
```

It's a much better idea to assign everything on your page a unique **id** or to give all similar objects a shared class so that you can target them more specifically from your JavaScript.

Discussion

The statement just shown is fragile for at least two reasons:

- It's effectively chaining down to the last child of the first child of the second `<div>` on the page (remember that arrays in JavaScript are zero-indexed, so the first `<div>` would be `[0]`). You might inadvertently change your own markup and insert an element above what used to be the first child, or below what used to be the last one.

- If you're used to doing development in a more traditional environment, you might not run into too many circumstances in which the HTML in your page changes without you doing it. Consider what happens to your code when Facebook changes the way something like `<fb:multi-friend-input>` is actually output by the FBML parser. If Facebook adds an extra `<div>`, your count is now off.

All of this is not to suggest that you shouldn't chain your JavaScript commands together. There are plenty of times when combining a few lines of code can help optimize your function by cutting down on computationally expensive operations, such as allocating memory. It's perfectly acceptable, for example, to optimize a few lines like:

```
var messageDiv = document.createElement('div');
messageDiv.setTextValue('Hi there!');
messageDiv.setStyle('color', 'red');
messageDiv.setStyle('border', '1px red solid');
messageDiv.addListener('click', closeMessage);
```

into a more compact single line like:

```
document.createElement('div').setTextValue('Hi there!')
.setStyle({color: 'red', border: '1px red solid'}).addListener('click', closeMessage);
```

The main difference lies in the dependence of the code on external factors. In this case, the entire line is self-contained and won't break, even if the entire structure of your page changes. Keep in mind that lines like that really benefit from a comment to remind you of what they're doing when you come back to them in six months' time, or to prevent your teammates from wanting to hunt you down and express their frustrations in very real and physical terms. Remember Golding's Law: always program as if the person who will be maintaining your program is a violent psychopath who knows where you live.

7.16 Linking to External FBJS Files

Problem

I have a large block of FBJS that I use throughout my application, and I'd really like to have the browser cache it for better client-side performance.

Solution

Facebook Platform supports linking to external FBJS files through the `<script>` tag with a `src` attribute, the same way you would with traditional JavaScript. Simply add a line to your source file and stick the JavaScript file on your server:

```
<script src="http://www.foo.com/bar.js"></script>
```

Your external file will get included in your rendered FBML pages, with a cache policy set to never expire.

Discussion

As with most traditional JavaScript you put into your app pages, your `<script>` tag will be rewritten by the FJBS parser into something you'll barely recognize. Our example would appear in the final page as:

```
<script src="http://apps.facebook.com/fbjs_get.php?src=
http%3A%2F%2Fwww.foo.com%2Fbar.js&appid=12345&pv=1&sig=xxxxxxxxxxxx"></script>
```

You can access that URL directly (not the one here, but the one from your own app), and you'll see your external JavaScript file after it's been run through the FBJS parser. If there's anything wrong with your script or the parser isn't able to do its thing, you'll simply get a 0 as the return value (i.e., a blank page with the only content being the character 0). All of your variable, object, and function names will get rewritten by `fbjs_get.php` the same way your inline JavaScript is.

7.17 Use Firebug (No, Seriously)

Problem

Unfortunately, I lack any form of extrasensory powers and have no idea why my HTML isn't rendering properly, what my Ajax calls are returning, or the first clue why my JavaScript is behaving like it's possessed.

Solution

Install Firebug, a Firefox add-on, and make your life considerably easier. Install it with a single click from *http://www.getfirebug.com/*, give your browser a quick restart, and then click on the little bug icon in the status bar at the bottom of your window and let the festivities begin.

If you're not running Firefox, you can still access some of this functionality by including the *firebug.js* JavaScript file in your pages (although this may fail when parsed through the FBJS parser). For more information, see *http://www.getfirebug.com/lite.html*. Do yourself a favor, though, and download Firefox and Firebug just to see how much easier this will make your life. You should still test in Internet Explorer and Safari, but your joy in building Facebook applications (and any other web project) will increase by the bucketload.

Discussion

Some web developers are born with a sixth sense that lets them do freaky things like writing flawless cross-browser HTML on the first try or crafting brilliant JavaScripts that make my head hurt to even contemplate. For the rest of us, there's Firebug. If you're a devout Internet Explorer or Safari user, you're going to want to just skip to the next recipe before you find your life changing in unexpected ways. If you're already a dedicated Firefox user, prepare to fall in love all over again. If you do any web development of any kind and don't yet know about Firebug, you'd better grab a seat. (You should really grab one anyway—isn't this book getting heavy?)

Real firebugs, known in some circles as *Pyrrhocoris apterus*, are members of the insect order *Hemiptera*, usually mate in April and May, and subsist primarily on a diet of seeds from lime trees and mallows. Lovely as they are, they certainly aren't going to help your web development efforts. Recognizing this shortfall, top-notch developers and Firefox contributors Blake Ross and Joe Hewitt built Firebug and reshaped web development forevermore. Firebug gives you the ability to inspect and edit HTML on the fly, tweak your CSS in place and see the results, visualize CSS metrics and the box model of your objects, monitor network activity and watch GET and POST requests from your page as they happen, debug and profile JavaScript, catch and monitor all of the exceptions and errors thrown by your code, explore the DOM and all of its properties, execute JavaScript on the fly, and log JavaScript errors, warnings, and info straight to the console.

 Just for the sake of this story having a happy and entirely relevant-to this-book ending, Blake and Joe were nice enough to go and sell their company, Parakey, to Facebook, where they now do amazing things, such as building the iPhone version of the Facebook site.

There are a bunch of uses for Firebug in building Facebook applications, not the least of which is figuring out what your JavaScript is doing and walking through the various ways that the FBML and FBJS parsers have modified your code. One of the most useful features is the ability to log to the console, as well as to output your objects in human-readable form. Firebug automatically adds a `console` object to any window in which it's enabled, which means you can freely call the functions in the console from inside your own code. Here are some of the most useful functions you can try in your own code:

```
console.log('What the heck is this: ',obj);
```
> Having a debugger that lets you step through your code is great, but sometimes you just want to dump some messages or the contents of a variable out to the console. `console.log( )` will join together all of the objects you pass in, and will automatically output a human-readable version of FBJS objects (if that *obj* variable

were a reference to a `div`, it would be something like `Object PRIV_obj=div#app12345_someDiv`).

`console.debug( )`, `console.info( )`, `console.warn( )`, and `console.error( )`

Logging stuff is fun and all, but once your console is full of information, you're going to wish you had a way to sort through it. In addition to the ever-handy `console.log( )` just mentioned, Firebug supports four other levels of console output in the form of `debug( )`, `info( )`, `warn( )`, and `error( )`.

`console.assert(`*`expression`*`)`

Tests to see whether *expression* resolves to `true`, and throws a logged exception if not.

`console.dir(`*`obj`*`)` and `console.dirxml(`*`node`*`)`

Outputs DOM and XML views of an object, respectively. The `console.dir( )` view is similar to what you would see if you used Firebug's DOM inspector, whereas `console.dirxml( )` outputs the same source tree that you would see in the HTML inspector.

`console.time( )` and `console.profile( )`

If you're having trouble with the performance of a block of JavaScript, these two functions can be lifesavers. Add a call to `console.time('timerName')` before your code and a complementary `console.timeEnd('timerName')` after, and you'll get precise time info. If that's not enough information for you, throw in `console.profile('profileName')` and `console.profileEnd('profileName')`, and you'll get an incredibly detailed breakdown of every call that gets made, how many times it gets called, how long it takes to run, exactly which file it's in, and the line it's contained on.

There's way more to the application than that, and we could probably fill a whole different O'Reilly book on the topic. In the meantime, check out *http://www.getfirebug.com/docs.html* for more information.

7.18 Accessing the DOM Behind FBJS

Problem

I need to see the actual DOM object that's behind an FBJS variable, but I can't figure out any way to get to it.

Solution and Discussion

Install Firebug (see Recipe 7.17 for more information), and then add a call to `console.dir(`*`obj`*`)` on your object. Firebug will give you a long listing of all of the functions that FBJS has added to your object (starting with things such as `addClassName( )`, `addEventListener( )`, `appendChild( )`, etc.), at the very top of which you will find a

`PRIV_obj` entry. If you open that up, you'll see the actual DOM object hiding behind the ultimate FBJS representation.

7.19 Ajax Library: Backface

Problem

I'd really like to do some nifty Ajax animation effects or use some cool interface widgets and drag-and-drop actions, but none of the traditional Ajax libraries work inside of Platform.

Solution

Backface is a library for creating draggable widgets within your Facebook Canvas. Created by Peter Svensson from Stockholm, Backface (a.k.a. The Library Formerly Known as Prince—or TLFKAP—after he discovered that applications including the word "face" are not allowed on Facebook) can be found at *http://apps.facebook.com/backface/* and includes links to the downloadable PHP sample app and source. Backface won't quench all of your Ajax cravings, but it will allow you to do some neat drag-and-drop stuff, and it has panes and resizable objects coming, all written in FBJS so they don't run afoul of the parser.

Once you've downloaded and unpacked *backface.zip*, you'll find some documentation, a demo, and *backface.inc*, the actual include file. If you're building your Facebook app in PHP, the easiest way to work with it is to `include(backface.inc)` in the page you want to use it on.

Discussion

Peter is pretty dedicated to the project and has been quick to respond to developers' requests for features. You can follow along on his blog at *http://unclescript.blogspot .com/*, or by keeping tabs on the latest news in the Backface app on Facebook. The original library was hacked together in one late November night and has grown by leaps and bounds as people have asked for new things, such as snap-backs (i.e., objects returning to their original position when you drop them somewhere they shouldn't go). Peter has received a few donations to help the cause and may be interested in co-contributors, so drop by his blog if you'd like to be part of the effort.

CHAPTER 8

Facebook Query Language (FQL)

Let's say that you'd been puttering around town in a beat-up old jalopy and you pulled up to a traffic light. You dig your jalopy in a very Archie kind of way, even though it's a little slow sometimes and uses a lot of gas, but it's your car and it's all you've known. And now let's say, while you're sitting there at the light, a brand new Formula 1 race car comes screaming up to a stop right next to you, tires smoking. Sure, your jalopy is nice and all, but think how much faster you could get your shopping done in that baby! Now think of your jalopy as the Facebook API and the sleek, sexy, speedy race car as FQL.

See, here's the dirty little secret about APIs: they're all the rage with the kids these days, and they're a joy to program in, but they're not particularly efficient when you're worried about your app scaling to hundreds of thousands of users. If you're building a Facebook app that you think will really take off and you want to make sure you're being as future-proof as possible, you should consider using FQL for key queries for the following reasons:

Decreased result sets

When you're working with the API and you request the friends of a specific user, you get all the info back about everybody and then parse through the results. FQL gives you the ability to limit the fields you want returned and to put more conditions on your queries, thereby reducing the size of the result set and the bandwidth consumed. If you change a key query from the API to FQL and save yourself 10k per request, and you get 100 requests per minute, you're saving 1 MB of transfer, which is about 1.4 GB per day.

Reduced requests

Some of the API calls require you to make a request, get back the results, parse through them, and then make more requests based on your findings (e.g., to get the names of user's friends, you get the list of their IDs and then call `users.getInfo` on them). You can often reduce that down to a single FQL query that uses a subquery to get the list, saving yourself a full roundtrip from the server.

If you already know SQL, FQL is like a natural extension in the same way that FBML naturally proceeds from HTML. If you're not comfortable with SQL, I recommend picking up a book such as *Head First SQL* by Lynn Beighley, *Learning MySQL* by Seyed M.M. "Saied" Tahaghoghi and Hugh E. Williams, or *MySQL Cookbook* by Paul Du-Bois. You'll find all of them, along with everything else O'Reilly publishes, on *http://safari.oreilly.com*.

We'll start off with a quick overview of the basics (and particularly how FQL is different than SQL), and then dive right into some practical recipes. This isn't intended to give you every possible FQL query you might need, but rather to give you a whole bunch of different tools that you can combine to build your own queries. If you're looking for a specific query for one table and can't find it, check the other recipes for similar situations.

8.1 Playing with FQL

Problem

I'd like to try out some of the FQL queries listed in this chapter, but I don't want to have to write a whole test page for it.

Solution

Facebook makes three great testing consoles available to developers, which you can find at *http://developers.facebook.com/tools.php*. There isn't one specifically for FQL, but if you look in the API Test Console's Method drop-down (*http://developers.facebook.com/tools.php?api*), you'll find an "fql.query" option, which will reveal a query field.

Discussion

Another cool thing you can do in the test console is play with the Response Format drop-down, which lets you toggle between getting your responses in XML, JSON, or Facebook PHP Client. You can also switch between the different applications that you're a developer for, which lets you take advantage of the shortcuts in Platform based around who the logged-in user is and which app he's currently in.

8.2 FQL Query Structure

Problem

What's the basic structure of an FQL query?

Solution

FQL mimics SQL directly here, so the basic structure is:

```
SELECT [fields] FROM [table] WHERE [conditions]
```

In addition, you can also make use of SQL-like `ORDER BY` and `LIMIT` clauses:

```
SELECT [fields] FROM [table] WHERE [conditions] ORDER BY
  [field] LIMIT [offset], [rowcount]
```

Discussion

Here are a few noteworthy differences between SQL and FQL that might trip you up if you're used to the former and not the latter:

- Most significantly, the `FROM` clause in FQL can include only a single table, so there's no official support for joins of any kind. You can sort of get around this by using subqueries, but note that the subqueries can't reference variables from the outer query's scope. An example of a very useful subquery: requesting all of the friends of the current user who have already installed your application so that you can exclude them from an `fb:multi-friend-selector` control:

```
SELECT uid FROM user WHERE has_added_app=1 and uid IN
  (SELECT uid2 FROM friend WHERE uid1 = $user)
```

- In order for Facebook to provide direct database access for apps, all queries have to be indexable so that they don't impose huge performance hits on the server. Facebook maintains a relatively short list of 17 tables that you can do queries on; see Recipe 8.4 for details.

 Indexing is a technique in which a lookup index is created on a specific column in a table in order to speed up queries where that column is in the `WHERE` clause. (That makes it much clearer, no?) It might help to think of a giant library in which all the books are arranged in alphabetical order by title. If you wanted to find all of the books I've written, you'd have to go through the entire library and look for my name on the spines—slow and highly inefficient. However, if all the books were numbered and I handed you an index organized by author, you could look me up, note all the IDs of the books I've written, and then walk directly up to them on the shelf. Of course, this query would be very quick because this is my first book, so you wouldn't have far to walk.

- One critical note: the indexing limitation isn't that your query can *only* use indexed columns in the `WHERE` clause, but rather that at least one of them has to be indexed. This is not explained very well in the Developers Wiki, which may lead you to conclude that you can query only on indexed columns. For example, if you're looking for all of the users who share my birthday, you can't do:

```
SELECT uid FROM user WHERE strpos(birthday, "September 27") = 0;
```

since `birthday` isn't an indexed field. You can, however, do:

```
SELECT uid FROM user WHERE strpos(birthday, "September 27")
  = 0 AND uid IN (SELECT uid2 FROM friend WHERE uid1 = 561415460)
```

which will find all of my friends with that birthday. Since the first query would have been automatically constrained to people whose birthdays I'm allowed to see anyway, they have almost the same result.

- Given that one of the goals of FQL is to reduce the amount of data exchanged, there is no support for SELECT *. Down with lazy programmers! You're just going to have to figure out the actual fields you want and list them in each query.

- Finally, note that the ORDER BY capability in FQL is limited to a single field rather than the multiple comma-separated fields supported by SQL. You'll get a 601 error ("Parser error: unexpected ',"") if you try to sneak one in.

8.3 Functions and Operators

Problem

What functions and operators are supported in FQL?

Solution

FQL supports a number of functions that will be very familiar to PHP developers (see Table 8-1).

Table 8-1. FQL functions

Function	Description
now( )	Returns the current time
rand( )	Generates a random number
strlen(string)	Returns the length of the string
concat(string, ...)	Concatenates strings together
substr(string, start, length)	Returns the specified substring
strpos(haystack, needle)	Returns the position of the needle in the haystack
lower(string)	Converts the string to lowercase
upper(string)	Converts the string to uppercase

The standard set of SQL-like operators are supported: =, >=, <, etc., parentheses for order of operations, and the arithmetic operators +, -, *, and /. FQL also supports the AND, OR, and NOT logical operators inside of queries.

Discussion

You can use the functions directly inline with your FQL queries:

```
SELECT upper(concat(first_name, " ", substr(last_name, 0, 1),
    ".")), birthday FROM user WHERE sex = "female" AND uid IN (SELECT uid2
    FROM friend WHERE uid1 = $user) LIMIT 5;
```

That may not be the most practical query ever constructed, but it will return user's first five female friends with their first name and last name's first initial in all caps. Do with it what you will.

8.4 Indexed Facebook Tables and Fields

Problem

Which Facebook tables can I run queries against?

Solution

As of this writing, Facebook maintains a list of 17 tables you can query against. The Platform Wiki is a great source of information about which columns are contained in which table, so you should check there for information on building your own queries (see *http://wiki.developers.facebook.com/index.php/FQL_Tables*).

 For a quick overview of database indexing, see the Discussion in Recipe 8.2.

The list of available tables, along with the indexed columns you can use in WHERE clauses, includes:

album

    Storage for albums created in the Facebook Photos app. You can query on:

- aid (album ID of the album you're looking for)
- cover_pid (photo ID of the photo used on the cover)
- owner (ID of the owner whose albums you're looking for)

    See Recipe 8.6 for more information.

cookies

    Browser cookies that your application might have dropped. This will only return cookies for your app, and there's no way to request cookies for a different app for Facebook in general. You can query on:

- uid (user ID associated with the cookie)

    See Recipe 8.10 for more information.

metrics

    Metrics for your application. These are limited to your app, and there's no way to request metrics for a different app. You can query on:

- end_time (end date and time that metrics were collected, in epoch seconds). Note that the query is indexable (and therefore allowed) only if the date range of results is bounded and less than 30 days. See Recipe 6.20 for more on epoch seconds.

- period (period, in seconds, for which you want data returned). Allowable values are one day (86400 seconds), one week (604800 seconds), or one month (2592000 seconds).

See Recipe 8.14 for more information.

event

Storage for the events created in the Facebook Events app. You can query on:

- eid (event ID of the event you're looking for)

See Recipe 8.18 for more information.

event member

Relationship table storing a specific user's status for a specific event. Check this table to find out a user's RSVP response for an event. You can query on:

- uid (user ID of the user whose events you're looking for)
- eid (event ID of the event whose users you're looking for)

See Recipe 8.19 for more information.

friend

Relationship table storing friendships between users. You can query on:

- uid1 (one of the two user IDs of the users you're checking)
- uid2 (the other user ID)

See Recipe 8.25 for more information.

friend request

Storage of pending friend requests for the current loggedinuser. Check this table to find out who has invited the current user to be friends. Note that you can't query for anyone other than the current user and that the table contains only pending requests, not a history of all requests. You can query on:

- uid_to (user ID of the friend receiving the requests; can only be the loggedinuser)

See Recipe 8.26 for more information.

friendlist

Storage of friend lists owned by the current loggedinuser. You can display the list only to the loggedinuser, as it's considered private. You can query on:

- owner (user ID for whom you want to find friend lists; can only be the loggedinuser)

See Recipe 8.31 for more information.

friendlist member

Relationship table showing which friends of a specific user are in a specific friend list. You can query this table only when the friend list is owned by the loggedinuser, and you can display this information only to the loggedinuser, as it's considered private. You can query on:

- flid (friend list ID of a friend list belonging to the loggedinuser)

See Recipe 8.32 for more information.

group

Storage for the groups created in the Facebook Groups app. You can query on:

- gid (group ID of the group you're looking for)

See Recipe 8.37 for more information.

group

Relationship table showing which users are in which groups. You can query on:

- uid (user ID of a user whose groups you're looking for)
- gid (group ID of a group whose members you're looking for)

See Recipe 8.32 for more information.

listing

Storage for the listings created in the Facebook Marketplace app. You can query on:

- listing_id (listing ID of the listing you're looking for)
- poster (user ID of the user whose listings you're looking for)

See Recipe 8.42 for more information.

page

Storage for the pages created in the Facebook Pages app. You can query on:

- page_id (page ID of the page you're looking for)
- name (name of the page you're looking for)

See Recipe 8.47 for more information.

page_fan

Relationship table showing which users are fans of which pages. You can query on:

- uid (user ID of the user whose pages you're looking for)

See Recipe 8.48 for more information.

photo

Storage for photos added to the Facebook Photos app. You can query on:

- pid (photo ID of the photo you're looking for)
- aid (album ID of the album whose photos you're looking for)

See Recipe 8.51 for more information.

photo_tag

Relationship table showing which photos have been tagged with which users. You can query on:

- pid (photo ID of the photo you're looking for)
- subject (user ID of the user who you're looking for in the photos)

See Recipe 8.52 for more information.

`user`

Storage for Facebook users. You can query on:

- `uid` (user ID of the user you're looking for)
- `name` (full name of the user you're looking for)

See Recipe 8.55 for more information.

8.5 Advanced Relational Database Table Optimization

—Pete Forde with Rowan Hick (see their bios in Contributors)

Problem

I have the problem everyone wants: popularity! Even with a proper caching strategy and sensible indexes in place, my application database is quickly becoming a bottleneck. Like most web applications, my resources tend to be frequently read, with relatively infrequent updates. I have adhered to common design best practices; my schema is properly normalized. What more can I do to scale my database throughput capacity?

Solution

The solutions listed next won't work for everyone, but there's a pretty good chance that they'll solve some of your problems.

Denormalization

Are you consistently joining the same tables together? You might consider adding redundant columns to your high-traffic tables so that you can reduce or eliminate joins. For example, given a `Users.province_id fk> Province.id` relationship, it might make sense to create a `Users.province` column and store the literal text value directly on the Users table.

Of course, they call these databases "relational" for a reason! By giving that up, you accept the burden of updating the same data in multiple places. You might have to change how your application retrieves these new redundant values. Profile to find bottlenecks, and weigh the tradeoff cost of each optimization.

In most cases, it's not recommended that you drop or abandon your normalized join tables completely; you should add redundant columns only for data that you require in the high-throughput scenario. You are taking referential integrity into your own hands.

Cached counters

One of the most common database tasks is to discover how many child records a parent record has, resulting in redundant and expensive counting operations. Most modern database platforms do an impressive job of caching query results under normal load, but at some point it's better to track this count ourselves.

Create columns on the parent table in which to store these counts, and verify that your application contains hooks to update this value any time a child record is added or removed. For example, given `Items.list_id fk> List.id`, you could add `List.items_count` to your table and eliminate the requirement to incur a count operation.

Precalculated sums

Any expensive data transformation operations should be performed at the time a record is written, regardless of whether the operation is triggered programmatically or through SQL. However, although SQL supports functions like `SUM()`, these tools are not encouraged for use during a highly concurrent read operation.

Similar to implementing a cached counter, you can add columns to store these precalculated values. Generally this is assuming that there is a parent and child foreign key relationship in place. Any time a dependent record is changed, these calculated sum values on the parent table will need to be regenerated.

Discussion

First off, give yourself a quick refresher of normalization and its awkward cousin, denormalization:

- *http://en.wikipedia.org/wiki/Database_normalization*
- *http://en.wikipedia.org/wiki/Denormalization*

To paraphrase Wikipedia, a denormalized data model is not the same as a data model that has not been normalized, and denormalization should only take place after a satisfactory level of normalization has taken place.

Using database constraints to enforce referential integrity on a set of write-heavy, normalized tables might prove slower than using a join! Don't ever forget that your relational database management system (RDBMS) is trying to do its best to speed things along, regardless of your attempts at optimization.

Note that database views might seem like a shortcut to denormalization, with all of the benefits of a join and none of the syntax requirements. However, most RDBMS systems provide views so that a security model can be attached; they still do all of the ugly joins behind the scenes.

Some object-relational mapping (ORM) toolkits, such as ActiveRecord, abstract traditional concepts such as foreign keys and constraints. This is fine—if yours is the only application that will be accessing this data.

Not all of these solutions will work for every application. You should extensively profile your application using tools like *ab* (Apache Benchmark) to verify a positive change before giving up the advantages of a normalized schema.

Next steps

It wasn't that long ago that programmers were not encouraged to have an opinion on database infrastructure, which was traditionally the realm of the database admin (DBA). Today, this is no longer the case. Developer Rowan Hick has some pointers for optimizing your database access:

- If you are using MySQL, bookmark this excellent resource: *http://www.mysqlper formanceblog.com/*.

- If you are using MySQL or Postgres, look into the EXPLAIN statement. It is invaluable for spotting where you have missed creating a key index, or are inadvertently doing full table scans. You should always watch for queries that take longer than you expect by looking at slow query logs, if your database supports them.

- Make sure that you understand table locking, with the goal of reducing updates to a table or even offloading updates to another denormalized table. See *http://dev .mysql.com/doc/refman/5.0/en/table-locking.html*.

- Eventually you might need to pursue more dramatic strategies, such as *sharding*. Sharding splits data across multiple tables and servers. For example, you might have users A–M on one server and N–Z on another.

- If you are using Rails, check out "How to avoid hanging yourself with Rails" at *http://work.rowanhick.com/hang.pdf* to optimize how you use ActiveRecord for better performance.

8.6 Album Table

Problem

What's the schema for the album table?

Solution

The album table holds all of the photo albums that users have created in the Facebook Photos application. Its fields are listed in Table 8-2. Queries to this table will only return data the current user is allowed to see (in other words, you can't request albums that this user isn't allowed to see). More information about this table, including an up-to-date listing of fields, can be found at *http://wiki.developers.facebook.com/index .php/Album_(FQL)*.

Table 8-2. album table fields

Name	Type	Index	Description
aid	int	•	Album ID.
cover_pid	int	•	pid (photo ID) of the photo that has been set as the cover of the album.
owner	int	•	uid (user ID) of the owner of this album (i.e., the user who created it).
name	string		Name of the album.
created	string		Creation date of the album.
modified	string		Date that the album was last updated, in epoch seconds (see Recipe 6.20 for an explanation of epoch seconds).
description	string		Description entered by the album's owner.
location	string		Location entered by the album's owner (e.g., Toronto, The Moon).
size	int		The number of photos in the album.
link	string		URL to the album (i.e., the actual Facebook URL for this album).

Note that only the fields marked as "Index" in this table can be used in an FQL query's WHERE clause, but any of the fields can appear in the SELECT.

Discussion

If you'd rather use the API to access albums, try the Photos.getAlbums( ) method.

8.7 Retrieving an Album

Problem

I need to retrieve a Facebook album using FQL.

Solution

This is your most basic album-related query:

```
SELECT aid, cover_pid, name, link FROM album WHERE owner = $uid;
```

Discussion

Since SELECT * isn't supported in FQL, you'll have to list out the actual fields you're looking for. This would be enough to let you display someone's albums with links back to the original. Remember that this query will only return albums that the current loggedinuser has permission to see.

8.8 Counting All of a User's Photos

Problem

I need to use FQL to count all of the photos that a user has uploaded to the Facebook Photos app.

Solution

This would be easier in real SQL, since you could use the sum( ) function to add up all the photos. We'll have to use a little PHP instead:

```php
<?php
$query = 'SELECT size FROM album WHERE owner = ' . $user . ';';
$sizes = $facebook->api_client->fql_query($query);

$totalPhotos = 0;
if($sizes){
    foreach($sizes as $album){
        $totalPhotos += $album['size'];
    }
}
?>
```

The variable totalPhotos will contain the count of all photos at the end, or zero if none were found.

Discussion

As with all FQL queries, this will only return photos that the current loggedinuser has access to, so you won't be able to query for photos that she can't see.

8.9 Retrieving Five Albums for a User

Problem

I need to retrieve some (or all) of the albums for a specific user from the Facebook Photos app using FQL.

Solution

The simplest form of this query is:

```
SELECT aid, cover_pid, name, link FROM album WHERE owner = $uid LIMIT 5;
```

Discussion

When you're imposing a limit on the data that gets returned, you might want to add an ORDER BY clause so that you're getting some logical subset. With the case of something like albums, it might make sense to get the five albums most recently updated by a user:

```
SELECT aid, cover_pid, name, link, modified FROM album
  WHERE owner = $uid ORDER BY modified DESC LIMIT 5;
```

The DESC added to the ORDER BY when using a timestamp as the ordering field will give you results in reverse chronological order (i.e., newest first).

8.10 Cookie Table

Problem

What's the schema for the cookie table?

Solution

The cookie table holds all of the browser cookies that your app has dropped. Its fields are listed in Table 8-3. There's no way to use this table to access cookies that other apps or Facebook might have dropped, so your queries will only return results for your app. More information about this table, including an up-to-date listing of fields, can be found at *http://wiki.developers.facebook.com/index.php/Cookies_(FQL)*.

Table 8-3. cookie table fields

Name	Type	Index	Description
uid	int	•	uid (user ID) associated with this cookie. This is the ID of the user who was using your application when the cookie was dropped.
name	string		Name of the cookie.
value	string		Value of the cookie.
expires	int		Expiry timestamp for the cookie. The cookie never expires if this is empty.
path	string		Path relative to your app's callback URL with which the cookie is associated (i.e., if your app's callback is *http://www.someserver.com/myapp/* and the path is *friends/add.php*, then it was dropped by the page *http://www.someserver.com/myapp/friends/add.php*).

Note that only the field marked as "Index" in this table can be used in an FQL query's WHERE clause, but any of the fields can appear in the SELECT.

Discussion

If you'd rather use the API to access cookies, try the Data.getCookies() and Data.setCookie() methods.

8.11 Retrieving All Cookies for a User

Problem

I need to retrieve all of the cookies dropped for a specific user using FQL.

Solution

The simplest query you could use is:

```
SELECT name, value FROM cookies WHERE uid = $uid;
```

Discussion

This query is automatically contextual to your app based on the API key you initialized the Facebook client with, so you'll only be able to pull back cookies dropped by your app.

8.12 Retrieving a Specific Cookie

Problem

I need to retrieve a specific cookie using FQL.

Solution

```
SELECT name, value, path from cookies WHERE name="$name" AND uid = $user;
```

Discussion

Remember that all FQL queries are scoped to your application, so if you specify the name of a cookie from a different app, you'll get back null.

8.13 Retrieving All Cookies for a Specific Path

Problem

I need to retrieve all of the cookies I've dropped for a specific page in my app using FQL.

Solution and Discussion

```
SELECT name, value, path from cookies WHERE path="$path" AND uid = $user;
```

8.14 Metrics Table

Problem

What's the schema for the `metrics` table?

Solution

The `metrics` table holds all of the metrics recorded for your application. Its fields are listed in Table 8-4. You can view the same metrics from inside the Facebook Insights app (*http://www.facebook.com/business/insights/app.php?id=12345*). Metrics are calculated at midnight Pacific time everyday, so you should convert your `date` values into epoch seconds based on midnight PST (see Recipe 6.20 for more about epoch seconds). More information about this table, including an up-to-date listing of fields, can be found at *http://wiki.developers.facebook.com/index.php/Metrics_(FQL)*.

Table 8-4. metrics table fields

Name	Type	Index	Description
end_time	int	•	The ending date for which these metrics were recorded, in epoch seconds. See Recipe 6.20 for an explanation of epoch seconds.
period	int	•	Length of time for which you want results, in seconds. Supported lengths are one day (86400 seconds), seven days (604800 seconds), and 30 days (2592000 seconds).
active_users	int		Number of active users in your app on this day.
unique_adds	int		Number of unique new users for your app on this day (if the same user added, removed, and then added it again, it only counts for one).
unique_removes	int		Number of unique removes for your app on this day (if the same user added, removed, added, and removed, it only counts for one).
unique_blocks	int		Number of unique blocks for your app on this day (if the same user blocked, unblocked, and blocked, it only counts for one).
unique_unblocks	int		Number of unique unblocks for your app on this day (if the same user blocked, unblocked, blocked, and unblocked, it only counts for one).
api_calls	int		Total number of API calls your app made on this day (e.g., two calls to `fql_query` would count as two here).
unique_api_calls	int		Unique API calls made by your app on this day (e.g., two calls to `fql_query` would count as only one here).

Name	Type	Index	Description
canvas_page_views	int		Number of Canvas pages your app served up on this day (two views of the same page count as two views here).
unique_canvas_page_views	int		Unique number of Canvas pages your app served up on this day (two views of the same page count as only one views here).
canvas_http_request_time_avg	int		The average time required to handle an HTTP request from your app, in milliseconds.
canvas_fbml_render_time_avg	int		The average time required to render an FBML page for your app, in milliseconds.
canvas_page_views_http_code_0	int		The number of Canvas pages that timed out.
canvas_page_views_http_code_200	int		The number of Canvas page requests that were successful (HTTP code 200 is success).
canvas_page_views_http_code_200ND	int		The number of Canvas page requests that were successful but returned no data (HTTP code 200 is success; ND is no data).
canvas_page_views_http_code_404	int		The number of Canvas page requests that couldn't be found (HTTP code 404 is resource not found).

Note that only the fields marked as "Index" in this table can be used in an FQL query's WHERE clause, but any of the fields can appear in the SELECT.

Discussion

If you'd rather use the API to access `metrics`, try the `Admin.getMetrics( )` method.

This table actually contains fields for every HTTP code, not just the ones listed here. Simply sub in the code you want and you should get results. For example, if you were looking for 301, which is "resource permanently moved," you could SELECT canvas_page_views_http_code_301.

8.15 Retrieving Yesterday's Metrics

Problem

I need to retrieve some of my metrics from yesterday.

Solution

Since the `date` field is in epoch seconds, you need to do a conversion before you can query on it:

```php
<?php
$hoursAhead = 3;
$period = 86400; // 86400 = one day, 604800 = one week, 2592000 = one month
```

```
$yesterday = mktime($hoursAhead,0,0,date("m"),date("d")-1,date("Y"));
$monthAgo = mktime($hoursAhead,0,0,date("m"),date("d")-30,date("Y"));
$query = 'SELECT api_calls from metrics WHERE end_time = ' .
$yesterday . ' AND period = ' . $period . ';';
$metrics = $facebook->api_client->fql_query($query);
?>
```

You'll need to substitute the number of hours that your server's time zone is ahead of PST into the first line, and also change the fields you want to retrieve in the actual query if you want something other than just the number of API calls.

Discussion

The hours ahead of PST is important because Facebook calculates metrics at midnight PST and considers a day from midnight to 11:59:59 p.m. PST. You should always set your date ranges based on that time zone. See Recipe 6.20 for more information about epoch seconds.

8.16 Retrieving Metrics for a Date Range

Problem

I need to retrieve some of my app's metrics for the last 30 days.

Solution

Since the `date` field is in epoch seconds, you need to do a conversion before you can query on it:

```
<?php
$hoursAhead = 3;
$period = 2592000; // 86400 = one day, 604800 = one week, 2592000 = one month

$yesterday = mktime($hoursAhead,0,0,date("m"),date("d")-1,date("Y"));
$monthAgo = mktime($hoursAhead,0,0,date("m"),date("d")-30,date("Y"));
$query = 'SELECT active_users from metrics WHERE end_time = ' .
$yesterday . ' AND period = ' . $period . ';';
$metrics = $facebook->api_client->fql_query($query);
?>
```

The variable `metrics` will now contain an array with a single element that contains the `active_users` for the 30-day period ending yesterday.

Discussion

The hours ahead of PST is important because Facebook calculates metrics at midnight PST and considers a day from midnight to 11:59:59 p.m. PST. You should always set your date ranges based on that time zone. See Recipe 6.20 for more information about epoch seconds.

8.17 Alerting Yourself

Problem

I'd like to receive email alerts when my app is serving up 200ND (No Data) or 404 (Not Found) errors.

Solution

Since you can make calls from any server to Facebook through the Client, you can schedule a `cron` job on your server to use something like `curl` to request a page that runs the following code:

```php
<?php
$hoursAhead = 3;
$appId = 12345;
$appName = 'My App name goes here';
$myEmail = 'me@mydomain.com';

$yesterday = mktime($hoursAhead,0,0,date("m"),date("d")-1,date("Y"));
$query = 'SELECT canvas_page_views_http_code_200ND, canvas_page_views
_http_code_404 from metrics WHERE end_time = ' . $yesterday . ' AND period = 86400;';
$metrics = $facebook->api_client->fql_query($query);

if($metrics && ($metrics[0]['canvas_page_views_http_code_200ND']
 > 0 || $metrics[0]['canvas_page_views_http_code_404'] > 0) ){
    $headers = 'From: do-not-reply@mydomain.com' . "\r\n" . 'X-Priority: 1';

    $message = $appName . ' had ' . $metrics[0]['canvas_page_views
_http_code_200ND'] . ' 200ND errors';
    $message .= ' and ' . $metrics[0]['canvas_page_views_http_code_404']
 . ' 404 errors';
    $message .= ' on ' . date('F dS, Y', $yesterday) . '.';
    $message .= ' View more info at http://www.facebook.com/business/
insights/app.php?id=' . $appId . '&tab=httpreq';

    $success = mail($myEmail, '[Facebook Errors]: ' . $appName, $message, $headers);
}
?>
```

The little bit of configuration at the top will customize this for your app.

Discussion

Note that this code requires you to have an SMTP server running locally on your server, which most of you will. You can check to see whether your server's PHP is at least configured to send mail by putting `phpinfo( )` into a page and loading it in your browser—look for `sendmail_path` and make sure there's a value there (you can't do this through Facebook because `phpinfo( )` outputs a `body` tag, which the FBML parser won't allow, so you'll have to hit your server directly at your callback URL).

Many PHP installs don't have a default "from" address configured, and most SMTP servers will reject email without one, so we're adding in an additional header just to be safe (along with setting the priority to the highest level so that you notice the alerts in your inbox).

If you need some help with setting up a `cron` job, check out Click Mojo's excellent tutorial at *http://www.clickmojo.com/code/cron-tutorial.html*.

8.18 Event Table

Problem

What's the schema for the event table?

Solution

The event table holds all of the events created in the Facebook Events application. Its fields are listed in Table 8-5. Queries to this table will only return data the current user is allowed to see (meaning you can't request events for users the current user isn't friends with). More information about this table, including an up-to-date listing of fields, can be found at *http://wiki.developers.facebook.com/index.php/Event_(FQL)*.

Table 8-5. event table fields

Name	Type	Index	Description
eid	int	•	eid (event ID) of this event.
name	string		Name of this event.
tagline	string		Tagline of this event.
nid	int		nid (network ID) of the network, as set by the creator when the event was created.
pic_small	string		URL of the small picture for this event, which has a maximum width of 50 px and a maximum height of 150 px. Might be empty if this field wasn't set by the creator.
pic_big	string		URL of the big picture for this event (max width of 200 px, max height of 600 px). Might be empty if this field wasn't set by the creator.
pic	string		URL of the picture for this event (max width of 100 px, max height of 300 px). Might be empty if this field wasn't set by the creator.
host	string		Name of the host of the event. Note that this can be set to a group when the event is created, but this will return only a `string`, not a `gid`.
description	string		Description of this event.
event_type	string		Type of this event. Can be any one of Party, Causes, Education, Meetings, Music/Arts, Sports, Trips, or Other.
event_subtype	string		Subtype of this event. Subtypes are tied to the type, so each type has between 3 and 20 options.
start_time	string		Start time in epoch seconds. See Recipe 6.20 for more about epoch seconds.

Name	Type	Index	Description
end_time	string		End time in epoch seconds. See Recipe 6.20 for more about epoch seconds.
creator	int		uid (user ID) of the user who created this event.
update_time	string		Last time this event was updated in epoch seconds. See Recipe 6.20 for more about epoch seconds.
location	string		Location of this event. This is a free text field, so this could be anything.
venue	array		An array containing the street address, city, state, country, latitude, and longitude of the venue.

Note that only the fields marked as "Index" in this table can be used in an FQL query's WHERE clause, but any of the fields can appear in the SELECT.

Discussion

If you'd rather use the API to access events, see the Events.get( ) method in Chapter 9.

8.19 Event Member Table

Problem

What's the schema of the event_member table?

Solution

The event_member table records the relationships between events and users, as well as their RSVP status. Its fields are listed in Table 8-6. Queries to this table will only return data the current user is allowed to see (meaning you can't request events for users the current user isn't friends with). More information about this table, including an up-to-date listing of fields, can be found at *http://wiki.developers.facebook.com/index.php/Event_member_(FQL)*.

Table 8-6. event_member table fields

Name	Type	Index	Description
eid	int	•	eid (Event ID) of this event.
uid	int	•	uid (User ID) of the Facebook user whose RSVP status is recorded in this entry.
rsvp_status	string		The user's RSVP status. Can be one of attending, declined, unsure, or not_replied.

Note that only the fields marked as "Index" in this table can be used in an FQL query's WHERE clause, but any of the fields can appear in the SELECT.

Discussion

If you'd rather use the API to access `event_members`, try the `Events.get()` and `Events.getMembers()` methods.

8.20 Retrieving an Event

Problem

I need to retrieve a Facebook event using FQL.

Solution

If you have the `eid` (event ID) of the event, this is easy:

```
SELECT eid, name, pic_small, description, start_time,
    end_time, location FROM event WHERE eid = $eid;
```

You can, of course, `SELECT` a different set of fields.

Discussion

The only place you can get an `eid` using FQL is from the `event_member` table (see Recipe 8.19). This query will only return events that the current `loggedinuser` has permission to see.

8.21 Retrieving Events Created by a User

Problem

I need to retrieve all of the Facebook events created by a specific user using FQL.

Solution

```
SELECT eid, name, pic_small, description, start_time,
    end_time, location FROM event WHERE creator = $user AND eid IN (SELECT eid
    FROM event_member WHERE uid = $user);
```

Discussion

This will return content only if the current `loggedinuser` can see the events of the user specified in `$user`.

8.22 Retrieving a User's Events

Problem

I need to retrieve a specific user's Facebook events using FQL.

Solution

Retrieving all of a specific user's events is easy:

```
SELECT eid, rsvp_status FROM event_member WHERE uid = $uid
```

Discussion

Keep in mind that this will return events only if the current `loggedinuser` is allowed to see them. If you query for a user that the `loggedinuser` isn't friends with, you'll get an empty results set.

8.23 Retrieving a User's Events with a Specific RSVP

Problem

I need to retrieve a specific user's event based on their RSVP.

Solution

```
SELECT eid, rsvp_status FROM event_member WHERE rsvp_status = $status AND uid = $user;
```

Discussion

There are four possible statuses for `event_member` records: `attending`, `declined`, `unsure`, or `not_replied`. Keep in mind that this solution will return events only if the current `loggedinuser` is allowed to see them.

8.24 Retrieving Events Two Users Are Attending

Problem

I need to find all of the events that two users are attending, using FQL.

Solution

Assuming the current `loggedinuser` is friends with both of these users (or otherwise allowed to see their events):

```
SELECT name FROM event WHERE eid IN (SELECT eid FROM
 event_member WHERE uid = $user1 AND eid IN (SELECT eid FROM event_member
 WHERE uid= $user2))
```

You'll need to plug the two IDs in as `user1` and `user2`.

Discussion

This should be pretty easy to extend for more than two users if you need to, and it shouldn't affect performance considerably, since the heavy lifting is done by the database.

8.25 Friend Table

Problem

What's the schema of the `friend` table?

Solution

The `friend` table records the friendship between two users. Its fields are listed in Table 8-7. Queries to this table will only return data the current user is allowed to see (meaning you can't request friendships for users the current `loggedinuser` isn't friends with). More information about this table, including an up-to-date listing of fields, can be found at *http://wiki.developers.facebook.com/index.php/Friend_(FQL)*.

Table 8-7. friend table fields

Name	Type	Index	Description
uid1	int	•	uid (user ID) of the first user
uid2	int	•	uid (user ID) of the second user

Discussion

If you'd rather use the API to access `friends`, try the `Friends.get( )` and the `Friends.areFriends( )` methods.

This table isn't all that useful on its own, since it contains only two data points, but it is very powerful when combined with the `user` table (see Recipe 8.55).

8.26 Friend Request Table

Problem

What's the schema for the `friend_request` table?

Solution

The `friend_request` table records the friendship requests between two users. Its fields are listed in Table 8-8. Queries to this table will only return data the current user is allowed to see (meaning you can't request friendships for users the current `loggedinuser` isn't friends with). More information about this table, including an up-to-date listing of fields, can be found at *http://wiki.developers.facebook.com/index.php/Friend_request_(FQL)*.

Table 8-8. friend_request table fields

Name	Type	Index	Description
uid_to	int	•	uid (user ID) of the user this request went to. You can query only on the current loggedinuser.
uid_from	int		uid (user ID) of the user this request came from.

Note that only the field marked as "Index" in this table can be used in an FQL query's `WHERE` clause, but any of the fields can appear in the `SELECT`.

Discussion

This table isn't all that useful on its own, since it contains only two data points, but you can combine it with other tables as a subquery.

8.27 Retrieving a User's Friends

Problem

I need to retrieve all of a specific user's friends using FQL.

Solution

This is a really simple query:

```
SELECT uid2 FROM friend WHERE uid1 = $uid;
```

Discussion

Luckily for FQL users everywhere, this query returns exactly the same result if you run it the other way around:

```
SELECT uid1 FROM friend WHERE uid2 = $uid;
```

You can run this query only when you're looking for the friends of the current `loggedinuser`, or you'll get an "Error 604: Can't lookup all friends of 12345; only for the logged in user" error (see Recipe 8.58 for more info).

8.28 Checking Whether Two Users are Friends

Problem

I need to check to see whether two users are friends using FQL.

Solution

If this query returns a result, user1 and user2 are friends:

```
SELECT uid1 FROM friend WHERE uid1 = $user1 AND uid2 = $user2;
```

Discussion

There are no privacy restrictions on this query in terms of errors, but you will get back an empty set if the current loggedinuser isn't allowed to see the friends for one of the two users.

8.29 Retrieving a User's Pending Friend Requests

Problem

I need to retrieve all of the pending friend requests for a specific user using FQL.

Solution

This query will return an empty set if there are no pending requests:

```
SELECT uid_from FROM friend_request WHERE uid_to = $uid;
```

Discussion

You can run this query only for the current loggedinuser or you'll get an "Error 604, Message: Can only lookup friend requests for logged in user" (see Recipe 8.58 for more information).

8.30 Checking for a Friend Request Between Two Users

Problem

I need to check to see whether there's a pending friend request between two specific users using FQL.

Solution

```
SELECT uid_to, uid_from FROM friend_request WHERE uid_from
= $user2 AND uid_to = $user1;
```

Discussion

You can run this query only when `user1` is the current `loggedinuser`.

8.31 Friend List Table

Problem

What's the schema for the `friendlist` table?

Solution

The `friendlist` table stores the friend lists created by users to organize their friends. Its fields are listed in Table 8-9. Queries to this table will only return data the current user is allowed to see (i.e., you can't request `friendlists` for users other than the current `loggedinuser`). More information about this table, including an up-to-date listing of fields, can be found at *http://wiki.developers.facebook.com/index.php/Friendlist_(FQL)*.

Table 8-9. friendlist table fields

Name	Type	Index	Description
flid	int		`flid` (friendlist ID) of this friend list.
name	string		Name of this friend list.
owner	int	•	`uid` (user ID) of the owner of this friend list. You can query only on the current `loggedinuser`.

Note that only the field marked as "Index" in this table can be used in an FQL query's `WHERE` clause, but any of the fields can appear in the `SELECT`.

Discussion

If you'd rather use the API to access `friendlists`, try the `Friends.getLists()` method.

8.32 Friend List Members Table

Problem

What's the schema for the `friendlist_member` table?

Solution

The `friendlist_member` table records the friends that a user has placed into his friend lists. Its fields are listed in Table 8-10. Queries to this table will only return data the current user is allowed to see (i.e., you can't request `friendlists` for users other than the current `loggedinuser`). More information about this table, including an up-to-date listing of fields, can be found at *http://wiki.developers.facebook.com/index.php/Friend list_member_(FQL)*.

Table 8-10. friendlist_member table fields

Name	Type	Index	Description
flid	int	•	flid (friendlist ID) of the friend list. You can only query for flids owned by the current loggedinuser.
uid	int		uid (user ID) of the friend that the current loggedinuser has placed in the friend list.

Note that only the field marked as "Index" in this table can be used in an FQL query's WHERE clause, but any of the fields can appear in the SELECT.

Discussion

If you'd rather use the API to access friendlist_members, try the Friends.getLists( ) method.

8.33 Retrieving a User's Friend Lists

Problem

I need to retrieve a specific user's friend lists using FQL.

Solution

```
SELECT flid, name FROM friendlist WHERE owner = $uid;
```

Discussion

You can run this query only when uid is the current loggedinuser.

8.34 Retrieving a Specific Friend List

Problem

I need to retrieve a specific friend list from a specific user using FQL.

Solution

```
SELECT flid, name FROM friendlist WHERE name = $name AND owner = $user;
```

Discussion

You can run this query only when uid is the current loggedinuser.

8.35 Retrieving Friends in Friend Lists

Problem

I need to use FQL to retrieve the friends that specific users have put in their friend lists.

Solution

You can pretty easily find all of the friends that the current `loggedinuser` has put into friend lists:

```
SELECT flid, uid FROM friendlist_member WHERE flid IN
  (SELECT flid FROM friendlist WHERE owner = $uid)
```

Discussion

You can run this query only when `uid` is the current `loggedinuser`.

8.36 Retrieving Friends in a Specific Friend List

Problem

I need to retrieve the friends from a specific user's specific friend list using FQL.

Solution

```
SELECT name FROM user WHERE uid IN (SELECT uid FROM friendlist
_member WHERE flid IN (SELECT flid FROM friendlist WHERE name = $name
 AND owner = $user));
```

Discussion

This will work only when `user` is the current `loggedinuser`.

8.37 Groups Table

Problem

What's the schema for the group table?

Solution

The group table stores the groups that have been created in the Facebook Groups app. Its fields are listed in Table 8-11. Queries to this table will only return data the current user is allowed to see (meaning you can't request groups that the current `loggedinuser` can't see). More information about this table, including an up-to-date listing of fields, can be found at *http://wiki.developers.facebook.com/index.php/Group _(FQL)*.

Table 8-11. group table fields

Name	Type	Index	Description
gid	int	•	Group ID of this group.
name	string		Name of this group.
nid	int		Network ID that this group belongs to, if any.
pic_small	string		URL of the small picture for this group (max width of 50 px and max height of 150 px). Might be empty if this field wasn't set by the creator.
pic_big	string		URL of the big picture for this group (max width of 200 px and max height of 600 px). Might be empty if this field wasn't set by the creator.
pic	string		URL of the picture for this group (max width of 100 px and max height of 300 px). Might be empty if this field wasn't set by the creator.
description	string		Description of this group.
group_type	string		Type of group. Can be any one of Business, Common Interest, Entertainment & Arts, Geography, Internet & Technology, Just for Fun, Music, Organizations, Sports & Recreation, or Student Groups.
group_subtype	string		Subtype of this group. Subtypes are tied to the type, and each has between 3 and 20 options.
recent_news	string		Contents of the Recent News as set by a group admin.
creator	int		User ID of the creator of the group.
update_time	string		Last time this event was updated in epoch seconds. See Recipe 6.20 for more about epoch seconds.
office	string		Contents of the office field as entered by the creator of the group.
website	string		Contents of the website field as entered by the creator of the group.
venue	array		An array containing the street address, city, state, and country of the venue of the group.

Note that only the field marked as "Index" in this table can be used in an FQL query's WHERE clause, but any of the fields can appear in the SELECT.

Discussion

If you'd rather use the API to access groups, try the Groups.get( ) method.

8.38 Group Member Table

Problem

What's the schema for the group_member table?

Solution

The `group_member` table records the relationships between **groups** and **users**. Its fields are listed in Table 8-12. Queries to this table will only return data the current user is allowed to see (i.e., you can't request **groups** that the current `loggedinuser` can't see). More information about this table, including an up-to-date listing of fields, can be found at *http://wiki.developers.facebook.com/index.php/Group_member_(FQL)*.

Table 8-12. group_member table fields

Name	Type	Index	Description
uid	int	•	User ID of this user.
gid	int	•	Group ID that this user belongs to.
posi tions	array		Any positions in the group that this user may occupy. If the user has no position in this group, positions will be null; otherwise, it will be an array listing each of her positions. Looks like the possible positions are ADMIN and OFFICER, but that's not documented anywhere.

Note that only the fields marked as "Index" in this table can be used in an FQL query's `WHERE` clause, but any of the fields can appear in the `SELECT`.

Discussion

If you'd rather use the API to access **groups**, try the `Groups.get()` and `Groups.getMembers()` methods.

8.39 Retrieving a Specific Group

Problem

I need to retrieve a specific group using FQL.

Solution

If you know the **gid** of the group, it's as easy as:

```
SELECT name, description FROM group WHERE gid = $gid;
```

It's a little trickier if you know the **name** of the group but not the **gid**. As long as the **user** is a member of the group, you can do this:

```
SELECT gid, nid, description FROM group WHERE name = $name
  AND gid IN (SELECT gid FROM group_member WHERE uid = $user);
```

Discussion

The current `loggedinuser` needs to be allowed to see the specified group or you'll get back an empty set. Two things to note if you're looking up a group by name:

- Groups aren't unique by name, so you may well get more than one result back.
- Remember that it's an exact match, so you'll need to get punctuation and capitalization exactly right.

8.40 Retrieving a User's Groups

Problem

I need to retrieve a specific user's groups using FQL.

Solution

You can't get a user's groups without using both the group and group_member tables:

```
SELECT name FROM group WHERE gid IN (SELECT gid FROM group_member WHERE uid = $uid);
```

Discussion

If the current loggedinuser doesn't have permission to see the groups that uid is in, you'll get an empty set.

8.41 Checking Whether Two Users Are in the Same Group

Problem

I need to check to see whether two specific users are in the same group using FQL.

Solution

Assuming the current loggedinuser is able to see both groups:

```
SELECT name FROM group WHERE gid IN (SELECT gid FROM
group_member WHERE uid = $user1 AND gid IN (SELECT gid FROM group_member
WHERE uid = $user2))
```

You'll need to plug the two IDs into user1 and user2.

Discussion

This should be pretty easy to extend for more than two users if you need to, and it shouldn't affect performance considerably, since the heavy lifting is done by the database. Just chain on an additional subquery for every additional user you need to check, and remember to add a closing bracket at the end.

8.42 Listing Table

Problem

What's the schema for the `listing` table?

Solution

The `listing` table stores the listings created in the Facebook Marketplace application. Its fields are listed in Table 8-13. Queries to this table will only return data the current user is allowed to see (i.e., you can't request `listing` that the current `loggedinuser` can't see). More information about this table, including an up-to-date listing of fields, can be found at *http://wiki.developers.facebook.com/index.php/Listings_(FQL)*.

Table 8-13. listing table fields

Name	Type	Index	Description
listing_id	int	•	Listing ID of this listing.
url	string		URL pointing to this listing on Facebook.
title	string		Title of this listing.
description	string		Description of this listing.
price	string		Price of this item as a string (rather than a float).
poster	int	•	User ID of the user who posted this item.
update_time	string		The last time this item was updated in epoch seconds. For more info about epoch seconds, see Recipe 6.20.
category	string		The top-level categories for listings are JOBS, FORSALE, HOUSING, FREE STUFF, and OTHER.
subcategory	string		Subcategories are the level below the category. Each category has about five subs (e.g., "For Sale" breaks down into "Books", "Furniture", "Tickets", "Electronics", "Cars", and "Other").
image_urls	array		An array of the images uploaded to this listing. Users can add four images when they create the listing and can add more after it's been created (which is a really effective user experience design trick to limit most people to four unless they're determined enough to add more).
condition	string		Condition of the item, if applicable. Either Used or New.
isbn	string		ISBN number, if applicable.
num_beds	int		Number of bedrooms, if applicable.
num_baths	int		Number of bathrooms, if applicable.
dogs	bool		Are dogs allowed? (if applicable)
cats	bool		Are cats allowed? (if applicable)
smoking	bool		Is smoking allowed? (if applicable)
square_footage	string		Square footage of the property, if applicable.

Name	Type	Index	Description
street	string		Street address of the property, if applicable.
crossstreet	string		Closest cross street to the property, if applicable.
postal	string		Postal/zip code of the property, if applicable.
rent	int		Monthly rent of the property, if applicable.
pay	int		Salary for the job, if applicable.

Note that only the fields marked as "Index" in this table can be used in an FQL query's WHERE clause, but any of the fields can appear in the SELECT.

Discussion

The design of this table is a little strange in that it has fields to accommodate every possible listing property in one table, rather than splitting them out into tables for each type of listing and using a central table to record the IDs of the children. Sometimes it's better to denormalize your data for performance reasons, and this approach means that all listings are in a single table with one index on listing_id, which is significantly faster than chaining down through relationships. For more information about denormalization, see Recipe 8.5 or *http://en.wikipedia.org/wiki/Denormalization*.

If you'd rather use the API to access listings, try the Marketplace.getListings( ) and Marketplace.search( ) methods.

8.43 Retrieving a Listing

Problem

I need to retrieve specific a listing from the Facebook Marketplace using FQL.

Solution

If you know the listing_id of the listing, it's as simple as:

```
SELECT url, title, description, price, poster FROM listing
  WHERE listing_id = $listing_id;
```

If you don't know the listing_id but it was posted by user and you do know the title, you can do:

```
SELECT listing_id, description FROM listing WHERE title = $title AND poster = $user;
```

Discussion

The current loggedinuser needs to be allowed to see the specified listing or you'll get back an empty set. Two things to note if you're looking up a listing by title:

- Listings aren't unique by title, so you may well get more than one result back.
- Remember that it's an exact match, so you'll need to get punctuation and capitalization exactly right.

8.44 Retrieving a User's Listings

Problem

I need to retrieve all of the listings posted by a specified user using FQL.

Solution

```
SELECT url, title, description, price FROM listing WHERE poster = $uid;
```

Discussion

The current `loggedinuser` needs to be able to see this listings posted by the user you're querying on, or you'll get back an empty set.

8.45 Retrieving a User's Friends' Listings

Problem

I need to retrieve all of a specified user's friends' listings using FQL.

Solution

```
SELECT title, url, description, price, category FROM
  listing WHERE poster IN (SELECT uid2 FROM friend WHERE uid1 = $user);
```

Discussion

Since this is based on a query on the `friend` table, you can make it only when `user` is the current `loggedinuser`.

8.46 Retrieving a User's Listings by Category

Problem

I need to retrieve all of a specified user's listings that are in a specific category.

Solution

```
SELECT title,listing_id, description, category FROM listing WHERE
  category = $category AND poster = $user;
```

Discussion

Unfortunately, there's no way to retrieve all of the listings in a category independently of the poster, as you ultimately need a `WHERE` clause that acts on either the `poster` or `listing_id` fields.

You can easily modify this recipe to search for all of the listings in a category from all of the user's friends:

```
SELECT title, url, description, price category FROM listing
  WHERE category = $category AND poster IN (SELECT uid2 FROM friend
  WHERE uid1 = $user);
```

8.47 Page Table

Problem

What's the schema for the page table?

Solution

The `page` table records information about Facebook Pages. Its fields are listed in Table 8-14. Queries to this table will only return data the current user is allowed to see (i.e., you can't request `pages` that the current `loggedinuser` can't see). More information about this table, including an up-to-date listing of fields, can be found at *http://wiki .developers.facebook.com/index.php/Page_(FQL)*.

Table 8-14. page table fields

Name	Type	Index	Description
page_id	int	•	Page ID of this Page.
name	string	•	Name of this Page.
pic_small	string		URL of the small picture for this Page (max width of 50 px and max height of 150 px). Might be empty if this field wasn't set by the creator.
pic_big	string		URL of the big picture for this Page (max width of 200 px and max height of 600 px). Might be empty if this field wasn't set by the creator.
pic_square	string		URL of the square picture for this Page (max width and height of 50 px). Might be empty if this field wasn't set by the creator.
pic	string		URL of the picture for this Page (max width of 100 px and max height of 300 px). Might be empty if this field wasn't set by the creator.
pic_large	string		URL of the large picture for this Page (max width of 396 px and max height of 1188 px). Might be empty if this field wasn't set by the creator.
type	string		Type of this Page.
website	string		External URL for the subject of this Page.
has_added_app	bool		Indicates whether this Page has your application installed.

Name	Type	Index	Description
founded	string		The date when the subject of this Page was founded, if applicable.
company_overview	string		Summary of the subject of this Page, if applicable.
mission	string		Mission statement of the organization that is the subject of this Page, if applicable.
products	string		Products offered by the company on this Page, if applicable.
location	string		Location of this Page, including the street, city, state, country, and zip code (or post code). Some of the fields may be blank.
parking	string		Type of parking available at the location of this Page.
public_transit	string		Type of public transportation available near the location of this Page, if applicable.
hours	string		Hours of operation for the Page being queried.
attire	string		Type of attire recommended by the Page being queried, if applicable.
payment_options	string		Forms of payment accepted by the Page being queried, if applicable.
culinary_team	string		Team of people preparing the food at the restaurant on this Page, if applicable.
general_manager	string		General manager of this Page, if applicable.
price_range	string		Price range for the products offered by this Page.
restaurant_services	string		Services offered by the restaurant on this Page, if applicable.
restaurant_specialties	string		House specials offered by the restaurant on this Page, if applicable.
release_date	string		Date the film on this Page was released, if applicable.
genre	string		Genre of music of the band on this Page, if applicable.
starring	string		Actors starring in the film on this Page, if applicable.
screenplay_by	string		Screenwriters of the film on this Page, if applicable.
directed_by	string		Director of the film on this Page, if applicable.
produced_by	string		Producers of the film on this Page, if applicable.
studio	string		Studio releasing the film on this Page, if applicable.
awards	string		Awards received by the film on this Page, if applicable.
plot_outline	string		Plot of the film on this Page, if applicable.
network	string		Network airing the TV show on this Page, if applicable.
season	int		Season of the TV show on this Page, if applicable.
schedule	string		Schedule of the TV show on this Page, if applicable.
written_by	string		Writers of the TV show on this Page, if applicable.
band_members	string		Members of the band on this Page, if applicable.
hometown	string		Home town of the band on this Page, if applicable.
current_location	string		Current location of the band on this Page, if applicable.
record_label	string		Record label for the band on this Page, if applicable.

Name	Type	Index	Description
booking_agent	string		Booking agent for the band on this Page, if applicable.
artists_we_like	string		Other bands and artists that the band on this Page likes, if applicable.
influences	string		Influences of the band on this Page, if applicable.
band_interests	string		Other interests of the band on this Page, if applicable.
bio	string		Artist biography of the band on this Page, if applicable.
affiliation	string		Political affiliation of the person on this Page, if applicable.
birthday	string		Birthday of the person featured on this Page, if applicable.
personal_info	string		Personal information about the artist on this Page, if applicable.
personal_interests	string		Other interests of the artist on this Page, if applicable.
members	string		Members of the cast of the TV show on this Page, if applicable.
built	string		Year the vehicle on this Page was built, if applicable.
features	string		Features of the vehicle on this Page, if applicable.
mpg	string		Fuel economy (in miles per gallon) of the vehicle featured on this Page, if applicable.
general_info	string		General information about the entity on this Page, if applicable.

Note that only the fields marked as "Index" in this table can be used in an FQL query's WHERE clause, but any of the fields can appear in the SELECT.

Discussion

Much like the schema for the listing table (see Recipe 8.42), the page table has been seriously denormalized for performance reasons. A normalized schema for this page would move all of the fields specific to one type of listing into a secondary table for that listing type.

If you'd rather use the API to access page, try the Pages.getInfo( ) method.

8.48 Page Fan Table

Problem

What's the schema for the page_fan table?

Solution

The page_fan table records the relationships between pages and users. Its fields are listed in Table 8-15. Queries to this table will only return data the current user is allowed to see (i.e., you can't request fans for pages that the current loggedinuser can't see).

More information about this table, including an up-to-date listing of fields, can be found at *http://wiki.developers.facebook.com/index.php/Page_fan_(FQL)*.

Table 8-15. page_fan table fields

Name	Type	Index	Description
uid	int	•	User ID of this user.
page_id	int		Page ID of the Page the user is a fan of.
type	string		Type of this Page. There are a way too many different Page types to enumerate here. You can see them on the Create a Page page (*http://www.facebook.com/pages/create.php*). They're generally stored in the database in all caps, with underscores in place of spaces (e.g., CONSUMER_PRODUCTS).

Note that only the field marked as "Index" in this table can be used in an FQL query's WHERE clause, but any of the fields can appear in the SELECT.

Discussion

There's a really obvious index missing from this table, which makes working with it a whole lot harder: page_id (although the field exists, the lack of an index on it means you can't include it in FQL queries as part of the WHERE clause). As it currently stands, you can find the Pages a user is a fan of but not the users who are fans of a Page. It would fit better with the general FQL model to enable that index but only return users that the current loggedinuser is friends with, so maybe that will come in time.

If you'd rather use the API to access page_fan, try the Pages.getInfo( ) and Pages.isFan( ) methods.

8.49 Retrieving a Page

Problem

I need to retrieve a specific Page using FQL.

Solution

If you know the page_id of the Page you want, this is easy:

```
SELECT name, type, pic_square FROM page WHERE page_id = $page_id;
```

If you don't know the page_id but do know the name, you can still find it, as long as you know a user who's a fan:

```
SELECT page_id, pic_square, type FROM page WHERE name = $name
    AND page_id IN (SELECT page_id FROM page_fan WHERE uid = $user;
```

Discussion

This is a little harder than some of the comparable queries on other tables because there's no way to do this without a subquery, which is dependent on having a uid. As noted earlier, the outcome is that this will work only when the current loggedinuser or one of his friends is a fan of the Page you're looking for.

You'll get an empty set if the current loggedinuser doesn't have permission to see the Pages of the user you're querying on.

8.50 Retrieving a User's Pages

Problem

I need to retrieve all of the Pages a specified user is a fan of using FQL.

Solution

```
SELECT name, type, pic_square FROM page WHERE page_id IN
  (SELECT page_id FROM page_fan WHERE uid = $user);
```

Discussion

You'll get an empty set if the current loggedinuser doesn't have permission to see the Pages of the user you're querying on.

8.51 Photo Table

Problem

What's the schema for the photo table?

Solution

The photo table stores the photos that have been created in the Facebook Photos app. Its fields are listed in Table 8-16. Queries to this table will only return data the current user is allowed to see (i.e., you can't request photos that the current loggedinuser can't see). More information about this table, including an up-to-date listing of fields, can be found at *http://wiki.developers.facebook.com/index.php/Photo_(FQL)*.

Table 8-16. photo table fields

Name	Type	Index	Description
pid	int	•	Photo ID of this photo.
aid	int	•	Album ID of this photo.
owner	int		User ID that this photo belongs to.

Name	Type	Index	Description
src_small	string		URL of the small picture for this photo (max width of 75 px and max height of 225 px). Might be empty if this field wasn't set by the creator.
src_big	string		URL of the big picture for this group (max width or height of 604 px). Might be empty if this field wasn't set by the creator.
src	string		URL of the picture for this photo (max width or height of 130 px). Might be empty if this field wasn't set by the creator.
link	string		URL to view this photo on Facebook.
caption	string		Caption for this photo.
created	string		Date this photo was created in epoch seconds. See Recipe 6.20 for more about epoch seconds.

Note that only the fields marked as "Index" in this table can be used in an FQL query's WHERE clause, but any of the fields can appear in the SELECT.

Discussion

If you'd rather use the API to access photos, try the Photos.get( ) method.

8.52 Photo Tag Table

Problem

What's the schema for the photo_tag table?

Solution

The photo_tag table contains the relationship between photos and the users who have been tagged in them. Its fields are listed in Table 8-17. Queries to this table will only return data the current user is allowed to see (i.e., you can't request photos that the current loggedinuser can't see). More information about this table, including an up-to-date listing of fields, can be found at *http://wiki.developers.facebook.com/index.php/ Photo_tag_(FQL)*.

Table 8-17. photo_tag table fields

Name	Type	Index	Description
pid	int	•	Photo ID of this photo.
subject	int	•	User ID of the person tagged in this photo.
text	string		The text entered for this tag.
xcoord	float		The *x* coordinate of the center of the tag square.
ycoord	float		The *y* coordinate of the center of the tag square.
created	int		The date this tag was created, in epoch seconds. See Recipe 6.20 for more about epoch seconds.

Note that only the fields marked as "Index" in this table can be used in an FQL query's WHERE clause, but any of the fields can appear in the SELECT.

Discussion

If you'd rather use the API to access photo_tags, try the Photos.get( ) and Photos.getTags( ) method.

8.53 Retrieving the 10 Most Recent Photos from a User

Problem

I need to retrieve the 10 most recently posted photos by a specific user using FQL.

Solution

```
SELECT pid, src, caption FROM photo WHERE aid IN (SELECT
 aid FROM album WHERE owner = $user) ORDER BY created DESC LIMIT 10;
```

Discussion

The owner field isn't indexed in the photo table, so we need to make a subquery into the album table to find photos owned by a specific user.

The ORDER BY and LIMIT clauses can be applied to any of the queries in this chapter to order and/or constrain the result set.

8.54 Retrieving All Photos a User Is Tagged In

Problem

I need to retrieve all of the photos that a specific user has been tagged in using FQL.

Solution

```
SELECT pid, src, caption FROM photo WHERE pid IN
 (SELECT pid FROM photo_tag WHERE subject = $user);
```

Discussion

This will return an empty set if the current loggedinuser doesn't have permission to see any of the photos or if user hasn't been tagged in any.

8.55 User Table

Problem

What's the schema for the user table?

Solution

The user table stores all the Facebook users. Its fields are listed in Table 8-18. Queries to this table will only return data the current user is allowed to see (meaning you can't request users that the current loggedinuser can't see). More information about this table, including an up-to-date listing of fields, can be found at *http://wiki.developers .facebook.com/index.php/User_(FQL)*.

Table 8-18. user table fields

Name	Type	Index	Description
uid	int	•	User ID of this user.
first_name	string		First name of this user.
last_name	string		Last name of this user.
name	string	•	Full name of this user, including any initials.
pic_small	string		URL of the small picture for this user (max width of 50 px and max height of 150 px). Might be empty.
pic_big	string		URL of the big picture for this user (max width of 200 px and max height of 600 px). Might be empty.
pic_square	string		URL of the square picture for this user (max width and height of 50 px). Might be empty.
pic	string		URL of the picture for this group (max width of 100 px and max height of 300 px). Might be empty.
affiliations	array		Array of networks that this user is a member of. Includes the nid (network ID), name, type (work, region, etc.), status, and year.
profile_update_time	string		Timestamp of the last update to this Profile, in epoch seconds. See Recipe 6.20 for more about epoch seconds.
timezone	string		Timezone the user is in, measured in offset from GMT (e.g., Eastern Daylight Time is stored as -4).
religion	string		User-created string.
birthday	string		String version of the date ("September 27, 1901").
sex	string		male, female, or empty string if unspecified.
hometown_location	array		An array containing the city, state, country, and zip code of this user's home town.
meeting_sex	array		An array containing the genders of other users that this user is interested in meeting.

Name	Type	Index	Description
meeting_for	array		An array containing some combination of "Friendship", "Networking", "Dating", or "A Relationship".
relationship_status	string		String with one of the following values: "Single", "In a Relationship", "Engaged", "Married", "It's Complicated", "In an Open Relationship", or an empty string if unspecified.
significant_other_id	int		uid (user ID) of this user's significant other, if specified.
political	string		Users can enter anything they'd like into this field, but it also presents an autocomplete list of options based on the party names of each country.
current_location	array		An array containing the city, state, country, and zip code of the user's current locations.
activities	string		User-created string.
interests	string		User-created string.
music	string		User-created string.
tv	string		User-created string.
movies	string		User-created string.
books	string		User-created string.
quotes	string		User-created string.
about_me	string		User-created string.
hs_info	array		An array of high school records containing the name, grad_year, and id of each high school.
education_history	array		An array of degrees that this user has earned, containing the name, year, degree, and array of concentrations for each school.
work_history	array		An array containing the company_name, position, description, start_date, end_date, and location array (city, state, country) for each position.
notes_count	int		Count of the notes that this user has posted.
wall_count	int		Count of the posts on this user's Wall.
status	array		An array containing this user's current message and time (epoch seconds timestamp for when the status was entered; see Recipe 6.20 for more about epoch seconds).
has_added_app	bool		Does this user have your app installed?
is_app_user	bool		Has this user logged into your app?
online_presence	string		One of active, idle, offline, or an empty string.

Note that only the fields marked as "Index" in this table can be used in an FQL query's WHERE clause, but any of the fields can appear in the SELECT.

Discussion

If you'd rather use the API to access **users**, try the `Users.getInfo( )` method.

8.56 App Friends

Problem

I need to find all of the friends of a specific user who have already installed my application.

Solution

```
SELECT uid FROM user WHERE has_added_app = 1 AND uid IN (SELECT
  uid2 FROM friend WHERE uid1 = $user);
```

Discussion

This particularly comes in handy when you're displaying an `fb:multi-friend-selector` control in FBML and want to exclude friends of the current `loggedinuser` who have already installed your app (see Recipe 6.46).

8.57 Birthday Friends

Problem

I need to find all of a specific user's friends whose birthdays are on a given day using FQL.

Solution

```
SELECT uid FROM user WHERE strpos(birthday, "September 27")
  = 0 AND uid IN (SELECT uid2 FROM friend WHERE uid1 = $uid)
```

Discussion

Rather than supporting the `LIKE` comparator from SQL, Facebook has included the ability to run a small set of PHP-like functions in your queries (see Recipe 8.3). We're using the `strpos( )` function here, which returns the position of the needle in the haystack (the first parameter—birthday—is known as the haystack, and the second parameter—"September 27"—is known as the needle). Since we're looking for people who share the same birthday and we don't care about the year, we want to return results where the string starts with "September 27", which would mean it's at position 0. In more traditional SQL, this query would have:

```
SELECT uid FROM user WHERE birthday LIKE "September 27%"
  AND uid IN (SELECT uid2 FROM friend WHERE uid1 = $uid)
```

You can, of course, substitute any day you'd like for "September 27", which just happens to be my birthday (please email cakes and other goodies). This query comes from the excellent Facebook Developers Wiki Sample FQL Queries page, which you'll find at *http://wiki.developers.facebook.com/index.php/Sample_FQL_Queries*.

8.58 600 Errors

Problem

My FQL doesn't work! I'm getting a 600 error!

Solution

Don't panic! 600-class errors are Facebook's way of telling you that there's something wrong with your FQL query. The possible error codes are listed in Table 8-19.

Table 8-19. FQL error codes

Error code	Description
601	Error while parsing the FQL statement.
602	The field you requested does not exist.
603	The table you requested does not exist.
604	Your statement is not indexable.
605	The function you called does not exist.
606	Wrong number of arguments passed into the function.

Discussion

Pay special attention to 604 errors, because they often have extra information in them about why the statement isn't indexable. As an example, `metrics` table queries are considered indexable only if the date range you're querying on isn't bigger than 30 days. If it is bigger, you'll get a 604 error, which tells you that the range is too big.

If you're getting an error and are having trouble tracking it down in the context of your code, try extracting the query and running it directly inside the API Test Console at *http://developers.facebook.com/tools.php?api*. If you select "fql.query" as the Method, you can play with FQL and see live results on the righthand side.

8.59 Preload FQL

Problem

I want to increase the performance of my pages that require the results of an FQL to do their initial rendering.

Solution and Discussion

Facebook has developed a preload FQL system that enables you to have Facebook send along the results of a specific FQL query when it requests FBML pages from your server. Since this is more reliant on an API call than on FQL, it's documented in the `Admin.SetAppProperties( )` API method (see Chapter 9). More information can also be found in the Developers Wiki at *http://wiki.developers.facebook.com/index.php/Preload _FQL*.

CHAPTER 9

Facebook API

You've done a bang-up job of planning, your brilliant, unpolished diamond is starting to shine with a beautiful design, you have stellar FBML built out on a standards-compliant framework, your FBJS screams Ajax cleanliness from 1,000 feet away, and you've mastered FQL queries like the back of your normalized (and partially denormalized) hand. Now what?

Time to dig into the Facebook Application Programming Interface (API). If you're unfamiliar with the concept of an API, read the first few recipes in this chapter carefully. The majority of the content here will cover the various API calls and how to get different types of data in and out of Facebook, with some extra attention at the end to some of the new beta features that have recently been introduced. As with the rest of this book, I'm going to cover the API using the official Facebook PHP Client, but it shouldn't be too hard to convert these examples into your language of choice.

In the interest of saving space (and trees!), I've omitted the code to set up a Facebook Client object and retrieve the active user from most of the recipes in this chapter. Since it's always the same, refer to Recipe 9.1 for reference.

You should be able to look up any of the API calls covered in this chapter by adding them to the end of the Facebook Developers Wiki URL. As an example, if you want more info on Users.getInfo( ), go to *http://wiki .developers.facebook.com/index.php/Users.getInfo*.

9.1 What's an API?

Problem

I keep hearing about this API thing. API this, API that. What's the deal?

Solution

According to Wikipedia:

> An application programming interface (API) is a source code interface that an operating system, library, or service provides to support requests made by computer programs.

In the case of Facebook, the API provides developers with external access to the very core functionality of Platform, in a way that enables you to build on top of it and integrate it directly into your application. All of the other pieces of Platform—FBML, FBJS, FQL, etc.—wouldn't exist without the API, but that's not true the other way around. There are lots of examples of really powerful APIs in web applications that exist without any means to do frontend development on top of them (see the upcoming Discussion for some examples).

Most APIs exist as a specification that explains what you can expect to receive back from a service when you make certain calls to it. The Facebook API is no different, and you can visit *http://wiki.developers.facebook.com/index.php/API* to see all of the API calls available and what they expect to receive from you and send back to you (e.g., `Pages.isFan( )` expects a `page_id` and a `uid` and returns XML containing either 0 for `false` or 1 for `true`). Luckily for you, Facebook has gone a little beyond the norm by also providing a full Client Library, which makes it easy to integrate API code into your application (see Recipe 9.2 for more info).

Generally speaking, you make a call to an API directly in your code and then use the response as you would any other variable. A quick example:

```php
<?php
include_once 'resources/includes/config.php';
include_once 'resources/includes/facebook.php';

global $api_key, $secret;

$facebook = new Facebook($api_key, $secret);
$facebook->require_frame();
$user = $facebook->require_login();

$fields = array('last_name', 'first_name');
$myUser = $facebook->api_client->users_getInfo($user, $fields);

echo $myUser[0]['first_name'] . ' ' . $myUser[0]['last_name'];?>
```

The end result of this code should be the current `loggedinuser`'s first name and last name separated by a space. Although this looks like a lot of code to get to that point, keep in mind that the first five lines are setup, which you need to do only once per page. Since this is our first actual, live code sample from the API, let's take a look at what we're doing in each section:

```php
include_once 'resources/includes/config.php';
include_once 'resources/includes/facebook.php';

global $api_key, $secret;
```

The *config.php* file includes the definition of the `api_key` and `secret` variables, which hold the API and secret keys for your application (you can find them in the Developers app, on your app's page: *http://www.facebook.com/developers/apps.php?app_id= 12345*, where 12345 is your app's ID). You don't have to set up your app that way, but I find it more convenient than embedding the keys in every page. The *facebook.php* file is the Client Library that includes all of the actual calls.

```
$facebook = new Facebook($api_key, $secret);
$facebook->require_frame();
$user = $facebook->require_login();
```

The first line instantiates a new instance of the Facebook Client Library, which we'll use to make all of our subsequent calls. The second checks to see whether we're inside of a frame (e.g., an iFrame), and then forces us to the login page to make sure that this session is valid. The call to `require_login( )` will force the user to hit a login screen if they aren't logged in and will then create a session and will return their `uid` (you'll get a `uid` either way).

 Users have the option of turning that session into an infinite session by checking the "Keep me logged into [Your App Name]" checkbox on the login screen. See Recipe 9.7 for more information.

```
$fields = array('last_name', 'first_name');
$myUser = $facebook->api_client->users_getInfo($user, $fields);
```

Since the `Users.getInfo( )` method requires an array of fields that we want returned, we start off by defining an array called `fields` and populating it. The call to `Users.getInfo( )` returns a multidimensional array with each item representing one user's data, but since we passed in only one `uid`, we can assume that we're only interested in the data at position 0 when we echo it:

```
echo $myUser[0]['first_name'] . ' ' . $myUser[0]['last_name'];?>
```

Discussion

APIs are truly wonderful things. It's fairly safe to say that they are one of the underlying technologies that makes this entire Web 2.0 revolution possible, and are therefore the golden goose that lays the golden eggs into our fat dotcom v2 pockets. Or, if you want to be a little less cynical, they're the glue that makes it easy to bind a whole bunch of independent services together into a new mashup app that is far greater than the sum of its parts.

There are a whole bunch of them, too. At the time this was written, the fantastic ProgrammableWeb site (*http://www.programmableweb.com/apis*), a repository of information about APIs, listed 760 different publicly available APIs in 55 categories. Google Maps is the most popular API for mashups, by quite a long way (47% of all mashups listed on ProgrammableWeb), with Flickr (11%), YouTube (8%), and

Amazon (8%) following behind. You can find a whole lot of information about each of those APIs in the directory section of that site (e.g., *http://www.programmableweb .com/api/google-maps*).

9.2 Getting Started with the Client Library

Problem

OK! I'm down with the API scene. How do I get started?

Solution

You need to download a Facebook Client Library in the language of your choice, get it installed on your server, and then get cracking! You'll find links to various Client Libraries at *http://developers.facebook.com/get_started.php*, but keep in mind that the only officially supported version is the PHP 4/5 library, and so using another language means relying on third parties to keep the library up-to-date.

In addition to the Wiki (*http://wiki.developers.facebook.com/index.php/API*), there's some documentation for the Client Library in the actual code files in the form of comments, and it's often easier to figure out how to use a function by just looking it up in the *facebookapi_php5_restlib.php* file than trying to find it on the Web.

Discussion

If you're running PHP, this should be as simple as downloading the library from Facebook, uploading to your server, and creating a *config.php* file with your app's API and secret keys. The PHP Client Library comes with the Footprints sample application, which will give you a very simple overview of an app that uses the API to set some Profile Actions and Boxes. There are also two more demo apps, Restaurants and Who's Showing Up, which show off Mock Ajax, FBJS, and the Data Store API, and the ability to build apps for users and Pages, respectively. You can find all three apps at *http://wiki .developers.facebook.com/index.php/Demos*.

If you're not running PHP, check the installation instructions that came with your Client Library.

9.3 RESTing with Facebook

Problem

I'm curious to know more about how my app communicates with Facebook. What kind of API is this?

Solution

This is a Representational State Transfer, or REST-like API, which means that calls are simply made over HTTP (using GET or POST) to the Facebook server. You'll be POSTing requests to *http://api.facebook.com/restserver.php* when you make calls from your server, but you can visit that URL directly if you're curious to see what a 101 error response looks like (and who isn't, really?).

Discussion

The alternative to REST is generally considered to be SOAP, a heavier-weight protocol that includes an additional message layer. The two are very similar in some regards (both generally use HTTP as their transport protocol and generally use XML to encode data), but there's a lot more overhead in implementing a SOAP-based API. More information about REST and SOAP can be found at *http://en.wikipedia.org/wiki/Representational_State_Transfer* and *http://en.wikipedia.org/wiki/SOAP*, respectively.

9.4 Storable Data

Problem

I want to make sure that I don't violate the Facebook Developer Terms of Service. What information am I allowed to retrieve from Platform and store in my own database?

Solution

The (short) list shown in Table 9-1 is all you're allowed to store.

Table 9-1. Storable data

Property	Description
Uid	User ID
Nid	Network ID
Eid	Event ID
Gid	Group ID
Pid	Photo ID
Aid	Album ID
flid	Friend list ID
listing_id	Marketplace Listing ID
page_id	Page ID
notes_count	Total number of notes written by a user
profile_update_time	Last time the user's Profile was updated

Discussion

The Developer Terms of Service can be found at *http://developers.facebook.com/terms .php*.

9.5 Authenticating Users

Problem

How do I log a user into my Platform app?

Solution

Users have to be logged into Facebook in order for you to make API calls on their behalf, so Facebook provides an automated authentication process that you can initiate by redirecting users to *http://www.facebook.com/login.php?api_key=1234567890&v=1.0* (where 1234567890 is your app's API key). This URL can accept a few parameters, as documented in the Discussion.

Discussion

The process works like Figure 9-1.

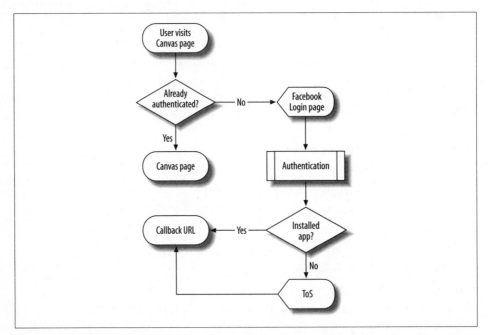

Figure 9-1. User authentication flow

Let's walk through the steps. Users start off by visiting a Canvas page in your app without logging into Facebook first, as shown in Figure 9-2.

Welcome to the Super Disco Napping Application!

You must be logged into Facebook to use this application.

facebook 🔒

Figure 9-2. Canvas page with login message

You can insert a standard Facebook login button anywhere you'd like with the following code:

```
<a href="http://www.facebook.com/login.php?api_key=1234567890
&v=1.0"><img src="http://static.ak.facebook.com/images/devsite/
facebook_login.gif"></a>
```

where 1234567890 is your app's API key (which isn't the same as your app's ID; the API key can be found in the Facebook Developers app and is usually about 30 characters long, made up of letters and numbers). When users click on that button, they'll get bumped over to a Facebook login page with your app's name in it, as in Figure 9-3.

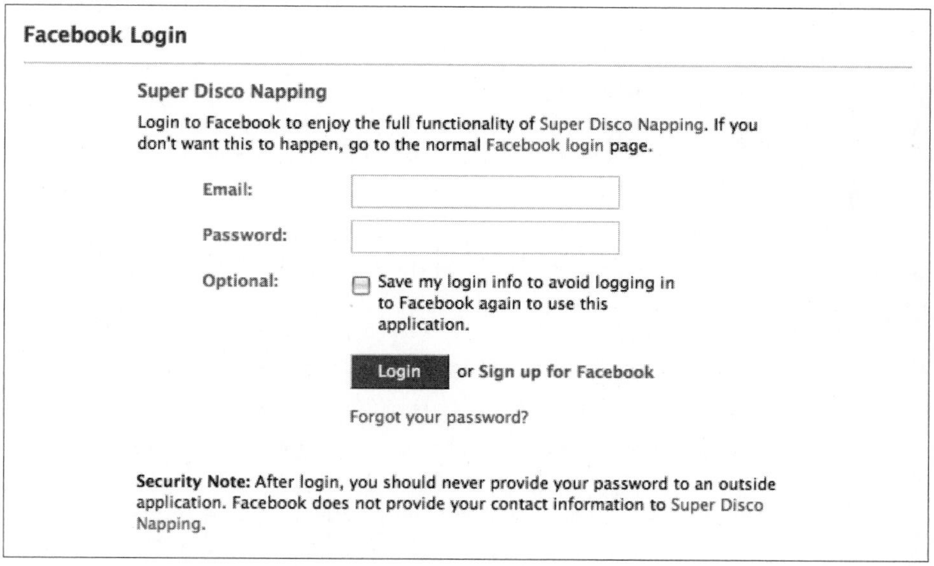

Facebook Login

Super Disco Napping

Login to Facebook to enjoy the full functionality of Super Disco Napping. If you don't want this to happen, go to the normal Facebook login page.

Email:

Password:

Optional: ☐ Save my login info to avoid logging in to Facebook again to use this application.

Login or Sign up for Facebook

Forgot your password?

Security Note: After login, you should never provide your password to an outside application. Facebook does not provide your contact information to Super Disco Napping.

Figure 9-3. Facebook Login page

If this user hasn't installed your app or agreed to its Terms of Service before, they'll be shown the ToS page (Figure 9-4).

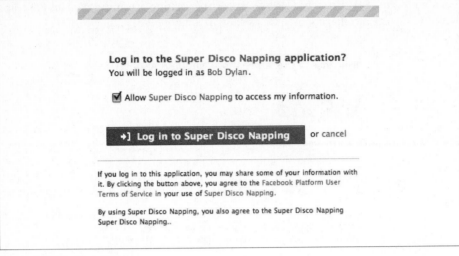

Figure 9-4. Facebook ToS page

Finally, they'll be sent to your app's callback URL, rather than to the page they started on. This is important because the callback URL isn't actually on Facebook, so you want to use this as an opportunity to store the auth_token variable you'll get passed and then redirect them to a page in your app:

```
$auth_token = $_GET['auth_token'];
```

You'll need to keep that auth_token handy if you're going to be making calls into the API from your server to Facebook without rendering them into a Canvas page. Note that auth_tokens expire, but you can create an infinite session instead (see Recipe 9.7 for more info).

The login URL (to which you send users to start this whole process) accepts a bunch of parameters that give you some control over the way it behaves; see Table 9-2.

Table 9-2. Parameters for login URL

Name	Type	Default	Description
api_key	string	N/A	Your application's API key (not ID). *This is required.*
v	float	N/A	The API version you're using. "1.0" is currently the only supported value. *This is required.*
auth_token	string	N/A	This is used only for desktop applications and is required when they make API calls. You can create this using the auth.createToken( ) method.
popup	bool	false	Forces the display of an alternate version of the login page without the Facebook navigation around it. For best results, you should open this in a pop-up window sized 646 × 436 pixels.
skipcookie	bool	false	Force Facebook to ignore the presence of a login cookie and always show the form. Might be useful if another Facebook user forgot to log out.

Name	Type	Default	Description
hide_checkbox	bool	false	Force Facebook to hide the "Save my login info" checkbox on the login form. Do this only if you want to force users to log in every time; otherwise, leave this as true.
next	string	false	Whatever you pass in here will get appended to the callback_url after login, so use this to maintain state.
canvas	bool	false	Force Facebook to return users to the Canvas page they came from rather than to your callback URL.

It's worth going into a little detail about how Facebook assembles the URL that users will be sent to after they log in. By default, this will just be the callback URL that you've specified for your application (which should be off-Facebook). For the sake of this example, let's assume that it's something like:

http://facebook.myserver.com/apps/myapp

Users will be directed to that URL after they've logged in, and you'll get an auth_token automatically added to the end of it:

*http://facebook.myserver.com/apps/myapp?auth_token=
aca27a78c5853267656280baa35642cb*

If you specify a next parameter, Facebook will append that to the end of your callback URL. You'll need to URL-encode the string so that it doesn't become part of the login URL when you put your login button onto your Canvas page, which you can do using any number of web-based tools, such as *http://ostermiller.org/calc/encode.html*. Continuing in the vein of our example, let's say that you wanted to append the time in epoch seconds, which you've calculated as 1212020040 (see Recipe 6.20 for more info about epoch seconds). In that case, you would pass "%3Ftime%3D1212020040" as the value for next, and Facebook will send users to:

*http://facebook.myserver.com/apps/myapp?time=1212020040&auth_token=
aca27a78c5853267656280baa35642cb*

Note that Facebook will automatically switch the separator before the auth_token from ? to & if it needs to.

Finally, if you specify true for the canvas parameter, Facebook will send users back to the page they came from rather than to your callback URL. You won't get an auth_token in that case (because you don't need to create a session key when you're making API calls from inside a Canvas page), but you will still get whatever you passed into next:

http://apps.facebook.com/myapp/?time=1212020040

9.6 Creating a Session Key

Problem

I need a session key so that I can make subsequent API calls from my app's server to Facebook. Where would I find such a thing?

Solution

If you've made a run down to the local Session Key Store and they're all out of stock, try the `Auth.createToken()` and `Auth.getSession()` methods. Desktop apps need to call `Auth.createToken()` to generate a token, whereas web apps will receive one appended to their callback URL when users log in (see Recipe 9.5 for more info).

Discussion

Session keys were undergoing some changes as this book was being written, largely to make the process of adding new applications and authenticating easier for users. Facebook has modified a number of its API methods so that they no longer require a session key (meaning that you can call them on behalf of users without users needing to have added your app), and Facebook is moving in the direction of making it possible for users to try your app out and gradually grant it more permissions, rather than a single, complex authentication page. Facebook is working toward having the following methods not require a key:

- `Auth.createToken()`
- `Auth.getSession()`
- `Fbml.refreshImgSrc()`
- `Fbml.refreshRefUrl()`
- `Fbml.setRefHandle()`
- `Marketplace.createListing()`
- `Marketplace.getCategories()`
- `Marketplace.getSubCategories()`
- `Marketplace.removeListing()`
- `Notifications.send()`
- `Notifications.sendEmail()`
- `Pages.getInfo()`
- `Pages.isAppAdded()`
- `Photos.addTag()`
- `Photos.createAlbum()`
- `Photos.upload()`

- `Profile.getFBML()`
- `Profile.setFBML()`
- `Users.hasAppPermission()`
- `Users.isAppUser()`
- `Users.setStatus()`

Since this new policy was evolving as this book was going to press, check the Wiki for more information about which methods do or don't require a key (specifically *http://wiki.developers.facebook.com/index.php/New_Design_Platform_Changes#Changes_to _Session_Keys* or *http://tinyurl.com/5czxej*).

9.7 Creating an Infinite Session Key

Problem

The user sessions that are created when my users log in expire too quickly. Is there a way to create an infinite session?

Solution

There are two ways to do this:

- If your users check the "Keep me logged into [Your App Name]" checkbox when logging into your app, their session with your app will go on forever and always.
- You can give users the option of creating a special infinite key code for you by sending them to the URL *http://www.facebook.com/code_gen.php?v=1.0&api_key =1234567890*, where 1234567890 is your app's API key (not your app's ID, but rather the full API key). This will prompt them to generate a key, which they can then give your app and you can pass into the `Auth.getSession()` as an `auth_token`. The `session_key` you get back will survive beyond the sands of time.

 Web-based Facebook apps used to be automatically granted infinite sessions but now need to manually create them (as of July 15, 2008), the same way that Desktop and Mobile apps have always had to.

Discussion

Infinite session keys are also useful when you have users accessing your app from a third-party site or if you're using a `cron` job to process things on a scheduled basis. There's no way for you to programmatically create an infinite session without expressed consent from your users, which is really for the best. The second option listed in the Solution is the more awkward of the two, since it requires sending them off into a Facebook process that doesn't automatically return them to your app. If users aren't logged in when you send them to that URL, they'll see a login page with the special message shown in Figure 9-5.

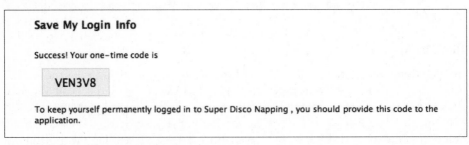

Facebook Login

Log in to Facebook to generate a one-time code that you can give to the application.

Email:

Password:

☑ Remember me

Login or Sign up for Facebook

Forgot your password?

Figure 9-5. Session key generator login

After they log in (or if they were already logged in), they'll see the confirmation page shown in Figure 9-6.

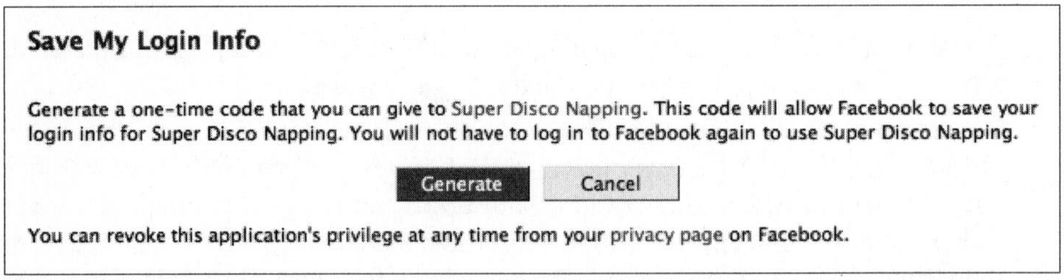

Save My Login Info

Generate a one-time code that you can give to Super Disco Napping. This code will allow Facebook to save your login info for Super Disco Napping. You will not have to log in to Facebook again to use Super Disco Napping.

Generate   Cancel

You can revoke this application's privilege at any time from your privacy page on Facebook.

Figure 9-6. Session key generator confirmation

If they click on the Generate button, they'll get a code they can give you, like the one shown in Figure 9-7.

Save My Login Info

Success! Your one-time code is

VEN3V8

To keep yourself permanently logged in to Super Disco Napping , you should provide this code to the application.

Figure 9-7. Session key generator code

Note that there's no way back to your app from that page, so although they now have the code (yay!), they need to figure out how to get back to give it to you on their own (boo!). When they've finally hacked their way back through the jungle and made it over the perilous river bridge, grab that code and pass it into a call to `Auth.getSession()` to produce your fabled infinite session key:

```
$return = $facebook->api_client->auth_getSession($userCode);
```

Look in `return['session_key']` to find the actual key.

A final note on the true infinite nature of the infinite key. As with all things in life, this is only mostly as good as it sounds. The key doesn't really last forever: if a user uninstalls and reinstalls your app, her key will expire and she'll have to go through this again (although this time she'll have an easier time navigating through the jungle).

 Facebook's list of storable items doesn't include a user's `session_key`, but it's pretty hard to work with the key if you don't store it (especially for infinite keys, which you're going to need to use again later). It's almost certainly not a violation of the Facebook Terms of Service, but you should be aware of it nonetheless.

9.8 Getting a Session (Desktop Only)

Problem

I have my `auth_token` and created my session, but now I need to retrieve it again after switching from HTTP to HTTPS.

Solution

If you established a session over HTTP but need to switch to HTTPS, you can retrieve a session key again by calling `Auth.getSession()` and passing in the `auth_token` you got when you called `Auth.createToken()`.

Discussion

This isn't required by web apps, as there's currently no way for a user to interact with your app over an HTTPS connection to *http://apps.facebook.com* (it will either bounce them back to HTTP automatically or give an error about using a security certificate for the wrong domain).

You can also pass a `generate_session_secret` boolean into `Auth.getSession()` if you'd like it to generate and return a temporary secret key associated with the session. You can use that secret instead of your app's API secret key for the duration of this session.

9.9 Creating an Auth Token (Desktop Only)

Problem

I need to create an auth token for my desktop Facebook app.

Solution

Use the `Auth.createToken( )` method, which requires no parameters beyond the standard `api_key`, `sig`, and `version`, and returns a key that can be used to create a session (see Recipe 9.6 for more info).

Discussion

This isn't required by web apps, which can just go directly to creating a session key.

9.10 Making Calls (Desktop Only)

Problem

How do I make a call to the Facebook API server from my desktop app?

Solution

Generally speaking, you prepare a request and then transmit it to the API server (see *http://api.facebook.com/restserver.php*) using POST over the HTTP protocol. The server will return an XML response.

Discussion

You could write your own code to manage the Facebook session and handle the server communication, but you might want to leverage the excellent work other people have been doing and use one of these libraries instead:

.NET
> Facebook and Microsoft have partnered to provide a Facebook Developer Kit built on Popfly and Visual Studio Express. You can get more information and downloads at *http://www.microsoft.com/express/samples/facebook/*. Even more information is available on CodePlex at *http://www.codeplex.com/FacebookToolkit*. An alternate library, Facebook.NET, which includes support for C# and VB.NET, can be found on CodePlex at *http://www.codeplex.com/FacebookNET*.

ActionScript
> The *facebook-actionscript-api* is an MIT-licensed library for secure communication between Flash/Flex apps and the Facebook server, written and maintained by Jason

Crist. More information and downloads are available at *http://code.google.com/p/facebook-actionscript-api/*.

Java

Facebook used to provide an official Java Client Library, but it has subsequently been discontinued. The *facebook-java-api* project has taken over with an open source version, which you can download at *http://code.google.com/p/facebook-java-api/*.

Ruby on Rails

Check out the Facebooker project at *http://facebooker.rubyforge.org/*. It's conveniently packaged as a gem, so you can just `gem install facebooker`.

Qt+KDE

Linux developers should check out the *libkfacebook* project, which is an asynchronous, GPL-licensed library for talking to the Facebook API with responses mapped to C++ objects. You can grab the source from Subversion at *svn://anonsvn.kde.org/home/kde/trunk/playground/pim/kfacebook*.

VB.NET

Independent developer Jay Lagorio has released a Client Library for Facebook that supports the API version 1.0 in VB.NET. More information and downloads are at *http://www.lagorio.net/windows/facebook/*.

You need to create an `auth_token` and then instantiate a session before you can make most of the calls in the API (but not, obviously, before you can make the calls to generate them). See Recipes 9.9 and 9.6, respectively, for more information on those processes.

9.11 Logging Out

Problem

How can I give my users a way to log out of Facebook?

Solution and Discussion

Just send them to *http://www.facebook.com/logout.php?confirm=1*.

9.12 Getting Allocations

Problem

I need to retrieve my allocations from Facebook so that I know how many Notifications I can send out per day.

Solution

Use the `Admin.getAllocations()` method:

```
$allocation = $facebook->api_client->admin_getAllocation('notifications_per_day');
```

Discussion

This method supports retrieving a number of different allocations, as shown in Table 9-3.

Table 9-3. Allocations

Allocation	Description
notifications_per_day	Number of Notifications your application can send per user per day
requests_per_day	Number of requests your application can send per user per day
emails_per_day	Number of email messages your application can send to a user per day
email_disable_message_location	Location of the disable message within emails sent by your application ("1" is at the bottom and "2" is the top)

For more information about allocations, see Recipe 2.16.

9.13 Getting Metrics

Problem

I want to retrieve my app's daily metrics for yesterday.

Solution

The `Admin.getMetrics()` method will return metrics for daily, weekly, or monthly periods:

```
$targetMetrics = array('active_users');
$monthAgo = strtotime('yesterday') - 24*60*60*29;
$yesterday = strtotime('yesterday');

$oneDay = $facebook->api_client->admin_getMetrics($monthAgo,
  $yesterday, 86400, $targetMetrics);
$sevenDays = $facebook->api_client->admin_getMetrics($monthAgo,
  $yesterday, 604800, $targetMetrics);
$thirtyDays = $facebook->api_client->admin_getMetrics($monthAgo,
  $yesterday, 2592000, $targetMetrics);
```

Discussion

`Admin.getMetrics()` accepts start and end dates, expressed in epoch time, a `period`, and an array containing a list of the specific metrics you're looking for (you have to use an array, even if you only want one back, or you'll get a long error message about needing an array). The `period` parameter, also expressed in epoch seconds, defines the period you want to receive metrics for: one day (86400 seconds), seven days (604800 seconds), or 30 days (2592000 seconds). See Recipe 6.20 for more information about epoch time. Your return value will always be a multidimensional array (which makes sense, since you're requesting an array), with each item containing a date and the specified metric. If you requested a one-day period of `active_users` and did a PHP `print_r` on that array, you might see:

```
Array
(
    [0] => Array
        (
            [active_users] => 1234340
        )
)
```

There are quite a few metrics you can request for your app (see Table 9-4), based on what you can graph on the Usage and HTTP Requests tabs of the Facebook Insights application (for more info, see Recipe 10.6).

Table 9-4. Metrics

Metric	Description
active_users	Active users
unique_adds	Users who added your application
unique_removes	Users who removed your application
unique_blocks	Users who blocked your application
unique_unblocks	Users who unblocked your application
api_calls	API calls made by your application
unique_api_calls	Users on whose behalf your application made API calls
canvas_page_views	Canvas page views
unique_canvas_page_views	Users who viewed your application's Canvas page
canvas_http_request_time_avg	Average time to fulfill an HTTP request to your application's Canvas page
canvas_fbml_render_time_avg	Average time to render FBML on your application's Canvas page
canvas_page_views_http_code_0	Canvas page views that timed out
canvas_page_views_http_code_100	HTTP code 100s—Continue
canvas_page_views_http_code_200	HTTP code 200s—OK
canvas_page_views_http_code_200ND	HTTP code 200s—OKs with no data
canvas_page_views_http_code_301	HTTP code 301s—Moved Permanently
canvas_page_views_http_code_302	HTTP code 302s—Found
canvas_page_views_http_code_303	HTTP code 303s—See Other
canvas_page_views_http_code_400	HTTP code 400s—Bad Request
canvas_page_views_http_code_401	HTTP code 401s—Unauthorized

Metric	Description
canvas_page_views_http_code_403	HTTP code 403s—Forbidden
canvas_page_views_http_code_404	HTTP code 404s—Not Found
canvas_page_views_http_code_405	HTTP code 405s—Method Not Allowed
canvas_page_views_http_code_413	HTTP code 413s—Request Entity Too Large
canvas_page_views_http_code_422	HTTP code 422s—Unprocessable Entity
canvas_page_views_http_code_500	HTTP code 500s—Internal Server Error
canvas_page_views_http_code_502	HTTP code 502s—Bad Gateway
canvas_page_views_http_code_503	HTTP code 503s—Service Unavailable
canvas_page_views_http_code_505	HTTP code 505s—HTTP Version Not Supported

FQL equivalent

If you'd prefer to use FQL to access your metrics, the equivalent query is:

```
SELECT active_users, canvas_page_views FROM metrics WHERE end_time
   = 1206946800 AND period = 86400
```

For more information, see Recipe 8.14.

9.14 Getting and Setting Application Properties

Problem

I need to retrieve or set some of the properties about my application.

Solution

Use the `Admin.getAppProperties()` method to retrieve properties:

```
$targetProps = array('application_name','description');
$properties = $facebook->api_client->admin_getAppProperties($targetProps);
```

Use the `Admin.setAppProperties()` method to set properties:

```
$setProps = array('description' => 'My new description!');
$return = $facebook->api_client->admin_setAppProperties($setProps);
```

Discussion

`Admin.getAppProperties()` returns an array, with each named element being one of the properties you requested. In addition to whatever you ask for, Facebook will always return your app's `canvasname`, `icon_url`, and `logo_url` appended to the end of the returned array.

`Admin.setAppPropoerties()` will return a code indicating whether it worked. Confusingly, it returns true as the value 1 if it works, which coincides with error code 1, which signifies an unknown error (see Recipe 9.16). If you're concerned it's not working, you can do a check using `Admin.getAppPropoerties( )`:

```
$setProps = array('description' => 'This was set using the new
 Admin.setAppProperties() method!');
$return = $facebook->api_client->admin_setAppProperties($setProps);

$getProps = array('description');
$newDesc = $facebook->api_client->admin_getAppProperties($getProps);

if($newDesc['description'] == $setProps['description']){
    echo 'Success!';
}
```

 These methods are currently marked as beta in the Developers Wiki, so treat them with a little caution and make sure to report any bugs you might find to the Facebook Bug Tracker, at *http://bugs.developers.face book.com*.

The list of properties you can specify in either method is pretty extensive and covers basically anything that you set in the Developer app (see Table 9-5, but for the most up-to-date list, refer to *http://wiki.developers.facebook.com/index.php/ApplicationPro perties*).

Table 9-5. Application properties

Property	Type	Description
application_name	string	Name of your application.
callback_url	string	Callback URL, which can't be longer than 100 characters and will be off-Facebook on your server.
post_install_url	string	URL where a user gets redirected after installing your app. Can't be longer than 100 characters.
edit_url	string	Appears to be an empty string.
dashboard_url	string	URL to your app's dashboard (generally the first page in your app, at *http://apps .facebook.com/yourapp*).
uninstall_url	string	URL where a user gets redirected after removing your application.
ip_list	string	IP addresses of the servers you've given permission to access Facebook's servers. This applies only to web-based apps.
email	string	Email address associated with your app, which Facebook uses to contact you (default value is your Facebook email address).
description	string	Description of your application.
use_iframe	bool	False (0) means you use FBML; true (1) means you use an iFrame.
desktop	bool	False (0) means a web-based app; true (1) means a desktop app.
is_mobile	bool	False (0) means you can't run on Facebook Mobile; true (1) means you can.

Property	Type	Description
default_fbml	string	Default FBML that appears in the user's Profile Box when she adds your app, before you've set something specific.
default_column	bool	False (0) means you want to appear in the narrow column (sidebar); true (1) means you want to appear in the wide column (body) of user Profiles.
message_url	string	URL that Facebook uses to display your message attachment content.
message_action	string	Label for message attachment action for your app, which can't be more than 20 characters.
about_url	string	URL for your app's About Page.
private_install	bool	False (0) means you use the News Feed and Mini-Feed; true (1) means they're disabled for your app.
installable	bool	False (0) means users can't install your app; true (1) means they can.
privacy_url	string	URL for your app's privacy terms.
help_url	string	URL for your app's help page.
see_all_url	string	Appears to be an empty string.
tos_url	string	URL for your app's Terms of Service.
dev_mode	bool	False (0) means developer mode is disabled; true (1) means it's enabled, which blocks anyone who isn't on the developer list from installing the app.
preload_fql	string	A preloaded FQL query.
default_action_fbml	string	Default FBML that appears in the user's Profile actions when he adds your application, before you've set something specific.
canvas_name	string	The Canvas name of your app (read-only).
icon_url	string	URL for your app's icon (read-only).
logo_url	string	A URL for your app's logo, as shown in the product directory and search listings (read-only).

9.15 Getting an App's 4-1-1

Problem

Is there any way for me to retrieve the general public information about an app?

Solution

Use the Application.getPublicInfo( ) method, and pass in any one of the following properties for the target app:

- application_id
- api_key
- application_canvas_name

Let's say, for example, that you want to retrieve some information about the Zerofoot-print Calculator. All three of the following will return the same array:

```
$appId = $facebook->api_client->application_getPublicInfo('8653633892');
$appAPI = $facebook->api_client->application_getPublicInfo
('d41570392c4b0d08a794f4a66b91a2a9');
$appCanvas = $facebook->api_client->admin_getPublicInfo('zfcalculator');
```

Discussion

The returned array includes the properties in Table 9-6.

Table 9-6. Properties returned by Application.getPublicInfo()

Property	Zerofootprint Calculator example
app_id	8653633892
api_key	d41570392c4b0d08a794f4a66b91a2a9
canvas_name	zfcalculator
display_name	Zerofootprint Calculator
icon_url	http://photos-892.ll.facebook.com/photos-ll-sctm/v43/8/8653633892/app_2_8653633892_7652.gif
logo_url	http://photos-892.ll.facebook.com/photos-ll-sctm/v43/8/8653633892/app_1_8653633892_3724.gif
developers	
company_name	Zerofootprint Inc.
description	The Zerofootprint Calculator helps you measure your footprint on the environment. It takes just one minute to use and calculates how many tonnes of carbon you produce through driving, travel, diet, and home.
daily_active_users	300
daily_active_percentage	1

The **developers** field is empty in this case because the application is set as having a company name instead of individual developers (you can change this setting for your app by editing the About Page).

This method is currently marked as beta in the Developers Wiki and is, in fact, so beta that it isn't included in the currently released version of the Facebook PHP Client Library, but it will be soon.

Treat it with a little caution and make sure to report any bugs you might find into the Facebook Bug Tracker at *http://bugs.developers.facebook .com.*

9.16 Batching Calls

Problem

I have a bunch of calls I need to make using the API, and I'd really like to batch them to get better performance.

Solution

Facebook has recently released a Batch API that does exactly that. The batching support is really easy to use and basically consists of wrapping the calls you want to make in `beginBatch( )` and `endBatch( )` statements.

If you were previously running this code as individual calls:

```
$friends = $facebook->api_client->friends_get();
$notifications = $facebook->api_client->notifications_get();
```

you could do the same thing as a batch by doing this:

```
$facebook->api_client->begin_batch();
$friends = &$facebook->api_client->friends_get();
$notifications = &$facebook->api_client->notifications_get();
$facebook->api_client->end_batch();
```

You won't see any significant performance gains on two calls, but you should if you push the Batch API to its limit and run 20 calls in a batch. See the Discussion for more information about what's really happening.

Discussion

The Batch API is currently in beta, so remember that you probably shouldn't build production code on it without being very careful, and you should report any bugs you might find into the Facebook Bug Tracker at *http://bugs.developers.facebook.com*.

Batching is considerably more efficient because it saves you roundtrips to the server on each call, and it lets Facebook process up to 20 calls in parallel at the same time. If you made each of those calls individually, you'd have to do them in series and would have 40 calls and responses instead of two. If you need to run the calls in your batch in the order you've listed them (rather than in parallel, which is the default), you can override the `batch_mode` variable in the Facebook Client Library:

```
// Default is 0, which is parallel
// (unless you've modified facebookapi_php5_restlib.php)
$facebook->api_client->batch_mode = FacebookRestClient::BATCH_MODE_DEFAULT;

// Explicitly setting the mode to parallel (0)
$facebook->api_client->batch_mode = FacebookRestClient::BATCH_MODE_SERVER_PARALLEL;

// Overriding the mode to serial (2)
// (don't forget to set it back!)
$facebook->api_client->batch_mode = FacebookRestClient::BATCH_MODE_SERIAL_ONLY;
```

Although this may change in the future, your batch will currently exit if there's an error in one of the calls, but any calls that you've made up to that point will still be committed. (In other words, this isn't a batched transaction in which the changes are committed only at the end; if you make any calls that modify Facebook-side data, they will still modify the data, even if the whole batch isn't successful.) If you're running in serial mode, try to optimize your code so that the calls most likely to result in errors happen at the end of the batch (e.g., something such as publishing to a News Feed will return an error if you've exceeded your allocations for the day).

Return by reference

Notice the ampersands (&) in front of the two calls inside the batch in the example in the Solution. This tells PHP that you want the return value from them as a reference rather than as a copy of the value. Without the ampersand there, PHP would normally return a copy of an array from a `Friends.get( )` call, rather than a reference to the actual data stored in memory. This might seem a little abstruse if you don't have a programming background, but stick with me because it's important.

Let's say that I'm your accountant and you really need to know how much money you spent on Big Gulp Slushies from 7-Eleven so far this year. If you pick up the phone and call me and I tell you that you spent $10,314 on crushed ice and syrup, you now have the value (and probably a serious bill from the dentist), and you can use it to do whatever you needed to do with it. The problem is that you spend about $28 a day on Big Gulp Slushies, and so that one-time value I passed you is true only at the moment I give it to you and immediately becomes untrue the next time you go into a 7-Eleven (which is probably where you phoned from, so that's a pretty short window of truth).

Now let's further suppose that I'm your accountant 50 years into the future and that we're actually connected by a telepathic data link (and, of course, that you aren't dead from Slushie overconsumption). When you go into the 7-Eleven and scan your thumb-print to pay for the fifth Big Gulp of the day, that transaction immediately shows up in my records. When you ping me on the ole telelink, instead of telling you that the value of your current purchases is $10,314, I pass you a reference to that number in my accounting system. The next time you swipe your thumb and buy a drink, the number updates on my end, and you automatically get the update since you have a reference to where the value is stored, rather than a copy.

OK! Back to Facebook. When you call `Friends.get( )` under nonbatch circumstances, it returns the value of the array of the friends for the user you requested. If the user has another tab open in her browser and accepts a new friend request in it, your copy of the value of her friends array is now out-of-date. This is a fairly unlikely occurrence when you've got her attention and she's looking at your page, but it's much more likely to happen when you're batching a number of API operations in which the 12th call might affect the values retrieved from the third call, which gets used in the 15th.

9.17 Getting and Setting Cookies

Problem

I need to get or set cookies for my application.

Solution

Use the `Data.setCookie( )` method to set a cookie (where **user** is the UID of the user you want to drop the cookie for):

```
$cookieReturn = $facebook->api_client->data_setCookie($user,
  'cookie_type', 'chocolate_chip');
```

Use the `Data.getCookies( )` method to get a cookie (where **user** is the UID of the user you want to retrieve the cookie for):

```
$cookie = $facebook->api_client->data_getCookies($user, 'cookie_type');
```

Discussion

You can specify optional **expires** and **path** settings for cookies when you drop them (the defaults are 24 hours and /, respectively):

```
$cookieReturn = $facebook->api_client->data_setCookie($user,
  'cookie_type', 'chocolate_chip', '1254079800', '/some/path/here');
```

Note that the **expires** argument is measured in epoch seconds (see Recipe 6.20 for more information about epoch time).

If you don't specify a cookie name for `Data.getCookies( )`, it will return all of the available cookies for the specified user.

Cookies in Facebook are handled differently than a regular browser-side cookie dropped by a regular web page. The cookies are actually managed by Platform and are associated with the user's account rather than residing in her browser, so they'll be present whenever that user logs into Facebook from any computer. Facebook will pass any unexpired cookies to your application with each request from a Canvas page to your callback URL, and will store any cookies you return (up to a limit of 50 cookies per app) so that you can access them next time. Some important things to note:

- You can use cookies to store data that you would otherwise have to roundtrip through API calls. This can be a very effective performance enhancement, since cookies are sent to you with each request. Keep in mind, however, that your request size will grow considerably if you fill it full of cookies. There's a careful balancing act at play here, but it's one that you can measure quite easily (check the average roundtrip time over a series of requests using the API, then compare to the average of the same number of roundtrips using cookies).

- Cookies without an **expires** attribute expire after 24 hours by default.

- Stored cookies are associated with the application ID and not with your callback URL's domain (which is great because it means you can move to a different server or address without issues).

- Facebook cookies have a path attribute just like regular cookies, which is evaluated relative to the callback URL of your application (rather than to a path on Facebook).

- You can drop and retrieve cookies for users who haven't logged into your application.

- Only web-based Facebook apps can use cookies. There is no cookie support for desktop apps.

- The cookie API calls do not require a session key.

 These methods are currently marked as beta in the Developers Wiki, so treat them with a little caution and make sure to report any bugs you might find into the Facebook Bug Tracker at *http:// bugs.developers.facebook.com*.

FQL equivalent

If you'd prefer to use FQL to access cookies, the equivalent query is:

```
SELECT uid, name, value, expires, path FROM cookies WHERE uid=12345 AND name='Foo'
```

For more information, see Recipe 8.10.

9.18 Getting Events

Problem

I need to retrieve an event.

Solution

Use the `Events.get( )` method, which allows you to filter for one user, a series of events, start/end times, and/or RSVP status. To filter for one user, specify `null` for the other filter parameters:

```
$events = $facebook->api_client->events_get(12345, null, null, null, null);
```

To retrieve one or more events, pass an array of event IDs (`eids`) as the second parameter:

```
$events = $facebook->api_client->events_get(null,
    array(14381739642,16044821668), null, null, null);
```

If you specify both a `uid` and an array of `eids`, Platform will return the events in the array that the user has on his list:

```
$events = $facebook->api_client->events_get(12345, array(14381739642,
  16044821668), null, null, null);
```

You can add in a start and/or end time (in epoch seconds; see Recipe 6.20 for more info) to further filter the results:

```
$events = $facebook->api_client->events_get(12345, array(14381739642,
  16044821668), 1209600000, 1214827199, null);
```

The final argument is to filter by a specific RSVP status, which are attending, unsure, declined, and not_replied:

```
$events = $facebook->api_client->events_get(12345, null, 1209600000,
  1214827199, 'declined');
```

Discussion

Events.get( ) will always return only those events that the current loggedinuser is allowed to see, regardless of who you specify as the uid filter (you'll get an empty set of events back if the user isn't allowed to see any of the events that should have been in the set).

The Client Library will return a multidimensional array in which each element contains all of the fields shown in Table 8-6.

FQL Equivalent

If you'd prefer to use FQL to access events, the equivalent query is:

```
SELECT eid, name, tagline FROM event WHERE eid IN (SELECT eid FROM
  event_member WHERE uid=uid)
```

See Recipe 8.18 for more information.

9.19 Getting Event Members

Problem

I need to retrieve the users who are attending an event.

Solution

Use the Events.getMembers( ) method:

```
$members = $facebook->api_client->events_getMembers($eid);
```

where eid is the ID of the event whose members you want to retrieve.

Discussion

This will return a multidimensional array in which the first level contains the different RSVP statuses and the second level is the uid (user ID) of the member who RSVPed.

The four possible statuses are attending, unsure, declined, and not_replied. If you wanted, for example, to list all of the people who are attending the event with eid 12345, you could do the following:

```
$members = $facebook->api_client->events_getMembers('12345');
if($members){
    if($members['attending']){
        echo '<ul>';
        for($counter = 0; $counter < count($members['attending']); $counter++){
            $uid = $members['attending'][$counter];
            echo '<li>';
            echo '    <fb:profile-pic uid="' . $uid . '"/>'
            echo '    <fb:name uid="' . $uid . '"/>';
            echo '</li>';
        }
        echo '</ul>';
    }
}
```

FQL equivalent

If you'd prefer to use FQL to access your event members, the equivalent query is:

```
SELECT uid, eid, rsvp_status FROM event_member WHERE eid=eid
```

See Recipe 8.19 for more information.

9.20 Refreshing FBML Caches

Problem

I need to tell Facebook to refresh its caches for some of my stored data.

Solution

If you're caching images, use the FBML.refreshImgSrc( ) method:

```
$return = $facebook->api_client->fbml_refreshImgSrc
('http://www.someserver.com/images/some_image.jpg');
```

If you're caching URLs, use the FBML.refreshRefUrl( ) method:

```
$return = $facebook->api_client->fbml_refreshRefUrl
('http://www.someserver.com/page.php');
```

Discussion

This returns true (1) if Facebook is able to locate an entry in its cache with the url you passed in and can refresh, or false (0) or blank if it can't.

9.21 Getting a (Ref) Handle on FBML

Problem

I want to put some FBML into Facebook's cache so that I can use it in a whole bunch of user Profiles.

Solution

Use the `FBML.setRefHandle( )` method:

```
$return = $facebook->api_client->fbml_setRefHandle('myHandle','FBML goes here');
```

Discussion

This will associate the `handle` you pass as the first parameter with the FBML content that you pass in the second one. You can then pull this content at any time using the `fb:ref` FBML tag (see Recipe 6.57 for more info).

This can be used only by web-based Facebook apps. Desktop apps are out of luck on this one.

9.22 Three Story Sizes: Working with Template Bundles

Problem

I'd like to be able to publish stories that take advantage of the one-line, short story, and full story formats introduced in the mid-2008 Profile redesign. What do I need to do?

Solution

In addition to splitting Profiles into multiple tabs, the Profile redesign also saw the advent of Feed stories appearing in one-line, short story, and full story formats. As a developer, you need to register "template bundles" with Facebook before you can publish stories in the different formats. Template bundles contain at least one of:

- One or more one-line story templates
- One or more short story templates
- One or more full story templates

You can specify multiple one-line templates by including them in a JSON-formatted array. Remember that order is very important here, and you want to include your most detailed template first and your least detailed last. For example:

```
{*actor*} just shared a {*nap-type*} with {*target*}.
{*actor*} just shared a nap with {*target*}.
{*actor*} just napped.
```

Tokens are always in the form {*token_name*}, and subsequent templates should only ever include a subset of the tokens used in the template prior (in other words, your templates should get less and less detailed without introducing new content). See the Discussion for more info about tokens. Facebook will always use the most flexible (i.e., the first) template for Mini-Feed stories, and it will try to aggregate stories together for News Feeds. Keep in mind that your least-specific template (i.e., the last one) has the highest likelihood of being used for aggregation, since it's the most likely to have content from all of the actors (see the Discussion for more about aggregation). Here's an example of template registration:

```
$oneLiners = array('{*actor*} just shared a {*nap-type*} with {*target*}.',
  '{*actor*} just shared a nap with {*target*}.', '{*actor*} just napped.');

$shortStories = array(
    array('template_title'=>'{*actor*} just shared a {*nap-type*}
  with {*target*}', 'template_body'=>'<p>It was {*status*}!</p>'),
    array('template_title'=>'{*actor*} just shared a nap with
  {*target*}','template_body'=>'<p>It was {*status*}!</p>'),
    array('template_title'=>'{*actor*} just napped.', '
template_body'=>'<p>It was {*status*}!</p>'));

$fullStories = array(
    array('template_title'=>'{*actor*} just shared a {*nap-type*}
  with {*target*}', 'template_body'=>'<p><img src=
"http://myserver.com/some_img.jpg" alt="Naps!"> It
  was {*status*}!</p>'),
    array('template_title'=>'{*actor*} just shared a nap with {*target*}
  ','template_body'=>'<p><img src="http://myserver.com/
some_img.jpg" alt="Naps!"> It was {*status*}!</p>'),
    array('template_title'=>'{*actor*} just napped.',
  'template_body'=>'<p><img src="http://myserver.com/some_img.jpg"
alt="Naps!"> It was {*status*}!</p>'));

$bundleId = $facebook->api_client->feed_registerTemplateBundle
($oneLiners, $shortStories, $fullStories);
```

A few notes:

- You have to include the one-line templates but can leave out either of the short or full templates by passing null into Feed.registerTemplateBundle( ).

- The template_title fields have to start with the {*actor*} token, but you're free to do whatever you'd like in the body fields.

- The bundle ID returned in the code here can be used with the other Feed API calls for publishing stories and managing template bundles.

Discussion

Registering your templates is just the first step. This Discussion will give you a quick tour of the other Feed API calls related to template bundles, as well as an example of what the stories look like.

Feed story example: Causes

Figures 9-8, 9-9, and 9-10 show examples of the three different story sizes from the Causes app.

Figure 9-8. Causes one-line story

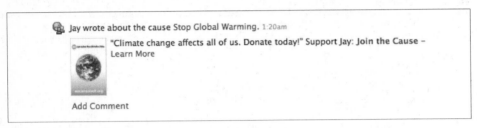

Figure 9-9. Causes short story

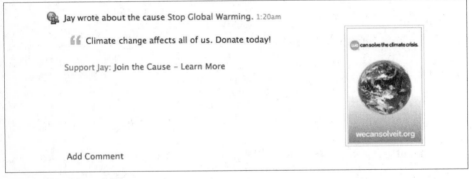

Figure 9-10. Causes full story

The "Add Comment" links are added by Facebook automatically.

About tokens

You can create as many tokens as you'd like in your feeds by defining them on the fly (anything wrapped with {* and *} automatically becomes a token). The only limitation on naming is that you can't conflict with one of the special tokens outlined later in this section.

There are two special tokens that you can include in your templates and don't need to define:

{*actor*}
   The user who originated the action that resulted in the story being published.

{*target*}

A list of the friends of the actor on whom or with whom the actor performed the action. The advantage to using this token over a custom one (e.g., {*friends*} or something similar) is that Facebook will automatically output the right text for the number of included targets (one friend just lists the name, two adds "and", three turns into a list ending in "and", etc.).

In both cases, Facebook will worry about substituting the right people into the story for you. In addition to those two tokens, you can also take advantage of a collection of additional templates that Facebook will handle for you. You can use exactly one of the following four tags in each story:

{*images*}

You can include up to four images in your story, so when you publish a story using `Feed.publishUserAction( )`, this token should map to an array containing four records, with required `src` keys and optional `href` keys if you'd like the images to be links.

{*flash*}

You can include a single Flash movie that fits into a box measuring 100 pixels high by 130 pixels wide. When you publish a story using `Feed.publishUserAction( )`, this token should map to an array containing a single entry with the required keys `swfsrc` (the location of the Flash movie) and `imgsrc` (the location of an image to display until the user clicks to activate). The default size is 30 pixels high by 100 pixels wide, so you'll need to specify an optional `height` (an integer between 30 and 100) and `width` (one of 100, 110, or 130) if you want to override the default.

{*mp3*}

You can include a single MP3 that Facebook will render as playable using its audio controller. You're required to include an `src` key (the location of the MP3), and you can include optional `title`, `album`, and `artist` keys (as strings).

{*video*}

You can include a single video that Facebook will make playable in the story. You're required to include the keys `video_src` (location of the video) and `preview_img` (image to display until the user clicks to activate). You can optionally include `video_title`, `video_type` (defaults to "application/x-shockwave-flash"), and `video_link` keys.

Getting all of your templates

Use the `Feed.getRegisteredTemplateBundles( )` method to retrieve all of the template bundles your application has previously registered:

```
$bundles = $facebook->api_client->feed_getRegisteredTemplateBundles();
```

You'll get back an array containing all of the templates, including their IDs for use in subsequent calls.

Getting a template bundle

Use the `Feed.getRegisteredTemplateBundleByID( )` method to retrieve a specific template bundle by ID:

```
$bundle = $facebook->api_client->feed_getRegisteredTemplateBundleByID(12345);
```

where 12345 is a valid template bundle ID.

Deactivating a template bundle

If you need to deactivate a template bundle you've previously registered, use the `Feed.deactivateTemplateBundleByID( )` method:

```
$result = $facebook->api_client->feed_deactivateTemplateBundleByID(12345);
```

where 12345 is a valid template bundle ID. The result will be `true` if the template was found and deactivated, and `false` if otherwise. Stories that were previously published with the deactivated template will still display in the News and Mini-Feeds, but you won't be able to publish to it anymore.

9.23 Publishing News and Mini-Feed Stories

Problem

I want to publish stories about my users' activities in my app so that their friends see them and become engaged.

Solution

Use the `Feed.publishUserAction( )` method:

```
$template_bundle_id = 12345678901;

$template_data = array(
    'nap-type'=>'Super Disco Nap',
    'status'=>'fabulous',
);

$target_ids = '12345,67890';

$result = $facebook->api_client->feed_publishUserAction
($template_bundle_id, json_encode($template_data), $target_ids);
```

You can optionally include a fourth parameter, `body_general`, to add additional body content to extend short story format posts. If these stories are being aggregated, Facebook will include one of the `body_general` parameters in the aggregated story. See Recipe 9.22 for more information about template bundles.

Discussion

Your app used to be limited to calling this function once every 12 hours for every user other than those listed as developers for your app (who will always see every story that you publish for testing purposes). At the time this book was going to press, it remained unclear as to whether that would continue to be the case with the Profile redesign.

Note that the `template_data` needs to be JSON-encoded when you pass it into the `Feed.publishUserAction( )` method.

Escaping JSON-Encoded URLs

The JSON-encoding step is easy if you're working in PHP 5.2 (or newer), since it includes a JSON encoder. This can become a particular pain with URLs that you might include in the `template_data` array, which need to have all the slashes escaped. If, for example, you have a token called {*photo*} and you need to substitute in the actual <a> tag linking to *http://flickr.com/photos/someuser/12345/*, you would need to include it as:

```
{"photo":"<a href{{=}}\"http:\/\/www.flickr.com\/photos\/someuser\/12345">Flickr<\/a>"}
```

Take a look at the PHP documentation for `json_encode( )`, which makes that a whole lot easier:

```
$titleData = json_encode(array('photo => '<a href=
"http://flickr.com/photos/someuser/12345/">Flickr</a>', ));
```

If you're working in an earlier version of PHP, check out the Zend JSON encoder at *http://framework.zend.com/manual/en/zend.json.html*. Developers working in other languages should find a similar library.

Stories may or may not show up in users' News Feeds, depending on a very complex and highly secretive algorithm that the Facebook team keeps locked up in a cage deep underground their Palo Alto lair. Thankfully, they released some details about how this works back in December 2007, which you can still read at *http://wiki.developers.facebook.com/index.php/FeedRankingFAQ* (note that this might be out-of-date or exactly accurate—such is the joy of proprietary algorithms).

`Feed.publishUserAction( )` will return either true (1) on success, false (0) on a permissions error, or one of the other Facebook error codes (see Recipe 9.58 for more information).

9.24 Story Aggregation

Problem

I've heard that Facebook aggregates stories together, but I don't know what that means.

Solution

If your app is growing in popularity and you have multiple users who are connected through part of the social graph, Facebook will aggregate the stories from your app about a given user's friends, and that aggregated story will have a much higher chance of showing up in their feed. You've likely seen this happen with Facebook's own stories, particularly about things such as Profile picture changes. Any of your stories that are published using the same registered template bundle can be aggregated automatically.

Discussion

Let's take a look at an example of aggregation. If our handy old Super Disco Napping application developed the ability to report on the post-napping brunch adventures of its users, it might publish a News story something like the one shown in Figure 9-11.

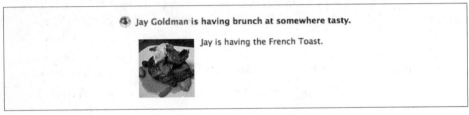

Figure 9-11. News story, non-aggregated

 The delicious photo of a delicious-looking plate of French toast is courtesy of urbanshoregirl, who published it on Flickr under a Creative Commons license. You can find the original photo at *http://flickr.com/photos/urbanshoregirl/101749649/*.

That's pretty interesting and might attract my friends' attention if it made it into their News Feeds, but it has to compete against all the other stories out there, so the odds are pretty slim (which I won't be after eating that plate of food). If we take advantage of aggregation, Facebook can pick out that my brunch story is the same as the ones published by my wife and our friend Jason, and it can aggregate them together into one story, as in Figure 9-12.

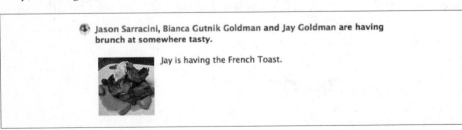

Figure 9-12. News story, aggregated

This News story is quite likely to be true, since we all have brunch together a lot. Unfortunately, it's only part of the story, since Jason's wife Athena isn't on Facebook. A more accurate aggregated story might be the one in Figure 9-13.

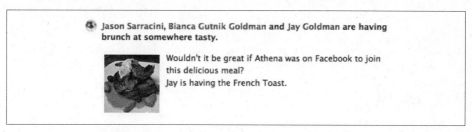

Jason Sarracini, Bianca Gutnik Goldman and Jay Goldman are having brunch at somewhere tasty.

Wouldn't it be great if Athena was on Facebook to join this delicious meal?
Jay is having the French Toast.

Figure 9-13. Factually accurate News story, aggregated

Aggregation used to be much more complicated before `Feed.publishUserAction( )` came along, requiring you to make sure that the content in the title and body of your stories was identical. Now that we have the joy of registered template bundles, Facebook will try to aggregate any stories that use the same templates, falling back to the simplest (i.e., the last) template in the one-line, short, or full story formats. For more information, see Recipe 9.22.

9.25 Setting Info Sections

Problem

My app has collected some fantastic info about my users, and I'd like to add it to their Info tabs as structured data.

Solution

The mid-2008 Profile redesign introduced the ability for applications to add sections to the new Info tab, accomplished through a new family of four API calls and a new FBML tag.

Setting an Info section is fairly simple, though the nested arrays can be a little confusing:

```
$info_fields = array(
    array(
        'field'=>'Favorite Naps',
        'items'=>array(
            array(
                'label'=>'Disco Nap',
                'link'=>'http://apps.facebook.com/superdisconapping/define/disconap'),
            array(
                'label'=>'Super Disco Nap',
                'link'=>'http://apps.facebook.com/superdisconapping/
define/superdisconap'),
            array(
```

```
                    'label'=>'Power Nap',
                    'link'=>'http://apps.facebook.com/superdisconapping/
        define/powernap'))),
            array(
                'field'=>'Favorite Napping Locales',
                'items'=>array(
                    array(
                        'label'=>'Car',
                        'link'=>'http://apps.facebook.com/superdisconapping/locale/car'),
                    array(
                        'label'=>'Office',
                        'link'=>'http://apps.facebook.com/superdisconapping/
        locale/office'))));

    $infoResult = $facebook->api_client->profile_setInfo('Super Disco
     Napping', 1, $info_fields, 12345);
```

If you read down from the top, `info_fields` is an array that contains a `field` name and an array of `items`. Each `item` contains, at a minimum, a `label` and a `link`, but can also contain `image`, `description`, and `sublabel` fields (the example here keeps it simple and uses only `label` and `link`). The actual call to `Profile.setInfo()` accepts a name for the Info section, either 1 for a text-based section or 5 for an object-based one (see the Discussion for more details), your array of data, and the `uid` of the user you're setting the section for.

Discussion

As outlined in Recipe 2.13, you can include either text-based or object-based sections. You can fit a lot more information into a much smaller area if you use the text-based option, but people are like magpies and are attracted to bright, shiny images, so you'll probably get more clicks if you go the object route.

Since the links on items can go anywhere, add as many links into your application as you can. Users surfing their friends' Info tabs will see your tantalizing links and follow them right into your app, where they will hopefully grant you access and install it themselves. In the example here, the Super Disco Napping app now includes a section that defines different types of naps and locations for taking them in, which would ideally be unprotected content that didn't require a login to access (both for attracting users and to open them up for indexing by search engines). Note that you can add only one Info box per application, so subsequent calls to `Profile.setInfo()` will simply overwrite earlier calls.

The other three tags are outlined next.

Getting Info sections

You can retrieve content you've set in an Info section by calling `Profile.getInfo()`:

```
    $infoSection = $facebook->api_client->profile_getInfo(561415460);
```

where 12345 is the `uid` for which you want to retrieve your section. This will return an array containing the same nested array structure you used to create the section (see the earlier example).

Adding options

Users can edit their Info section right on the Info tab, so it's a really good idea to pre-populate the options they can add (especially if you're using an object-based section). Call the `Profile.setInfoOptions()` method to add some options for the type-ahead control:

```
$options = array(
    array(
        'label'=>'Siesta',
        'link'=>'http://apps.facebook.com/superdisconapping/define/siesta'),
    array(
        'label'=>'Cat Nap',
        'link'=>'http://apps.facebook.com/superdisconapping/define/catnap'));

$infoOptionsResult = $facebook->api_client->profile_setInfoOptions
($options,'Favorite Naps');
```

The second parameter is the name of the field set when you called `Profile.setInfo()`.

Getting Options

You can retrieve the options defined for a field by calling the method `Profile.getInfoOptions()`:

```
$infoOptions = $facebook->api_client->profile_getInfoOptions('Favorite Naps');
```

9.26 FQL Queries

Problem

I need to run an FQL query.

Solution and Discussion

See Chapter 8, which covers FQL in great detail.

9.27 Friends?

Problem

I need to determine whether two (or more) users are friends.

Solution

Use the `Friends.areFriends()` method:

```
$areFriends = $facebook->api_client->friends_areFriends('12345', '67890');
```

The method also accepts two arrays and will let you know whether each pair (pulling the member at the same position in each array) is a friend:

```
$aUsers = array('12345', '67890', '11223');
$bUsers = array('33445', '66778', '99100');
$areFriends = $facebook->api_client->friends_areFriends($aUsers, $bUsers);
```

Discussion

Either way, the `Friends.areFriends()` returns a multidimensional array in which each element contains `uid1`, `uid2`, and `are_friends` elements (with the latter being `true`, `false`, or empty if the members aren't visible due to privacy rules or don't exist, which is the case with our fictional users here):

```
Array
(
    [0] => Array
        (
            [uid1] => 12345
            [uid2] => 33445
            [are_friends] =>
        )

    [1] => Array
        (
            [uid1] => 67890
            [uid2] => 66778
            [are_friends] =>
        )

    [2] => Array
        (
            [uid1] => 11223
            [uid2] => 99100
            [are_friends] =>
        )
)
```

Since the method is symmetric, both arrays need to have the same number of elements in them or you'll get an invalid parameter error.

FQL equivalent

If you'd prefer to use FQL to access friends, the equivalent query is:

```
SELECT uid1, uid2 FROM friend WHERE uid1=uid1 AND uid2=uid2
```

See Recipe 8.28 for more information.

9.28 Get Friends

Problem

I need to retrieve all of the current `loggedinuser`'s friends.

Solution

Use the `Friends.get( )` method:

```
$friends = $facebook->api_client->friends_get();
```

You can optionally specify a `flid` (friend list ID) if you want to narrow the scope of the retrieval down to a single friend list:

```
$friends = $facebook->api_client->friends_get(12345);
```

You can find the `flid`s for this user by calling `Friends.getLists( )` (see Recipe 9.30).

Discussion

`Friends.get( )` returns an array of `uid`s for the matching friends.

This method will only return friends of the current `loggedinuser`. There is no way to call this for a different user. It is against the terms of use of Facebook Platform to store the returned values from this call.

FQL equivalent

If you'd prefer to use FQL to access friends, the equivalent query is:

```
SELECT uid2 FROM friend WHERE uid1=$uid
```

See Recipe 8.27 for more information.

9.29 Get Friends Who Use My App

Problem

I need to retrieve all of the current `loggedinuser`'s friends who already have my app installed.

Solution

Use the `Friends.getAppUsers( )` method:

```
$friends = $facebook->api_client->friends_getAppUsers();
```

This method has no parameters, and it can be called only for the combination of the current `loggedinuser` and your application.

Discussion

`Friends.getAppUsers( )` returns an array of `uids` of the friends who have your app installed. It is against the terms of use of Facebook Platform to store the returned values from this call.

FQL equivalent

If you'd prefer to use FQL to access friends, the equivalent query is:

```
SELECT uid FROM user WHERE uid IN (SELECT uid2 FROM friend WHERE uid1=$uid)
  AND is_app_user
```

See Recipe 8.56 for more information.

9.30 Get Friend Lists

Problem

I need to retrieve all of the friend lists for the current `loggedinuser`.

Solution

Use the `Friends.getLists( )` method:

```
$friendLists = $facebook->api_client->friends_getLists();
```

This method has no parameters, and it can be called only for the current `loggedinuser`.

Discussion

`Friends.getLists( )` returns an array of the `flids` (friend list IDs) for the current `loggedinuser`. You can retrieve the members of a friend list by calling `Friends.get( )` and passing in the `flid` (see Recipe 9.28).

You're allowed to store the returned friend lists, but you should check them periodically because changes users make won't be reported back to you. Friend lists are considered private, so you can't share this information with anyone else.

FQL equivalent

If you'd prefer to use FQL to access friend lists, the equivalent query is:

```
SELECT flid, name FROM friendlist WHERE owner = $uid;
```

See Recipe 8.33 for more information.

9.31 Get Groups

Problem

I need to retrieve information about a set of groups, based on either a list of users or group IDs.

Solution

Use the Groups.get( ) method:

```
$groups = $facebook->api_client->groups_get();
```

If you specify no filters, you'll get all the groups for the current loggedinuser. You can specify a different user's uid to filter for them:

```
$groups = $facebook->api_client->groups_get(12345);
```

In that case, you'll get something back only if the current loggedinuser is allowed to see the groups for the user you've specified. If you have one or more gids (group IDs) and just want to pull information on them, you can do that too:

```
$targetGroups = array('2248774311', '14740918186');
$groups = $facebook->api_client->groups_get(null, $targetGroups);
```

Discussion

Groups.get( ) returns a multidimensional array of group records, with each element containing the fields listed in Recipe 8.37.

FQL equivalent

If you'd prefer to use FQL to access groups, the equivalent query is:

```
SELECT gid, name, description FROM group WHERE gid IN (SELECT gid FROM
  group_member WHERE uid=$uid) AND gid IN ($gids)
```

See Recipe 8.37 for more information.

9.32 Get Group Members

Problem

I need to find all of the members of a group.

Solution

Use the Groups.getMembers( ) method:

```
$members = $facebook->api_client->groups_getMembers(12345);
```

where 12345 is the gid (group ID) of your target group.

Description

`Groups.getMembers( )` returns a multidimensional array in which the first level of elements are the four membership types (`members`, `admins`, `officers`, `not_replied`), each containing the appropriate set of `uids` representing all of the members of that category whom the current `loggedinuser` is allowed to see. Note that the `members` array contains all of the `admins` and `officers` but does not overlap with the `not_replied` array. These lists are not filtered for users of your application, so note that they might contain users who don't have it installed.

FQL equivalent

If you'd prefer to use FQL to access group members, the equivalent query is:

```
SELECT uid, gid, positions FROM group_member WHERE gid=$gid
```

See Recipe 8.42 for more information.

9.33 Creating/Modifying Marketplace Listings

Problem

I need to create or modify a Facebook Marketplace listing from inside my application.

Solution

Creating and modifying listings both use the incorrectly named `Marketplace.createListing( )` method. If you're creating a new listing, pass a 0 for the `lid` (listing ID):

```
$attributes = array('title'=>'Bees!','category'=>'FORSALE',
 'subcategory'=>'GENERAL','description'=>'Great big hive full
 of bees for sale. Makes great honey.');
$listing = $facebook->api_client->marketplace_createListing(0, true, $attributes);
```

If you're modifying an existing listing, pass the listing's `lid`:

```
$attributes = array('title'=>'Free Bees!','category'=>'FORSALE',
 'subcategory'=>'GENERAL','description'=>'I\'m covered in beeeeeees!
 Please take them. Please.');
$listing = $facebook->api_client->marketplace_createListing
(23464075249, true, $attributes);
```

Discussion

This method (along with `Users.setStatus( )`) requires that users grant your application an extended permission. If you call it without having the permission granted, you'll get back a 280 error ("Creating and modifying listings requires the extended permission `create_listing`"). See Recipe 9.52 for more information on extended permissions.

The `attributes` array can contain settings for any of the properties of a Marketplace listing, which you can find in Recipe 8.42.

The middle parameter is a boolean indicating whether the entry should show up on the user's Profile. Passing `true` will publish a News story about the user, like the one shown in Figure 9-14.

Figure 9-14. News Feed of new listing

There's one more parameter you can pass in: a `uid` to indicate who should own the new listing. This is ignored for desktop applications, and it will be honored for web apps only if that user has granted the extended permission. If you're not using the Client Library, this parameter is required if you don't pass in a `session_key`.

9.34 Get Marketplace Listings

Problem

I need to retrieve Marketplace listings, based on either a list of users or listing IDs.

Solution

Use the `Marketplace.getListings()` method:

```
$listings = $facebook->api_client->marketplace_getListings('1234567', null);
```

where 1234567 is the `lid` (listing ID).

If you specify no `uid` (user ID) as the second parameter, you'll get the listings you've asked for with no filtering. You can specify a `uid` without `lid`s to retrieve all the listings owned by one user:

```
$groups = $facebook->api_client->marketplace_getListings(null, 12345);
```

Both parameters can be specified as arrays as well:

```
$targetListings = array('1234567', '8901234');
$targetUsers = array('12345', '67890', '11223');
$listings = $facebook->api_client->marketplace_getListings
($targetListings, $targetUsers);
```

Discussion

`Marketplace.getListings( )` returns a multidimensional array of listing records, with each element containing the fields listed in Table 8-13.

FQL equivalent

If you'd prefer to use FQL to access listings, the equivalent query is:

```
SELECT listing_id, url, title, description FROM listings WHERE poster in
  ($uids) AND listing_id in ($listing_ids)
```

See Table 8-13 for more information.

9.35 Get Marketplace Categories and Subcategories

Problem

I need to pull in the list of Marketplace categories and subcategories.

Solution

Use the `Marketplace.getCategories( )` method:

```
$categories = $facebook->api_client->marketplace_getCategories();
```

Once you have a category, use the `Marketplace.getSubCategories( )` method to retrieve its subcategories:

```
$subcategories = $facebook->api_client->marketplace_getSubCategories('FORSALE');
```

Discussion

You can quite easily combine the two methods to generate a `<select>` representing the hierarchy of the Marketplace:

```
$categories = $facebook->api_client->marketplace_getCategories();
if($categories){
    echo '<select>';
    foreach($categories as $category){
        echo '<option value="' . $category . '">'. $category . '</option>';
        $subcategories = $facebook->api_client->marketplace_
getSubCategories($category);
        if($subcategories){
            foreach($subcategories as $subcategory){
                echo '<option value="' . $subcategory . '"> '
. $subcategory . '</option>';
            }
        }
    }
    echo '</select>';
}
```

9.36 Deleting Marketplace Listings

Problem

I need to delete a Marketplace listing.

Solution

Use the `Marketplace.removeListing()` method:

```
$result = $facebook->api_client->marketplace_removeListing('1234567');
```

You can optionally specify a status to make it clear why the listing is being removed. Valid statuses are `SUCCESS`, `DEFAULT`, or `NOT_SUCCESS` (the default is, unsurprisingly, `DEFAULT`):

```
$result = $facebook->api_client->marketplace_removeListing('1234567', 'SUCCESS');
```

Discussion

You can also tag a `uid` on the end to specify whose listings you're deleting if they are not the current `loggedinuser` (this will be ignored for desktop apps). `Marketplace.removeListing()` will return true (1) on success, and false (0) or an error on failure.

9.37 Searching the Marketplace

Problem

I need to search the Marketplace.

Solution

Use the `Marketplace.search()` method:

```
$results = $facebook->api_client->marketplace_search(null, null, 'donuts');
```

The first two parameters are optional category and subcategory filters:

```
$results = $facebook->api_client->marketplace_search('JOBS', null, 'donuts');
```

Discussion

`Marketplace.search()` returns a multidimensional array in which each element is a listing containing the fields found in Table 8-13 in Recipe 8.42.

9.38 Sending Notifications

Problem

I need to send Notifications out to my users and their friends.

Solution

Use the `Notifications.send( )` method to send on-Facebook Notifications:

```
$to_ids = array('12345', '67890');
$result = $facebook->api_client->notifications_send($to_ids,
 'Your super disco nap is over! Time to wake up!');
```

You can send a Notification to the current `loggedinuser` by passing an empty string for `to_ids`. If you send the Notification to other users, make sure that the content starts with a verb because Facebook will prepend your text with the user's name (e.g., "Jay Goldman..."). The prepending doesn't happen if you send the Notification to the current `loggedinuser`.

The second parameter is the actual content for the Notification and allows for some FBML and markup, so you can experiment to find out what's allowable. `Notifications.send( )` returns a comma-separated list of the users it was able to send the Notification to.

Use the `Notifications.sendEmail( )` method to send off-Facebook Notifications:

```
$recipients = array('12345', '67890');

$subject = 'Hello Disco Nappers!';

$text = 'This is a reminder that it\'s almost time for you to take your
 next Disco Nap!';

$fbml = 'This is a reminder about your forthcoming Disco Nap with
 <fb:name uid="11223" useyou="false" />!';

$result = $facebook->api_client->notifications_sendEmail($recipients,
 $subject, $text, $fbml);
```

Every application has an imposed limit on the number of emails you can send per day, which you can find in your Facebook Insights application, on the Allocations tab (see *http://www.new.facebook.com/business/insights/app.php?id=12345&tab=allocations*, where 12345 is your app's ID). Desktop apps have to pass a session key and can send email only to the current user identified in that session. Some tags are prohibited in the `fbml` parameter, so try experimenting to see what you can get away with. `Notifications.sendEmail( )` returns a comma-separated list of the users it was able to send the Notification to.

Discussion

Notifications have got to be one of the most contentious issues for Facebook app developers. On the one hand, they make up the bread and butter of how a lot of applications grow their user bases. On the other hand, they're the pain in the inbox that users most often lament when complaining about how Facebook applications are ruining their Facebook experience. We've all logged in to find an overwhelming avalanche of Notifications, but we're also tickled pink when we find out that it's our turn in a Scrabulous game or that someone has stolen our Two Headed Serpent in PackRat.

Notifications are a mechanism for your application to alert your users that something has happened in your app that requires their attention. Your Notifications page on Facebook will show Notifications that you've both received and sent, as in Figures 9-15 and 9-16.

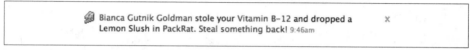

Figure 9-15. PackRat Notification received

Figure 9-16. PackRat Notification sent

As described in Recipe 2.16, your application has an allocated number of Notifications that you can send per day, based on how users have received your Notifications in the past. Since users who mark your Notifications as spam today affect the number of Notifications you can send tomorrow, it's critical to your app's success that you spend time on a Notification strategy that will keep your so-called "spamminess" rating as low as possible. There's no one strategy that will work for all apps, but here's some general advice.

Sending to friends

You can send Notifications only to the current `loggedinuser` or to her friends who have your app installed. This works well for games such as PackRat, since you can only play with your friends anyway. It works much less well in a game in which you can challenge players who aren't your friends, since there's no way to send them a notification when it's their turn. You can get around this by creating infinite sessions for them and storing their `session_keys` in your database, and then making an API call on their behalf to send them a Notification, though this can become quite tedious. See Recipe 9.7 for more information.

Monitoring allocations

Here are two ways you can monitor your allocation of Notifications:

1. Check the Allocations tab in the Facebook Insights application for your app (*http://www.facebook.com/business/insights/app.php?id=123456789&tab=allocations*, where 12345679 is your app's ID).

2. Use the `Admin.getAllocation( )` method. See Recipe 9.12 for more info.

You should generally keep an eye on those numbers, but you should be particularly watchful when you make a change to the Notifications sent by your app, as that's most likely to trigger a change in the way recipients are receiving them.

9.39 Get Notifications

Problem

I need to retrieve all of the outstanding Notifications for the current user.

Solution

Use the `Notifications.get( )` method:

```
$notifications = $facebook->api_client->notifications_get();
```

Discussion

`Notifications.get( )` returns a multidimensional array in which the elements are different Notification types (messages, pokes, shares, friend requests, group invites, and event invites), with each one containing different information depending on its type. Messages, pokes, and shares all contain an `unread` count and the `most_recent` ID of the relevant content type, friend requests contains the `uids` of the users who have made the outstanding requests, and group and event invites contain the `gids` and `eids` of the relevant groups and events.

Facebook encourages developers who are building apps that notify users of new messages, pokes, and shares to use the following logic:

```
if (unread > 0 && most_recent > old_most_recent) {
    display_notification();
}
old_most_recent = most_recent;
```

9.40 Get Pages

Problem

I need to find all of the Pages that the current user is a fan of.

Solution

Use the `Pages.getInfo( )` method:

```
$fields = array('name','pic_small','has_added_app');
$pages = $facebook->api_client->pages_getInfo(null,$fields,null,null);
```

Discussion

The four parameters are filters that allow you to constrain the result set. The first is for `pageids` (Page IDs), which allows you to retrieve info for a specific Page or a set of Pages:

```
$pages = array('25975037248', '5603889283');
$fields = array('name','pic_small','has_added_app');
$pages = $facebook->api_client->pages_getInfo($pages,$fields,null,null);
```

The second parameter is the set of fields you'd like returned in your results, which can include any of the fields listed in Table 8-15. The third is for `uids` and allows you to return the Pages for a different user (or set of users), provided that the current `loggedinuser` is allowed to see that info:

```
$users = array('567770429');
$fields = array('name','pic_small','has_added_app');
$pages = $facebook->api_client->pages_getInfo(null,$fields,$users,null);
```

The final parameter is for Page type and lets you filter the results down to a specified list. There doesn't appear to be an easy way to get the list of possible types, but they are generally an all-uppercase version of the type's name that you see when creating the page, with spaces replaced by underscores (e.g., "RETAIL", "MUSICIAN", "LOCAL_TECHNOLOGY_TELECOMMUNICATIONS_SERVICES", etc.).

FQL equivalent

If you'd prefer to use FQL to access Pages, the equivalent query is:

```
SELECT fields FROM page WHERE page_id IN (SELECT page_id FROM page_fan
  WHERE uid = $uid AND type = $type)
```

See Table 8-15 in Recipe 8.48 for more information.

9.41 Checking Page Properties

Problem

I need to find out if a user is the admin of a Page, or if a Page has my app installed, or whether a user is a fan of a specific Page.

Solution

Use the `Pages.isAdmin( )` method to find out whether the current `loggedinuser` is an admin of a specific Page:

```
$result = $facebook->api_client->pages_isAdmin('123456789');
```

where 123456789 is the `pageid` of the Page you're interested in.

Use the `Pages.isFan( )` method to find out whether a user is a fan of a specific Page:

```
$result = $facebook->api_client->pages_isFan('123456789', '12345');
```

where 123456789 is the `pageid` of the Page you're interested in, and 12345 is the optional `uid` of the user you want to check for (it defaults to the current `loggedinuser` if you leave it off).

Use the `Pages.hasAppAdded( )` method to find out if a specific Page has your app added:

```
$result = $facebook->api_client->pages_hasAppAdded('123456789');
```

where 123456789 is the `pageid` of the Page you're interested in.

Discussion

All three methods return true (1) if the thing you're checking is true, or false (0) if it isn't (or the `pageid` can't be found).

9.42 Create a Photo Album

Problem

I need to create a photo album.

Solution

Use the `Photos.createAlbum( )` method, which unfortunately isn't supported in the PHP Client Library (see Recipe 9.57):

```
$album = $facebook->api_client->photos_createAlbum('Test Album',
'Testville','This is a test');
```

Discussion

This method will return an array containing the information about your newly created album:

```
Array
(
    [aid] => 12345679012345
    [cover_pid] => 0
    [owner] => 12345
    [name] => Test Album
    [created] => 1212878578
    [modified] => 1212878578
    [description] => This is a test
    [location] => Testville
    [link] => http://www.facebook.com/album.php?aid=12345679012345&id=12345
```

```
            [size] => 0
    )
```

You're allowed to store the `aid` (album ID) and the `uid` of the owner, but nothing else. The returned `cover_pid` value will always be 0 because this album was just created and doesn't contain any photos yet.

9.43 Get Photo Albums

Problem

I need to retrieve a user's photo albums.

Solution

Use the `Photos.getAlbums( )` method:

```
$albums = $facebook->api_client->photos_getAlbums('12345');
```

You can specify a `uid` and/or an array of `aids` (album IDs) to retrieve specific albums:

```
$targetAlbums = array('9876543210987654321','12345');
$albums = $facebook->api_client->photos_getAlbums(null,$targetAlbums);
```

Specifying both will return only the albums from the list that belong to the user.

Discussion

This method will return a multidimensional array of photos, with each photo containing:

```
[0] => Array
        (
            [pid] => 1234567890123456789
            [aid] => 9876543210987654321
            [owner] => 1345
            [src] => http://photos-f.ak.facebook.com/photos-ak-sf2p/
v283/16/97/12345/s....jpg
            [src_big] => http://photos-f.ak.facebook.com/photos-ak-sf2p/
v283/16/97/561415460/n....jpg
            [src_small] => http://photos-f.ak.facebook.com/
photos-ak-sf2p/v283/16/97/561415460/t....jpg
            [link] => http://www.facebook.com/photo.php?pid=1122334&id=12345
            [caption] =>
            [created] => 1212879873
        )
```

The `created` field is expressed in epoch seconds (see Recipe 6.20 for more information about epoch time).

9.44 Get Photos

Problem

I need to retrieve specific photos, either because they contain a specific user, are in a specific album, or I have their pids (photo IDs).

Solution

Use the Photos.get( ) method. To retrieve photos of a specific user, call:

```
$photos = $facebook->api_client->photos_get('561415460',null,null);
```

To retrieve photos from a specific album, get the aid using Photos.getAlbums( ) and then pass it as the middle parameter (note that the aid shown in the URL when you're looking at a specific album isn't the album's real aid and won't retrieve the photos here):

```
$photos = $facebook->api_client->photos_get(null,'1234567890123456789',null);
```

To retrieve specific photos, pass an array of aids as the final parameter:

```
$targetPhotos = array('1234567890123456789','9876543210987654321');
$photos = $facebook->api_client->photos_get(null,null,$targetPhotos);
```

You can combine the three parameters in any way you'd like, allowing you to filter for photos from specific albums that have been tagged with a specific user, or the subset of a specific set of photos that have been tagged with a specific user, etc.

Discussion

This method will return a multidimensional array of photo elements, each containing the following:

```
[0] => Array
        (
            [pid] => 1234567890123456789
            [aid] => 9876543210987654321
            [owner] => 1345
            [src] => http://photos-f.ak.facebook.com/photos-ak-sf2p/
v283/16/97/12345/s....jpg
            [src_big] => http://photos-f.ak.facebook.com/photos-ak-
sf2p/v283/16/97/561415460/n....jpg
            [src_small] => http://photos-f.ak.facebook.com/
photos-ak-sf2p/v283/16/97/561415460/t....jpg
            [link] => http://www.facebook.com/photo.php?pid=1122334&id=12345
            [caption] =>
            [created] => 1212879873
        )
```

FQL equivalent

If you'd prefer to use FQL to access photos, the equivalent query is:

```
SELECT pid, aid, owner, src FROM photo WHERE pid IN (SELECT pid FROM
  photo_tag WHERE subject=$subj_id) AND aid=$aid AND pid IN ($pids)
```

See Recipe 8.52 for more information.

9.45 Uploading a Photo

Problem

I need to upload a new Facebook photo.

Solution

Use the `Photos.upload( )` method, which currently is not supported in the PHP Client Library (see Recipe 9.57). Luckily, Jeremy Blanchard, Paul Wells, and Kevin Pazirandeh have developed an unofficial extension that supports uploading, which you'll find at *http://wiki.eyermonkey.com/Facebook_Photo_Uploads*.

If you're making API calls directly from your own code or are using a different Client Library, this won't be so important to you. The syntax for their method is very similar to what's outlined on the Developers Wiki, with the notable exception of the `filename` argument:

```
$result = $facebook->api_client->photos_upload($filename, $aid, $caption);
```

In this case, `filename` is a URL pointing to the image you want to add to Facebook (it has to be somewhere on the Web already); `aid` is the album ID you want to add the photo to; and `caption` is an optional caption describing the image. The Wiki defines this function as accepting raw data to upload the image with, which means you could actually take a file from the user's local computer and upload it instead of requiring it to be on the Web.

Discussion

Uploading images from a local computer is hard to do properly, due to security constraints. Facebook's own uploader uses a Java applet to get around sandbox issues that prevent things such as Flash and JavaScript from accessing the local filesystem. With enough experimentation, you should be able to build an HTML form into a page in your Facebook app that makes a multipart submission to your server, including a file upload field, and then you should be able to use this Client Library extension to upload the image into Facebook from there.

9.46 Adding Tags to Photos

Problem

I need to add tags to photos that have been stored in the Facebook Photos app.

Solution

Use the `Photos.addTag()` method, which unfortunately isn't supported in the PHP Client Library (see Recipe 9.57):

```
$result = $facebook->api_client->photos_addTag('1234567890123456789',
'12345',null,50,50,null,null);
```

The parameters, in order, are the `pid` (photo ID) of the target photo; the `uid` (user ID) of the user you're tagging (set to null if this is a text tag); the text to tag (set to null if this is a user tag); the *x* coordinate of the tag; the *y* coordinate of the tag; a JSON-formatted array of tag information; and the `uid` of the owner of the photo (if it isn't the current `loggedinuser`).

Discussion

Tags can only be added to pending photos owned by either the current `loggedinuser` or the user specified in the last argument, unless your app has been granted the `photo_upload` extended permission (see Recipe 9.52 for more information).

The parameters for `Photos.addTag()` are pretty self-explanatory, except for the optional `tags` JSON-formatted array. If you pass a `tags` array, the `tag_id`, `tag_text`, `x`, and `y` parameters are ignored. The tags string should be constructed of `x` and `y` values accompanied by either a `tag_uid` or `tag_text`:

```
[{"x":"30.0","y":"30.0","tag_uid":12345}, {"x":"70.0","y":"70.0","tag_text":"
Joe's skateboard"}]
```

If you're building your app in PHP 5.2 or higher, you can create a regular PHP array and then use the built-in JSON encoder (other languages may have equivalent functions; check your documentation):

```
$tags = array(array('x'=>50,'y'=>50,'tag_uid'=>'12345'),
array('x'=>25,'y'=>40,'tag_text'=>'Pizza!'));
$result = $facebook->api_client->photos_addTag('1234567890123456789'
,null,null,null,null,json_encode($tags),null);
```

9.47 Getting and Setting Profile FBML

Problem

I want to get and set the contents of my users' Profile Boxes and Profile Action links.

Solution

Use the `Profle.getFBML( )` and `Profile.setFBML( )` methods to manipulate the contents of your app's Profile Box.

Discussion

The process of setting FBML is similar to the process that takes place behind the scenes when a user requests a page from your app (see Recipe 4.1). In this case, the process is less symmetrical, since you initiate an update to Facebook's cache that they'll later display. The FBML update flow is illustrated in Figure 9-17.

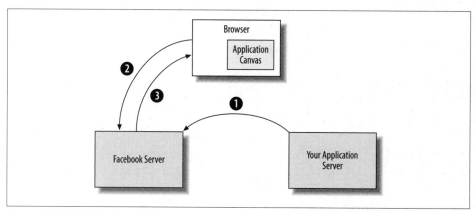

Figure 9-17. FBML update flow

The FBML you set is cached on Facebook's servers to make displaying Profiles as quick as possible, so you'll need to use `Profile.setFBML( )` again if you want to update the cache:

1. Whenever your app feels the need to update Profile FBML, you call `Profile.setFBML( )` from your app server and send your new content to Facebook's servers, where it gets cached. This generally happens either because you have a user currently logged in who has done something Profile-worthy, or because you have a scheduled job (possibly using `cron`) that has resulted in a calculation.

2. A visitor to one of your users' Profiles requests the page from Facebook.

3. Facebook renders your cached FBML into HTML (along with all of the other cached Profile Boxes and Action links for this user) and serves it back to the visitor's browser.

There are four parts to setting the FBML: the wide Profile Box, the narrow Profile Box, the main Profile Box, and the mobile Profile Box. The main Profile Box was added in the mid-2008 Profile redesign and gives apps the opportunity to have a version of their Profile Box added to the Wall page, limited to a height of 250 pixels.

We're going to leave the mobile Box out for now and just focus on the other three. Here are three important things to note in the code shown next:

- The wide and narrow Boxes are passed together as the Profile argument.

- The first argument used to be markup, but it's been deprecated. It's still in the method call in the PHP Client Library, so you have to pass a null for it.

- The fourth argument used to be profile_action, but it's also been deprecated with the mid-2008 Profile redesign, so pass a null there, too:

```
$title = '<fb:title>Super Disco Naps</fb:title>';
$title .= '<fb:subtitle seeallurl="http://apps.facebook.com/superdisconaps/all">';
$title .= 'Displaying 10 of 3200 naps ';
$title .= '<fb:action href="http://apps.facebook.com/superdisconaps/nap.php">';
$title .= 'Take a Nap!';
$title .= '</fb:action>';
$title .= '</fb:subtitle>';

$wide = '<fb:wide>';
$wide .= $title;
$wide .= 'This is the wide profile box for <fb:name uid="'. $user . '"
 useyou="false" firstnameonly="true"/>!';
$wide .= '</fb:wide>';

$narrow = '<fb:narrow>';
$narrow .= $title;
$narrow .= 'This is the narrow profile box <fb:name uid="'. $user . '"
 useyou="false" firstnameonly="true"/>!';
$narrow .= '</fb:narrow>';

$narrowMain = '<p>This is the main narrow profile box <fb:name uid="'.
 $user . '" useyou="false" firstnameonly="true"/>!</p>';

// $markup, $uid, $profile, $profile_action, $mobile_profile, $profile_main
$result = $facebook->api_client->profile_setFBML(null, 12345, $wide . $narrow,
 null, null, $narrowMain);
```

Retrieving FBML for a Profile Box is as simple as:

```
$boxFBML = $facebook->api_client->profile_getFBML(12345, 1);
$mainFBML = $facebook->api_client->profile_getFBML(12345, 2);
```

The first parameter is the uid of the user you want to retrieve for, and the second is either 1 for the wide and narrow Boxes or 2 for the main Profile's narrow Box.

Don't forget that you can preview your FBML using the FBML Test Console (*http://developers.facebook.com/tools.php?fbml*) before you post it, to make sure it renders correctly.

9.48 Get a User's Info

Problem

I need to retrieve info about a specific user.

Solution

Use the `Users.getInfo( )` method:

```
$uids = array('12345');
$fields = array('first_name','last_name');
$users = $facebook->api_client->users_getInfo($uids, $fields);
```

Discussion

You can query on any of the fields that make up the user table, which are documented in Figure 9-1. You might run into some of the privacy restrictions built-in to Platform, which limit the `meeting_for`, `meeting_sex`, `religion`, and `significant_other_id` fields to being visible to an app only when it has been added by a user. Users also have the option to limit the visibility of all fields except `affiliations`, `first_name`, `last_name`, `name`, and `uid`.

FQL equivalent

If you'd prefer to use FQL to access users, the equivalent query is:

```
SELECT uid, name, birthday FROM user WHERE uid IN ($uids)
```

See Recipe 8.55 for more information.

9.49 Get Logged-In User

Problem

I need to find the current `loggedinuser`'s uid.

Solution

Use the very simple `Users.getLoggedInUser( )` method:

```
$currentUser = $facebook->api_client->users_getLoggedInUser();
```

Discussion

`Users.getLoggedInUser( )` returns the `uid` of the current `loggedinuser`.

9.50 Has a User Added My App?

Problem

I need to check whether a user has added my app.

Solution

Use the `Users.isAppAdded()` method:

```
$hasAdded = $facebook->api_client->users_isAppAdded();
```

Discussion

`Users.isAppAdded()` returns a boolean indicating whether the specified user has installed your app. This will check for the current `loggedinuser` by default, but web-based Facebook apps can also pass in a different `uid`:

```
$hasAdded = $facebook->api_client->users_isAppAdded('12345');
```

9.51 Setting Status

Problem

I need to set the Facebook status of my users.

Solution

Use the `Users.setStatus()` method, which unfortunately isn't supported in the PHP Client Library (see Recipe 9.57):

```
$result = $facebook->api_client->Users_setStatus('setting his status
using the API!',false);
```

The parameters, in order, are the `status` and whether or not to `clear` the status. Passing true for `clear` will ignore the `status` you pass in and leave it blank.

Discussion

You can set the status only for users who have given your application the `status_update` extended permission (see Recipe 9.52 for more information).

`Users.setStatus()` will also accept two additional parameters: a boolean called `status_includes_verb`, which will prepend "is" to the front of your `status` if you pass `false`, and a `uid` of the user for which you want to set the status (which is ignored for desktop apps and is required for web apps only if you don't have a valid session).

9.52 Extended Permissions

Problem

I've planned out a great app, but it's going to require my users to give permission to do some things that are beyond the usual set of options, such as setting their status or creating Marketplace listings. How do they let me know it's OK?

Solution

Table 9-7 lists three extended permissions that users can grant an application.

Table 9-7. Extended permissions

Permission	Description
status_update	Your application can call Users.setStatus( ) for this user.
photo_upload	You can already upload photos and add tags for all users with the Photos.upload( ) and Photos.addTag( ) methods, but both will go into a pending state and require approval. Granting this permission allows your app to bypass that step.
create_listing	Your application can create new Marketplace listings on behalf of this user.

The permissions are granted one at a time by sending users to *http://www.facebook.com/authorize.php?api_key=YOUR_API_KEY&v=1.0&ext_perm=PERMISSION_NAME* (see example page in Figure 9-18), substituting your API key and the permission's name from Table 9-7.

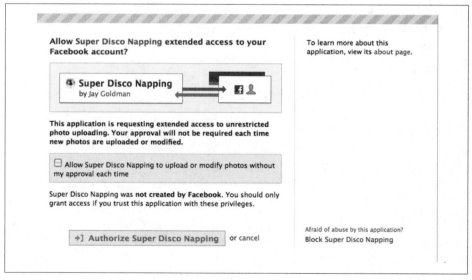

Figure 9-18. Extended permissions

Discussion

You can add two more parameters to the URL, next and next_cancel, which are URL-encoded URLS you'd like the user sent to when they're finished granting permission or if they cancel, respectively:

http://www.facebook.com/authorize.php?api_key=YOUR_API_KEY&v=1.0&ext
_perm=PERMISSION_NAME&next=http%3A%2F%2Fapps.facebook.com
%2Fmyapp%2Fpermissions.php&next_cancel=http%3A%2F%2Fapps.facebook
.com%2Fmyapp%2Fcancel.php

If you don't provide those URLs, users will see a Facebook message letting them know they can return to the app if they save (canceling just goes back one page in their history), as in Figure 9-19.

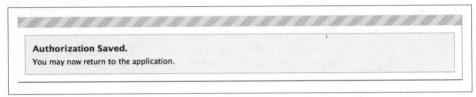

Figure 9-19. Extended permissions message

Users can revoke extended permissions on their Edit Apps page, at *http://www.facebook.com/editapps.php*.

You can check to see whether a user has granted a certain permission to your app by calling the API's Users.hasAppPermission( ) method (see Recipe 9.53 for more info).

9.53 Checking Extended Permissions

Problem

How can I check to see whether a user has granted my app extended permissions?

Solution

Use the Users.hasAppPermission( ) method, which is not currently included in the PHP Client Library (see Recipe 9.57):

```
$permission = $facebook->api_client->Users_hasAppPermission('status_update');
```

Discussion

This will return true (1) or false (0). There are three extended permissions you can check for:

status_update
> You can set the user's status with Users.setStatus( ).

`create_listing`
> You can create Marketplace listings for the user.

`photo_upload`
> You can upload photos and set tags on nonpending photos.

See Recipe 9.52 for more information.

9.54 Storing Data with the Data Store API

Problem

I need a place to store some data for my app, and I don't want to use my own database or a third-party service. Is there somewhere I can stick it inside of Facebook?

Solution

Facebook recently introduced the Data Store API, which was still in beta as this book went to press. The approach is to provide specialized storage, highly targeted and optimized to the kind of data that app developers need to store, rather than taking the more generalized approach of Amazon SimpleDB. The API is grouped into the areas:

Specialized tables
> One of the advantages of using the Data Store API is specialized tables, designed and optimized to store the kinds of data for which your app is most likely to need storage. The initial pass only includes a User Preference table, but Facebook is looking for feedback from app developers about the types of tables they might be interested in.

Distributed tables
> Most web developers understand databases well enough to administer a single server but lack the experience necessary to design and maintain a complicated, scalable, distributed system. Using the Data Store API gives you access to a well-managed distributed system for free, designed to allow your tables to grow to millions of records without a significant performance loss.

Associations
> If you've read Chapter 8 and checked out some of the performance recommendations around indexing or already have a good level of database design knowledge, you'll be familiar with how indexing can deliver a substantial speed increase. This is true in a traditional database but loses its effectiveness in a distributed scheme because there's no centralized directory telling the index where to find data. Facebook has solved this problem with associations, which describe the relationship between two pieces of data (e.g., a husband and wife or a gift giver and receiver).

Since this API will appeal only to a smaller subset of readers, and since it's in early beta and subject to change, I'm only going to cover a few quick examples and leave the rest up to the Wiki's documentation, which you'll find at *http://wiki.developers.facebook .com/index.php/Data_Store_API_documentation*.

To store and retrieve a user preference:

```
$prefId = 31;
$prefValue = 'black';
$setResult = $facebook->api_client->data_setUserPreference($prefId, $prefValue);
$getResult = $facebook->api_client->data_getUserPreference($prefId);
```

You can store up to 201 preferences per user per application, identified by the numeric IDs 0–200. One important note: the Data Store API will clear out a preference set to either zero (0) or an empty string, which it treats as the same thing. If you need to set a preference to the value 0, you'll need to come up with a scheme that you'll later recognize, since setting it to 0 will remove it (e.g., "n:0", or "zero", or "nil", etc.). Both of the methods shown in the code sample also have a sibling batch mode version: Data.setUserPreferences( ) and Data.getUserPreferences( ). The former takes an associative array of key/value pairs and a boolean indicating whether new preferences should overwrite (true) or merge into (false) existing ones:

```
$prefBatch = array(31=>'red', 42=>'potato', 68=>'rubber golve');
$setResult = $facebook->api_client->data_setUserPreferences($prefBatch, true);
$getResult = $facebook->api_client->data_getUserPreferences();
```

There are no arguments for Data.getUserPreferences( ), which will return a multidimensional array containing all of the preferences for this user in this app:

```
Array
(
    [0] => Array
        (
            [pref_id] => 31
            [value] => red
        )

    [1] => Array
        (
            [pref_id] => 42
            [value] => potato
        )

    [2] => Array
        (
            [pref_id] => 68
            [value] => rubber golve
        )

)
```

The term "object type" in the Data Store API is effectively what you would think of as a "table" in a traditional database. You can create as many object types as you'd like and can then add as many properties (i.e., fields or columns) as you need. Here's some sample code for defining a new object type for storing a dog, adding properties, getting a description of our new type, and then dropping it. Note that property names can be up to 32 characters long and can consist of lowercase letters (a–z), numbers (0–9), and underscores. There are currently three supported types: integers (1), strings (2), and blobs of text (3):

```
// Create the Object Type
$facebook->api_client->data_createObjectType('dog');

// Define some Properties
$facebook->api_client->data_defineObjectProperty('dog','name',2); // 2 = string
$facebook->api_client->data_defineObjectProperty('dog','breed',1); // 1 = int
$facebook->api_client->data_defineObjectProperty('dog','cat_friendly',1);
$facebook->api_client->data_defineObjectProperty('dog',
'description',3); // 3 = text blob

// Make some changes
$facebook->api_client->data_renameObjectProperty('dog','description','bio');
$facebook->api_client->data_undefineObjectProperty('dog',
'cat_friendly');
$facebook->api_client->data_renameObjectType('dog','canine');

// Retrieve the type(s)
$objectTypes = $facebook->api_client->data_getObjectTypes(); // Get all types
$myObjectType = $facebook->api_client->data_getObjectType('canine'); // Get the type

// Drop it
$facebook->api_client->data_dropObjectType('canine'); // Bye!
```

Once you've created your object types, you can create objects (think rows in a database table) based on them:

```
// Create an object
$objProps = array('name'=>'Findley','breed'=>1,'bio'=>'Best dog!');
$objId = $facebook->api_client->data_createObject('canine',json_encode($objProps));

// Update it
// true = replace values, fales = merge
$objProps = array('name'=>'Findley','breed'=>1,'bio'=>'Best dog in the world!');
$facebook->api_client->data_updateObject($objId,json_encode($objProps),true);

// Get the properties
$findleyProperties = $facebook->api_client->data_getObject($objId);
$findleyBio = $facebook->api_client->data_getObject($objId,'bio');
```

The last part of the Data Store API is creating associations, which act as indexes to speed up queries across the distributed tables. Associations can be one-way (a person owns a car but a car doesn't own a person), symmetrical two-way (a spouse is a spouse in both directions), or asymmetrical two-way (a husband to a wife is not the same as a wife to a husband). Assuming we have an object type called 'person', let's define the relationship between people and their dogs:

```
// Define an association
$info1 = array('alias'=>'owner','person',false);
$info2 = array('alias'=>'canine','person',false);
```

```
// 1 = one way
// 2 = two way symmetrical
// 3 = two way asymmetrical (requires the other direction to be named)
$facebook->api_client->data_defineAssociation('owner_of_pet',3,
$info1,$info2,'pet_of_owner');

$myAssoc = $facebook->api_client->data_getAssociationDefinition('owner_of_pet');
```

When we're done with our associations, we can undefine them (make sure you undefine both sides of a two-way asymmetrical association):

```
$facebook->api_client->data_undefineAssociation('owner_of_pet');
$facebook->api_client->data_undefineAssociation('pet_of_owner');
```

As with object types and objects, we can now create actual instances of the association we just defined:

```
// Create objects
$objProps = array('name'=>'Findley','breed'=>1,'bio'=>'Best dog in the world!');
$dogId = $facebook->api_client->data_createObject('canine',json_encode($objProps));
$objProps = array('name'=>'Jay','bio'=>'Best dog owner in the world!');
$ownerId = $facebook->api_client->data_createObject('person',json_encode($objProps));

// Set an association
$facebook->api_client->data_setAssociation('owner_of_pet',$ownerId,$dogId);
$jaysDogs = $facebook->api_client->data_getAssociatedObjects('owner_of_
pet',$ownerId,false);
$findleysOwners = $facebook->api_client->data_getAssociatedObjects
('pet_of_owner',$dogId,false);
```

As mentioned earlier, this recipe covers only the basics of the Data Store API, and so you'll want to consult the Wiki for more detailed info.

Discussion

Although there are some definite advantages in using the Data Store API (mostly around performance and ease of implementation), it also means you can't share the data that you store in there with any other frontends. If you're following my architecture advice (see Recipe 4.2), you might want to consider storing this information in your own database so that other frontends can share the same info.

9.55 Granting Permissions to Other Applications Via the Permissions API

Problem

I'm building a whole family of applications, and I'm writing an additional one for myself that is going to aggregate all of the daily metrics and allocations from its siblings into one convenient place. How can I have one app gather stats for another?

(How's that for a contrived example? There aren't many times when you'll need these calls otherwise, but maybe you have more imagination than I do.)

Solution

The Permissions API, which was still in beta at the time of this writing, enables you to grant and revoke permissions for one app to call three `Admin` methods on behalf of another app. The three available methods are:

- `Admin.getAppProperties()` (see Recipe 9.14)
- `Admin.getMetrics()` (see Recipe 9.13)
- `Admin.getAllocations()` (see Recipe 9.12)

You'll need to know the API key of the application you're granting permissions to. You can grant on the `Admin` namespace in general if you want to give permission to call any of the methods:

```
$permissions = array('admin.');
$result = $facebook->api_client->permissions_grantApiAccess
('456eaf416a25820f18568b7cb0848c3c', $permissions);
```

That would grant permission for my Super Disco Napping app to have access to your stuff, which I highly recommend you do so that I can sneak peaks at what's going on. If you decided you wanted to limit me to getting just allocations and metrics, you could modify the call to narrow the permissions:

```
$permissions = array('admin.getAllocation','admin.getMetrics');
$result = $facebook->api_client->permissions_grantApiAccess
('456eaf416a25820f18568b7cb0848c3c', $permissions);
```

Discussion

`Permissions.grantApiAccess()` returns true (1) if successful or false (0) if it fails. You only need to call this once for each grant you want to do, but it will continue to succeed if you call it multiple times, and it won't fail with any kind of "Permission already granted" error.

You can check to see which permissions have been granted to your application by another application by using the `Permissions.checkAvailableApiAccess()` method and passing in the API key of the other app:

```
$result = $facebook->api_client->permissions_checkAvailableApiAccess
('456eaf416a25820f8568b7cb0848c3c');
```

In this case, `result` would contain an array of permissions that the Super Disco Napping application granted to your app, if any. You can also do the reverse and check to see which permissions your app has granted to another app by calling:

```
$result = $facebook->api_client->permissions_checkGrantedApiAccess
('456eaf416a25820f1868b7cb0848c3c');
```

which would, in this case, return an array of permissions you had granted to the Super Disco Napping app.

Revoking API access works just like granting it, but with a different method call:

```
$permissions = array('admin.getAllocation','admin.getMetrics');
$result = $facebook->api_client->permissions_revokeApiAccess
('456eaf416a25820f18568b7cb0848c3c', $permissions);
```

9.56 Post-Remove (Uninstall) URL

Problem

I'd like to be able to collect some statistics when users remove my application, but I don't get any kind of notice from Facebook.

Solution

You can specify a Post-Remove URL in your app's settings, which Facebook will ping with a POST request when a user removes your app.

Discussion

The important thing to note is that users won't be sent to the URL when they remove it, but rather that you'll get a POST request from Facebook with some useful information, listed in Table 9-8.

Table 9-8. Post-remove URL parameters

Name	Type	Description
fb_sig_uninstall	bool	This will always be true (1).
fb_sig_time	string	The uninstall timestamp in epoch seconds (see Recipe 6.20 for more info on epoch time).
fb_sig_user	int	uid (user ID) of the user who removed the app.
fb_sig_api_key	string	API key of the app being uninstalled.
fb_sig	string	Signature of the POST, made up of the other parameters and the app's secret key hashed into an MD5 hash.

You should verify that the POST requests you receive are valid by building your own version of `fb_sig` and then checking that they match:

```
$sig = '';
ksort($_POST);
foreach ($_POST as $key => $value) {
    if (substr($key, 0, 7) == 'fb_sig_') {
        $sig .= substr($key, 7) . '=' . $value;
    }
}
$sig .= $secret;
```

```
$verify = md5($sig);

if ($verify == $_POST['fb_sig'] && $_POST['fb_uninstall'] == true) {
    // The signatures match and this is an uninstall request,
    // so go ahead and do it
} else {
    // This is a forged request or not an uninstall, so track it
    // for later inquiry
}
```

Note that this assumes you already have a `secret` variable on this page that contains your app's secret key.

9.57 Adding Missing PHP Client Library Methods

Problem

Some of the methods documented in this chapter throw a "Call to undefined method" error when I try to use them!

Solution

The bad news: five methods listed in the Developers Wiki are missing from the official Facebook PHP 4/5 Client Library: `Photos.createAlbum( )`, `Photos.upload( )`, `photos.addTag( )`, `Users.hasAppPermission( )`, and `Users.setStatus( )`. The good news: you can add some of them yourself! The only tricky one is `Photos.upload( )` because it requires you to submit raw data from a file upload field, so you might instead want to look at the extended version of the Client Library mentioned in Recipe 9.45.

These instructions are for the PHP 5 version of the Client Library, but you should be able to apply them to the PHP 4 version as well:

1. Back up the copy of *facebookapi_php5_restlib.php* on your server, just in case we break something. You could also install them into an entirely new file and include it too, so that you don't have to remember to make the same changes in future versions of the Client Library.

2. Open the nonbackup version in a text editor.

3. You can either insert all the new methods in one group, or you can find the right place in the file to insert them so that they're with the related functions that the Client Library does include. I recommend the latter, so scroll down to line 596 and insert these two functions:

```
/**
* Creates a new Photo album
* @param string $name : name of the new album
* @param string $location : location of the new album
* @param string $description : description of the new album
* @param int $uid : album creator. null for session user
* @return array
```

```
    */
    public function &photos_createAlbum($name, $location, $description, $uid=null){
        return $this->call_method('facebook.photos.createAlbum',
                            array('name' => $name,
                                  'location' => $location,
                                  'description' => $description,
                                  'uid' => $uid));

    }

    /**
     * Adds Tags to a Photos
     * @param int $pid : Photo ID of the target Photo
     * @param int $tag_uid : uid of the user being tagged (or tag_text, not both)
     * @param string $tag_text : text being tagged (or tag_uid, not both)
     * @param float $x : x location of the tag box
     * @param float $y : y location of the tag box
     * @param string $tags : JSON formatted array of tags
     * @param int $owner_uid : uid of the Photo owner. null for session user
     * @return boolean
     */
    public function &photos_addTag($pid, $tag_uid, $tag_text, $x, $y, $tags, $owner_uid){
        return $this->call_method('facebook.photos.addTag',
                            array('pid' => $pid,
                                  'tag_uid' => $tag_uid,
                                  'tag_text' => $tag_text,
                                  'x' => $x,
                                  'y' => $y,
                                  'tags' => $tags,
                                  'owner_uid' => $owner_uid));

    }
```

4. Scroll down to line 626 and insert these two functions:

```
    /**
     * Returns whether or not the user has a requested extended permission
     * @param string $ext_perm : name of the extended permission to check
     * @param int $uid : optional uid to check for. null for session user
     * @return boolean
     */
    public function &users_hasAppPermission($ext_perm,$uid=null) {
        return $this->call_method('facebook.users.hasAppPermission',
                            array('ext_perm' => $ext_perm, 'uid' => $uid));
    }

    /**
     * Sets the user's status
     * @param string $status : The status message to set
     * @param boolean $clear : Set to true to clear the status
     * @param boolean $status_includes_verb : If set to false, "is" will be prepended
     * @param int $uid : uid of the target user. null for session user
     * @return boolean
     */
    public function &users_setStatus($status, $clear, $status_includes_verb, $uid=null) {
        return $this->call_method('facebook.users.setStatus',
```

```
                    array('status' => $status,
                          'clear' => $clear,
                          'status_includes_verb' => $status_includes_verb,
                          'uid' => $uid));
    }
```

Discussion

I actually opened a bug for this situation in Facebook's Bugzilla system, so it will hope-fully get resolved in the future, and then you can use this recipe to line your birdcage.

9.58 Error Codes

Problem

My API calls don't work! I'm getting errors back!

Solution

Don't panic! 100- and 200-class errors are Facebook's way of telling you that there's something wrong with your API calls. The possible error codes are listed in Table 9-9.

Table 9-9. API error codes

Error code	Description
1	An unknown error occurred. Please resubmit the request.
2	The service is not available at this time.
4	The application has reached the maximum number of requests allowed. More requests are allowed once the time window has completed.
5	The request came from a remote address not allowed by this application.
100	One of the parameters specified was missing or invalid.
101	The API key submitted is not associated with any known application.
102	The session key was improperly submitted or has reached its timeout. Direct the user to log in again to obtain another key.
103	The submitted call_id was not greater than the previous call_id for this session.
104	Incorrect signature.
200	The application does not have permission to operate on the passed-in uid parameter.

Discussion

The long, long list of Facebook error codes can be found at *http://wiki.developers.face book.com/index.php/Error_codes*.

If you're getting an error and are having trouble tracking it down in the context of your code, try extracting the call and running it directly inside the API Test Console found at *http://developers.facebook.com/tools.php?api*.

CHAPTER 10

Marketing Your App

You've released the world's greatest Facebook application, and all 500 of your closest friends have it installed. Your install base is slowly climbing, and your daily active stat looks good so far. Great riches await you, if you can just figure out how to get from here to there. Now what?

Marketing Facebook apps is no different from marketing any other kind of web app, widget, doohickey, or thingamabob. Some people have a natural flair for this kind of thing, while others have a natural flair for writing programming language compilers. It's unlikely that you're the kind of person with an instinct for both, so if you're in the latter camp and are serious about the success of your app, you might want to find someone in the former to help you out.

The bad news: there's no magic bullet or panacea that will instantly turn your app into a Top 10 and bring dump trucks filled with money to your doorstep. The good news: if you work as hard at promoting your app as you did at designing and building it, you can be very successful and earn a really good living doing this. This chapter looks at a few different avenues you have available for marketing your app, as well as a few techniques you can use to assess where you're at and decide how to move forward.

10.1 Attracting Users Through Facebook Ads

—Alain Chesnais (see his bio in Contributors)

Problem

I launched my app a month ago, but I still only have a handful of users!

Solution

You need to promote your app to make your potential users aware of its existence. The most effective way to do so is through advertising.

Discussion

A common mistake many developers make is to assume that simply building an app is enough to have it go viral and reach millions of users overnight. Good apps only really go viral after they have attained a sufficient number of users. To see why this is true, let's assume that your app has launched and you get one new user virally every day for every hundred users you currently have. That's 1% growth every day. Let's assume that you start off with 10 of your best friends signing up and let it run. This type of viral growth is exponential, but the startup phase can be painfully slow. In this particular case, it would get you to 13 users in a month and 60 users after 6 months.

So what can you do about it? The key thing to do when launching a new app is to promote it and let people know that they should be trying it out. There are currently tens of thousands of apps on Facebook. You want users to know about yours. Your best bet is to run advertisements within Facebook, and the most obvious way is to use Facebook's ads. These appear randomly in users' Notifications or in the ad slot on the lefthand side of each Facebook page. You bid for ad placement for given demographics and pay for the placement. Try different ads and aim at different demographics to see which are the most productive.

Let's look at how we might promote our SceneCaster application. You can start a new ad by visiting *http://www.new.facebook.com/ads/create/*. First we are asked what we want to advertise. Choose the application you want to promote from the drop-down menu shown in Figure 10-1.

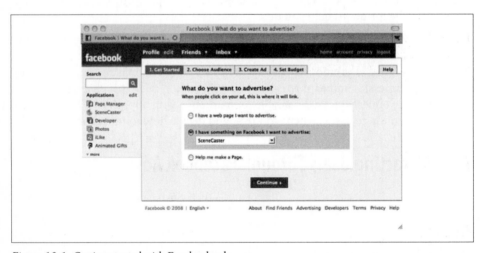

Figure 10-1. Getting started with Facebook ads

Next, you are asked to choose your target demographic. You don't want to take a scattershot approach here. Understand who might use your application and target them specifically. In this case, we assume that we want to target people in the U.S. who are over 18 and have expressed interest in interior design, interior decorating, or architecture, as shown in Figure 10-2. We'll later craft our messaging explicitly for them.

Figure 10-2. Choose Audience page

Now we're ready to create the ad. Choose a tagline, some descriptive text, and an image (Figure 10-3).

Figure 10-3. Create Ad page

We're now ready for the final step: setting your budget. In this dialog (Figure 10-4), you will be asked whether you want to pay per click or pay per view. Try each and see which performs best. You'll also be prompted to set a bid price. Facebook suggests values that correspond to current bids for similar demographics. It's a good starting point, but you should try different values and see which gets you the best results per unit cost. Facebook also builds in a safety net so that you don't blow your budget with an unexpected success.

Figure 10-4. Set Budget page

Another approach to consider is buying ads on the large app aggregators, such as Slide or Rock You. Buying ads on their apps (which include Super Wall and FunWall) can gain you large numbers of viewers at a reasonable cost.

There is no single solution that works in all cases. Your best approach is to try several and see which campaigns work best for your app. The key to success is to measure the success of each campaign, and to keep doing this over time. Your success rate will change as users become familiar with your ad, and so refreshing the ad and measuring its success will help you acquire a maximum number of users.

To get a sense of how well this can work, let's take SceneCaster as an example. We launched the application in late September 2007 and did not promote it at first. We wanted to get the kinks out before launching our marketing effort to promote it. In early December we had reached a total of 3,000 users and decided to launch our marketing campaign, using a combination of Facebook ads and ads with Rock You. Within two weeks we skyrocketed to become the most active application on Facebook. By Christmas we had reached a total of 100,000 users. Roughly six months later we reached 1,000,000. We've now ramped down our spending in terms of dollars spent per total number of users we have, and let the viral nature of the app kick in to help attract new users.

For me, the key to a successful launch is to pay attention to your promotion. Set yourself a budget for how much you want to spend to kick-start your app. This will help you decide how long you want to maintain your ad campaigns and give you a clear understanding of how much you are willing to spend. The next step concerns how you maintain and maximize your viral aspect. Facebook gives you several tools to achieve this, specifically Notifications, requests, and friend invitations. Your key challenge will be to find a good trade-off between communicating enough and being perceived as spam. There is no magic formula here. Once again, the best way to find this out is to measure your success. Whenever you modify the number of Notifications and request opportunities, you should check to see the percentage of new users compared to the total number of users. One thing to look at specifically is the number of remove requests. This is often linked to over-communication and means that your communications are being perceived as spam. At one point we dramatically increased the amount of messaging we were generating and immediately saw a decrease in our rate of net new users. We quickly pulled back and tried alternate approaches.

The final recommendation that I would make is to keep refreshing the content of your app. Users will tend to come back more often if they expect to find new content. Taking the SceneCaster app as an example, our landing canvas shows you the top users and creations of the day, every day. We also update our catalog once a week; that way, users who create content expect to find new objects to work with every week. Finally, you want to establish a sense of relationship with your users. Again, using the SceneCaster example, we asked one of our best designers to be the community leader. He selects the user of the day and the scene of the day every workday. He also maintains a blog that is frequently updated and posted on the landing page, so that we are constantly communicating with our users to keep them abreast of what is new.

10.2 Monetize, Measure, and Market with SocialMedia

Problem

I need a toolkit of services and opportunities to earn revenue and attract users to my app.

Solution

SocialMedia Networks offers a whole platform for app developers to monetize, measure, and market their applications on Facebook, Bebo, MySpace, and hi5. You can find more information and sign up at *http://www.socialmedia.com*.

Discussion

SocialMedia shares a lot in common with other ad platforms for social networks, such as Cubics (see Recipe 10.3). SocialMedia's platform is divided into three pieces, as shown in Figure 10-5.

Figure 10-5. SocialMedia's Three-M platform (from http://socialmedia.com/developers)

Monetize

SocialMedia has developed a number of innovative ad formats for display inside of your applications that are designed for Facebook Platform, not just the Web at large, including Canvas (645 × 60 pixels), Television (300 × 250 pixels), Interstitial (600 × 500 pixels), and Leaderboard (728 × 90 pixels). You simply need to register, specify one of your apps, and paste the generated `fb:iframe` tag into your page.

Measure

Once you have a SocialMedia account, you'll have access to their dashboards and Appsaholic app-tracking tools (see Recipe 2.1 for more info on Appsaholic). The dashboards offer most of the same information that you can find in Facebook Insights, but also lets you compare your performance against other, similar apps.

Market

The flip side to monetizing through SocialMedia is buying ads in other apps to promote your own. SocialMedia has built a useful little viral calculator (*http://socialmedia.com/?q=market*) that will help you get a sense of how far you can stretch your budget in terms of new user acquisitions.

 If you're running an ad blocker such as AdBlock Plus in Firefox, you'll have some trouble browsing SocialMedia's website. Most ad blocker blacklists have something like *.socialmedia.com/*, preventing the site's CSS and images from loading. Make sure to disable it or add some better filters so you can learn more about their services.

10.3 Social Network Advertising with Cubics

Problem

I keep hearing about Cubics as an alternative to AdSense or SocialMedia. What is it?

Solution

Cubics is a platform for inserting ads into social networks, including Facebook, My-Space, Friendster, Bebo, and hi5. They both buy and sell ad inventory, so you can work with them to monetize your app and promote it into other apps.

Discussion

Cubics and SocialMedia are fairly closely related, in that they're both ad platforms for social networking sites (see Recipe 10.2). In Cubics parlance, you're either an Advertiser (you have purchased ads to promote your app or product) or a Publisher (you have an app in which you host Cubics ads). You have the option of doing either CPM (cost per thousand impressions) or CPC (cost per click) campaigns, and they have a bunch of targeting options, as shown in Figure 10-6, that are quite similar to Facebook's (see Recipe 10.1).

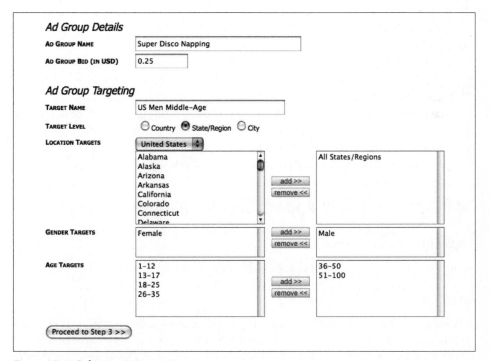

Figure 10-6. Cubics targeting options

Again, if you're running an ad blocker such as AdBlock Plus in Firefox, you'll have some trouble browsing Cubic's website. Most ad blocker blacklists have something like *.cubics.com/*, preventing the site's CSS and images from loading. Make sure to disable it or add some better filters so you can learn more about their services.

10.4 Other Ad Networks

Problem

I already know about SocialMedia and Cubics. Are there any other Facebook ad networks?

Solution

Sure are! Among many others (which are just a Google search away), take a look at:

fbExchange
> *http://www.fbexchange.com*

Lookery
> *http://www.lookery.com*

Slide
> *http://www.slide.com/advertise*

Rock You
> *http://www.rockyou.com/corp/facebook/ad.php*

Discussion

It's always worth experimenting with different ways of attracting users, but make sure it's not detrimental (e.g., if it's a really annoying experience, you'll attract the wrong kinds of users or scare the right kind off) and that the cost you're paying is worth it compared to other platforms that fit in the same budget.

10.5 Spreading Your App via Google AdWords

Problem

I'd like to advertise my app on Google AdWords. Will that generate a lot of traffic?

Solution

AdWords is a great platform for promoting non-Facebook sites, but it's not ideal for getting people into your app. Most of the people who are in the right frame of mind to install Facebook apps are on Facebook, which means that ads they see while they're on Google are going to be less effective at getting them to install. You can find out more, and sign up, at *http://adwords.google.com*.

Discussion

As with everything else, you might find that AdWords works extremely well for your app's unique circumstances where it has failed for others. Keep close tabs on the traffic you earn from it by driving users to unique AdWords landing pages within your app, and make sure that you're getting your money's worth by checking what users do after they've arrived. (AdWords is always pay-per-click, so it's more a question of whether they install or invite friends.)

10.6 Measuring Your Success

—Jeffrey Tseng (see his bio in Contributors)

Problem

Which metrics are important to measure in order to ensure a successful application?

Solution

The two key metrics that need to be closely monitored to ensure a successful application are:

- The viral factor, sometimes known as the "*k-factor*," an indication of viral growth
- An engagement metric, oftentimes application-specific, as an indication of how much the user interacts with your application

Discussion

Metrics are one of the keys to developing a Facebook application. Similar to any consumer web application, it is almost impossible to predict user behavior. As such, the most successful application developers tune their apps extensively through the process of trial and error. To accomplish this, developers must use metrics to measure the effectiveness of the changes they have made to their applications so that they can quickly iterate to achieve their goal of creating a successful application.

Virality

K-factor = [(total number of users converted through installs) + (total number of users converted through Notifications) + (total number of users converted through emails) + (total number of users converted through Feeds) + (total number of users converted through Profiles)] / total number of installs.

The k-factor indicates how viral, or how rapid and self-sustaining, the growth is. This number represents the number of new users that an existing user gets to install your application. If the k-factor is less than 1, the application cannot have self-sustaining organic growth. When the k-factor is 1, the application has linear growth. If the number is greater than 1, the application has "gone viral" and has self-sustaining organic growth. The goal is to obtain a k-factor of greater than 1.2 for rapid growth of your application.

Engagement

Although user session time is a good indication of engagement on the Web, there are more appropriate engagement metrics for Facebook applications. With Facebook apps, the goal is to increase the interaction of the user with the application itself, because increased engagement results in increased monetization. Engagement can be broadly classified in two categories:

- Application-specific engagement (for a gaming app, this could be how often a user performs a specific game action)
- Social engagement, which is a count of the number of Facebook channels used by users who already have the application installed

Optimizing for both types of metrics will result in the user performing the desired actions on your site (application-specific engagement), or re-engaging other app users, in turn generating more active users of your application (social engagement).

How to measure

So, how does one actually go about acquiring these metrics? The first step should be to instrument your application with Google Analytics. Though Google Analytics is really designed for the broad Web, it gives you basic information about the overall health of your Facebook app by providing you the page view count and average session time, as well as other basic metrics.

To calculate and tune the k-factor, there are a couple of possible approaches. One is to query your application data to mine for these metrics. This may seem relatively simple to do, but as your applications grow larger, the queries will become slower and start to interfere with the performance of your app. Therefore, it is not a recommended long-term solution, but it is a good starting point. The alternative is to use third-party software, such as the Kontagent analytics suite, to collect and process this data for you. It generally takes a few hours to instrument your existing application, but the result provides you deep social analytics, much like Google Analytics, tailored for social networks. Kontagent analytics provide you with virality rates, conversion, and deep metrics on all your communication channels, as well as metrics that correlate user characteristics with social behavior. You can find more information at *http://www.kont agent.com*.

10.7 Work the Integration Points

Problem

I don't really have a budget to spend on advertising my app to attract users. Is there anything I can do on-Facebook?

Solution

Work the integration points like there's no tomorrow. See Recipe 2.8 for more information about the different points and how best to use them.

Discussion

Spreading through the social graph is still the most powerful mechanism for attracting users because those users tend to be much higher-value (they are drawn to your app because their friends use it, rather than because they come across it in an ad). Experiment aggressively during the early days of your app to figure out what works as content in invitations, requests, message attachments, etc., and then make sure you don't get lazy and allow competitors to bypass you on any one of the points. As with the different ad networks, make sure you're measuring your success at the different points so that you can quickly adjust if things aren't panning out (see Recipe 10.6).

10.8 Continuous Improvement Through A/B Testing

Problem

I want to continuously improve my ability to attract new users, but I don't know how to keep evaluating what's working.

Solution

A/B testing comes from the world of hi-fidelity audio systems, in which people stand in neutral rooms and toggle back and forth between the "A" and "B" speakers connected to an amplifier, to decide whether they should buy the ones that cost twice as much as your mortgage or the ones that are more expensive than a university education. Luckily for you, A/B testing isn't just for audiophiles anymore! The same principle can be applied to web or Facebook apps: develop "A" and "B" alternatives, show "A" to a test group and "B" to another test group, and see which one is better at a predefined metric. You might, for example, try different invite texts to see which attracts users faster or at a higher response rate.

Discussion

Implementing your own A/B test framework is doable, but that's like saying it's possible to climb Mount Everest. If you're just getting started, don't invest a huge amount of time in building something that isn't core to your application, because it just drags you away from the important stuff. Take a look at efforts such as The Fountain Project (*http://www.fountainproject.com/*), which provides an A/B system for testing Facebook invitations.

10.9 The Great Apps Program

Problem

My app is a really outstanding example of building on Facebook Platform and I'd like to see it celebrated by Facebook.

Solution

Apply to the Facebook Great Apps Program! You can learn more at *http://developers .facebook.com/greatapps.php*.

Discussion

Facebook, recognizing the need to celebrate truly great applications, launched the Great Apps Program at the f8 conference in July 2008. If your app does an exceptional job of meeting Facebook's 10 Guiding Principles (*http://developers.facebook.com/get _started.php?tab=principles*), has a minimum user base, and has a consistent record of complying with Platform policies, you stand a chance of being accepted, although it's worth noting that they expect to add only 10–15 apps over the first year.

As a Great App, you'll enjoy:

Increased visibility
Your app will get promoted at the same level as Facebook's own apps, including the weight and visibility given to your News Feed items.

Early access to features
Great Apps will be given sneak peaks at new stuff and will be able to help test these features before the general masses.

Support from Facebook
The Facebook team has committed to working closely with the developers of Great Apps, providing them with feedback and better usage data to help improve their user experience.

The program launched with two Great Apps in place: iLike and Causes. It's too early to really provide any guidance about how to shape your app to get accepted, other than to say that it's worth reviewing what these apps have done and how they excel at the Guiding Principles.

10.10 Application Verification Program

Problem

The world of apps is getting too crowded, and I feel like users just don't trust apps the way they used to. How can I get them to know that my app is legit?

Solution

If you're faced with being MC Hammer (i.e., being 2 legit, 2 legit 2 quit), consider the Application Verification Program launched at the 2008 f8 conference. More information is at *http://developers.facebook.com/verification.php*.

Discussion

Interested developers can submit their apps, along with a processing fee, and Facebook will verify and certify that the app:

- Uses major integration points in the manner they were intended
- Triggers communication between users and friends appropriately
- Has relevant and appropriate content in communications

Verified applications will receive a badge on their About Page, heightened presence in the Application Directory, and more visibility in some Facebook communication channels compared to their unverified peers. Generally speaking, if your app complies with Facebook's Platform Policy (*http://wiki.developers.facebook.com/index.php/Platform _Policy*) and meets (or exceeds!) the Guiding Principles (*http://developers.facebook .com/principles.php*), you should have no trouble.

Index

We'd like to hear your suggestions for improving our indexes. Send email to *index@oreilly.com*.

Z

About the Author

Jay has been providing a human side to technology for over 10 years, as a technologist, user experience specialist, and visual designer. His career has been focused on the interaction between people and technology, and his insights have helped greatly improve products on mobile, web, and desktop platforms, including IBM DB2, Mozilla Firefox, and several Facebook apps. Jay led Radiant Core's Professional Services Team on a wide variety of award-winning engagements across many industries, and he is now helping tech startups change the world as a consultant on products, technology, and design. He has been instrumental in the continued growth of the BarCamp community in Toronto and was one of the co-conductors of the very successful TransitCamp event held in partnership with the Toronto Transit Commission. Jay has been published in *Harvard Business Review* and lives in Toronto with his beautiful wife, Bianca, and their lovely little dog, Mr. Findley Mordecai Goldman.

Jay can help make your project better—find him at *http://jaygoldman.com*.

Colophon

The animal on the cover of *Facebook Cookbook* is a slow loris (*Nycticebus coucang*). The loris likely gets its name from the Dutch word *lores*, which means sluggish. Also known as the bashful monkey, the slow loris is about 10 to 15 inches long and weighs 3 to 5 pounds. It has a round head, small ears covered by fur, and a tail so short it's almost invisible. The loris has large, circular eyes that are fixed in place—like an owl, it must rotate its head to change points of view. Slow lorises vary in color from gray to white, depending on location, and they have dark rings around their eyes and a dark stripe running along their backs. They live in tropical evergreen rain forests across southeast Asia.

Lorises are nocturnal and arboreal, sleeping by day in tree hollows or branches and becoming active at sunset. Unlike most primates, lorises do not leap through trees. They move slowly and deliberately, using their strong opposable thumbs to grab hold of branches, although they can move quickly if alarmed. Slow lorises are excellent climbers and are able to hang from branches for long periods of time, as specialized blood vessels allow them to grip on for hours.

The slow loris is one of only a few poisonous primates. A special tissue in its inner elbows secretes a toxin. When the loris feels threatened, it folds its arms around its head, allowing it to take the toxin into its mouth. The loris then delivers the toxin via biting. It may also make a buzzing or hissing sound when disturbed.

The cover image is from Lydekker's *Royal Natural History*. The cover font is Adobe ITC Garamond. The text font is Linotype Birka; the heading font is Adobe Myriad Condensed; and the code font is LucasFont's TheSansMonoCondensed.